"With the plague of addictions found in the church today, those called to a ministry of hope and healing must be prepared for the plethora of struggles that will come their way. This in-depth guide should be at the top of your list as you pour grace into hurting lives and lead people toward recovery."

—**Mark Laaser,** cofounder of Faithful and True and bestselling author of *Healing the Wounds of Sexual Addiction*

"This fills the gap that is there for many in the helping profession."

—**Stephen Arterburn,** founder and chairman of New Life Ministries, cohost of Christian radio talk show *New Life Live!*, and bestselling author of the Every Man series

"An excellent and invaluable resource for pastors, lay leaders, and counselors dealing with ministry for those trapped in addiction—especially for those inside the church doors. Addiction knows no boundaries, and those in leadership in the church need this kind of educational tool."

—**David Stoop,** psychologist, coauthor of the *Life Recovery Bible* and cohost of Christian radio talk show *New Life Live!*

"The tool you hold in your hand is much needed in today's broken world. The pages contain a broad and yet in-depth spectrum of advice and guidance to help you impact those struggling in addictions."

—**John Baker**, founder of Celebrate Recovery

The Quick-Reference Guide to

# ADDICTIONS
# AND RECOVERY
# COUNSELING

*40 Topics, Spiritual Insights,*
*and Easy-to-Use Action Steps*

## DR. TIM CLINTON
### and
## DR. ERIC SCALISE

BakerBooks
*a division of Baker Publishing Group*
Grand Rapids, Michigan

© 2013 by Tim Clinton

Published by Baker Books
a division of Baker Publishing Group
P.O. Box 6287, Grand Rapids, MI 49516-6287
www.bakerbooks.com

Printed in the United States of America

Library of Congress Cataloging-in-Publication Data is on file at the Library of Congress, Washington, DC.

ISBN 978-0-8010-7232-1

13   14   15   16   17   18   19        7   6   5   4   3   2   1

In keeping with biblical principles of creation stewardship, Baker Publishing Group advocates the responsible use of our natural resources. As a member of the Green Press Initiative, our company uses recycled paper when possible. The text paper of this book is composed in part of post-consumer waste.

green press INITIATIVE

# Contents

Acknowledgments   7

Introduction   9

**Part 1  Addictions and Recovery Overview**

1. Disease and Choice   24
2. Trauma and Comorbidity   37
3. Treatment Protocols   45
4. Spiritual Applications   53
5. Recovery and Relapse Prevention   61

**Part 2  Substance Abuse Addictions**

6. Alcohol   70
7. Caffeine   78
8. Cocaine and Crack Cocaine   83
9. Depressants   89
10. Diuretics and Weight Loss   96
11. Hallucinogens   104
12. Inhalants   118
13. Marijuana and Hashish   126
14. Narcotics and Opiates   134
15. Nicotine   146
16. Prescription Drugs   154
17. Stimulants   160

**Part 3  Behavioral Addictions**

18. Bodybuilding and Body Image   170
19. Cutting and Self-Harm   176
20. Eating Disorders   182
21. Fetishes and Bizarre Interests   188
22. Food Addictions   193

23. Gambling   199
24. Hoarding   206
25. Internet Use and Gaming   212
26. Kleptomania and Stealing   218
27. Pornography and Sexual Addiction   226
28. Shopping and Excessive Collecting   233
29. Technology and Social Networking   239
30. Voyeurism and Exhibitionism   246

**Part 4  Process Addictions**

31. Adrenaline and Thrill Seeking   256
32. Anger and Rage   263
33. Anxiety and Worry   271
34. Chronic Stress and Self-Imposed Pressure   279
35. Co-dependency and Toxic Relationships   288
36. Cults and the Occult   296
37. Narcissism and Attention Seeking   310
38. Obsessions and Compulsions   318
39. Religious Addiction and Toxic Faith   329
40. Workaholism and Performance   339

Appendix: Chemical Dependency Assessment   349

Notes   356

# Acknowledgments

Special thanks to the following individuals for their hard work, dedication, and research assistance in this project.

Tyler Anderson
Laura Captari
Whitney Cope
Amazing Grace Danso
Adam Holcomb

Hitomi Makino
Meredith Mitchell
Brent Sprinkle
Betel Yosef

# Introduction

Substance abuse and other addictive problems are prevalent in almost every segment of society today. The issues and concerns that are created cross all ethnic, cultural, educational, socioeconomic, gender, and age barriers. While there has been an upward trend in elder and prescription abuse over the past decade, adolescent rates have stabilized somewhat. Yet, when considering the various forms that addiction can take, the statistics are staggering (sources include the U.S. Department of Health and Human Services, U.S. Department of Justice, National Center for Health Statistics, Centers for Disease Control and Prevention, and U.S. Bureau of Labor Statistics):

- There are an estimated 15 million alcoholics and 10 million drug addicts (other than alcohol) in the United States. Forty percent of all family problems brought to domestic court are alcohol related; 75 percent of all juvenile delinquents have at least one alcoholic parent. More than 150,000 teens use cocaine and 500,000 use marijuana one or more times per week. In addition, nearly 500,000 junior and senior high students are weekly binge drinkers. An estimated 10–15 million adolescents need treatment for drug and alcohol abuse each year.
- An estimated 5–7 million people are addicted to prescription drugs.
- Every addict directly affects at least 5 other people. In a recent Gallup poll, 41 percent of those polled indicated that they had suffered physical, psychological, or social harm as a result of someone else's drinking or drugging (double the level reported in 1974).
- There are 40–80 million Americans who suffer from compulsive overeating and 5–15 percent will die from its consequences in any given year. Some 20 billion dollars is spent annually by Americans seeking to lose weight.
- Close to 100,000 adolescent girls, or 1–2 percent, and 4–5 percent of college-age women struggle with anorexia and/or bulimia.
- There are 2.5 million pathological gamblers and another 3 million compulsive gamblers in the United States. Gambling has become a 500-billion-dollar industry. The suicide rate for this population is 20 times higher than the national average. Some 50 million family members are said to be adversely affected.

- There are currently more than 300 million pornographic websites with an estimated 6–8 percent of the population diagnosed with some level of sexual addiction.
- No one really knows how many workaholics there are since this addiction has received comparatively little attention up until now. One study indicated that more than 10 million adults average 65–70 hours of work each week.

One of the more common debates in the public eye centers on whether addictive problems are disease-based (primarily genetic or biological) or choice-based (primarily habits or social environment). Major theoretical orientations include moral theory, disease theory, behavioral theory, social learning theory, and systems theory. Often people of faith incorporate the sinful nature of fallen man into the equation. Romans 7:14–25 is a poignant reminder of this: "But I see another law at work in me, waging war against the law of my mind and making me a prisoner of the law of sin at work within me (v. 23).

Even though children of alcoholics are said to be four times more likely to become alcoholics than children of nonalcoholics, initial theories of a single alcoholism gene have been disproven. Nevertheless, biological determinants cannot simply be ignored or discarded. Years of qualified research have now clearly demonstrated that addiction is influenced both by multiple genetic traits, called "polygenic" or addictive inheritance, and by a complex array of psychosocial dynamics. However, it is important to keep in mind that susceptibility does not necessarily imply inevitability. If genetics and biology were all encompassing, no one would ever be able to use free choice to move toward recovery. Alcoholics Anonymous and other 12-step approaches have consistently demonstrated the principle of choice.

Recent research continues to explore the neurobiology of addiction. In all brain functioning, neurotransmitters (chemical messengers) are released by the electrical impulses of a neuron and record sensory experiences called imprints. These imprints are encoded, passed along appropriate pathways (across a synapse), and stored (usually at the unconscious level). Dopamine is one of the major agents related to the "pleasure pathway" to or through the limbic system (where the feeling of pleasure is produced and regulated) and the development of addiction. Studies have shown that addictive substances (as well as behaviors) can adversely affect the nucleus accumbens, a circuit of specialized nerve cells within the limbic system. The amygdala—an almond-shaped mass of nuclei located deep within the temporal lobe of the brain, which plays a primary role in the processing and memory of emotional reactions—in essence, hijacks normal messaging that passes through the neocortex, where cognition is managed, and creates new neural pathways that enhance the addictive process. The brain has a natural blood-brain barrier that normally does not allow water-soluble molecules to pass through capillary walls. A substance is considered to be psychoactive when it can penetrate that barrier and create changes in neurochemistry and subsequent brain functioning.

Most practitioners who work in this field also understand and consider the needs-based aspect of addictive behavior that seems to fuel the dynamic. This can include the need to be insulated from worry and anxiety, the need to reduce manipulating guilt feelings, the need for approval and acceptance, the need to maintain a sense of control and power in one's environment, the need to avoid pain (physical, emotional, and psychological), and the need to be a perfect person and measure up to the expectations of others.

As such, all addictions typically fit into four basic categories:

1. *Addictions that stimulate*—activities or substances that provide arousal and ecstasy, usually resulting in a release of adrenaline
2. *Addictions that tranquilize*—activities or substances that calm, comfort, or reduce tension or anxiety, usually resulting in a release of endorphins
3. *Addictions that serve some psychological need*—such as self-punishment, codependency, workaholism
4. *Addictions that satisfy unique appetites*—involving both psychological and physiological components, such as pornography and some fetishes

*The Diagnostic and Statistical Manual of Mental Disorders IV*-Text Revision (DSM-IV-TR) quantifies the difference between substance use/abuse and dependency. The latter can be characterized as a maladaptive pattern of substance use leading to clinically significant impairment or distress that can include tolerance, withdrawal symptoms, and increased usage in spite of the fact that doing so is ultimately destructive. Usually addicts do not become dependent on a substance or activity immediately, but only after progressing through a number of distinct stages. These stages—partially based on the work of addiction researcher E. Morton Jellinek—are:

1. *Experimentation: Desired Release or the Exploratory Phase.* In this phase the person is motivated by curiosity or a desire for acceptance or escape, does not go overboard, and learns that the effects are controlled by the level of intake. There are usually few, if any, consequences.
2. *Occasional Use or Doing: Diminishing Returns or the Prodromal Phase.* In this phase the person experiences periodic disruptions at work, school, or home, needs more of the substance or activity to get the same effect, and has more actual seeking behavior. Still, the behavior occurs primarily in a social context where the person is frequently guided by a more experienced "user."
3. *Regular Use or Doing: Demanding Response or the Crucial Phase.* In this phase the person begins obsessing more and is preoccupied with using or doing, begins to do it more on their own, may experience a periodic loss of control, begins to break their own self-imposed rules that regulate the behavior, experiences increased shame and guilt, and looks for ways to hide the behavior.
4. *Addiction and Dependence: Destructive Results or the Chronic Phase.* In this phase the person needs the substance or behavior to survive, cope, and get by in daily living or functioning and experiences a deterioration in mental, emotional, physical, moral, and spiritual health.

Though otherwise unique, all addictive behaviors throughout these stages provide short-term gain, but lead to long-term pain.

Despite the nature of the addiction, all addictions have a number of common identifiers:

- They serve the purpose of removing a person from their true feelings.
- They serve as a form of escape.
- They totally control the addict, and the control transcends all logic or reason.
- They override the ability and/or willingness to delay self-gratification.
- They always involve pleasure.
- They involve psychological dependence.
- They are ultimately destructive and unhealthy.
- They eventually take priority over all of life's other issues.
- They lead to a system of denial and minimization.

From a biblical perspective, addiction in all its various forms results in the formation of spiritual strongholds and bondage in the life of the addict. There are several verses in both the Old and New Testaments that speak to this subject. The Greek word *pharmakon*—a feminine noun from which the words *pharmacy*, *pharmacist*, and *pharmaceutical* are derived—is used to describe a curative or medicinal drug. It's interesting that a derivative with the same root, *pharmakeia*, relates to things like sorcery, the occult, witchcraft, illicit drugs, and incantations associated with drugs. These terms can be found in Galatians 5:20–21 and Revelation 9:20–21 (translated as "sorcery" or "witchcraft" in each case). The human body is remarkably (even divinely) balanced chemically, and it is interesting to note that when balance is disrupted (either from introducing chemicals into the system that are not necessary or through other conditions such as psychosis and schizophrenia), spiritual doors (mostly destructive) seem to be opened within the person's soul. Thus when it comes to the treatment arena of addictions, we frequently find ourselves in a spiritual battle with the client.

The apostle Paul understood the battle clearly. Listen to his discourse in Romans 7:14–25 regarding this powerful dynamic, as well as his conclusion that it is Christ who is the deliverer:

> We know that the law is spiritual; but I am unspiritual, sold as a slave to sin. I do not understand what I do. For what I want to do I do not do, but what I hate I do. And if I do what I do not want to do, I agree that the law is good. As it is, it is no longer I myself who do it, but it is sin living in me. For I know that good itself does not dwell in me, that is, in my sinful nature. For I have the desire to do what is good, but I cannot carry it out. For I do not do the good I want to do, but the evil I do not want to do—this I keep on doing. Now if I do what I do not want to do, it is no longer I who do it, but it is sin living in me that does it.
>
> So I find this law at work: Although I want to do good, evil is right there with me. For in my inner being I delight in God's law; but I see another law at work in me, waging war against the law of my mind and making me a prisoner of the law of sin at work within me. What a wretched man I am! Who will rescue me from this body that is subject to death? Thanks be to God, who delivers me through Jesus Christ our Lord!

Here's an insightful look at another Scripture, Proverbs 23:30–35 (NASB), that speaks to some of the spiritual dynamics related to addiction, as well as the poor or sinful choices made by an individual:

- *"Those who go . . ."*—An addict begins an intentional quest for relief from his or her pain.
- *"When it sparkles in the cup . . ."*—The seductiveness of alcohol is evident.
- *". . . bites like a serpent . . . stings like a viper . . ."*—The pain relief of the alcohol has now become the main problem, but the addict continues the cycle until recovery or death.
- *". . . eyes will see strange things. . . . Your heart will utter perverse things . . ."*—A distorted perspective on life, relationships, attitudes, and behaviors that becomes an acting out of pain in the heart.
- *"They have struck me, but I was not hurt; they have beaten me, but I did not feel it . . ."*—The denial of addicts is so strong that they cannot see how the addiction is destroying everything around them. They are out of touch with reality.
- *"When shall I awake, that I may seek another drink?"*—Even with all the pain, addicts believe that the alcohol will solve their problems.

Most people do not sincerely desire or set out to become addicts and have their lives completely destroyed as a result of their abuse or the behaviors they are engaging in. Yet many end up in that place of isolation and brokenness. The journey down this long and empty road is one that can be seen within the addictive cycle below:

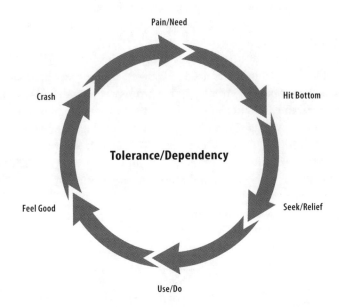

Here is how the cycle works:

1. The person has an unmet *need* in their life or a significant source of *pain*. The pain or need can be physical, emotional, psychological, relational, or spiritual. All the individual knows is that he or she is hurting.
2. This pain or need eventually results in the *person hitting bottom*. In other words, they become about as miserable and desperate as they can imagine. Often this is a place of hopelessness and despair.

3. Once the person bottoms out, the natural human desire is to *seek relief* from the pain or help with the need, and so the search begins.
4. The seeking motive results in the person *using* and/or *doing* something that he or she believes will bring a level of relief. For some, it's drugs or alcohol; for others it could be food, gambling, sex, the need for control, co-dependent relationships, or a number of other things.
5. The initial result is that the person *feels good*. They experience some *relief*—remember the motive to begin with.
6. Unfortunately the relief is usually short-lived. Often guilt, shame, and other consequences enter the picture, causing a *crash* (much like the proverbial hangover). The person comes to realize that the temporary reprieve was not worth it and did not solve the problem.

The impact of the crash actually becomes an additive factor to the original pain or need. This means the person does not end up in the same place after going "around the mountain." Now they feel even greater pain or need and hit bottom a little bit harder, which means the desire for relief is a little stronger, which means it now requires a little more of whatever the person used or did to bring them to the same level of relief. This is where the deception of addiction can be found. Since the person had to use or do more, the reality is that it took them higher and deeper toward addiction, but it didn't feel that way. Once again the resulting crash is greater, and this becomes a downward spiral. The technical terms for the process are *tolerance* and *dependency*.

The good news is that there are exit doors off this merry-go-round. One is at the top of the cycle. Counselors need to address, as best they can, the motivating source of a client's pain or need. In other words, what is driving the behavior? There may be some limitations in how directly these areas can be fully unpacked on an emotional level (for example, early childhood abuse); however, the second exit door offers additional opportunities. This primarily regards what the person used or did to seek relief. Part of the treatment process is to help clients understand and incorporate healthier and more God-honoring responses to what may be going on in their life.

Consider the following passage of Scripture from 2 Kings 17:16–17 (NASB). This was during a time of Israel's history when the people, by and large, had deserted their singular devotion to God and began committing what the Bible refers to as spiritual adultery. Several words have been emphasized, which speak to an important process.

> They *forsook* all the commands of the LORD their God and *made* for themselves two idols cast in the shape of calves, and an Asherah pole. They *bowed* down to all the starry hosts, and they *worshiped* Baal. They *sacrificed* their sons and daughters in the fire. They practiced divination and sought omens and sold themselves to do evil in the eyes of the LORD, arousing his anger.

From a Christian perspective, addictions are sometimes referred to as *spiritual strongholds*. It may not sound too profound, but a good definition for a stronghold is something that has a *strong hold* on a person. In the 2 Kings passage above, a progression can be seen that *begins with a choice* and ends with a generational impact.

1. The Israelites' *first choice* was to *forsake* God. In this context, it means they willfully turned their backs on Him to walk in a manner that was contrary to what He desired for them. All addictions involve moral choices. While the research clearly indicates a genetic predisposition for some individuals (especially in the case of alcohol dependency), it does not mean a person will be automatically compelled to take the first drink. Choices are still made. However, once that person consumes alcohol, he would have to fight much harder within himself—than other individuals without the same genetic makeup—not to take the next drink. In a pure disease model, choice would not be a factor. For example, if a person had cancer, usually she would not merely wake up one morning and say, "I choose not to have cancer," and it would then disappear. However, when it comes to an addiction, people can make choices (step 3 in the 12-step program) to live differently. If choice were not an option, no one would ever move from addiction to sobriety and into the recovery process.

2. The Israelites' *second choice* was they *made* idols. In other words, they took what was already in their hearts and minds and spirits and then brought it into reality with tangible objects. When it comes to addiction, people must first make a choice in their heart and mind and then bring their desire into reality, whether it is a bottle, a line of cocaine, a pornographic image, a food item, a slot machine, and so on. The object or behavior brings their desire into reality.

3. The Israelites' *third choice* was they *worshiped* what they had made. Worship at its most basic level is simply giving someone or something one's time and attention in such a way it is elevated in prominence and priority. People can worship many things other than God. In the addictive progression (from experimentation to occasional using to regular using to dependency), individuals begin to spend more and more time and give more and more attention to the object or behavior they have set in front of them.

4. The Israelites' *fourth choice* was they *served* Baal (the idol they fashioned and then worshiped). The Hebrew word for serve here is *abad*, and it does not mean to serve in the positive connotation of assisting or helping another. The literal translation is "to be in bondage to" or "enslaved" by something. The progression from an act of the will, to bringing something into one's life, to giving it greater priority, may then result in bondage and enslavement (addiction and dependency) to the object or behavior.

5. The Israelites' *fifth choice* was they *sacrificed* their children as a result of their choices, and in essence passed the problems to the next generation. Baal worship at the time included human sacrifice among other abominations. When it comes to addictions, we often see the negative impact on the addict's family members and loved ones.

So now let's go back to the beginning of the process. If forsaking God is the first step down a path leading to destructive consequences, then from a biblical perspective, *confession, repentance,* and *godly sorrow* become the first steps back to sanity and a healthier lifestyle. In his letter to the Corinthians, the apostle Paul says,

Godly sorrow brings repentance that leads to salvation and leaves no regret, but worldly sorrow brings death. See what this godly sorrow has produced in you: what earnestness, what eagerness to clear yourselves, what indignation, what alarm, what longing, what concern, what readiness to see justice done.

2 Corinthians 7:10–11

Throughout this Quick-Reference Guide, various types of addiction will be examined (substance abuse addictions, behavioral addictions, and process addictions); however, it is important to keep in mind that while biological, genetic, and sociocultural influences may all be factors, human beings' sinful nature, our moral choices, and the need for God's grace and forgiveness must also be integrated into the process when completing assessments and developing appropriate treatment protocols. Considering the whole person (physically, emotionally, mentally, relationally, and spiritually) is essential. The clinical dynamics are important, but without repentance and godly sorrow, the discussion would be incomplete. Look at the first three steps from AA/NA (Alcoholics Anonymous/Narcotics Anonymous):

- We admitted we were powerless over our addiction and that our lives had become unmanageable.
- We came to believe that a Power greater than ourselves could restore us to sanity.
- We made a decision to turn our will and our lives over to the care of God as we understood Him.

Addiction is a complex phenomenon involving genetic and biological factors, as well as psychosocial and spiritual dynamics. The good news from a treatment perspective is that those we work with still have choices. The orientation of the caregiver is also important. Some counselors are more naturally priests—they love to comfort the disturbed. Others are more naturally prophets—they love to disturb the comfortable. While an adept and skilled counselor is able to move between both orientations, addictions work does require a certain comfort level with confrontation due to the prevalence among addicts of denial and the tendency to minimize issues. Accountability and increasing the utilization of appropriate support systems are critical components for any treatment strategy. Recovery is rarely a solo journey.

"Two are better than one, because they have a good return for their labor: If either of them falls down, one can help the other up. But pity anyone who falls and has no one to help them up" (Eccles. 4:9–10).

# THE ROAD TO RECOVERY

## Step 1—Recognize and Admit: The Role of Confession and Breaking the Power of the Secret

The first thing an addict must be willing to do is face himself or herself with courageous but brutal honesty and say, "This is me! It's not about the other person.

I recognize and admit that I have the problem. In fact I may be the problem." People can carry the "secret" of their struggle for years and the only thing they experience is the growing power it has over every aspect of their lives. Honest reflection is critical if one is to break through the fear and shame and take personal responsibility for what needs to be done. First John 1:9 says, "If we *confess* our sins, He is faithful and righteous to forgive us our sins and to cleanse us from all unrighteousness" (NASB). Confession requires bringing things into the light where they become visible (see Ephesians 5:13). The child cries out at the "monster under the bed" until the light is turned on. Only then are things seen for what they really are. The same is true when it comes to an addiction. Bring it into God's light where the Great Physician can perform the necessary surgery.

## Step 2—Clean Out the Infection: The Role of Grieving and Breaking the Power of Denial

There is a need for the painful and/or distorted emotions within the addict to be addressed and resolved so the potential for healing and restoration can exist. Otherwise sinful and destructive patterns will continue to have a negative impact on life. These emotional wounds may become infected, and infections have a natural way of spreading. It will not be easy or pleasant—no infection is attractive—but the source of pain needs to be cleansed. Just like a parent who must touch and gently clean the scraped knee of their child, so too God must be allowed to "touch" the sensitive, hurting, and broken places in the addict's life. And He graciously provides opportunities throughout Scripture. David and other psalmists were constantly crying out before God and there was no minimizing or denying the reality of what they were wrestling with. Psalm 62:8 says, "*Pour out* your heart before Him; God is a refuge for us" (NASB). Only then can a healing salve and bandage be applied. When addicts turn to God with their greatest fears and deepest griefs, they will always encounter the safest hands. This requires repentance and godly sorrow.

## Step 3—Renew the Mind: The Role of Truth and Breaking the Power of Unbelief

A wrongful and unbalanced belief system usually contributes to an addictive lifestyle. How people think about the beliefs they carry may have so distorted the truth that they are now bound by the lie that is lived out. The enemy of the soul is a liar and a deceiver, but the ability of God's Word to give discernment, clarity, direction, hope, wisdom, and changed thinking is evident. The addict is transformed by the renewing of their mind (Rom. 12:2) and the washing of His Word (Eph. 5:26). Just as the rain softens the ground, making it easier to weed the garden, so truth has a way of softening one's "heart ground," allowing God to pull out the things that tend to choke life. He is a faithful gardener, but when an addict's heart is hard and closed, He usually is able to get only what's at the surface and not down to the root of the matter. His grace and truth must be allowed to wash over every part of the person. The result will be not only new life but life in great abundance.

## Step 4—Exercise the Will: The Role of Accountability and Breaking the Power of Fear

While owning the problem, dealing with damaged emotions, and having a renewed mind are all important, they are not enough. Concrete and proactive steps must be taken through confession, repentance, obedience, and accountability. Every journey really does begin with a first step. Committed action is usually the result of strong conviction and is evidence that the addict is ready to move on and beyond the past. The apostle Paul told the Philippians that he was "forgetting what lies behind and reaching forward to what lies ahead" (3:13 NASB). The truth, however, is that most addicts cannot do it alone—they need others to walk with them. Someone once said that accountability is the breakfast of champions, but too many people skip the most important meal of the day. Isolation is Satan's primary tactic to take out a believer. The person who is alone is an easier target. In 1 Kings 4:1–19 there is a list of Solomon's key officials. Embedded in this list is a priest named Zabud, who is called "the king's friend" (NASB). Solomon, the wisest man who ever lived, had the insight to have someone in his inner circle whose primary role was apparently that of friend. Who is the addict's Zabud? They must identify these accountability partners and ask them to prayerfully consider taking the journey with them.

# THE THREE LEGS OF HELPING MINISTRY

This Quick-Reference Guide is designed for mental health practitioners, as well as pastors and ministry leaders, and lay caregivers—like the three legs of a three-legged stool—who desire to understand better and help those struggling with various forms of addiction. We have written this book to apply to those in each category—each leg of our three-legged stool metaphor. We advance the ideas that helping ministry in the church is made up of *pastors*, who serve in a central oversight role, as clients nearly always return to the role of parishioners; of *professional Christian counselors and clinicians*, who often serve many churches in a given geographic area; and of *lay helpers*, who have been trained and serve in the church through both individual and group leadership roles.

People serving at all three levels must develop both the character and the servant qualities that reflect the grace and truth of Christ Himself. God has also distributed His gifts liberally throughout the church to perform the various ministry tasks that are central to any healthy church, not the least of which is *caring for the broken and hurting*. No matter how skilled or equipped we become, unless we rely directly on the Spirit of God to work in and through us to do the ministry of God, our service will not bear kingdom fruit.

God will bring us to those who are caught in the bondage of addiction whom He wants to love and heal through us. We must learn to depend on Him to touch others in a supernatural way—so people can exclaim, "God showed up in that counseling session today!" The apostle Paul said in 2 Corinthians 4:6–7, "For God, who said, 'Let light shine out of darkness,' made his light shine in our hearts to give us the light of the knowledge of God's glory displayed in the face of Christ. But we have this treasure in jars of clay to show that this all-surpassing power is from God and not from us."

## Pastor or Church Staff

If you are a pastor or church staff member, you know that many who walk through the doors of your church have wrestled with substance abuse, chemical dependency, and other forms of addiction. This guide will assist you in:

- delivering effective counseling and short-term strategies to assist those who seek pastoral care
- teaching others and developing sermons about addiction, recovery, and how to live and walk in freedom
- providing essential resources and materials for staff and lay leaders in your church to equip them and advance their helping ministries

## Mental Health Practitioner

If you are a mental health practitioner and licensed or certified in one of the six major clinical disciplines, you are likely already familiar with most of the topics in this book. However, this guide will assist you in:

- reviewing the definitions and assessment questions that are critical in your initial session with a new client
- understanding and incorporating a biblical worldview of the client's problem as you develop an appropriate treatment plan
- delivering information to your clients that best helps them get unstuck and move forward more resolutely with right thinking and focused action regarding the treatment process

## Lay Counselor

If you are a lay counselor, this book will guide you in planning and delivering the best care you can from beginning to end. We recommend that you read through the entire book, highlighting the material most useful to you in either individual or group formats. This guide will assist you in:

- understanding and accurately assessing the addict's problem
- guiding your discussions and delivery of helpful suggestions without assuming too much control or yielding too little influence
- reminding you of key principles and guiding you in the process of moving effectively from problem identification to resolution
- reminding you of the limits of lay ministry and assisting you in making constructive referrals to others with more training and/or expertise

# USING THE QUICK-REFERENCE GUIDE FOR ADDICTION AND RECOVERY

This guide includes chapters on forty of the most prevalent issues we see as professionals and ministry leaders in the field of addiction and recovery. You will see we have divided each topic into an outline format consisting of eight parts that follow the logic of the counseling process. The goal and purpose of these eight segments are as follows:

1. **Portraits.** Each topic begins with a number of short vignettes that tell a common story about people struggling with the issue at hand. We have tried to tell stories like ones you may encounter with the people you serve.

2. **Definitions and Key Thoughts.** This section begins with a clear definition of the issue in nontechnical language. Then we add a variety of ideas and data points to help you gain a fuller understanding of the issue and how it impacts lives and may harm the individuals who struggle with it.

3. **Assessment Interview.** This section may begin by suggesting a framework in which to approach making a thorough assessment and is followed by a series of specific questions for gaining a more complete understanding of the individual's problem(s).

4. **Wise Counsel.** One or more key ideas are presented here that should serve as an overarching guide to your interventions—wise counsel that will help you frame your interventions in a better way. These key insights will give you an edge in understanding and working with the men and women you encounter.

5. **Action Steps.** This section—along with Wise Counsel—will guide you in what to do in your counseling interventions. It helps you construct a logical road map that will guide you and your client from problem identification to resolution in specific, measured steps—client action steps. Without a good action plan, it is too easy to leave someone confused and drifting rather than moving in a determined way toward concrete goals for change. Most Action Steps will be directed at the individuals you are counseling. Any added notes for the counselor will be in italics.

6. **Biblical Insights.** Here we provide relevant Bible passages and commentary to assist you in your counseling work from beginning to end. Embedding the entire process in a biblical framework and calling on the Lord's power to do the impossible are essential to authentic Christian counseling. You may choose to give your clients some of these verses as homework—ask them to meditate on them and/or memorize them—or you may want to use these passages as guides for the intervention process.

7. **Prayer Starter.** While not appropriate in every situation, many Christians want—and expect—prayer to be an integral part of the helping process. You should ask clients for their consent before praying. Even if they do not join you, make it your habit to pray silently or in pre- or post-session reflection for each of your clients. Since prayer is a critical aspect of spiritual intervention, we offer a few lines of prayer that can serve as effective introductions to taking counseling vertical, inviting God directly into the healing process.

8. **Recommended Resources.** Here we list some of the best-known and predominantly Christian resources for further reading and study. Although by no means an exhaustive list, it will direct you to resources that will also reference additional works, allowing you to go as deep as you want in further study of an issue.

As you learn more about addiction and recovery, know that your desire to break the silence as you help and care for people honors God. Christian counseling is a strong, effective, case-based form of discipleship. In fact it is often the door the hurting people walk through to break the chains of pain, misperception, and destructive habits that have kept them from being fully alive to God. We are honored to be partners with you in God's work, and we trust that God will continue to use you in powerful ways to touch the brokenhearted and bring wholeness and healing.

# ADDITIONAL RESOURCES

The American Association of Christian Counselors (AACC) is a ministry and professional organization of nearly fifty thousand members in the United States and around the world. They are dedicated to providing and delivering the finest resources available to pastors, professional counselors, and lay helpers in whatever role or setting they serve. With their award-winning magazine, *Christian Counseling Today*, and courses available through Light University, they also deliver a comprehensive range of education, training, and conference opportunities to equip you fully for the work of helping ministries in whatever form they take. While some of these resources are noted at the end of the following chapters, several essential texts include:

- *The Bible for Hope: Caring for People God's Way* by Tim Clinton and many leading contributors (Thomas Nelson, 2006).
- *Caring for People God's Way* (and *Marriage and Family Counseling* and *Healthy Sexuality*—books in the same series) by Tim Clinton, Archibald Hart, and George Ohlschlager (Thomas Nelson, 2009).
- *Competent Christian Counseling: Foundations and Practices of Compassionate Soul Care* by Tim Clinton, George Ohlschlager, and many other leading contributors (WaterBrook, 2002).
- AACC's Light University also provides various biblical counseling video-based training programs, including: *Caring for People God's Way, Breaking Free, Addictions and Recovery, Stress and Trauma Care, Caring for Teens God's Way, Marriage Works, Healthy Sexuality, Extraordinary Women,* the *Geneva Series,* the *Courageous Living Series, Sexual Addiction,* and others.
- Please visit www.aacc.net for other resources, services, and training opportunities offered by the AACC for the growth and betterment of the church.

# REFERENCES

American Psychiatric Association. *Diagnostic and Statistical Manual of Mental Disorders*: DSM-IV-TR, 1994, 181–83.

Jellinek, E. M. "Phases of Alcohol Addiction." *Quarterly Journal of Studies on Alcohol* 13, 1952, 673–74.

McNeece, C. A., and D. M. DiNitto. *Chemical Dependency: A Systems Approach*. 3rd ed. Pearson Education, 2005.

Stevens, P., and R. L. Smith. *Substance Abuse Counseling: Theory and Practice*. 3rd ed. Pearson Education, 2005.

# PART 1

# Addictions and Recovery Overview

This section provides a comprehensive look at important aspects of addiction and recovery.

In considering assessment factors and treatment protocols—including sound counseling and psychological principles—it is essential to maintain a biblically based and biblically sound orientation (including confession, repentance, and godly sorrow) regarding the care and counsel of those individuals who struggle with addiction and dependency, especially as they are moving toward freedom and wholeness in Christ.

Remember the four basic steps that were presented in the introduction regarding the Road to Recovery:

1. *Recognize and admit:* the role of confession and breaking the power of the secret
2. *Clean out the infection:* the role of grieving and breaking the power of denial
3. *Renew the mind:* the role of truth and breaking the power of unbelief
4. *Exercise the will:* the role of accountability and breaking the power of fear

# 1 Disease and Choice

## 1 PORTRAITS

- "Pastor, I need help! My marriage is falling apart!" Becky begins in her call to your office. "My husband gets drunk almost every week but won't admit he has a problem!" She cries, "For years, I have had to put up with his behavior, his yelling, his anger! And yesterday he was fired! I can't stand it anymore."

- Dan worries about his mother, Marie, a sixty-five-year-old who seems depressed and unmotivated to do anything. He is concerned about her going to doctors all the time. It was five years ago that she first consulted a doctor about her back pain and she continues to go, often switching doctors. Dan is beginning to wonder if she is becoming addicted to her pain medication.

- David, who is in eighth grade, smoked weed this summer for the first time. He was with school friends and heard it was a "soft drug," one that is not so bad. He was just curious and thought it was cool to give it a try. The first time he didn't get high, but when he tried more, he got high. He loved it. "It was amazing how it worked on my mind!" Now he smokes marijuana daily to regain the euphoric feeling of that first experience.

## 2 DEFINITIONS AND KEY THOUGHTS

### Alarming Trends and Statistics

- *Addiction* is a serious problem, impacting many individuals and families.

- About *3 million Americans* aged 12 or older used an illicit drug for the first time within the past year—about 8,100 new users per day.[1]

- In 2009, *72.5 percent of students in ninth through twelfth grade* reported having had at least one drink of alcohol, and 41.8 percent of them had at least one drink within 30 days of the survey.[2] Likewise, 36.8 percent of students reported having *used marijuana* before and 20.8 percent had used marijuana at least once within 30 days of the survey.[3]

- *Heavy drinking* was reported by 6.7 percent of the population aged 12 or older, or 16.9 million people.[4]

- *Approximately 79,000 deaths are attributed to problem drinking* each year.[5] This represents nearly 40 percent of all traffic fatalities in the United States. Furthermore, it is estimated that 1.6 million hospitalizations and 4 million emergency room visits can be attributed to alcohol-related problems.[6]

- Numerous studies have established the consequences of substance abuse on families. *One out of 4 children is exposed to alcohol abuse or dependence in the family.* Drug and alcohol use are associated with violence, child neglect, abuse, delinquency, poor academic performance, occupational problems, divorce, and homelessness.

- Of the incidents of *domestic violence*, 80 percent are associated with alcohol abuse.[7] Alcohol and drug use also contribute to infant morbidity and mortality.

- *Long-term alcohol and drug abuse* are associated with cancer, cardiovascular disease, neurological damage, psychiatric problems, HIV, and other blood-borne diseases.

- The *economic consequences* of alcohol and drug abuse are staggering. Statistics show that drug abuse and drug addiction cost Americans more than 600 billion dollars annually (for healthcare expenses, lost job wages, traffic accidents, crime, and so on).[8]

## Key Characteristics

- Webster's dictionary defines addiction as "*the state of being enslaved to a habit or practice or to something that is psychologically or physically habit-forming, as narcotics, to such an extent that its cessation causes severe trauma.*" Note that people can be addicted not only to a particular chemical but also to activities (known as behavioral or process addictions), such as gambling, pornography, and compulsive shopping. These are compulsions that people have difficulty stopping even though they are aware of negative consequences.

- *Drugs* are simply chemicals that make changes in the body's chemistry or internal makeup.

- *Drug misuse* refers to using drugs for purposes or conditions for which they are not suited or for appropriate purposes but improper dosages.

- *Drug abuse* is simply defined as a pattern of harmful use of any substance or habitual activity for the purpose of altering one's mood. People abuse drugs to forget or not feel painful feelings such as loneliness, anxiety, depression, and anger.

- *Tolerance* is a phenomenon that occurs when a substance is used repeatedly and the same dose of the substance begins to have less effect. This is the reason a person who is addicted to a drug must increase the amount of drug intake to have the desired effects.

- *Physical dependence* means that the body has adapted to the presence of the chemical and *withdrawal syndrome* appears as the drug level in the system drops—when the person stops taking the drug. Withdrawal syndrome varies from one class of drugs to another.

- *Psychological dependence* (also called *behavioral dependence*) is defined by observable behavior, such as frequency of using a drug or by the amount of time or effort an individual spends in obtaining the drug.

## Methods of Use and Abuse

- There are several ways a drug can be administered. They include:

  - *Ingestion*—swallowing
  - *Injection*—needles (usually the fastest method)
  - *Inhalation*—huffing or breathing in orally
  - *Insufflation*—snorting, sniffing or breathing in nasally
  - *Interception*—absorbed into the skin through a patch, for example

- To fully understand the impact of how a given chemical will impact a user, it is important to understand the concept of pharmacology—the principles that influence how a given drug is metabolized within the human body and how this process will influence the potential side effects that could be experienced as a result. The critical elements in the process include the method by which a given drug is administered, its *bioavailability* (the process by which a substance is absorbed and then transported and distributed throughout the human body), and the concepts of *biotransformation* (the process by which the body breaks down and modifies perceived toxins so they can be safely eliminated from the body). The chosen method or "route" of administration is also important because this will impact the speed by which the drug will begin to affect the body, how the substance is distributed, and how quickly the user will begin to experience the effects and intensity of the substance.

- There are several methods by which a drug can be introduced to the body, of which the most common are *enteral* and *parenteral* forms of administration. When a drug is given enterally, it is usually taken in the form of a *tablet* or *capsule*. This allows the substance to be absorbed and broken down by the gastrointestinal tract. A *second method* by which a drug can be given enterally is *sublingual*. The drug dissolves under the tongue and is absorbed by the blood rich tissues located there. By choosing to administer a drug in this manner, it is possible to avoid the initial metabolizing effect and maximize the potential of a given compound. A *third method* of enteral administration and one rarely used by medical professionals or recreational drug users is introducing the compound into the body *rectally*.

  - The *parenteral* form of drug administration involves *injecting* a given substance directly into the body. This method is preferred in circumstances where it is important for the user to experience the desired effects rapidly. The gastrointestinal tract is avoided, allowing the drug to have maximum effect. There are several forms of parenteral administration.
  - The *subcutaneous* method requires that a given amount of the substance be injected just under the skin. While the onset of desired effects is much slower, the drug is allowed to establish a reservoir just under the skin, which can then be released into the body at a later time.

— The drug can also be *injected into muscle tissue* within the body. Due to the large amount of blood supplied to muscle tissue, the substance is absorbed much more quickly into circulation.

— The drug might be administered parenterally via *intravenous injection.* Although there are several factors that can influence the speed by which the effects of a given drug will be experienced by the user, this method seems to be the fastest. By injecting the substance directly into a vein, the drug is allowed to immediately circulate in the bloodstream.

## Models of Addiction

- What causes addiction and dependency? *Multiple models* have been suggested.

  — The *disease model* explains that there is a legitimate and verifiable difference between those who are addicted and those who are not. Addiction is viewed as a *progressive disease,* making people incapable of not using their drug of choice once they start. The drawback of this model is that by claiming it is an incurable disease, addicts are more likely to *avoid responsibility for change.*

  — The *genetic model* focuses on *differences in genetic and physiological processes* to explain addiction. Family, twin, and adoption studies suggest that 40–60 percent of an individual's risk for an addiction to alcohol is genetic. However, this does not mean individuals with certain genes will necessarily become addicted to a particular drug, for it is a matter of susceptibility or genetic predisposition. For example, in some people with certain genes, it is harder to quit once they start than for others.

  — The *biological model* focuses on *unique biological conditions*, such as abnormal drug metabolism and brain sensitivity to explain addiction. It is known that highly addictive drugs such as stimulants can spur the dopamine pathway within the brain, resulting in a feeling of being high. This causes the body to produce less dopamine. Studies with brain-scanning technology show the difference in brain structure activity between brains that have been influenced by drugs and healthy brains. However, these studies tend to show some of the physiological consequences produced by drug usage and not necessarily the causes of dependence.

  — The *choice model (moral model)* states that the individual person and his or her choices are the primary cause of an addiction problem. The model is based on the idea that each individual has *free choice and is responsible* for their behaviors. Alcohol and drug consumption are viewed as choices. Scriptures teach that each person has a moral responsibility before God, as Hebrews 4:13 says, "Nothing in all creation is hidden from God's sight. Everything is uncovered and laid bare before the eyes of him to whom we must give account." However, under the *choice model* of addiction, the addicts are often labeled as weak, with poor willpower or other *moral failings. This kind of contempt is destructive and not helpful for their recovery.*

— The *personality model* considers addiction as rooted in an *abnormality of personality*, which may be characterized by poor impulse control, a lowered self-esteem, poor coping skills, egocentricity, and manipulative traits.[9] There are frequent correlations between drug abuse and *antisocial personality disorder, and juvenile delinquency.* However, this does not fully explain whether abnormality of personality causes addiction.

— The *coping/social learning model* considers one's *psycho-emotional development* as playing an important role in addictive behaviors. People with addiction problems are seen as emotionally wounded. Many have experienced severe trauma in childhood. For example, the research on sex addicts has shown that 81 percent have been sexually abused, 74 percent have been physically abused, and 97 percent emotionally abused.[10] Addiction is considered as a *coping mechanism* to alleviate emotional pain.

— The *sociocultural model* points to the *role of society, environmental factors,* and *subcultures* in shaping an individual's addiction. In essence, addiction is viewed as a learned behavior from others. For example, alcohol consumption is powerfully influenced by the availability of alcohol and social interactions. The level of availability to illicit drugs may vary depending on the family environment, socioeconomic status, peer pressure, educational or prevention programs, legal regulations, and so on. *Social support and accountability are essential for recovery from addiction.*

— The *spiritual model* views addiction as stemming from a *lack of spirituality, a lack of faith-based values, and disconnection from God,* who is seen as the source of light, truth, love, and wellness. This model suggests that recovery from addiction requires a restored relationship with God. The Word of God does not imply that alcohol (wine) in and of itself is evil. In fact, alcohol consumption was part of everyday customs and prevailing biblical cultures and was also used for various celebrations, as well as for medicinal purposes. Yet the Bible is clear that *drunkenness is sinful* (see Gal. 5:21). The Scriptures also acknowledge the battle between the desires of the flesh (lust, craving, and so on) and the Spirit's desires (see Gal. 5). We are not to gratify the sinful desires of the heart but to live by the Spirit (Rom. 6:12; 8:5; Gal. 5:16).

• Which model is the most accurate? Scientific studies have shown the consequences of addiction in the brain but have not conclusively proven a biological causality. There may be genetic factors involved in one's vulnerability, yet that does not mean everyone from an alcoholic family will develop addiction. Likewise, social environment is influential, but everyone has a choice to take or not to take the drug when being offered. *If choice were never part of the equation and the process were purely biological, genetic, or disease-based, then it would be questionable as to whether anyone could move toward sobriety and recovery.* The fact remains that thousands of individuals do become sober.

- Today there is a definition of addiction that is commonly accepted as a *bio-psycho-social-spiritual phenomenon.* Addiction is considered as having *a myriad of causations and contributing factors,* which provide multiple pathways to recovery. These factors all impact one's vulnerability to addiction and should be considered in the recovery process. All the aspects mentioned above exist simultaneously. Each has a unique identity that helps define the problem. People have unique personalities and do not live in isolation from family, friends, community, and the larger society. We cannot ignore the reality that *the past influences the present* and we live in an imperfect and fallen world where drugs, alcohol, and other kinds of addictive temptations exist. We are *responsible for our choices* before God and will one day give an account for those choices. However, even though we are all sinners and have rebelled against a holy God by making sinful choices, His mercy and grace are available to all who call on His name (see Heb. 4:14–16).

## The Effects of Addiction

- *Compulsion.* There are three elements to compulsion: *reinforcement, craving,* and *habit.* Reinforcement occurs when the addictive substance or behavior is first engaged. The effect of the substance or the feeling it produces (such as pleasure, stimulus, or relief from pain) reinforces the user. Craving means that your brain sends intense signals that the drug or behavior is needed. Continual use becomes a habit and part of your lifestyle.
- *Loss of control.* The addict senses that the addiction is out of his or her control. Typically the person cannot predict or determine when or how much of the drug will be consumed.
- *Negative consequences.* The addict continues to use despite all the painful consequences to himself or herself and to others. These include poor physical health, mental problems, family problems, interpersonal relationship difficulties, poor job or school performance, financial problems, falling into habitual sin, and separation from God.
- *Tolerance.* When the substance is used continually, the body begins to tolerate the drug's or behavior's pharmacological effects. As a result, *the body needs an increased amount* of the chemical or behavior to produce the same effect.
- *Withdrawal.* When drug use is stopped, the addict experiences unpleasant effects. Symptoms vary depending on the substance and the amount used; withdrawal can be life-threatening and may require careful medical attention (*detoxification*), as in the case of alcohol.

## Signs and Symptoms of Addiction

- *Eyes*—bloodshot, watery, extremely dilated or pinpoint pupils, inability to focus on or track objects
- *Nose*—runny, irritated membranes

- *Odor*—bad body and/or breath odor
- *Needle tracks*—skin boils and sores, injection points
- *Unusual emotional extremes*—hysterical crying or laughter, depression, confusion, agitation, and negative response to authority
- *Unusual dispositional extremes*—over-stimulated or constantly sleepy or lethargic
- *Appetite extremes*—no appetite or very little, particularly for sweets and liquids
- *Fear complex*—paranoia, convinced someone is after them, very suspicious, becoming overly defensive or arguing about trivial things, increased secrecy
- *Physical ill health*—body deterioration in tone, skin color, stance, and weight
- *Mental ill health*—emotional extremes, loss of interest in former goals, unresponsive, increased irresponsibility at home, work, or school
- *Moral and spiritual ill health*—former values destroyed and abnormal ideas and ideals adopted in their place, lying, stealing, gambling, shoplifting, and other immoral or illegal behavior

## The Neurobiology of Addiction

- There are three major parts of the brain: the *hindbrain*, the *midbrain*, and the *forebrain*.
- The forebrain includes the *cortex/neo-cortex* (cognition/thinking) and interacts with the *limbic system* (affect/emotions).
- The feeling of pleasure is produced and regulated by a circuit of specialized nerve cells within the limbic system and is called the *nucleus accumbens*.
- The brain has approximately 100 billion *neurons* (cells)—a strongly stimulated neuron can fire 1,000 times per second.
- A small gland called the *amygdala* plays a primary role in the processing and memory of emotional reactions. In some ways it acts much like a traffic cop at a busy intersection. However, the amygdala can redirect rationale and balanced thinking away from the forebrain and send an intense message of pleasure directly to the limbic system.
- *Neurotransmitters* are chemical *messengers* released by the electrical impulses of a neuron, which record sensory experiences called *imprints*. These imprints are encoded, passed along appropriate pathways (across a *synapse*), and stored (usually at the unconscious level). Dopamine is one of the major agents related to the "pleasure pathway" to and/or through the limbic system and in the development of addiction.
- Drugs interfere with the brain's normal functioning and natural chemicals (neurotransmitters and the limbic system) that carry signals from one cell (neuron) to another (receptor). *Serotonin, dopamine,* and *norepinephrine* are the three primary neurotransmitters in the brain. Neurotransmitter levels and functioning are moderated by certain chemicals either *introduced* into the body (for example, through substance use) or *produced* (as by adrenaline) through certain behaviors (for example, through gambling or sex).

- The brain has a natural *blood-brain barrier* that normally does not allow water-soluble molecules to pass through capillary walls. A substance is considered to be *psychoactive* when it can penetrate that barrier and create changes in neuro-chemistry and subsequent brain functioning.

- *First Corinthians 6:19* is a helpful reminder: "Do you not know that *your bodies are temples* of the Holy Spirit, who is in you, whom you have received from God? You are not your own."

| Neurotransmitter | Primary Function | Chemicals with Greatest Impact and Interaction |
|---|---|---|
| Serotonin | Regulates mood, increases self-confidence, creates a feeling of safety and security, can increase sleepiness and appetite. | alcohol, cocaine, amphetamines |
| Dopamine | Regulates mood, cognition, sleep, attention and memory; influences motivation and the punishment/reward system. | heroin, PCP, caffeine, amphetamines |
| Norepinephrine | Impacts the fight/flight syndrome, acts as both a stress hormone and as a neurotransmitter, affects heart rate and glucose levels, impacts attention and focus. | caffeine, cocaine, amphetamines |
| Acetylcholine | Activates muscles (contraction), affects memory and cognition, is the primary neurotransmitter within the autonomic nervous system, regulates brain processing speed. | marijuana, LSD, PCP, nicotine, cocaine, amphetamines |
| Gamma-aminobutyric Acid (GABA) | Reduces excessive brain activity, reduces the impact of stress and irritability, promotes a state of calm, helps in relaxation, and reduces anxiety. | alcohol, benzodiazepines |
| Epinephrine (Adrenaline) | Initiates the flight/fight syndrome, acts as both a stress hormone and a neurotransmitter, promotes secondary release of endorphins. | nicotine, cocaine, amphetamines |
| Endorphins | Prevents nerve cells from releasing more pain signals, increases feelings of well-being. | heroin, nicotine |

# ASSESSMENT INTERVIEW 3

One of the difficulties in recovering from addiction is that many who are addicted deny their problem. The important role you will play in the initial assessment is to help individuals be honest with themselves and become more aware of the effects and consequences of their addiction.

The counselor's respect for the counselee is essential to begin working together. It will make it easier for clients to become honest and open if you show your genuine interest, accept them as individuals, and ask the right questions in nonjudgmental ways. The following are some helpful questions that can be asked:

1. What brought you here for counseling? Has anyone ever said that your use of _____ is a problem? How do you view the situation?
2. How often and how much do you use currently (per day or per week)?
3. Have you ever consulted a medical doctor or counselor about this problem?
4. Who in your immediate or extended family has had similar problems?
5. When did you first start using and how long have you been using?
6. How do you think your use of _____ is affecting your spouse and your family?
7. How do you think your use of _____ is affecting your job or school performance or other activities?
8. Have you tried to stop using? What kind of help did you seek? At what point do you think the process broke down or failed?
9. Have you ever done anything while under the influence, such as breaking a law, that you later regretted doing? If so, what did you do?
10. When, where, and under what circumstances do you use? More specifically, can you describe the last time you used? What happened? Whom were you with? Where were you? How were you feeling just before you used and just after?
11. On a scale of 1 to 10, with 10 being very bad, how bad do you feel about this problem?
12. On a scale of 1 to 10, with 10 being very motivated, how motivated are you to change? How hopeful do you feel about the fact that one day you may not have this problem?
13. Describe your life if you did not have this problem.
14. What kind of obstacles do you think you will face and have to overcome if you are committed to change?

*For a more thorough and formal assessment, please see the appendix.*

# 4 WISE COUNSEL

While knowing various factors are involved in the development of addiction—as we have reviewed above—we cannot, in an isolated way, simply allow the counselee to blame others (for example, family members) or circumstances (peer pressure, the environment one was raised in, traumatic events, and so on) for his or her addiction. This would not lead to intervention and change. It is most important in the recovery process that the addict *recognize the problem* and *own the responsibility* for change. Without this awareness and a sense of ownership (where choices are made), the recovery process would not be initiated. The counselor's role is to help the client come to this point.

Another essential element of addiction counseling is *safety*. The danger of the Choice Model (more specifically, the Moral Model) is that the counselee may be viewed as weak, with poor willpower, or as immoral. This kind of judgmental attitude toward the client does not help the person move to a healthier place in life but may discourage him or her from believing an opportunity for change exists. The individual may already be feeling ashamed, hopeless, and helpless (on top of any initial denial). Your acceptance, respect, empathy, and genuine understanding of the person are essential components in creating the right environment for transformation to develop. This is where the *bio-psycho-social-spiritual model* of addiction is helpful. Addiction is a complex phenomenon and each person is in a unique situation. Stand alongside the client and together seek to understand how each factor (biological, psychological, emotional, relational, and spiritual) is contributing to continued bondage to a certain drug or behavior.

# ACTION STEPS 5

## 1. Seek Medical Help

- Realize the powerful effects of drugs on the body, because the body may have adapted and developed strong tolerance and/or dependence. A thorough physical exam and consultation may be indicated.
- Sudden abstinence may result in life-threatening symptoms. A doctor should be consulted to determine if medically supervised detoxification (detox) is required. This medical procedure can cause withdrawal symptoms that need to be carefully monitored.

## 2. Become Aware of Yourself and the Nature of the Addiction

- Your counselor will help you consider how addiction is affecting your life. What would you like your life to be like?
- The first step is admitting that you have a problem. If you do not want to change, it is unlikely that you will change.

## 3. Seek Accountability and Professional Help

- Change, even that which is desired and sought after, can be difficult and complex. Change is often scary, and you will need caring professionals who know how to help you navigate this path in a productive way.
- Along with professional help, you will need accountability for the change to be maintained over time. Recovery is a journey, and you may frequently face difficult obstacles. You will need someone who cares about you and supports you through this process.

## 4. Make Sure You Are Ready to Change

- Your counselor will help you count the cost. Even though the advantages of stopping use may be great, it is also important to note there will be challenges related to neurobiological factors, self-deception, denial, and the fallen nature of mankind.
- When you realize that you actually want to change, it becomes easier to make a commitment to a plan.

## 5. Make Action Plans for Real Change

- With the right support and help, you can establish obtainable goals and develop a plan and strategy for change.
- Plans should be specific, detailing the old behaviors that need to be extinguished and the new behaviors to adopt.

## 6. Stick to the Plan

- Your counselor will help you implement the plan and assist you in taking each step toward change.
- Each new action is important. The new behavior must be practiced over time to create a new habit.
- Old habits and behaviors may remain attractive. If you indulge in them again (called a relapse), don't give up. You have probably lived with the old habits for a long time and it takes time to change patterns and recover. Review and address the plan if necessary, seek appropriate accountability, and start again.

# 6 BIBLICAL INSIGHTS

*I do not understand what I do. For what I want to do I do not do, but what I hate I do.*

*Romans 7:15*

Having fleshly desires comes with being human. Though your client is a Christian, he or she will still have struggles and temptations. Even the apostle Paul wrestled within himself. Recognize there is a battle between the flesh and the Holy Spirit who dwells in us (Gal. 5:17).

*But each person is tempted when they are dragged away by their own evil desire and enticed. Then, after desire has conceived, it gives birth to sin; and sin, when it is full-grown, gives birth to death.*

*James 1:14–15*

These desires can drive deep down in a person (Eph. 2:3; 4:22). When desire is conceived, or when someone is driven by these passions, it gives birth to sin. This leads to obeying the lust (Rom. 6:12). Sin is serious, deserving of God's anger and wrath (Rom. 1:32; 6:23).

The only salvation from sin and from God's anger is found in Jesus Christ (1 Cor. 15:55–57; Heb. 7:27; 1 Pet. 2:24; 1 John 2:2).

*What a wretched man I am! Who will rescue me from this body that is subject to death? Thanks be to God, who delivers me through Jesus Christ our Lord!*

*Romans 7:24–25*

While the Spirit in him wants to do what is pleasing to God, another power makes Paul a slave to the sin that is still in him (Rom. 7:23). Paul understood the dilemma and complexity of change. So does God! He never abandons us. He understands everything we go through.

God offered His own Son as a sacrifice for our sins. While we were still sinners, He demonstrated His love for us. God saved us! He continues to care for our every need and sees our struggles. He longs for us to come to Him.

Once a person receives Jesus as Savior and Lord, the person becomes His child and God gives His Spirit. The Holy Spirit helps in this battle and in human weakness (Acts 1:8). By yielding to Him, an addict will have victory over the flesh.

## PRAYER STARTER 7

Lord, thank You for _____'s willingness to come here and face his (her) addiction. We acknowledge that You know everything that goes on with _____. Thank You for Your love and compassionate understanding. You see the struggles, the physical dependence, painful emotions, and his (her) past and future. We are here to say we need You. We confess our brokenness and our dependence on Your grace. Apart from You, we cannot do anything good. You see our fleshly desires that war against who You want us to be. Yet Your goal for us is to be holy as You are holy. We give You control over every aspect of our lives. Give _____ strength in each step as he (she) moves toward recovery . . .

## RECOMMENDED RESOURCES 8

Anderson, Neil T. *Freedom from Addiction: Breaking the Bondage of Addiction and Finding Freedom in Christ.* Gospel Light, 1996.

Arterburn, Stephen, and David Stoop. *The Book of Life Recovery.* Tyndale, 2012.

Clinebell, Howard. *Understanding and Counseling Persons with Alcohol, Drug, and Behavioral Addictions.* Abingdon, 1998.

Clinton, Tim. *Turn Your Life Around.* FaithWords, 2006.

Clinton, Tim, Archibald Hart, and George Ohlschlager. *Caring for People God's Way.* Thomas Nelson, 2006.

Dunn, Jerry. *God Is for the Alcoholics.* Moody, 1986.

Hersh, Sharon. *The Last Addiction: Why Self Help Is Not Enough.* WaterBrook, 2008.

Murphey, Cecil. *When Someone You Love Abuses Drugs and Alcohol.* Beacon Hill Press, 2004.

Rice, Michael. *The Choice Theory Approach to Drug and Alcohol Abuse.* Madeira, 2009.

## Websites

Alcoholics Anonymous: www.aa.org/

Celebrate Recovery: www.celebraterecovery.com/

Substance Abuse and Mental Health Services Administration: (SAMHSA): www.samhsa.gov/

# Trauma and Comorbidity 2

## PORTRAITS 1

- "As a child, I was beaten up by my own father. . . ." Dan starts telling his life story. "We didn't know when he would come home drunk again and I was always terrified. It was like walking on eggshells all the time." Now Dan, as a father of three small children, is frustrated that he finds himself doing the same as his father did. "I told myself I would never do this to my own kids . . . but I can't stop screaming at them and drinking!"

- Tina, a twenty-two-year-old crack addict, comes for counseling and says that she is in an abusive relationship. Her boyfriend slaps and punches her; he threatens to kill her if she leaves him. She explains that she has been physically abused since she was four years old. Her father died in a shooting accident and then her mother moved in with another man. This man did something so awful to her that she is not ready to talk about it yet. Tina says her childhood was fragmented. "It feels like I'm always outside of my body." She is confused with her frame of reference and seems terrified as she speaks. Violence, sex, and drugs have been major themes throughout her life.

- Stephen, a thirty-three-year-old Army veteran with the National Guard who recently returned from deployment in Afghanistan, has been having a hard time adjusting to civilian life. He has not been able to keep a job for longer than a month. He feels exhausted, extremely anxious, stressed all the time, and helpless. He cannot control his agitation and anger, which is beginning to affect his marriage. Stephen feels lonely deep inside and is emotionally disconnected from his wife and children. He has difficulty falling asleep. Every night he is afraid that hundreds of haunting war memories will intrude on his sleep. He drinks to "calm down" and he knows he needs help.

## DEFINITIONS AND KEY THOUGHTS 2

- *Comorbidity* is the condition where one person has two or more disorders or illnesses simultaneously or sequentially. The term implies interactions between them, with one illness influencing the course and prognosis of the other(s).[1]

- *Dual diagnosis* is a term often used for comorbidity. This term, however, is used more specifically in referring to a condition where one person has a substance addiction (abuse/dependence) and a mental illness (such as depression, anxiety, borderline personality disorder, and so on).

- *Dual diagnoses are common.* For example, people diagnosed with drug addictions are about twice as likely to suffer from mood disorders (depression, bipolar disorder, and so on) and anxiety disorders (generalized anxiety disorder, obsessive-compulsive disorder, post-traumatic stress disorder [PTSD], and others) compared to the general population. Those who are diagnosed with mood or anxiety disorders are two times more likely to have addiction-related problems. Those diagnosed with a behavioral disorder (such as conduct disorder or antisocial personality disorder) are also twice as likely to have addiction problems.[2]

- Among *adolescents*, the prevalence of substance use, abuse, or dependence is 6–33 percent (depending on the method of study), and 61–68 percent of these youth have at least one comorbid psychiatric diagnosis. Externalizing disorders (such as conduct disorder, attention deficit hyperactive disorder, and oppositional defiant disorder) are more common than internalizing disorders (mood and anxiety disorders) among adolescents.[3]

- *PTSD is one of the anxiety disorders.* It is characterized by (1) being exposed to a traumatic experience—danger to self (for example, physical and sexual abuse, serious injury, combat trauma) or witnessing danger to others; (2) recalling or re-experiencing a traumatic event and responding with unwanted thoughts and feelings of fear, horror, shock, and helplessness; (3) avoiding trauma-associated thoughts, feelings, and triggers; and (4) experiencing increased arousal such as difficulty falling asleep or staying asleep, irritability, or outbursts of anger.[4]

- *"Fight-flight"* reactions are natural when we are in real or anticipated danger. However, this normal reaction process is damaged in people with PTSD. They display fight-flight reactions (both physically and psychologically) when they are no longer in any actual danger.

- In recent years and especially among returning combat veterans, clinicians and researchers have become aware of the high occurrence in the *dual diagnosis of PTSD and substance abuse diagnoses (abuse/dependence).* Among patients with substance use disorders, 20–30 percent meet criteria for PTSD. The rate is generally higher for women (30–59 percent).[5] It is estimated that 75 percent of Vietnam veterans meet diagnostic criteria for lifetime substance dependence.[6]

- *Dual diagnosis is more problematic than a single diagnosis.* Those who have both a diagnosis of PTSD and substance addiction have *more severe symptoms* than those with a single diagnosis. PTSD symptoms include emotional and physiological arousal (unwanted recollection of trauma with feelings of fear, horror, shock, difficulty sleeping, irritability, startle response, and so on) and avoidance of these intense arousal symptoms. It is typically more difficult to treat than those with a single diagnosis. Treatment is longer and highly challenging for both professionals and clients. More frequent relapse and events requiring hospitalization have been reported among this population. The use of substances seems to worsen the effectiveness of medication as well.[7]

- Researchers have come up with two explanations for the connection between PTSD and substance abuse. *The first model is that drug abuse precedes PTSD.* In the search for drugs, substance abusers repeatedly place themselves in dangerous situations, which often results in greater exposure to traumatic events. Chronic use of substances leads to higher levels of arousal and increased sensitivity to stress, which can also lead to vulnerability in the development of PTSD. *The second model suggests PTSD precedes drug abuse.* Those who suffer from symptoms of PTSD use substances to cope with their intense emotional and physiological arousal. Patients actually report symptom relief from depressants, such as alcohol, cannabis, opioids, and benzodiazepines.[8]

- People who struggle with *both chemical dependence/abuse and PTSD* need to be treated with integrated care. This requires professionals who are equipped to attend to their psychological needs and medical professionals who are able to provide medical care, including detox services. Treatment must be multifaceted, not only supporting a client's recovery from addiction but also addressing his or her thoughts and emotions (or management of emotions) to strengthen life and social skills.

# ASSESSMENT INTERVIEW 3

## Counselor Responsibility

In cases of ongoing trauma, if the client is in immediate danger, he or she must first be taken to a safe environment. Trauma such as abuse, when experienced as a child, has severe consequences on future physical, emotional, and mental health. If your client is a minor and you suspect abuse or neglect, it is your moral responsibility to report it to the appropriate agencies, such as local law enforcement, the Department of Social and Health Services, or Child Protective Services. Licensed clinicians are mandated by the state and their regulatory boards to report cases involving known or alleged abuse.

## Rule Outs

1. On a scale of 1 to 10, with 1 being great and 10 being extremely depressed, how are you feeling today?
2. Do you have any thoughts of hurting yourself? Do you have thoughts about ending your life? Do you have any plans to harm yourself or end your life? *If suicidal tendencies are evident, seek professional help for your client immediately.*

## Questions for the Client

Assessments should include questions concerning both substance use and psychosocial history.

1. What brought you here today? Is this the first time you have sought help?
2. Have you experienced or witnessed an event in your past that was extremely scary, horrifying, traumatic, physically harmful, and/or life-threatening?

3. Do you have distressing memories of the event, such as images, thoughts, or perceptions? Do you have distressing dreams or nightmares about the event?

4. Do you find yourself trying to avoid these thoughts and feelings while talking about the trauma?

5. Are you in any immediate danger? Is someone threatening you? If so, what kind of boundaries have you set? Have you tried to stop the abuse? If so, what happened?

6. During the past month, how often have you felt each of the following: depressed, worthless, hopeless, anxious, nervous, or restless? On a scale of 1 to 10, with 10 being very intense, how intense were these feelings?

7. How are any of these emotions affecting work or school?

8. How are these feelings impacting your friendships, working relationships, and marriage and family relationships?

9. Are you currently using alcohol or other substances? Are you engaged in a habit that you feel you cannot stop? On a scale of 1 to 10, with 10 being very strongly, how strongly do you believe you need these substances to function?

10. Have you ever felt you should reduce your drinking or use of a substance? Do you lie about how much or how often you drink or use?

11. How much, where, and when do you use? Describe how you were feeling and what went through your mind both before and after your last use of the substance.

12. Have you consulted a medical provider about drinking, other drug use, or your intense emotions? Have you sought other professional help with a counselor or psychologist? If so, please describe the process and what led you to stop treatment.

13. What do you believe about yourself? How do think God sees you and how do you see God in your life?

# 4 WISE COUNSEL

Often those who suffer from a dual diagnosis need comprehensive treatment services. What they go through is not simple. While there must be teaching and encouragement from the Word of God, simply sharing Scriptures does not necessarily address every underlying psychological and medical issue. When people have intense emotions and experience difficulty in managing them, they may struggle in connecting with the Scriptures you share. They may even have difficulty connecting with you. A team of medical professionals, psychotherapists, social workers, and caring friends and family is sometimes required.

To make things more complicated, under the same diagnosis, individual symptoms and needs can vary from one person to another. Some require hospitalization or a detox program to break the cycle of addiction. Some require medication. Others need social skill training and/or stress management training. Some may need life-skill education, such as money management or job interviewing preparation. A comprehensive assessment and understanding of each person is essential for an effective intervention plan.

Interpersonal trauma (emotional, physical, and sexual abuse) is a boundary violation. Healing from such a violation requires sensitivity and gentle care, where the victims can regain safety, trust, and healthy relationship boundaries. Your genuine presence as a caregiver is important. You need to accept them for who they are and meet them where they are in the moment. Through your loving presence, they will come to embrace the safety and love of God.

Working with those who have a dual diagnosis can be especially challenging. Abstinence is difficult to attain for this population. It requires much patience on your part, because relapses will undoubtedly occur. The love of Christ must be your motivation as a counselor. Keep loving your clients as Christ loves them, regardless of the ups and downs in their overall progress. Do not expect quick results or healing. Set small and obtainable goals, such as making and keeping appointments, staying accountable, setting appropriate personal boundaries, and learning about mental illness.

Individuals with dual diagnosis tend to have shame and guilt feelings before God. To cope with negative emotions, they start the addiction cycle. Knowing what they are doing is wrong, guilt and shame increase, creating more distance from God. Helping these clients accept God's grace and forgiveness is an important goal.

# ACTION STEPS : 5

## 1. Admit That You Have a Problem

- If you do not admit that you have a problem, you will not do anything to change.
- Consider the impact of your addiction and your intense emotional and physiological distress.
- At the same time, ask yourself honestly how motivated you are to work toward recovery. What has kept you in the past from embracing change and healing? What are you afraid will happen if you start this recovery process?
- Stop blaming others or your past. You cannot change people or what has happened. All you can do is allow God to change you.

## 2. Seek Professional Help

- Your best chance of recovery is from a team of professionals who can assist you with both the addiction and the mental health issues.
- Educate yourself about available treatment services. Treatment options include inpatient detox programs, residential rehab centers, outpatient individual psychotherapy, family therapy, group counseling, medications, and peer recovery groups (for example, Alcohol Anonymous, 12-step programs).

### 3. Believe That You Will Be Healed

- The impact of trauma is severe, yet in Christ, you have a future. Refuse to see yourself as a victim. You are a survivor. Realize you have a choice to stay where you are or to take another step toward recovery.
- You may dream of a quick recovery but be realistic and make sure to set small and attainable goals. Your focus should be to achieve each goal one step at a time.
- Be patient with yourself. Healing takes time. Do not compare your progress with another person's recovery. You might relapse, but remember that this is often a part of the recovery process. God's love for you is patient and He will not give up on you (1 Cor. 1:4–7). Do not be discouraged!

### 4. Seek God, the Ultimate Healer

- You might feel guilty before God. You might feel distant from Him. However, take courage to seek and understand Him through reading the Scriptures and meditating on them. He wants you to know Him as the gracious and compassionate God that He is. He knows all about your problems, your past, and your heart cries.

### 5. Seek Accountability

- The healing process is complex. You might feel scared and alone. For your recovery, you need not only caring professionals but also those who share the same struggles as you do and can journey with you. There is power in understanding that you are not alone. Draw close to your professional helpers, as well as to your peer support. When you slip and fall, it does not necessarily mean you have to go all the way back to square one.

## 6  BIBLICAL INSIGHTS

*If we confess our sins, he is faithful and just and will forgive us our sins and purify us from all unrighteousness.*

1 John 1:9

If a person has never asked God for forgiveness of sins, this is the most important decision to make. It means believing and trusting in Jesus Christ, who died for our forgiveness. Scripture tells us to believe in the Lord Jesus Christ and be saved (Rom. 10:9, 13).

Even though clients have asked Christ to save them from sin and its penalty, they may still feel distant or guilty before God. Confessing sin, including addictions to drugs and alcohol or other bad habits and the lies they have believed, is important. Help them acknowledge they gave their heart and body to these things, but when they ask for forgiveness, God forgives them. It is guaranteed and He keeps His promises. Have them take time to meditate on this promise: you are forgiven.

*God opposes the proud but shows favor to the humble. Submit yourselves, then, to God. Resist the devil, and he will flee from you. Come near to God and he will come near to you.*

*James 4:6–8*

God has compassion for those who are broken and humble. He is always ready and available when someone comes humbly to Him. When a person recognizes his or her need of Him and for His forgiveness, healing, and growth, He is delighted to give grace, strength, and restoration.

*He was despised and rejected by mankind, a man of suffering, and familiar with pain. Like one from whom people hide their faces he was despised, and we held him in low esteem. Surely he took up our pain and bore our suffering, yet we considered him punished by God, stricken by him, and afflicted. But he was pierced for our transgressions, he was crushed for our iniquities; the punishment that brought us peace was on him, and by his wounds we are healed. We all, like sheep, have gone astray, each of us has turned to our own way; and the LORD has laid on him the iniquity of us all.*

*Isaiah 53:3–6*

It was traumatic and very unfortunate that your clients have had to witness horrible things or were mistreated and abused by others. Who really understands their pain? Who else has been mistreated like they have? The Lord Jesus went through all of it. He sees their suffering. God invites them to participate in His sufferings. This healing process is an opportunity to understand Jesus Christ more completely.

*Love is patient, love is kind. It does not envy, it does not boast, it is not proud. It does not dishonor others, it is not self-seeking, it is not easily angered, it keeps no record of wrongs. Love does not delight in evil but rejoices with the truth. It always protects, always trusts, always hopes, always perseveres. Love never fails.*

*1 Corinthians 13:4–8*

This is how God loves us. God is patient and gentle. When we are discouraged by seeing our own failures and relapses, we must look to Jesus, who is not surprised with our failures. He knows we are weak and His love never fails. His love endures forever.

# 7 PRAYER STARTER

Lord, Jesus, thank You for Your forgiveness and Your warm invitation for _____ to be adopted into Your family. He (she) is Your child. You deeply and dearly love him (her). You see his (her) innermost and intense pain and every detail of what has happened to him (her). You see all of his (her) fears. Lord, guide _____ to Your light. We know we will be safe in Your presence. I ask _____ to be filled with Your loving presence right now . . .

# 8 RECOMMENDED RESOURCES

Adsit, Chris. *The Combat Trauma Healing Manual: Christ-Centered Solutions for Combat Trauma.* Military Ministry Press, 2008.

Clinton, Tim, Archibald Hart, and George Ohlschlager. *Caring for People God's Way: Personal and Emotional Issues, Addictions, Grief, and Trauma.* Thomas Nelson, 2006.

Evans, Katie, and Michael Sullivan. *Dual Diagnosis: Counseling the Mentally Ill Substance Abuser.* Guilford Press, 2001.

———. *Treating Addicted Survivors of Trauma.* Guilford Press, 2004.

Ferrini, Cindi. *Balancing the Active Life: Reclaiming Life after Trauma.* Tate Publishing, 2011.

Gingrich, Heather Davediuk. *Restoring the Shattered Self: A Christian Counselor's Guide to Complex Trauma.* IVP Academic, 2013.

Laaser, Mark. *Healing the Wounds of Sexual Addiction.* Zondervan, 2004.

Ortman, Dennis. *The Dual Diagnosis Recovery Sourcebook: A Physical, Mental, and Spiritual Approach to Addiction with an Emotional Disorder.* Lowell House, 2001.

Roberts, Candyce. *Help for the Fractured Soul: Experiencing Healing and Deliverance from Deep Trauma.* Chosen, 2012.

Smith, Gary. *Radical Compassion: Finding Christ in the Heart of the Poor.* Loyola Press, 2002.

Wright, H. Norman. *The Complete Guide to Crisis and Trauma Counseling: What to Do and Say When It Matters Most!* Regal, 2011.

## Websites

Brookhaven Hospital: www.brookhavenhospital.com/ptsd-treatment/

Capstone Treatment Center: www.capstonetreatmentcenter.com/

The Christian Treatment Center: www.thechristiantreatmentcenter.com/our-program

Keystone Treatment Center: www.keystonetreatment.com

Meier Clinics: www.meierclinics.com/

The Minirth Clinic: www.theminirthclinic.com/

New Life Recovery: www.newliferecovery.net/ChristianBasedDrugRehabChristian-RelatedAddictionTreatmentCenter.htm

Timberline Knolls: www.timberlineknolls.com/information/christian-path

# Treatment Protocols   **3**

- Isabelle has been diagnosed with a life-threatening cancer. All she can think about is beating this disease, so she consults specialists, those who understand her specific cancer and who have expertise in relevant treatment protocols. She is looking for the most effective treatment she can find to give her the best chance for recovery. Perhaps you have had someone in your counseling office with a serious addiction problem. You and your client would be as eager to find the best treatment possible, just as in the case of a cancer diagnosis.

- Alice has a son, Benjamin, who is sixteen years old. Just last week, she was astonished to hear that he was suspended from school due to theft and possession of illegal drugs. She thought he was a good kid and would never get in trouble with drugs. Now Alice learns that Benjamin has been heavily involved in marijuana, cocaine, and methamphetamines. She is both furious and very worried at the same time. How did he get involved in these things? Where does he go from here? What is the first step? He says he is sorry, but will everything be okay if he can just stop using the drugs? How can he get help? What are his options? What about his faith in God?

## DEFINITIONS AND KEY THOUGHTS  **2**

### Statistics and Current Practice

- The *prevalence of substance abuse* in the United States is high and the needs for treatment are tremendous. It is estimated that 23.2 million people aged 12 and older need addiction treatment.[1] Only 10 percent of those who need services actually receive professional care.

- Overall, studies show the *outcome of treatment is poor*. The majority of those who initially receive care do not complete treatment.[2] Half of those who complete a treatment regimen seem to relapse and resume problematic alcohol or drug use within 6 months.[3] Indicators show the average success rate for a treatment center is 2–20 percent.

- Traditionally *complications-driven approaches* (attending to gastrointestinal, psychiatric, orthopedic, or trauma-related consequences) or *diagnosis-and-program-driven approaches* (recovery from addiction is the central focus and programs are prepackaged in terms of length, content, and structure) have been commonly practiced.[4] These approaches are often not comprehensive enough to meet individual client's unique needs.

- Recently, *individualized treatment approaches* with comprehensive assessment and multiple-level treatments have become the standard.[5] This shift reflects the importance of understanding the *individual differences and unique needs* of clients and of addressing the *underlying issues* behind addiction problems that are not necessarily the focus of traditional approaches. Furthermore, practitioners have been encouraged to seek *outcome-informed treatment approaches* that utilize client feedback—rather than only the practitioner's evaluation or objective data—to evaluate how the treatment is matching the client's needs as well as its overall effectiveness.[6]

- Recovery requires the correct treatment, the appropriate service, and optimal setting to best effect a positive outcome. This decision about treatment depends on various factors of addiction (severity, length of use, types of drugs, and so on), and the individual's physical, emotional, social, and spiritual needs.

## Levels of Care

The American Society of Addiction Medicine defines five levels of care that each client fits into at one time or another.

- *Level 0.5: Early intervention*—This level of care is not treatment but the combination of psychoeducation and assessment, targeted for individuals who are at risk of developing addiction problems or for those for whom there is not yet enough information to give a diagnosis. If the individual is in immediate danger, he or she is transferred to an appropriate level care. If the client is not in immediate danger, yet requires outpatient treatment, an attempt is made to facilitate such treatment where he/she will be assisted to increase awareness of the consequences of substance abuse.

- *Level I: Outpatient treatment*—Organized services such as individual counseling and group counseling are offered in nonresidential facilities. Services are provided in regularly scheduled sessions. This level of care is designed to treat individuals with clinical severity and to help them achieve permanent change in addiction-related behaviors, mental functioning, lifestyle, and behavioral issues.

- *Level II: Intensive outpatient treatment/partial hospitalization*—Organized outpatient services are delivered during the day, before or after work or school, or on weekends. This level of care includes essential education and treatment components, while allowing clients to apply learned skills in their "real world" environment.

- *Level III: Residential/inpatient treatment*—Organized services in a twenty-four-hour live-in setting (for example, halfway house, therapeutic rehabilitation facility, therapeutic community) provided by addiction treatment professionals and mental health practitioners. This level of care is designed for individuals who need a safe and stable living environment to obtain the necessary recovery skills.

- *Level IV: Medically managed intensive inpatient treatment*—Planned twenty-four-hour programs in a hospital are provided by an interdisciplinary team of addiction-credentialed clinicians, including physicians and physiatrists. Services include medical evaluation, medical management, and treatment for mental and substance-related disorders. This level of care is designed for those whose problems are so severe that they need biomedical, psychiatric, and nursing care.[7]

## Treatment Planning

- The National Curriculum Committee of the Addiction Technology Transfer Centers (ATTC) defines *treatment planning* as "a collaborative process through which the counselor and client develop desired treatment outcomes and identify the strategies for achieving them."[8]
- *Comprehensive assessment* must precede treatment planning. The components of clinical assessment include a history of alcohol and drug use, both current status and the history of physical health, mental health, substance use, treatment history, work history and career issues, socioeconomic status, lifestyle, legal status, family issues, spirituality, education, basic life skills, and the use of community resources.[9]
- After a relevant and thorough assessment has been made, the therapist summarizes the findings for the client. Collaboratively the therapist and client *prioritize the client's needs and concerns*. At this point, they also discuss the level of readiness for treatment. They formulate measurable treatment outcomes or treatment goals and identify the strategies for each outcome.
- The *treatment goal* may vary depending on the individual's view or model of addiction. For example, embracing a disease model (which suggests the client has a disease such that he cannot control the progression of use), the treatment goal will be total abstinence. For others who view social drinking, for example, as acceptable, a treatment goal may be to work toward controlled social drinking.[10]

## Treatment Strategies

- *Self-control of behavior training* equips clients with techniques to monitor and change their own behaviors.
- *Contingency management* identifies and manipulates environmental contingencies that reward or punish the addictive behavior.
- *Enhancing motivation for change* facilitates a client's motivation to change behaviors and maintain the changed behavioral patterns.
- *Skill training* trains clients on problem solving, decision making, relaxation, assertiveness, and social skills.
- *Marriage and family therapy*, based on systems theory, changes unhealthy relationships or family interactions that maintain addictive behaviors and involves family members to support the recovery process.
- *Cognitive therapy* helps clients change appraisals of self and the environment.

- *Aversive conditioning* couples substance use with an unpleasant experience.
- *Accountability and self-help groups* are structured support groups where members are held accountable for each other's recovery and abstinence, share testimonies, and gain personal responsibility and coping skills, which are helpful for recovery.
- *Pharmacotherapies*

  — *Detoxification (detox)* is an initial medical procedure to alleviate unpleasant withdrawal symptoms due to abrupt termination of drug use.
  — *Agonist/Substitution Therapy* induces cross-tolerance with safer agents to prevent relapse and cravings (for example, nicotine-replacement medications for tobacco dependence).
  — *Antagonist Therapy* induces extinction of the pleasurable experience that the abused drug provides (for example, Naltrexone for heroin dependence).
  — *Aversion Therapy* produces an aversive reaction when clients use the drug (for example, Disulfiram for alcohol, which produces headache, vomiting, and breathing difficulty in the presence of alcohol).[11]

## Elements of a Good Treatment Plan

- The plan treats the whole person.
- Goals and objectives are written.
- The plan considers needed skill training and education.
- Goals and objectives are based on the client's strengths.
- Goals and objectives are achievable.
- Goals and objectives are measurable.
- The treatment plan creates a sense of ownership.
- The plan is proactive rather than reactive.
- The plan identifies potential relapse triggers.
- The client does not feel alone. "Two are better than one, because they have a good return for their labor: If either of them falls down, one can help the other up. But pity anyone who falls and has no one to help them up. . . . A cord of three strands is not quickly broken" (Eccles. 4:9–10, 12).

# 3  ASSESSMENT INTERVIEW

Initial steps in working with individuals with addiction problems should include building rapport, gathering information comprehensively or systematically, and reviewing the treatment options that are suitable for a client's needs and goals.

1. Tell me what brought you here. Briefly tell me your life story.
2. What drugs are you using? How long, how often, and how much are you using? Tell me the symptoms you experience when you are using and when you quit.

3. Have you been diagnosed with any mental illnesses in the past?
4. Do you become aggressive toward others or do you have thoughts of harming yourself while using?
5. Have you sought treatment for this problem before? What was effective and what did not work?
6. Can you tell me the impact of substance use on your current life problems (in your job, marriage, family, relationships, school)?
7. On a scale of 1 to 10 where 10 is very ready, how ready are you to receive treatment and to work toward change?
8. What kind of social support systems do you have? How supportive do you believe your family will be as you work toward your goals? Do you have support from your workplace, school, church, or community?
9. What financial resources do you have?
10. Describe your relationship with God. Where is He in your struggles with addiction?

# WISE COUNSEL 4

Discerning the best treatment option for an individual is not a simple task. There are three key components in this task.

First, this is a collaborative process with the client. It is ultimately his or her decision and commitment to change. You should be available to support, facilitate, and assist in the process of making decisions about the client's recovery from addiction. You must establish rapport with clients early on and should maintain the collaborative working alliance throughout the course of treatment. Clients need to feel safe, understood, accepted, and they need to believe that you are there for them.

Second, as a helper you must discern if the individual needs immediate care. It is imperative to screen for any signs that the client has tried to injure self or others. Collect information on their use of drugs (frequency, length, intensity of intoxication, and severity of withdrawal symptoms). Withdrawal from certain drugs can be fatal. Accordingly, you must refer them to appropriate treatment facilities. Helpers must not hesitate to refer clients to medical professionals and to consult with other helping professionals.

Third, choosing appropriate treatment options requires a comprehensive understanding of each client and prioritizing their treatment needs. It is your role to ask guiding questions so that you and the client together may clarify goals. For each goal, explore strategies to achieve the desired outcome and in a collaborative manner, develop a mutually acceptable plan of action. Once the strategy is determined, you must patiently stay with the client's course of treatment by monitoring, supporting, and evaluating progress.

# 5 ACTION STEPS

## 1. Slow Down and Get Ready for Change

- Often addiction makes a person feel out of control. Intense urges and cravings make you feel that there are no other options. You have to learn how to slow down. When you slow down and reflect on your life and where you have been, grieving over the addiction may take place, along with an understanding of what could be lost—valued relationships, family, work, finances, health, dreams, or your relationship with God.

- You need to consider honestly if you are willing to let go of your addiction. While realizing how thoroughly addiction has taken over your life, you may face fears in letting go of a comfortable escape mechanism. Drinking and drugs replace boredom, loneliness, emptiness, hopelessness, or simply the reality of life. Are you ready for change?

## 2. Be Open to Seeking Help

- You should be aware of the powerful effects addiction can have on the body. It may be important to visit a doctor for consultation. Depending on the kind of drugs, dosage, and frequency, withdrawal may be fatal and require careful medical attention.

- Mental health professionals may be needed to explore treatment options. You may feel overwhelmed with various problems in your life and you may also be feeling lost. Talking to a professional will be helpful in mapping out problems, needs, priorities, obtainable goals, and steps and strategies to obtain those goals.

- You need to be active in seeking a faith community and other supportive and available resources. You must understand the roles that both isolation and accountability play in the process, especially when experiencing loneliness. Seeking out and depending on loving and wise friends who will lift you up and encourage you is important. Recovering addicts need someone who genuinely cares about and supports them.

## 3. Rest in God's Power

- Helping professionals can assist you in choosing an appropriate treatment plan and work through it with you. Accountability partners in self-help groups are valuable and helpful for recovery. However, ultimately, it is God who knows all the ups and downs in a person's life. He is the One who gives power over bad habits and our sinful nature. Transformation comes from and through the power of the Holy Spirit.

- Facing God honestly may be a challenge, but it is only through Him that hope is found. Do you experience God as angry or distant? Or do you believe that God has forgiven you? Can you rely on God and His power for recovery? Can you rely on His gracious faithfulness even if you fall back into the addiction?

# BIBLICAL INSIGHTS : 6

*Jesus answered, "It is written: 'Worship the Lord your God and serve him only.'"*

*Luke 4:8*

Often clients have good intentions. They may be willing to just quit alcohol or drugs "cold turkey" or may have already tried many times. The results of these self-efforts may have been failure after failure. If so, they know that recovery can be a rather complicated and overwhelming process. They may have realized it is not something to be handled alone and that freedom from addiction is a lordship issue—defining who one's master really is. Victory over addiction is God's business and it requires the person to surrender completely to Him.

*The fear of the LORD is the beginning of wisdom, and knowledge of the Holy One is understanding.*

*Proverbs 9:10*

First, clients must fear the Lord, for it is the beginning of wisdom. Since this is a battle that people are not equipped to fight by themselves, they need God's power and wisdom. Tactful strategies are necessary to fight against the flesh and addiction. God's wisdom is there for those who fear Him and seek Him. He gives generously to all without reproach (see James 1:5).

*Plans fail for lack of counsel, but with many advisers they succeed.*

*Proverbs 15:22*

Clients must surround themselves with wise counsel. Caring counselors who come alongside an addict can help plan how to gain freedom from addiction and guide each step.

# PRAYER STARTER : 7

Lord, we come into Your presence, acknowledging our dependence on You. You know everything that goes on in our lives. Please give _____ courage, for he (she) is ready to face this problem, which is bigger than we can handle by ourselves. Thank You for Your discernment, wisdom, and power that are available to us. We trust in Your unfailing love. Lord, please order our steps and give us a plan that honors You and brings freedom . . .

# 8 : RECOMMENDED RESOURCES

Anderson, Neil T., Mike Quarles, and Julia Quarles. *Freedom from Addiction: Breaking the Bondage of Addiction and Finding Freedom in Christ.* Gospel Light, 1996.

Belzman, Michael. *Handbook for Christ-Centered Substance Abuse and Addiction Counselors.* Xulon Press, 2011.

Benda, Brent B., and Thomas F. McGovern. *Spirituality and Religiousness and Alcohol/ Other Drug Problems: Treatment and Recovery Perspectives.* Haworth Press, 2006.

Clinebell, Harvard. *Understanding and Counseling Persons with Alcohol, Drug, and Behavioral Addictions.* Abingdon Press, 1998.

Clinton, Tim. *Turn Your Life Around.* FaithWords, 2006.

Erickson, Carlton K. *The Science of Addiction: From Neurobiology to Treatment.* W. W. Norton, 2007.

Jones, Bishop Samuel. *Breaking the Spirit of Addiction: Counseling Guide.* Xulon Press, 2011.

## Websites

Alcohol Drug Abuse Help and Resource Center: www.addicthelp.com/addiction-treatment.asp

Drug Addiction Support Organization: www.drug-addiction-support.org/Christian-Treatment.html

National Institute of Drug Abuse (NIDA): www.drugabuse.gov/

New Life Recovery (Christian Addiction Treatment Drug Rehab Centers): www.newliferecovery.net/ChristianBasedDrugRehabChristianRelatedAddictionTreatmentCenter.html

Substance Abuse and Mental Health Services Administration (SAMHSA): www.samhsa.gov/

# Spiritual Applications    **4**

## PORTRAITS : 1

- Chris grew up in an alcoholic home and swore he would never follow in his parents' footsteps. However, at the age of seventeen, he started experimenting with alcohol at the high school parties he attended. Though he made himself believe it was merely recreational, Chris's life started spinning out of control due to his drinking. He hit rock bottom when he was caught driving drunk and received a DUI. From that point on, he recognized he was beginning to lead the same kind of life his parents did. He has been involved in Alcoholics Anonymous for the last five years and has truly benefitted from the relationships he's built there and by AA's leading him to a closer relationship with the Lord.

- Lauren, after being kicked out of her parents' house, became heavily addicted to heroin in her mid-twenties. After just a few months of use, she unintentionally overdosed and was taken to the emergency room by a friend. After recovering in the hospital, Lauren admitted herself into a twenty-eight-day treatment facility to learn how to maintain sobriety. After completing that process, she joined Narcotics Anonymous. However, she soon found that the group did not focus as heavily on Christian principles as she would have liked. Recently her church started a Celebrate Recovery group, and Lauren has found the kind of spiritual guidance there she needs.

- Bill has been in recovery from alcoholism for seven years, and he has finally reached a point where he feels capable of ministering to others who are struggling with similar difficulties. He is seeking counseling to make sure he is strong enough to take on a leadership role in a support group. He trusts that God has successfully led him through recovery and he is passionate about helping others feel the same freedom he has finally been able to embrace. However, he is afraid of the triggers he will experience when working with others who are still battling their addiction.

## DEFINITIONS AND KEY THOUGHTS : 2

- *Spiritual applications* to addiction recovery are seen in many of the current models of treatment used today. One of the most well-known and widely used models is the *12 Steps*, originally created for Alcoholics Anonymous. Throughout the years, these steps have been replicated and expanded for other recovery groups. More

53

recently, faith-oriented approaches to addiction recovery have dwindled with a shift toward an all-inclusive focus that is tolerant of most religious groups and belief systems. In whatever manner in which one's understanding or concept of God may vary (for example, God as you understand Him, a higher power, etc.), research suggests that many Christian principles including surrender, forgiveness, meditation, and prayer do aid in the recovery process.

- *Alcoholics Anonymous*, which began on June 10, 1935, was started by two alcoholics, Dr. Bob Smith and Bill Wilson, who worked with one another to maintain sobriety.[1] Today AA has more than 2 million members in more than 160 countries, including 1.2 million members in the United States alone.[2]

  — AA claims to be a *spiritual organization*, not a religious group.[3]
  — The organization avoids the hierarchical structure—treatment professionals at the top and clients at the bottom—that many recovery and treatment centers employ. Rather it maintains its roots in the principle of one alcoholic helping another through the recovery process of his or her addiction.[4]
  — AA first defined the 12 Steps to recovery that many other programs have now utilized and expanded.[5]

- The 12 Steps from a *Christian perspective*[6]

  — *Step 1*: We admit that by ourselves, we are powerless over (name of the addiction) and that our lives have become unmanageable. "We know that the law is spiritual; but I am unspiritual, sold as a slave to sin" (Rom. 7:14).
  — *Step 2*: We come to believe that God, through Jesus Christ, can restore us to sanity. "For it is God who works in you to will and to act in order to fulfill his good purpose" (Phil. 2:13).
  — *Step 3*: We make a decision to turn our lives over to God through Jesus Christ. "Therefore, I urge you, brothers and sisters, in view of God's mercy, to offer your bodies as a living sacrifice, holy and pleasing to God—this is your true and proper worship" (Rom. 12:1).
  — *Step 4*: We make a searching and fearless moral inventory of ourselves. "Let us examine our ways and test them, and let us return to the LORD" (Lam. 3:40).
  — *Step 5*: We admit to God, to ourselves, and to another human being the exact nature of our wrongs. "Therefore confess your sins to each other and pray for each other so that you may be healed. The prayer of a righteous person is powerful and effective" (James 5:16).
  — *Step 6*: We commit ourselves to obedience to God, desiring that He remove patterns of sin from our lives. "Humble yourselves before the Lord, and he will lift you up" (James 4:10).
  — *Step 7*: We humbly ask God to renew our minds so that our sinful patterns can be transformed into patterns of righteousness. "Do not conform to the pattern of this world, but be transformed by the renewing of your

mind. Then you will be able to test and approve what God's will is—his good, pleasing and perfect will" (Rom. 12:2).

— *Step 8*: We make a list of all persons we have harmed, and become willing to make amends to them all. "Do to others as you would have them do to you" (Luke 6:31).

— *Step 9*: We make direct amends to such people where possible, except when doing so will injure them or others. "Therefore, if you are offering your gift at the altar and there remember that your brother or sister has something against you, leave your gift there in front of the altar. First go and be reconciled to them; then come and offer your gift" (Matt. 5:23–24).

— *Step 10*: We continue to take personal inventory, and when we are wrong, promptly admit it. "So, if you think you are standing firm, be careful that you don't fall!" (1 Cor. 10:12).

— *Step 11*: We seek to grow in our relationship with Jesus Christ through prayer, meditation, and obedience, praying for wisdom and power to carry out His will. "If any of you lacks wisdom, you should ask God, who gives generously to all without finding fault, and it will be given to you. But when you ask, you must believe and not doubt, because the one who doubts is like a wave of the sea, blown and tossed by the wind" (James 1:5–6).

— *Step 12*: Having a spiritual awakening, we try to carry the message of Christ's grace and restoration power to others who are addicted and dependent, and to practice these principles in all of our affairs. "Brothers and sisters, if someone is caught in a sin, you who live by the Spirit should restore that person gently. But watch yourselves, or you also may be tempted" (Gal. 6:1).

• *Celebrate Recovery* was developed in 1990 by Saddleback Church, one of the largest evangelical churches in the United States, located in Lake Forest, California.[7] Their purpose is to help those struggling with addiction discover Jesus Christ, "the one and only true Higher Power," through becoming free from addictive, compulsive, and dysfunctional behaviors.[8]

— The program expands the 12 Steps and is more specifically Christ-centered than AA.

— The focus is on the Beatitudes described in Matthew 5 as the foundation for freedom from addiction and the recovery process.

• *Spiritual surrender* includes a willingness to give up control to the Lord. It involves the act of dying to oneself (Luke 9:23–24) and choosing to give God His rightful place in one's life.[9]

— Alcoholics Anonymous, Celebrate Recovery, and other 12–step programs utilize the concept of surrender. Steps 3, 4, and 5 of AA's model reflect the ideas of spiritual surrender. Similarly, principles 3, 4, and 5 of Celebrate

Recovery's model describe the act of surrendering one's addiction to the Lord, believing that He is capable of providing healing.[10]

— Spiritual surrender is the "key agent of change in recovery from substance abuse and addiction."[11]

- *Confession* is another avenue of healing and recovery. This idea is included in AA's steps 4 and 5, and Celebrate Recovery's principles 4, 5, and 6. When dealing with addiction, it is important to acknowledge that one's past has likely been filled with hurt, pain, and shortcomings that developed directly or indirectly from the addiction. Part of the healing and recovery process includes acknowledging the ways in which the addict has wronged another person and working to confess these things to God and the other party unless doing so would be harmful to them or others.

  — Confession is defined as a public or private behavior in which individuals recognize that they have violated someone and seek forgiveness for this violation.[12]

  — Confession may have substantial effects on physical, psychological, and spiritual health.[13]

  — Confession has a liberating and guilt-relieving effect. It may allow the addict an opportunity to relieve tension, experience acceptance and reconciliation, resolve guilt feelings, and take responsibility for improving him- or herself.[14]

- *Meditation on Scripture and contemplative/centering prayer.*[15]

  — Meditation is included in step 11 of the AA model and principle 7 of the Celebrate Recovery model.

  — Contemplative prayer is different from traditional meditation in that it is completely focused on the "awareness of the presence of a loving God and on forgetting oneself into God through grace and love."[16]

  — Meditation on God's Word in a contemplative fashion offers the addict a means of connecting with God in a way that traditional meditation does not seem to offer. Most 12-step models do not necessarily focus on Christ per se, but refer to God as a person's Higher Power. Anyone can utilize meditation; however, Christians will meditate on Christ and Scripture, as this often strengthens the bond they feel with Him.

# 3  ASSESSMENT INTERVIEW

1. How important is spirituality to your recovery?
2. Are you willing to get well? (As emphasized in "Working with Couples from a Spiritual Perspective" by M. R. Laaser)[17]
3. Have you attended any support groups that have incorporated Scripture and/or spiritual principles? If so, how were they helpful?
4. How important is spirituality to your daily life?

5. What is your vision for a sober future?
6. What needs and/or desires are being fulfilled through your addiction? ·
7. Describe your concept of God and how He has helped you move past your addiction.
8. Are you a member of a church? Have you found help with your addiction there?
9. As a sober individual, would you consider helping others with their addictions?
10. What do you believe God thinks about addiction? What does His Word have to say on the subject?
11. Do you engage in prayer and/or meditation to maintain sobriety?

## WISE COUNSEL 4

The success of Alcoholics Anonymous and other 12-step support groups suggests that relationships are the key to treating and overcoming addiction. When working with those who are struggling with addiction, it is important for counselors to address strongly the concept of building and maintaining relationships with their clients. The benefits to an addict of being supported, affirmed, and led by those who have been through comparable experiences are incalculable.

Similarly one must not neglect the spiritual aspect of addiction and recovery. As scientist and philosopher Blaise Pascal wrote, "There is a God shaped vacuum in the heart of every man which cannot be filled by any created thing, but only by God, the Creator, made known through Jesus."[18] It seems that those who wrestle with addiction are working to fill this vacuum with all the wrong things. They are grasping for something, anything that will make them feel whole. More often than not, there is an underlying issue the addict is trying to resolve. Whether this is past abuse or trauma, familial problems, loss, physical pain, or any other form of hurt, the addict has resorted to numbing his or her pain with a substance or behavior that will ultimately fail the person. The roots of addiction can be incredibly complex; however, addressing the spiritual needs of the addict may help significantly in the recovery process. Counselors must not neglect to address these needs, as ultimately they can be satisfied only through a relationship with Jesus Christ.

## ACTION STEPS 5

### 1. Consult a Spiritual Leader

- In order to address your felt needs related to recovery from a spiritual perspective, it is essential that you consult with a spiritual leader, such as a pastor or Christian counselor. This leadership will provide you with guidance and a foundation for developing and growing in a vibrant walk with the Lord.
- A Christian counselor will be able to apply biblical principles to mental health and addiction issues. Such a combination of expertise may be most effective in dealing with addiction from a spiritual perspective. When seeing a counselor,

you can address the desire for spiritual principles to be applied in the counseling exchange.

## 2. Maintain Accountability

- Part of maintaining sobriety and growing in faith includes seeking accountability. This may be a relationship with a pastor, small group leader, or a mature Christian friend.
- You should find someone whom you trust and with whom you are willing to share your journey. Such support and encouragement will encourage your continued recovery from addiction.

## 3. Surrender Your Life to the Lord

- Part of being spiritually mature includes the willingness to relinquish control to God. To live sober, you must surrender your daily battles, struggles, and triggers to the lordship of Jesus Christ, trusting that He is faithful to bring peace, protection, and help in even the most tempting circumstances.
- The act of surrender can be deeply freeing. Consult with a trusted pastor or Christian mentor to learn how this may be carried out in daily activities.

## 4. Study the Bible

- Studying and meditating on Scripture can provide strength and insight to get through the days of recovery. Accepting God's Word and trusting in His promises will allow you to face each day with wisdom and the courage it takes to prevent relapse.
- Consider joining a Bible study with a friend or church group. Christian accountability and growth will allow you to build healthy relationships that will aid in the recovery process and with relapse prevention.

## 5. Pray

- The Bible instructs us to be constantly in prayer (1 Thess. 5:17). In dealing with recovery and sobriety, it is absolutely essential that you be mindful of talking with God and discussing your life with Him.
- As you talk with God in prayer, your fears and anxieties will be minimized and you will gain understanding. The Bible states that when we pray about our concerns, we will receive the peace of God, which surpasses all understanding (Phil. 4:6–7). Learn to trust that the Lord can meet your needs and rest in His assurance and sovereignty.

## BIBLICAL INSIGHTS 6

*All Scripture is God-breathed and is useful for teaching, rebuking, correcting and training in righteousness.*

2 Timothy 3:16

This passage informs us of the authority and usefulness of Scripture. In resolving that Scripture is relevant, authoritative, and applicable to all of life's circumstances, we may be able to more completely apply it to our daily battles. For the individual searching for ways in which to deal with addiction through spiritual means, accepting the authority of Scripture is the very foundation for doing just that.

*But I tell you that everyone will have to give account on the day of judgment for every empty word they have spoken.*

Matthew 12:36

This counsel ought to lead us to humbly contemplate our conversations with others. When working with those struggling with addiction, it is important that the counselor think through his or her statements very carefully. The Lord holds us accountable for all that we say, and in addressing this sensitive area of counseling, it is imperative we consider fully what we are saying and how we are correcting, explaining, and rebuking others. We should be mindful of taming our tongues so that we speak words that are pleasing to God (see James 3:1–12).

*As for God, his way is perfect: the LORD's word is flawless; he shields all who take refuge in him.*

Psalm 18:30

The Lord offers protection for all who trust in Him. Part of this trust process includes believing that His Word is flawless. In doing so, the believer ensnared by addiction may accept this authoritative source of correction, wisdom, and understanding, and then overcome his or her addiction through applying the knowledge of Scripture to daily living.

## PRAYER STARTER 7

Dear Lord, I thank You for _____'s interest in healing and recovery. Thank You for giving him (her) the boldness, the strength, and the humility to seek help with this issue. Lord, I pray that You give us wisdom as we look to You. Help us to be sensitive to the work of Your Holy Spirit and to search openly for answers. Thank You for all You are going to accomplish in _____'s life through this situation. Thank You that even when we don't have all of the answers, You do. Please give _____ courage as he (she) begins this journey of healing, growth, understanding, and recovery . . .

# 8 RECOMMENDED RESOURCES

Anderson, Neil, Mike Quarles, and Julia Quarles. *One Day at a Time: The Devotional for Overcomers*. Gospel Light, 2000.

Arterburn, Stephen, and David Stoop. *The Book of Life Recovery*. Tyndale, 2012.

Baker, John. *Celebrate Recovery Bible: NIV*. Zondervan, 2007.

Hontz, Marilyn. *Shame Lifter: Replacing Your Fears and Tears with Forgiveness, Truth, and Hope*. Tyndale, 2009.

May, Gerald. *Addiction and Grace: Love and Spirituality in the Healing of Addiction*. HarperOne, 2006.

Morgan, Oliver J., and Merle Jordan, eds. *Addiction and Spirituality: A Multidisciplinary Approach*. Chalice Press, 1999.

Rohr, Richard. *Breathing under Water: Spirituality and the Twelve Steps*. Franciscan Media, 2011.

Williams, Don. *12 Steps with Jesus*. Gospel Light, 2004.

## Websites

www.celebraterecovery.com

# Recovery and Relapse Prevention 5

## PORTRAITS 1

- Chad was born into the family of a preacher. Growing up he experienced little grace from his parents or his church and, as a result, was convinced of God's disdain for him and his actions. As a teen he experimented with drugs in an attempt to rebel against his upbringing. What began as a recreational weekend activity with friends spiraled quickly out of control as Chad entered his twenties. He became heavily addicted to alcohol and drugs, lost friendships and his relationship with his parents, was convicted of two DUIs, and lost his job all before the age of twenty-nine. When life seemed to be too difficult to manage any longer, a friend introduced Chad to the Celebrate Recovery (CR) group at his church. Certain that he had reached rock bottom, Chad went to the group the next Friday night. After getting a sponsor and beginning to work through the CR principles, he has found himself starting over as a sober adult.
- Growing up in an addicted family, Katie swore that she would never participate in such activities. As a child she worked to cover up her family's chaos by excelling at school and in sports. In college, however, Katie grew tired of trying to look and act perfect and soon found herself caught in the trap of a relationship with a man who was secretly addicted to prescription drugs. Katie was lost in this codependent relationship for a few years before finally acknowledging the fact that she was entering a cycle nearly the same as the one her family had always been in. Through the help of a counselor, Katie ended the relationship and has worked through her codependent tendencies, finally experiencing freedom from expectations and addicted loved ones.
- Ron has been sober for five months but continues to struggle with the consequences of his addiction—a divorce, poor health, and financial uncertainty. Initially Ron found freedom while spending a couple of weeks in an intensive inpatient program. Now, though, as he faces the ups and downs of daily life, he is tempted to deal with the stress through again resorting to cocaine.

## DEFINITIONS AND KEY THOUGHTS 2

- *Relapse* is defined as the heavy return to the addiction after a period of abstinence.[1]
- *Lapse* is defined as returning to the addiction one time following a period of abstinence.[2]

**61**

- The *rate of relapse* varies widely and depends on the substance used.[3]
- *Risk factors* vary from person to person, so counseling and/or treatment should be geared toward acknowledging these individual differences and working with them.
- Relapse rates for addictive diseases range from 50 to 90 percent.[4]
- Studies show that *women* in treatment *relapse less frequently* than men, partly because women are more likely to engage in *group counseling*.[5]
- *Relapse triggers* are events and/or specific factors that increase the risk of reusing a drug or repeating a behavior. Treatment strategies call for identifying potential triggers and building safeguards and roadblocks around them.

# 3 ASSESSMENT INTERVIEW

1. What has your life been like since becoming sober?
2. How have you been tempted to go back to your addiction?
3. Are you seeking accountability in your recovery process?
4. Have you sought help from a support group?
5. Do you have any persistent medical conditions that have resulted from your addiction? If so, how have you dealt with these?
6. Describe your close relationships since beginning the recovery process.
7. Describe your relationship with God since beginning the recovery process.
8. How do you plan to remain abstinent?
9. Do you engage in prayer and/or meditation to help maintain sobriety?
10. What are your goals for preventing relapse in the future?
11. What are potential relapse triggers related to your addiction and how have you addressed them in treatment?

# 4 WISE COUNSEL

It is important for the client to understand the most effective ways of recovering from his or her addiction and the ways in which relapse may be prevented. Addictions are complex and encompass many facets of the lives that are affected by their consequences. It is therefore key to address each of these triggers and work with the client to better understand how a life of recovery may be different.

Counselors should encourage the client to seek continued support from groups like Alcoholics Anonymous, Narcotics Anonymous, and Celebrate Recovery, as research suggests participating in a support group greatly increases one's ability to maintain sobriety. Even after years of sober living, relapse is only one decision away. Support from others who have experienced similar circumstances is incredibly healing and therapeutic. Similarly, after gaining wisdom and insight through sobriety, clients may be interested in using the knowledge they have to lead others.

Counselors should also be sensitive to a client's relationships following the initial phase of recovery. Some relationships will likely need to be mended; others may need to end if they are toxic to the client's recovery. Encourage the client's relationship development with those who are supportive and reassuring of his or her continued recovery.

## ACTION STEPS : 5

### 1. Seek Medical Care

- To rule out any possible physical conditions that have resulted from addiction, it is important to seek a medical and/or psychiatric assessment and care from a physician. The assurance that your health is satisfactory or the understanding of physical ailments and how to treat and overcome them will help in the recovery process.
- Don't avoid getting help and insight from health care professionals. Recovery includes improving mental, emotional, physical, relational, and spiritual health, and cannot be overlooked in the weeks and months following the initial stages of this process.

### 2. Develop a Plan

- It is important in recovery to develop a detailed plan for how you will identify relapse triggers and overcome temptations and situations that could cause you to fall back into the same addicted patterns. Write down your plan during the early stages of treatment and recovery to prevent relapse in the following months and years.
- The road to recovery is a process. In developing goals and a plan for maintaining sobriety, you may be better able to face the struggles that could lead you to reenter the trap of addiction. An effective plan may include seeking accountability, avoiding situations or settings that are not conducive to recovery, discussing temptations with trusted individuals, or finding ways to move your thoughts away from the addiction.[6]

### 3. Find a Support Group

- Being able to relate and work through recovery with the support of others is essential to relapse prevention. God indicated our need for human relationship and connection when He said that it is not good for man to be alone (Gen. 2:18). Find a healthy group that can offer support in the ongoing effort to live a healthier life. The writer of Hebrews encourages believers to "consider how to stimulate one another to love and good deeds, not forsaking our own assembling together" (Heb. 10:24).
- There are many well-known recovery groups, including Alcoholics Anonymous and Narcotics Anonymous, as well as faith-based support groups like Celebrate Recovery, which are known to increase one's ability to maintain abstinence.

- Those who do not participate in any kind of recovery group or have no accountability partners often relapse because they lack support when it is most needed.[7]
- Consider your needs, desires, faith, and personality when choosing to be part of a support group. Once you identify a group, you will need to invest in that group and trust the recovery process.

## 4. Study the Bible

- Studying and meditating on Scripture can provide strength and insight to get through the tough days inherent in any recovery. Accepting God's Word and trusting in His promises will help you face each day with wisdom and the courage it takes to prevent relapse.
- Also consider joining a Bible study with a friend or church group. Christian accountability and growth will allow you to build healthy relationships, which aid in the recovery process and with relapse prevention.[8]

## 5. Exercise

- Exercise stimulates the brain and body and can be a tremendous help in recovery. Exercise can reduce stress and may become an outlet for releasing stress and tension built up throughout the day.
- Maintaining proper exercise patterns can be difficult, so accountability is a good idea. If possible, include a friend or family member in your exercise plan; join an exercise class at the local gym; enter a run that has a good cause and train over the weeks and months leading up to it.

## 6. Pay Attention to Nutrition

- Good dietary habits can help recovery as they contribute to physical and mental health. Eating frequent mini-meals throughout the day helps sustain energy levels and moods. Eating fresh fruits and vegetables, foods made with whole grains, and limiting caffeine intake by choosing decaffeinated coffee and herbal teas are smart choices. Similarly, limiting the amount of red meat and sugars to maintain proper digestion and energy levels is suggested.[9]

# 6  BIBLICAL INSIGHTS

*Cast all your anxiety on him because he cares for you.*

*1 Peter 5:7*

God calls all those who follow Him to cast their anxieties on Him, trusting that He is fully capable of handling them. We can trust that we serve a God who brings peace to all who are weary and is able to sustain us despite our worries. He wants us to bring our burdens to Him, trusting that He will meet us right where we are.

*One thing I do: Forgetting what is behind and straining toward what is ahead, I press on toward the goal to win the prize for which God has called me heavenward in Christ Jesus.*

*Philippians 3:13–14*

This counsel encourages us to trust in the hope that we have in Jesus. We are called to accept the past, but not dwell on it, and move forward, trusting in all that God has done in our lives. We can trust that recovery and relapse prevention are possible through the strength and direction that God gives to us.

*I have told you these things, so that in me you may have peace. In this world you will have trouble. But take heart! I have overcome the world.*

*John 16:33*

The Lord offers peace to us in our time of confusion, fear, anxiety, change, and new beginnings. God does not promise that all of our struggles and burdens will disappear once we give our lives to Him. He does, however, offer us peace and assurance in Him, which is more than enough to face the ups and downs that life inevitably brings. He calls us to trust in Him—the One who overcame the world!

*I waited patiently for the LORD; he turned to me and heard my cry. He lifted me out of the slimy pit, out of the mud and mire; he set my feet on a rock and gave me a firm place to stand.*

*Psalm 40:1–2*

Looking back on all that we have overcome is a great reminder of God's work within us. We can trust that He hears us when we call to Him. He wants to be a part of the details of our lives, and by recognizing how He's come through in our past, we can believe that He will do the very same thing for us as we face future obstacles and burdens.

*Do you not know? Have you not heard? The LORD is the everlasting God, the Creator of the ends of the earth. He will not grow tired or weary, and his understanding no one can fathom. He gives strength to the weary and increases the power of the weak. Even youths grow tired and weary, and young men stumble and fall; but those who hope in the LORD will renew their strength. They will soar on wings like eagles; they will run and not grow weary, they will walk and not be faint.*

*Isaiah 40:28–31*

When we work through relapse prevention and the recovery process, it is normal and likely that we will feel exhausted by our efforts for maintaining a healthier life. Hard work is needed to make the necessary changes. When it feels as if it is too much for us to handle, God assures us that those who trust and hope in Him will be sustained by His immeasurable strength and boundless peace. Our troubles are not too much for Him to take care of. He is more than willing to meet us in our need and give us strength when we feel as though we aren't capable of facing another difficult day.

# 7 : PRAYER STARTER

Lord, thank You for all the work You have already done in _____'s life. We thank You that You have saved him (her) from the addictive patterns of the past and have led him (her) to seek help in recovery. I pray that You give _____ guidance, wisdom, and strength as he (she) faces a sober future. Thank You for _____'s desire to remain healthy and sober. Please reduce the triggers and temptations in his (her) life and guard his (her) heart and mind as he (she) continues on this journey . . .

# 8 : RECOMMENDED RESOURCES

Anderson, Neil. *Overcoming Addictive Behavior.* The Victory over the Darkness Series. Gospel Light, 1999.

Anderson, Neil T., Mike Quarles, and Julia Quarles. *One Day at a Time: The Devotional for Overcomers.* Gospel Light, 2000.

Arterburn, Stephen, and David Stoop. *The Book of Life Recovery.* Tyndale, 2012.

Baker, John. *Celebrate Recovery Bible: NIV.* Zondervan, 2007.

Conyers, Beverly. *Everything Changes: Help for Families of Newly Recovering Addicts.* Hazelden Foundation, 2009.

Hontz, Marilyn. *Shame Lifter: Replacing Your Fears and Tears with Forgiveness, Truth, and Hope.* Tyndale, 2009.

Laaser, Mark. *Healing Wounds of Sexual Addiction.* Zondervan, 2004.

Lutzer, Erwin W. *Putting Your Past behind You: Finding Hope for Life's Deepest Hurts.* Moody, 1997.

May, Gerald. *Addiction and Grace: Love and Spirituality in the Healing of Addiction.* HarperOne, 2006.

Quick, Daryl. *The Healing Journey for Adult Children of Alcoholics.* InterVarsity, 2011.

Rohr, Richard. *Breathing under Water: Spirituality and the Twelve Steps.* Franciscan Media, 2011.

Urschel, Harold. *Healing the Addicted Brain: The Revolutionary, Science-Based Alcoholism and Addiction Recovery Program.* Sourcebooks, 2009.

Williams, Don. *12 Steps with Jesus.* Gospel Light, 2004.

Have your way ✓
Feel the light ✓
*Laura* Like a star ✓
Welcome to the
the last get found
How we roll ✓
Safe ✓
Walkon' the water
Glow
Hanging on ✓
Headphoes ✓

.org
raterecovery.com
ww.coda.org
a.org

# PART 2

# Substance Abuse Addictions

This section provides a comprehensive look at important aspects of substance addiction and recovery.

Chemical dependency is a term often used interchangeably with other terms such as *substance abuse*, *drug addiction*, and *alcoholism*, to name a few. The common feature, however, is an addiction to some mood-altering chemical wherein the addict is unable to stop the behavior in spite of significant health-related, economic, legal, vocational, social, and/or spiritual consequences. Chemical dependency also crosses all demographic boundaries (race, gender, age, educational level, economic status, and religious orientation). While disease models are prevalent in the field, biblically based and Christ-centered factors are often critical to successful treatment and recovery.

Remember the four basic steps that were presented in the introduction regarding the Road to Recovery:

1. *Recognize and admit:* the role of confession and breaking the power of the secret
2. *Clean out the infection:* the role of grieving and breaking the power of denial
3. *Renew the mind:* the role of truth and breaking the power of unbelief
4. *Exercise the will:* the role of accountability and breaking the power of fear

# 6   Alcohol

## 1   PORTRAITS

- Jim sits in his hotel room alone wondering how he got to this place in his life. He thought he had his life under control but today he found out otherwise. He came home drunk again, and his wife had had enough. She told him to get out of the house or she was going to call the police. He feels angry with her for treating him this way but he knows she is right. *This is not who I want to be. I need help*, he admits to himself.

- Lindsay is a smart, talented teenager with a bright future ahead of her. She took her first drink at a friend's house when she was fourteen. Now at eighteen she parties regularly with her friends. She doesn't want to be left out of the fun, and many of her peers get involved in these parties. To her it's just not that big a deal. Her parents, however, have seen a dramatic drop in her grades and growing disinterest toward the activities she usually enjoys. Not knowing what to do, they decide to take her to a counselor.

- Charles has known alcohol to be a part of his life for as long as he can remember. His dad gave him his first drink when he was only eight years old. At forty-six he cannot imagine life without alcohol. He is constantly looking for a job, because his drinking interferes with his ability to keep a job. Today he woke up in the hospital after he blacked out last night. As he is getting older, he worries about his health. He has tried several times to stop drinking but nothing has ever worked. *What is wrong with me? Why can't I stop?* he wonders. He walks into the counseling office again, demoralized for relapsing and without any hope.

## 2   DEFINITIONS AND KEY THOUGHTS

- Alcohol is a *depressant* that affects the central nervous system and slows down response time.
- It is derived through the *fermentation* of fruits, vegetables, and grains.
- *Common names for alcohol* are booze, hooch, brew, chug, jack, and juice.
- Abuse of substances and alcohol is the *number one cause of preventable death* in the United States and is the most prevalent mental health issue in our society.
- There are an estimated *119 million alcohol users* in the United States.[1]
- *Beer* is the most common beverage consumed today.[2]

- Of all *domestic assaults*, 56 percent are alcohol-related.[3]
- In 2006, 32 percent of all traffic fatalities in the United States involved *drunk drivers*.[4]
- Alcohol raises *significant health concerns*, including serious injury and even death. It affects almost every organ of the body. For the heavy drinker, a single large dose of alcohol can cause the pancreas (which controls the digestive and endocrine systems) to hemorrhage or depress the respiratory center in the medulla (lower half of the brain stem), leading to death. Many alcohol users will develop *cirrhosis*, which is scarring of the liver, as well as poor liver function.[5]
- *Delirium tremens* (DTs), a severe form of alcohol withdrawal, is considered a medical emergency and can be fatal. Usually it occurs with people who are heavy drinkers (for example, seven to eight pints of beer every day for several months) and around seventy-two hours after the last drink. Some symptoms include body tremors, confusion, restlessness, fatigue, rapid mood changes, and vomiting.[6]
- The body will develop *tolerance* to the effects of alcohol over time as it tries to maintain normal functioning in the presence of the chemical. However, the lethal dose of alcohol remains the same regardless of the tolerance level.
- Alcohol affects more than just the person consuming it. People who come in contact with that person can also be affected in a variety of ways, especially the family. It is estimated that there are *at least four or five people negatively impacted by every addicted person.*
- Some alcohol users are capable of living a normal life while still ingesting the substance. These people are referred to as *functional alcoholics*. It is important to note that while, at present, their life may seem to be uninterrupted, the tendency is for the problem to get worse. Even though functional alcoholics do not see their drinking as a problem, they are still drinking at dangerous levels and are at risk of several health concerns.

## ASSESSMENT INTERVIEW 3

The CAGE test is a simple four-question survey administered either orally or on paper that is very accurate and gives the counselor a basic idea of the severity of the problem. If two questions are answered yes, then problems with alcohol are present and further assessment is warranted.

1. Have you ever felt you should **C**ut down on your drinking?
2. Have you ever been **A**nnoyed when people have commented on your drinking?
3. Have you ever felt **G**uilty or bad about your drinking?
4. Have you ever had an **E**ye-opener first thing in the morning to steady your nerves or get rid of a hangover?

## General Questions

1. How often do you drink? (Keep in mind that alcoholics are good manipulators. They need to be so they can keep drinking. Usually a person's answer to this question is understated due to denial.)
2. How much do you drink at one time?
3. What emotions are you feeling when you drink?
4. Have you ever tried to stop drinking?
5. When did you have your first drink? (A lot of times, heavy drinkers will remember vividly the first time they ever consumed alcohol, as it has become an emotional memory for them because of its life-changing effects.)
6. How long have you been drinking?
7. What amount did you drink a year ago compared with the amount of alcohol you drink today?
8. How does alcohol affect your job or school performance?
9. How do you see your drinking problem affecting your marriage and/or other relationships? Will this change in the future?
10. Where do you most often drink? Why is that?
11. Do you drink alone or with others?
12. If someone else, say a spouse or friend, had the same symptoms as you have, would you think that person had a problem?

# 4 WISE COUNSEL

## For the Alcoholic

First, when dealing with clients who abuse alcohol, attend to any pressing medical issues. If there is an immediate threat to the client's life or medical well-being, this should determine your first course of action. Never overlook the potential risk alcohol has on bodily health, even if the client seems to be in a healthy state.

Be mindful of your biases and assumptions regarding alcohol and alcoholics. Not all who drink are homeless or jobless or have an unkempt appearance. Alcoholism does not discriminate between race or social status. If your client is Christian, often they are afraid of being discovered, as drinking, especially when it is excessive, is highly looked down on in many Christian circles. Reassure them of confidentiality and make your office a safe place for them to share their problem.

Be aware that clients who are addicted to alcohol will most likely be in denial about the severity of the problem. In some cases, they will not admit to even having a problem. The identified problem drinker as well as their family will use denial to avoid doing something about the problem because it will upset the norm. It is important for you to confront the denial sensitively and appropriately and in a timely manner.

## For the Spouse and Family

*Codependency* is a maladaptive and problematic way of seeking identity and self-worth outside of the self. The spouse of a client who is addicted to alcohol may be most at risk for developing codependency. Some symptoms of codependency are an obsession with controlling the environment and people, extreme personal sacrifices to "cure" the alcohol abuser, using external sources for self-worth, and being enmeshed (over-involved) with their spouse. They often feel hyper-responsible for the choices or behaviors of the user. Detachment from the addict is the goal for the codependent person.

Regarding young children, look and listen for signs of possible neglect and/or abuse. Maybe the user has been driving under the influence with the children in the vehicle. Take immediate steps to protect the user and the children. Sometimes this may necessitate the need for direct (but appropriate) confrontation with the user, making other family members aware of the problem, and/or contacting Child Protective Services if there is a lack of response or the situation warrants. When the child is old enough, encourage him or her to say no to car rides with a parent under the influence and to call for help. If abuse is present, report it immediately and develop a plan to get the children out of danger.

If any family member engages in cover-up or enabling behavior, gently confront them and encourage more honest and open responses to the addict's behavior. This will encourage a change of behavior in the person struggling with alcohol abuse.

Frequently families will not talk or express feelings about the user's behavior in an effort to maintain a general sense of stability. Also, they are often told not to trust anyone else with the problem because there is power in holding on to the "secret." It is important that they establish a support system.

# ACTION STEPS 5

## For the Alcoholic

### 1. Consult Your Physician

- Realize that your body may be at risk due to the alcohol's presence in your system. Withdrawal can be fatal for heavy drinkers and it needs to be monitored by a medical professional.

### 2. Be Honest with Yourself

- You need to see how the alcohol use/abuse has become unmanageable and how it has negatively impacted your life.
- If nothing changes, then nothing changes. Do not continue to manipulate people and/or your surroundings to maintain the addiction. Address this issue honestly and make a change.

### 3. Seek Out Professional Help

- To overcome an addiction, you will need support as well as professional help. Find a local therapist and make an appointment. Also consider joining a support group. Currently Alcoholics Anonymous is the number-one program in America to deal with this issue. There are also Christian-based support groups such as Celebrate Recovery that can help.

### 4. Seek Out God's Strength

- Realize that your willpower is not enough to free you from the bondage to alcohol. You need someone transcendent and stronger than your addiction to work through you—you need God in your life.
- Pray and ask God to aid you in your recovery.
- Constantly fill your spirit with godly influences. Read the Word of God daily.

### 5. Be Accountable

- Talk to a pastor, friend, or trusted person and ask for help. You cannot do this alone. Isolation is a recipe for relapse and continued addiction.
- Have these individuals ask you about your behavior. Answering directly to someone will help motivate change in your life.
- Write out a contract regarding the amount of time you want to go without drinking. You and your accountability partner should sign it.

## For the Spouse or Family

### 1. Seek Support

- It is important that you establish a broad-based support system in your life to help you through this problem.
- Find out if there is a support group that you can be involved in at your church or another organization. Al-Anon, Adult Children of Alcoholics, and Families Anonymous provide support groups for families dealing with the problem of alcohol.

### 2. See a Therapist

- In addition to a support system, it may be wise to see a professional who can help equip you with the right tools for better coping with the situation.

### 3. Focus on Yourself

- Make self-care more of a priority. Don't allow yourself to be distracted with everyone else's problems, while ignoring your own. This is detrimental to your well-being.
- Focus on your achievements and the positives in your life. Acknowledge that you deserve to be treated with respect and dignity.
- Pay attention to your own behavior and ask yourself why you do what you do.

## 4. Detach from the User

- Realize that you cannot cure the user or make the necessary choices regarding treatment and recovery. Sometimes the best thing you can do is let him or her experience the consequences of their actions.
- Learn to set appropriate boundaries and say no. This will also help you develop a healthy sense of self-worth.

# BIBLICAL INSIGHTS : 6

*Do you not know that your bodies are temples of the Holy Spirit, who is in you, whom you have received from God? You are not your own; you were bought at a price. Therefore honor God with your bodies.*

*1 Corinthians 6:19–20*

As believers, our body is a temple of the Holy Spirit and not our own; it belongs to God. We need to be conscious of what substances we put in our bodies and whether or not this will result in glorifying God.

*Wine is a mocker and beer a brawler; whoever is led astray by them is not wise.*

*Proverbs 20:1*

Both wine and beer are personified in this verse, demonstrating the potential for wine to mock the person who drinks it and beer to make one aggressive. They both have the ability to lead someone astray.

*Who has woe? Who has sorrow? Who has strife? Who has complaints? Who has needless bruises? Who has bloodshot eyes? Those who linger over wine, who go to sample bowls of mixed wine. Do not gaze at wine when it is red, when it sparkles in the cup, when it goes down smoothly! In the end it bites like a snake and poisons like a viper. Your eyes will see strange sights, and your mind will imagine confusing things. You will be like one sleeping on the high seas, lying on top of the rigging. "They hit me," you will say, "but I'm not hurt! They beat me, but I don't feel it! When will I wake up so I can find another drink?"*

*Proverbs 23:29–35*

The questions at the beginning of this passage show that alcohol causes problems emotionally (woe and sorrow), socially (contentions and complaints), and physically (wounds without cause and redness of eyes). The problem of alcohol is complex and must be treated with care. A person struggling with addiction to alcohol can be demoralized as their problem has touched every aspect of life. They see no escape from it.

Alcohol can be very tempting as it is smooth and alluring, but a warning is given that shows the true nature of alcohol. The result of its seduction is described as a painful snake bite and as something that leaves you always wanting more in the morning. It renders the drinker a slave to it.

*Be very careful, then, how you live—not as unwise but as wise, making the most of every opportunity, because the days are evil. Therefore do not be foolish, but understand what the Lord's will is. Do not get drunk on wine, which leads to debauchery. Instead, be filled with the Spirit.*

*Ephesians 5:15–18*

Not only does this passage give a negative command, "do not get drunk on wine," it also gives a positive one, "be filled with the Spirit." This is a command to let yourself be controlled by the Holy Spirit instead of alcohol. We need to pay attention to how we live.

We become filled with the Spirit when are in relationship with God and constantly feed on the Word of God, praying for wisdom, strength, and grace.

This verse shows how drinking is a wasteful activity. It is not the best way to spend your time. By giving up alcohol, one has more time to spend with family, friends, and the things of God, making each and every day count.

# 7 PRAYER STARTER

Lord, I thank You for the life of _____ and his (her) willingness to face this issue in his (her) life. It's not easy and I thank You for the bravery and courage _____ has shown. We pray that You will provide power over any addiction to alcohol and strength for _____ to see the recovery process through. Be with his (her) family and the people around him (her); comfort them and give them a spirit of support . . .

# 8 RECOMMENDED RESOURCES

Arterburn, Stephen, and David Stoop. *The Book of Life Recovery*. Tyndale, 2012.

Clinebell, Howard. *Understanding and Counseling Persons with Alcohol, Drug, and Behavioral Addictions*. Abingdon, 1998.

Clinton, Tim. *Turn Your Life Around*. FaithWords, 2006.

Davis, Martin M. *The Gospel and the Twelve Steps: Following Jesus on the Path of Recovery*. Winepress, 2005.

Kuhar, Michael. *The Addicted Brain: Why We Abuse Drugs, Alcohol, and Nicotine*. Pearson Education, 2012.

Weaver, Andrew, Harold Koenig, and Howard Stone. *Pastoral Care of Alcohol Abusers*. Creative Pastoral Care and Counseling Series. Fortress, 2009.

Welch, Edward T. *Addictions: A Banquet in the Grave: Finding Hope in the Power of the Gospel*. P&R, 2001.

## Websites

Adult Children of Alcoholics: www.adultchildren.org

Al-Anon Family Groups: www.al-anon.alateen.org/

Alcoholics Anonymous: www.aa.org

Celebrate Recovery: www.celebraterecovery.com

Codependents Anonymous: www.coda.org

Help Guide: www.helpguide.org/mental/alcohol_abuse_alcoholism_signs_effects_ treatment.htm

National Institute on Alcohol Abuse and Alcoholism: www.niaaa.nih.gov/

WebMD: www.webmd.com/mental-health/alcohol-abuse/alcohol-abuse-and-de pendence-topic-overview

# 7 Caffeine

## 1 PORTRAITS

- Justin is a twenty-two-year-old single man with a love for gaming. He lives with his parents and has no job, so all his free time is spent playing video games. He loves to drink soda and energy drinks while he plays, saying they help him keep more alert. Usually he drinks more at night to help him stay awake so he can play longer, sometimes through the entire night. Recently he started waking up in the afternoon with severe headaches and a higher level of anxiety than normal. He finds that his headache goes away once he starts playing video games again (with a soda in hand). Justin is addicted to caffeine and has yet to see it as a problem.

- "I have to stay up and get this done! I can't afford another bad grade," Karen says as she takes another gulp of energy drink. Karen is working on a paper that counts for a significant portion of her grade. Due to procrastination and bad time management, she finds herself having to stay up again, the night before the assignment is due. In fact, this is not an uncommon situation for her at all. About three or four nights every week, she feels that she must stay up late to handle all the work of her heavy class load. Before going back to her dorm to work on homework, Karen always stops by the vending machine and gets two or three energy drinks to help her through the night.

- Mary has three young children and just recently took a job. Normally she must get up early to get the kids to school and herself to work. After work she picks them up from day care and takes the oldest to basketball practice. In the evening she has to make dinner for her family and several nights a week has to rush off to church to help with various projects and ministries. To help her through her day, Mary usually drinks five to six cups of coffee. Recently she visited her doctor and found that she has high blood pressure. Something has to change.

## 2 DEFINITIONS AND KEY THOUGHTS

- Caffeine is classified as a *central nervous system stimulant*, along with amphetamine, cocaine, nicotine, and ecstasy. It can be found in at least 63 different plants.
- Products that may contain caffeine are *coffee, tea, soft drinks, energy drinks, energy shots, yogurt, coffee-flavored ice cream, chocolate, chocolate milk, cocoa products, Midol, Excedrin, NoDoz, and Vivarin.*

- Caffeine is the world's *most consumed psychoactive substance* with an estimated 90 percent of Americans partaking of it on a daily basis.[1]
- The average American consumes *280 milligrams of caffeine per day* (that equals 7 cans of soda or 17 ounces of coffee).[2]
- A study noted at the Johns Hopkins Medicine website (the official communications link for both Johns Hopkins Hospital and Johns Hopkins University School of Medicine) shows that just 100 milligrams of caffeine per day (around one cup of coffee) can cause *physical dependence and withdrawal symptoms* if stopped.[3]
- The most common withdrawal symptom is *headaches*, along with others, such as *fatigue, forgetfulness, irritability, mood changes, trouble sleeping, nausea/vomiting, trouble focusing, drowsiness, work difficulty, and muscle pain.*
- The *half-life of caffeine is six hours*, meaning if you drink coffee in the late afternoon, 50 percent of the caffeine's effect is still in your body and could interfere with the amount and quality of your sleep that night.
- Common reasons people give for ingesting caffeine include *increasing alertness or memory function, relieving mental or physical fatigue, desiring or craving more caffeine, and to avoid withdrawal symptoms.*
- For most adults the caffeine product of choice is coffee, whereas minors prefer soft drinks.
- *Caffeine-free products* are not completely caffeine-free. There still exists a small amount of caffeine in the product.

## ASSESSMENT INTERVIEW 3

1. In the last three to six months, how many soft drinks, if any, have you consumed daily?
2. In the last three to six months, how many cups of coffee, if any, have you consumed daily?
3. Has anyone ever told you that you should cut down on your caffeine intake?
4. Do you find yourself wishing you could cut down on your caffeine intake?
5. Have you ever tried to stop ingesting caffeine? Why do you think it failed?
6. What is the longest period of time you have been without caffeine in your system?
7. In what ways do you believe caffeine is beneficial to you?
8. In what ways do you believe caffeine is harmful to you?
9. When you stop taking in caffeine, do you notice any side effects?
10. Have you ever consumed caffeine to relieve a physical discomfort, such as headache, nausea, fatigue, or other discomfort?
11. Would you say that the amount of caffeine you consume has changed over time? If so, how?
12. Do you find it easier to complete daily tasks when you have had caffeine?
13. When did you first notice that your intake of caffeine was a problem?
14. How often do you think about consuming more caffeine?

# 4 | WISE COUNSEL

Usually clients will attribute their withdrawal symptoms to something else besides caffeine because they do not see their caffeine intake as a problem. The counselor's job, then, is to help the client realize the negative effects caffeine is having on his or her life. Be sure to listen attentively and rephrase what clients have said to you, providing them with insight into their own lives.

Caffeine dependence is not considered to be life-threatening; however, the lethal dose of caffeine is around seven to ten grams. To consume that much caffeine, you would have to drink one hundred cups of coffee within a 24-hour period, so a lethal dose is extremely rare. Nonetheless, deaths have been reported due to caffeine consumption. In addition, caffeine can act as a trigger, setting off other health problems, such as high blood pressure, and can increase the risk for coronary heart disease. Make sure you assess the overall health of your client and how high levels of caffeine could affect his or her health.

# 5 | ACTION STEPS

## 1. Become Aware of Your Caffeine Intake

- Just paying attention to the amount of caffeine you consume daily can be an important motivating factor in changing your behavior. Also it may help you understand the reasons you consume so much caffeine.
- Start paying attention to the amount and quality of sleep you get each night in proportion to how much caffeine you consume. Do you still feel tired in the mornings when you know you went to bed on time? Do you notice that your ability to concentrate is low?
- It would be a good practice to keep a log of every time you eat or drink a product that contains caffeine.

## 2. Become Educated

- You need to understand the reasons why excessive caffeine consumption should be monitored. Research the possible harm caffeine can have on your body. Either search the internet or call your local doctor or health care professional and ask for information on caffeine.
- Learn how caffeine affects your body. Caffeine is a chemical stimulant and will cause changes in your body. Be health conscious as you monitor caffeine intake.
- If you take caffeine for energy, ask your doctor how you can boost your energy naturally by using supplements or vitamins.

## 3. Develop a Plan

- Set a goal. How do you want to change your caffeine consumption? Assess your desires and explicitly state your desired goal.
- It is not effective to simply decide to quit caffeine "cold turkey," as this may cause serious withdrawal symptoms (they can mimic symptoms of stronger stimulant drugs). It is recommended that you lower the amount of caffeine intake gradually over a period of time until you reach your goal.
- Consult your physician to aid you in developing a plan that is tailored to your specific needs. Every person is different and will need an individualized plan.

## 4. Stay Committed

- It is important that you follow through on your plan. While at the grocery store, make it a priority not to purchase products containing caffeine.
- Do not keep products that contain caffeine near you if they will tempt you. Be smart about what situations you put yourself in. For example, if you go out to eat, decide before going that you will drink only something that is noncaffeinated.
- Tell others about your goal and make yourself accountable to someone. This will help keep you on track.

## 5. Create a Reward System

- When you are making progress and accomplishing your goals, reward yourself. Enjoy your progress. Find something you like to do or want to have and promise not to get it until you reach your caffeine goal. This will help motivate you to consume less caffeine.

# BIBLICAL INSIGHTS 6

*I know what it is to be in need, and I know what it is to have plenty. I have learned the secret of being content in any and every situation, whether well fed or hungry, whether living in plenty or in want. I can do all this through him who gives me strength.*

*Philippians 4:12–13*

The apostle Paul was declaring the strength of the Lord in this verse. Whether he was in need or had plenty, he could do anything because of the strength and power of Christ. This verse applies to all areas of life, even to caffeine addiction.

Whether this is a small task or big task, God will provide enough strength and grace for you to get through it.

*"I have the right to do anything," you say—but not everything is beneficial. "I have the right to do anything"—but I will not be mastered by anything.*

*1 Corinthians 6:12*

This verse can apply to addiction to caffeine. It is okay to have caffeine, but we need to examine the benefits and the costs of consuming too much and determine if it is helpful to us.

This verse also tells us that our body is the Lord's and we should not let any other thing dominate or control it. The goal here, then, is to eliminate caffeine's control over your body by submitting your body to the Lord's control.

## 7 PRAYER STARTER

God, I thank You for sending Your Son to die for us so we don't have to live in bondage to substances on this earth. Give _____ Your strength to overcome this problem in his (her) life. Caffeine has control over _____'s body, so I pray that he (she) will submit his (her) body to You so that You can work in his (her) life . . .

## 8 RECOMMENDED RESOURCES

Anderson, Neil T. *Freedom from Addiction: Breaking the Bondage of Addiction and Finding Freedom in Christ*. Gospel Light, 1997.

Buchholz, David. *Heal Your Headache*. Workman, 2002.

Cherniske, Stephen. *Caffeine Blues: Wake Up to the Hidden Dangers of America's #1 Drug*. Warner, 1998.

Clinton, Tim. *Turn Your Life Around*. FaithWords, 2006.

Kuhar, Michael. *The Addicted Brain: Why We Abuse Drugs, Alcohol, and Nicotine*. Pearson Education, 2012.

Kushner, Marina. *Confessions of a Caffeine Addict*. SCR, 2010.

———. *The Truth about Caffeine*. SCR, 2009.

### Websites

Caffeine Awareness: www.caffeineawareness.org/

Johns Hopkins Medical Center: www.caffeinedependence.org/caffeine_dependence.html

Medicine Net: www.medicinenet.com/caffeine/article.htm

Web MD: www.webmd.com/balance/caffeine-myths-and-facts

# Cocaine and Crack Cocaine $\quad$ 8

## PORTRAITS $\quad$ 1

- Jane was a college student on her way to earning a bachelor's degree in communications. This year was going to be different, as she was able to get her own apartment. When moving in, she met a guy who lived next door. He was handsome and charming. They started dating within a week and were having a great time. One night her boyfriend brought back some cocaine and offered it to Jane. Without thinking, she took it and began enjoying her time with her boyfriend and cocaine. Soon it turned into her just enjoying the cocaine. Her boyfriend left town, and all she could think about was how to get the next line of coke. Her grades dropped and now she can no longer afford her apartment. She can't help thinking how stupid she has been. With the threat of eviction, she decides to get help.

- John was enraged. His dealer did not deliver his drugs on time, and he could not wait any longer for his cocaine. Finally his dealer arrived, and John, feeling desperate, hit him hard with a pipe he found and took the drugs. Now he is in jail for assault and battery and does not know what to think or do. He is ordered to go to a treatment program and he does so reluctantly.

- Miguel is a sixteen-year-old boy who enjoys skateboarding with his friends at the local park. One night one of his friends who is considerably older offers him some coke. He uses it and is amazed at the high. He finds out it helps him overcome his fear of heights, allowing him to do better on his skateboard. Before long his mom notices some things missing around the house and confronts Miguel about it. Of course, he denies taking anything. One night Miguel's mom catches him stealing her jewelry to fund his drug use. Furious, she reprimands him and tells him he is going to get sober or she will call the police.

## DEFINITIONS AND KEY THOUGHTS $\quad$ 2

- *Cocaine is an illegal drug* in the United States.
- It is a chemical obtained from the leaves of the *coca plant*.
- It is classified as a *central nervous system stimulant* that causes feelings of *euphoria* as well as *increases body temperature, blood pressure, and heart rate.* It can also be used as a local anesthetic.

- A cocaine user, when high, will feel a sense of intense euphoria *increasing libido*. This is referred to as the *flash* or *rush*.
- Types of cocaine include the *white powder* that is extracted from the coca leaves and *crack cocaine,* which looks like small *rock crystals*.
- Some street names for cocaine and crack cocaine are *coke, blow, Peruvian lady, snow, all-American drug, beam, candy, rocks, white dragon, line*.
- There are several methods by which a user can abuse cocaine or crack cocaine. Methods include: *snorting* (insufflation), *injection* (intravenous), *by mouth* (sublingual), *anal* (rectal), *vaginally*, and *smoking* (inhalation).
- According to the National Household Survey on Drug Abuse in 2001, an estimated 1.7 million (0.7 percent) Americans ages 12 or older were current cocaine users and 406,000 (0.2 percent) were crack cocaine users. The majority of cocaine users are between the ages of 18 and 34.[1]
- Each year, cocaine accounts for one of a significant *number of admissions for drug treatment* in the United States.[2]
- Cocaine has a *strong risk factor* as an *addictive substance*. Culture has portrayed the drug as always being addictive to everyone who uses it. However, of those who have used cocaine, only 24.9 percent were diagnosed as being *dependent* on the drug.[3]
- Several medical concerns and *side effects* of using this drug include:

  — heart attacks and hypertension
  — respiratory failure
  — anxiety and panic reactions
  — formication (the feeling that insects are crawling on your skin; sometimes cocaine users will have scratches on their body indicating that they have been scratching at themselves from this side effect)

- Cocaine is reported as being a *strong risk factor* for *suicide and homicide*. It is estimated that 20 percent of all suicides among people sixty years old and under were cocaine-related.[4]
- *Post-cocaine depression* is referred to as *crashing*. Often this is accompanied by *depression* that impacts cognition, affect, and physical well-being. This, in turn, will motivate another use to alleviate the pain of depression. During a crash, *suicide* is a high concern.
- Signs to look for in a person addicted to cocaine include *lack of money* because cocaine is expensive. Cocaine acts as an appetite suppressant, so *weight loss* is usually noticeable. Often users go long periods of time without eating. Since the substance is a stimulant, a user's *sleep pattern* is usually disrupted and he or she may sleep at odd hours of the day.
- Some girls struggling with *body image* might abuse cocaine to help them stop eating. This is a serious medical concern. The underlying psychological issue may not be the cocaine abuse but anorexia.

- Most users do not abuse cocaine only but other substances as well, which compounds the *health risks*. When cocaine is used with alcohol, small amounts of the cocaine are transformed into *coca ethylene*, which is *extremely toxic* to the body.

# ASSESSMENT INTERVIEW 3

## Rule Outs

1. Have you ever or do you currently have thoughts of hurting yourself?
2. What thoughts have you had that can be considered violent while under the influence? Do you have any intention of hurting others?

## General Questions

*Note: These questions will all refer to cocaine use as well as crack cocaine use, even though the term crack cocaine may be omitted.*

1. How often and how much do you use cocaine or crack cocaine currently (per day and per week)?
2. What other substances, if any, have you used with cocaine?
3. Have you consulted a medical doctor about your cocaine use?
4. Have you previously been in a treatment program?
5. Have others ever commented on your cocaine use? What was said?
6. What, if any, changes have you noticed in your work or school performance, other activities, mood, and relationships since you have been on the drug?
7. On a scale of 1 to 10, with 10 being the worst, how much of a problem is your cocaine use?
8. Have you ever stolen from family and friends or broken the law to support your habit?
9. During what circumstances of life do you feel the most need to use cocaine?
10. When was the first time you used cocaine?
11. Do you see yourself being cocaine-free in the future?

# WISE COUNSEL 4

As when interviewing a person who uses any drug, it is always important to assess the overall health of the individual and rule out any pressing medical concerns. Withdrawal from cocaine usually has *no physical symptoms* but is often accompanied by depression, anxiety, paranoia, lack of pleasure, and agitation. Make sure your client is not at risk for suicide or a danger to others before releasing him or her from your office.

Since one of the side effects of cocaine is a raised libido, it increases the chance that couples will abuse cocaine together. They think this heightens or intensifies their physical pleasure in their relationship. They will not see cocaine as a *destroyer of relationships*, but as a strengthener of relationships. However, this is never the case. When counseling a couple, you need to highlight and emphasize the ways in which cocaine has destroyed or hurt their relationship and offer hope and healing from that brokenness.

Be sensitive in your judgments of those who are addicted to cocaine. Do not look on them as weak or morally inferior. Instead see them as people whom God created with *intrinsic value*. In fact, when people have an addiction, they are abusing substances because they are searching for something greater in life. So in one sense, you could say that they are in touch with themselves because they sense emptiness inside, but in their attempts to fill the emptiness they have become lost. As their counselor, you can take this perfect opportunity to share the love of Christ with them and help them find fulfillment in Him.

Be aware that cocaine abusers will often attempt to manipulate you and try to say how the drug is beneficial. Listen for inconsistencies in their story and point out the difference in what they think the drug is doing for them and the real impact.

# 5 ACTION STEPS

## 1. Consult Your Physician

- Cocaine affects your body in a variety of ways and *can lead to death or serious injury.* Get a medical professional to give you an overall health assessment.

## 2. See a Substance Abuse Counselor or Mental Health Professional

- Recovering from an addiction to cocaine is not an easy process and there are a lot of benefits in having someone to work with you throughout the process. That person will have your best interest in mind and will provide you with the necessary tools to help you overcome your dependency.
- You can find local therapists and counselors online using various websites, such as www.treatment4addiction.com and www.healthgrades.com.
- Find someone in your life who will hold you accountable, perhaps a friend, relative, counselor, or abstinence group. You can join a Narcotics Anonymous (NA) meeting near you.

## 3. Accept Yourself

- Change will not occur if you approach your recovery with a critical attitude toward yourself. To be free, you need to be honest with yourself and then accept responsibility.
- If you beat yourself up for your choices and actions in the past, you end up feeling worse about yourself. Condemning yourself will hinder deep positive change. Be proactive and take responsibility but also understand that God's grace and forgiveness are freely available to those who ask.

## 4. Realize Christ's Love

- Stop looking to cocaine to fill the emptiness you feel inside or to cover up your pain. Instead get involved with a local church, surround yourself with people who will be good influences, and reach out to God and ask for help.
- God's love is enough to fulfill our every longing, and you can find pleasure by submitting to Him.

## 5. Focus on the Present

- Break free from the bondage of past mistakes and the irrational fears of the future. Focus on the here and now and put all your energy into recovery.

# BIBLICAL INSIGHTS : 6

*Clothe yourselves with the Lord Jesus Christ, and do not think about how to gratify the desires of the flesh.*

*Romans 13:14*

This verse gives us the secret to living chaste lives. Instead of thinking about doing your next line of cocaine, think about Christ and pray for strength.

As soon as tempting thoughts surface, train yourself to take them captive and think on positive things.

*For the grace of God has appeared that offers salvation to all people. It teaches us to say "No" to ungodliness and worldly passions, and to live self-controlled, upright and godly lives in this present age.*

*Titus 2:11–12*

Salvation is available to all—it is a free gift. We can have complete freedom through God's power from any substance that is holding us down.

When we experience God's grace through our salvation and His presence in our lives, we are led to say no to cocaine or other things that promise to give us fulfillment but really just leave us empty.

*But God demonstrates his own love for us in this: While we were still sinners, Christ died for us.*

*Romans 5:8*

*So I say, walk by the Spirit, and you will not gratify the desires of the flesh.*

*Galatians 5:16*

For believers, the way to conquer being controlled by any substance (desires of the flesh) is to walk in the Spirit. The Holy Spirit lives in us but will not automatically save us from our evil desires. The Spirit waits for us to depend on Him, waits for us to walk in Him. Once you do that, He promises that through His power He will help you resist your desire for cocaine.

## 7 PRAYER STARTER

Thank You for Your love for us, God. We know the only way _____ will be able to overcome his (her) addiction to cocaine is through the power of the Holy Spirit's leading. We ask for freedom from this terrible bondage and protection from the evil one. I pray that _____ will be motivated to seek Your help in this time of need and that he (she) will depend on You . . .

## 8 RECOMMENDED RESOURCES

Clinebell, Howard. *Understanding and Counseling Persons with Alcohol, Drug, and Behavioral Addictions.* Abingdon, 1998.

Clinton, Tim. *Turn Your Life Around.* FaithWords, 2006.

Kuhar, Michael. *The Addicted Brain: Why We Abuse Drugs, Alcohol, and Nicotine.* Pearson Education, 2012.

Lookadoo, Justin. *The Dirt on Drugs.* Revell, 2008.

Murphey, Cecil. *When Someone You Love Abuses Drugs or Alcohol.* Beacon Hill Press, 2004.

Washton, Arnold M. *Cocaine Addiction: Treatment, Recovery, and Relapse Prevention.* W. W. Norton, 1991.

### Websites

Addictions and Recovery: www.addictionsandrecovery.org/cocaine.htm

Celebrate Recovery: www.celebraterecovery.com

Cocaine Anonymous: www.ca.org/

Medicine Net: www.medicinenet.com/cocaine_and_crack_abuse/article.htm

Narcotics Anonymous: www.na.org

National Institute on Drug Abuse: www.drugabuse.gov/publications/drugfacts/cocaine

Web MD: www.webmd.com

# Depressants 9

- Gary is a businessman who is good at what he does. He is constantly traveling around the country, speaking at seminars and meeting with officials of various companies. As a result, sleep is something hard to come by in Gary's life. He got a prescription for some sleeping pills that would help him sleep better. At first it worked, but then he realized the effects wore off. He started taking more pills and this seemed to help for a while. At a hotel one night, after he had taken his normal dosage of pills, he was walking to his bed when he became disoriented and fell. He knocked over a glass vase and cut his arm badly. At the hospital, the doctor strongly recommended that he go see a counselor about his sleeping habits.

- Today is Friday, the day Chris gets paid. On the way home, he stopped by a gas station and purchased his beer to drink away the stress of the week. Now he is sitting on the couch, watching TV, and still drinking. He just wants to relax. The next thing he knows he is waking up as someone is shaking him. He had passed out from too much alcohol.

- "No, I think I'll just stay home tonight. I have a lot of homework," Jill told her high school friends who were inviting her out for the evening. It wasn't her workload, though, that made her turn down an evening with friends. It was the high level of anxiety in her life that seems to come up out of nowhere. She has been on medication for several months now and has seen a counselor. Since Jill's family is new in the area, they are seeking a new counselor for Jill and hoping this issue will get resolved once and for all. A new problem has arisen, as Jill's parents have noticed she has been going through her medication faster than prescribed.

## DEFINITIONS AND KEY THOUGHTS 2

- *Depressant* is an umbrella term used to describe various types of drugs that, when taken, *depress or decrease function in certain parts of the brain.* They are substances that *slow down the normal function of the central nervous system.* They are *the opposite of stimulants*, which increase brain function.

- Due to the effects of these drugs, they are usually referred to as *downers.*

- The most common reasons people use depressants are to *gain a sense of relaxation, help with trouble sleeping, relieve stress,* or *calm feelings of anxiety or panic.*

- All depressants have the potential to be abused and *can become physically addictive.*

- Depressants are still widely used for medicinal purposes. As a result, these drugs are not manufactured in clandestine laboratories but are *legitimate drugs that can be abused.*

- In 2010 there were 7 million (2.7 percent) persons in the U.S. ages 12 or older who had used prescription-type psychotherapeutic drugs *nonmedically* within the preceding month.[1]

- The *level of intoxication* and the *effects that are observed* from using depressants follow a continuum, from mild to fatal:

  — *Mild*: sedation, slurred speech, disorientation, ataxia (loss of muscle coordination), nystagmus (involuntary eye movement)

  — *Moderate*: coma (can be aroused by pain), hypoventilation (respiratory depression), depression of deep tendon reflexes

  — *Severe*: deep coma, gag reflex absent, apnea, hypotension (low blood pressure), shock, hypothermia

  — *Death*

- *Withdrawal from depressants can be fatal. Delirium tremens* (DTs) and seizures are always a concern. Some symptoms of DTs include *body tremors, confusion, restlessness, fatigue, rapid mood changes, and vomiting.*[2] A milder form of withdrawal can include *anxiety and insomnia*, conditions that may have moved the individual to abuse the drug in the first place.

- Depressants should never be taken with other depressant substances, especially alcohol, because of the *increased chance of overdosing.*

- Various depression and anxiety medications can increase *suicide ideation and behavior* and, therefore, are always a risk.

- Depressants include drugs that are used as *sedatives* and *hypnotics.* Specific groupings of sedative-hypnotic drugs by chemical makeup include: barbiturates, benzodiazepines, alcohol, inhalants, gamma-hydroxybutyrate (GHB), and major tranquilizers.

## Barbiturates

- Barbiturates are depressants that have been used to treat anxiety. Although benzodiazepines have largely replaced barbiturates, they are still available and abused. In the medical community, they are minimally used for *certain surgical procedures, control of brain swelling, treatment for migraine headaches, emergency treatment for seizures, and control of epilepsy.* Thiopental is also used for lethal injections.

- Street names are *barbs, yellows, red birds,* and *tooies.*

- Thousands of barbiturates were produced, but only fifty ever reached clinical use. Today roughly *twenty different barbiturates* still exist in practice. Less than 10 percent of all prescriptions are for barbiturates.[3]

- Common barbiturates include amobarbital (Amytal), aprobarbital (Alurate), butabarbital (Butisol), phenobarbital (Luminal), secobarbital (Seconal), and talbutal (Lotusate). All barbiturates are classified by duration of action.
- Users of barbiturates will often experience a decreased sexual drive, dizziness, a floating feeling, disorientation, a hangover the following day, and photosensitivity. Some have also experienced a drop of eight I.Q. points.

## Benzodiazepines

- Benzodiazepines are an *antianxiety* medication used to treat anxiety, insomnia, muscle strains, and seizures.
- Street names are *tranks, candy,* and *sleeping pills.*
- Currently they are the *most frequently prescribed* class of psychotropic medications in the world.[4]
- Common benzodiazepines are diazepam (Valium), chlordiazepoxide (Librium), flunitrazepam (Rohypnol or "roofies," the date-rape drug), alprazolam (Xanax), and clonazepam (Klonopin).
- *Side effects* include sedation, hangovers, euphoria, irritability, depressive reaction, and rage.

## Gamma-Hydroxybutyrate (GHB)

- GHB is a *central nervous system depressant* that occurs naturally in the human body and can also be created synthetically. The problem arises when too much is introduced into the system.
- Usually seen in a club or rave settings, this drug has a similar effect on the body as MDMA (*Ecstasy*) and *alcohol.*
- It has a reputation for being *a date-rape drug* similar to Rohypnol. It leaves users vulnerable to being taken advantage of.
- Originally it was approved by the FDA as a medication *to treat narcolepsy,* as it is a mild to moderate sedative.
- Some common street names for the drug are *liquid ecstasy, liquid X, fantasy, Georgia Home Boy, G,* and *Mils.*

## Major Tranquilizers

- Major tranquilizers are referred to as antipsychotics. These medications are used to treat *severe psychosis* (auditory and visual hallucinations), such as *schizophrenia, delusional disorder,* and *bipolar disorder.*
- Some highly used antipsychotics include haloperidol (Haldol), benperidol, chlorpromazine (Thorazine), perphenazine, clozapine (Clozaril), and flupenthixol.
- Some *side effects* of these drugs and others are agranulocytosis, which is loss of white blood cells used to help fight infection, drowsiness, dizziness when

changing positions, blurred vision, rapid heartbeat, sensitivity to the sun, skin rashes, and menstrual problems for women.

## Alcohol

See chapter 6, Alcohol.

## Inhalants

See chapter 12, Inhalants.

# 3 ASSESSMENT INTERVIEW

## Rule Outs

1. Have you ever had or do you currently have any thoughts about hurting yourself?
2. How extensive is the abuse of your drug of choice? Are you at risk of going through withdrawal now?

## General Questions

1. What medications are you currently taking and how much? Are you exceeding the amount prescribed or taking them for purposes other than for what they are intended?
2. In what situations do you think you are most vulnerable to misuse or abuse of your drug of choice?
3. What are your best times and your worst times? What is it that distinguishes between the two?
4. What has been said to you regarding the use of your drug of choice? Do you agree or disagree with what has been said?
5. What is the number one thing you want to change in your life? Does your drug of choice affect that in any way?
6. At what level are you functioning now? Tell me about a typical day.
7. Have you experienced any pain or other health concerns?
8. Do you abuse more than one depressant at a time? Are you aware of the major risks involved with this behavior?
9. On a scale of 1 to 10, with 1 being healthy and 10 being extremely depressed, where would you put yourself today?
10. What circumstances in life cause you the most anxiety? How do you usually cope with them?

# WISE COUNSEL :4

First, when dealing with depressants, always ask about suicide intentions and whether or not a client is at risk. Many depressants increase the risk of suicide. It would be a good idea to consult with a client's doctor, if they have one, about any medications they are on and possible side effects. You may not understand all the medical implications of prescription drugs but don't worry. You can ask a medical professional to guide you. Withdrawal from depressants can be fatal because of DTs. Find out if your client is at risk for withdrawal.

Many people who abuse depressants are often anxiety ridden or depressed (creating a comorbid situation). Discuss with them the reasons they are feeling this way. You could be dealing with a client who is abusing a substance and dealing with anxiety or depression at the same time. Each problem complicates the other. It is best to assess the substance abuse first to make sure there are no pressing medical concerns. When this has been assessed, it is beneficial to be able to deal with both the abuse and the anxiety and/or depression simultaneously. If one of these issues (abuse or depression) goes unresolved, it will often hinder the treatment progress in the other area.

Since many of the depressant drugs are legal in the United States, some clients may try to rationalize their behavior by saying that the substance is not illegal, therefore they are not technically in the wrong. Some will underestimate the amount of medication they use beyond the prescribed limit. Other clients will tell you how they needed extra doses because their health issue flared up. In all of these instances, the client is avoiding responsibility for their behavior. Point out the negative consequences of their actions and confront them about their rationalizations.

# ACTION STEPS :5

## 1. Get a Medical Checkup

- Safety is an important issue when chemicals that affect the body in dangerous ways are abused.
- Be sure to have a medical professional monitor your detoxification period.

## 2. Do Not Drive

- Depressants are drugs that affect awareness and slow down reaction time. Driving or operating certain kinds of machinery while under the influence is very dangerous and often illegal.
- *Counselors should encourage family members to say no to car rides when the client is driving. Special precaution is needed by someone abusing a depressant.*
- Abuse is a potential factor in dealing with alcohol or other depressants. If abuse is present, professional help should be sought immediately.

### 3. Set Goals

- Set goals for yourself and gain a fresh direction for your life.
- Surround yourself with encouraging people and an atmosphere that is conducive to accomplishing your goals.
- Make a commitment not to mix alcohol with your medications.
- Pray for the courage and strength to be able to follow through with your commitments.

### 4. Get Help

- Chances are that you have some level of anxiety or depression in your life if you are abusing a depressant. These underlying issues need to be dealt with on a professional level with a certified counselor.
- Learn and work on coping strategies for dealing with the stresses in your life.

### 5. Sign a Contract

- Accountability is a necessity in the recovery from any addiction.
- It is a good idea to sign a contract with a counselor or friend that states you will not abuse your drug of choice.

## 6 BIBLICAL INSIGHTS

*Humble yourselves, therefore, under God's mighty hand, that he may lift you up in due time. Cast all your anxiety on him because he cares for you.*

*1 Peter 5:6–7*

We need to allow ourselves to be humbled before God and ask for His help in our time of need. We can do this because we can be confident that Christ cares for us and wants to see us restored.

Instead of self-medicating your anxieties, cast them on God and let your worries be known.

*Finally, be strong in the Lord and in his mighty power. Put on the full armor of God, so that you can take your stand against the devil's schemes.*

*Ephesians 6:10–11*

When we try to do right and overcome an addiction, Satan will always try to thwart our efforts. We need to put on the armor of God so we can fight against the evil one.

*Anxiety weighs down the heart, but a kind word cheers it up.*

Proverbs 12:25

Surround yourself with good influences who will build you up and not tear you down. This will be one of the most helpful steps in your journey to recovery. Hearing a good word when you need it will refresh your soul and can give you much-needed motivation.

## PRAYER STARTER 7

Lord, You said that You have come to set the captives free. I pray that You will do that in the life of _____. Right now he (she) needs Your strength to lay aside this substance that has entrapped him (her). I pray that You surround him (her) with Your love and take his (her) burdens from him (her). We know that You care for us; thank You . . .

## RECOMMENDED RESOURCES 8

Benda, Brent B., and Thomas F. McGovern. *Spirituality and Religiousness and Alcohol/Other Drug Problems: Treatment and Recovery Perspectives.* Haworth Press, 2006.

Hart, Archibald. *The Anxiety Cure.* Thomas Nelson, 2001.

———. *Sleep—It Does a Family Good: How Busy Families Can Overcome Sleep Deprivation.* Tyndale, 2010.

Kuhar, Michael. *The Addicted Brain: Why We Abuse Drugs, Alcohol, and Nicotine.* Pearson Education, 2012.

McKeever, Bridget C. *Hidden Addictions: A Pastoral Response to the Abuse of Legal Drugs.* Haworth Press, 1998.

Warren, Kay. *Choose Joy: Because Happiness Isn't Enough.* Revell, 2012.

### Website

Substance Abuse and Mental Health Services Administration: www.samhsa.gov/

# 10 Diuretics and Weight Loss

## 1 PORTRAITS

- Jill competes in pageants all over the state and has won several contests. She just turned sixteen and now has her driver's license. With so much pressure to look pretty and maintain a certain body type, she has been going to the local pharmacy after school and picking up some Xpel. She knows it's a stupid idea but she does it anyway because every little bit helps. She started taking the pills before each pageant. Now she takes them after almost every meal to make sure she doesn't gain any weight. One day Jill's mom was helping her clean up her room and found the bottle of pills. Distraught, she immediately pursued counseling for her daughter, hoping it would help.

- Ben has been a football player since the children's league and has plans to go as far as he can. He is extremely motivated and will do whatever it takes to get to the NFL. He is on a college team right now and is excelling. One of the reasons for his success is that he has been experimenting with steroids for enhanced performance on the field—he's also been using other drugs for pleasure off the field. Knowing there are routine drug tests, Ben always purges his system with diuretics before each practice, hoping to mask his extracurricular experimentation. During a practice Ben collapses on the field and is rushed to the hospital. When he comes to, he doesn't know if it was the drugs, steroids, or diuretics that sent him to the hospital but he does know he has made a big mistake.

- Claire rushed into the shower to get ready for her next class. She turned on the hot water and felt her skin crawling. Dizziness overcame her and she dropped to her knees. Her vision slowly went black and her last thought was, *At least I will die skinny.* Her roommate found her and shook her awake. Claire was terrified. For the past three years, she had been taking laxatives every day to lose weight. When she was in high school, Claire had been teased and bullied for being fat. In college she decided to go on a secret diet of one bowl of cereal a day with coffee or tea. When she fell in the shower, it was a wake-up call. *I don't want to risk my life just to be skinny,* she decided.

# DEFINITIONS AND KEY THOUGHTS : 2

## Diuretics

- A diuretic, sometimes called a water pill, is used to *accelerate the rate of urination* by targeting the kidneys.
- Medically, diuretics are used to *treat a number of physical maladies,*[1] such as:

  - idiopathic edema (tissue swelling or bloating associated with premenstrual syndrome in women)
  - hypertension (high blood pressure)
  - glaucoma
  - osteoporosis
  - diabetes
  - kidney disorders, such as kidney stones
  - heart failure
  - cases of drug overdose or poisoning to help flush out the harmful substance

- There are three classifications of diuretics differing in function and targeting certain areas of the body: *loop diuretics, thiazides, and potassium-sparing diuretics.*
- You can obtain diuretics from a *prescription as well as in over-the-counter (OTC) forms,* with the prescribed forms being more potent. Some common OTC diuretics are Diurex, Xpel, Arbuterol, Expelis, Midol, and H2O Lean. Anyone can purchase these at a local pharmacy, *even minors.*
- In 2009, 7,563 (0.7 percent) of all emergency department visits were for *nonmedical use of diuretics* as opposed to 3,625 visits in 2004.[2]
- In a study of 275 *bulimic women,* 44.1 percent had abused diuretics. The majority of that population said they abused diuretics for the specific purpose of weight loss.[3]
- Some side effects of diuretic abuse are:

  - low sodium in the blood (hyponatremia) and other electrolyte imbalances
  - softening of bones
  - dizziness
  - headaches
  - increased thirst
  - muscle cramps
  - nausea
  - dehydration
  - increased blood sugar levels
  - increased cholesterol
  - rash

— joint disorders (gout)

— impotence

— menstrual irregularities

— breast enlargement in men (gynecomastia)

- When abused, diuretics can cause *organ damage* by depriving the body of enough of the vital fluids and electrolytes it needs, *organ failure, and even death.*

- Stopping the use of diuretics can produce withdrawal symptoms, such as *cramping, fatigue, constipation, bloating, and mood swings.*

- When diuretics are discontinued, sometimes *reflex fluid retention* takes place, with the body holding on to water for a short period of time before the fluid levels return to normal. This may cause the client to continue abusing the substance, believing that edema is still present when, in fact, it is *drug-induced.*[4]

- Diuretics, because of their effect, are frequently used by users of illicit drugs to *mask the evidence of drug use in a urine test.* Therefore, diuretic use could be a potential *indicator for abuse of other drugs.* More times than not, an abuser will abuse more than one drug.

## Laxatives

- Laxatives are another substance abused for weight loss by *targeting the large intestine.*

- Many who abuse laxatives do so *to expel the food just eaten* before the body has time to absorb the calories. *This will not work* because laxatives target the large intestines and the large intestines do not digest food, but hold the excess undigested food from the small intestine. So the body has already absorbed the calories. Apparent weight loss will be felt, however, only because of the loss of water and other fluids in the body. *The dehydration of the body is temporary weight loss.* When the body is rehydrated the weight will return.

- The abuse of diuretics and laxatives is most commonly seen with people struggling with *bulimia* and *anorexia nervosa,* because the substance seems to purge the body of the food just eaten.

- A review of several studies states that anywhere from *38 to 75 percent of women* who are diagnosed with *bulimia* will abuse laxatives.[5]

- In one study of fifty-one women, about 50 percent of the *anorexic individuals* abused laxatives.[6]

- People struggling with anorexia nervosa, depression, weight loss connected to sports (athletes), and poor body image may be abusing diuretics or laxatives. Therefore, *abuse of diuretics or laxatives is usually a warning sign for other serious problems, the most common being eating disorders.*

- After a prolonged period of time of abusing laxatives, the body will no longer respond to the substance and the individual will need to take more to produce the desired effect. This is called *laxative dependency.*

## Ipecac Syrup

- People struggling with an eating disorder may abuse *ipecac syrup*. Its intended use is to induce vomiting in case of swallowing toxic materials or poison. As a result, it is readily available.
- Its ability to *completely purge the stomach* attracts abusers and is most abused by clients who have just started purging and are having difficulty doing so. Some chronic users abuse it regularly when the gag reflex is damaged or no longer present.
- Abuse can be *fatal* by causing *cardiomyopathy* (deterioration of the heart muscle). Other problems associated with this drug are myopathy (weak muscles), shock, coma, seizure, cramping, high blood pressure, and dehydration.[7]
- In one study, twenty-eight out of one hundred women struggling with *bulimia nervosa* indicated they had abused ipecac syrup.[8]

# ASSESSMENT INTERVIEW 3

## Rule Outs

1. Do you have any thoughts about hurting yourself?
2. When was the last time you ate? Did you keep the food down?

## General Questions

1. What brought you in for counseling? What was the thought that made you decide to commit to doing this?
2. How long have you been abusing diuretics and when was your first experience with them?
3. How often and how much do you abuse them now?
4. What is the primary feeling you experience when you are using a diuretic?
5. Who knows about your struggle?
6. When you look in the mirror, what do you see?
7. What do others say about your weight or body image? Do you believe them?
8. Can you see that your abuse of these substances is affecting other activities and areas in your life?
9. If one morning when you woke up, you realized all of your problems were gone, what would your life be like?
10. How do you see yourself in relation to others? Are your emotions, problems, and thoughts more or less important than those of others? Do you feel people judge you often?

# 4 WISE COUNSEL

Abuse of diuretics, laxatives, or ipecac syrup carries with it several health concerns, some mild and some severe. A client's state of health and risk of medical emergency should always be a number-one concern. Consult with the client's doctor about any medications they may be taking.

When talking to doctors the client has seen in the past, ask about the amount of prescribed diuretics. Many clients who are abusing prescription diuretics visit multiple doctors, not telling them about their other prescriptions, thus being able to get additional prescriptions. Let the doctor know about any manipulation on the client's part.

Most individuals abusing diuretics or laxatives do so because of low self-esteem issues related to body image or perceived body image. When low self-esteem or self-hatred is present, they are at risk for suicide, social anxiety, or severe depression. Do not be afraid to address these issues because not doing so could be damaging to the client.

Many who struggle with body image have several negative beliefs about themselves that are not based in facts. A few of these beliefs are: *My problems are not important to anyone; I am really fat compared to others; No one will ever love me unless I am skinny; I need others' approval to feel good about myself.* It is imperative that these negative beliefs are teased out and dealt with. Start by showing empathy for the client and talk in terms of how hard it must be to be in their situation. Next reframe their beliefs and offer positive and encouraging affirmation that is based in reality, such as "You are handling this very well, and you are a strong person." Once their cognitions start to change, they will be better able to overcome.

Be aware that you may have a client who is either too young or too inexperienced to know that substances can be abused to achieve weight loss. If you ask them about suspected substance abuse, you may be inadvertently exposing them to an unhealthy way of losing weight that they didn't know about. Be sure to explain the seriousness of substance abuse and the health risks involved to prevent initiation or experimentation with a new substance.

Many who have an eating disorder feel the need to control their food intake because other areas of their life are out of control. Help the client work through these feelings and help them establish a healthy feeling of control. Encourage the client by reminding them of God's sovereignty.

# 5 ACTION STEPS

## 1. Seek Professional Help

- If you are abusing diuretics or laxatives, you are putting your body in danger of several health problems. A doctor needs to be notified and a precautionary checkup needs to be performed.
- Your counselor will help you find a mental health professional or counselor who specializes in this area of treatment. Knowing what to do and being educated are important in recovery. Being able to share your story in a safe place is also beneficial.

## 2. Take Inventory

- Search yourself and find your strengths and weaknesses, your assets and liabilities, and your good and bad traits. This is not for the purpose of self-condemnation, but to help you discover self-esteem and help you realize the tools you have to combat negative feelings. It also points out the areas of your life where you are weak and need to be careful or they may cause you to relapse.
- Be courageous when taking inventory. It is hard to be honest with yourself. Honesty and openness are the most important factors involved in recovery.

## 3. Target Negative Beliefs

- Identify the triggers for negative beliefs, the things in life that cause you to think negatively about yourself, and decide that when they surface, you will not listen to them. Become aware of what contributes to your negative beliefs.
- Carry an index card on which you have written positive phrases you want to believe about yourself. Read it aloud when you are tempted to despair.
- Take your positives and outweigh the negatives when it comes to attributions, life experiences, significant relationships, achievements, etc.

## 4. Surrender to God

- Ask God for strength in the times when all you can think about are the negatives.
- Realize who you are compared to God and that you will not be able to recover without Him. Depend on Him.
- Give the Lord control over your life.

## 5. Be Accountable

- Tell someone you trust in your life about your struggles and give them permission to ask you about what's in your medicine cabinet.
- Give them permission to ask you about your purchases to make sure you are not giving in to temptations to buy diuretics or laxatives.

# BIBLICAL INSIGHTS 6

*For it is God who works in you to will and to act in order to fulfill his good purpose.*

*Philippians 2:13*

God works through us to show His power. We must allow Him to do this in our lives. He is the great Enabler. While we strive to overcome, God will come along beside us and help.

*But he said to me, "My grace is sufficient for you, for my power is made perfect in weakness." Therefore I will boast all the more gladly about my weaknesses, so that Christ's power may rest on me. That is why, for Christ's sake, I delight in weaknesses, in insults, in hardships, in persecutions, in difficulties. For when I am weak, then I am strong.*

*2 Corinthians 12:9–10*

The apostle Paul realized in these verses that he was weak, much like how people feel who are abusing drugs. Christ worked through him and made him strong because He is strong. Paul then could say His grace is sufficient. When we are weak, we can depend on God to be strong for us.

*Let us examine our ways and test them, and let us return to the Lord.*

*Lamentations 3:40*

The Scriptures tell us always to examine ourselves and keep inventory. Only when we are aware of our shortcomings can we ask God for specific help in our need.

In this passage, Jeremiah had just realized God was not a judge in heaven simply inflicting pain on him, but a loving, faithful God who was disciplining Israel and calling them back to Himself. He was then writing this passage urging others to examine their beliefs and to come to the same conclusion.

Likewise, we need to examine our view of God and ourselves and see if we have any faulty beliefs, namely about weight. If we do, we must take these beliefs to God and pray for right thinking.

# 7 PRAYER STARTER

Lord, I pray for _____ and the struggle he (she) is going through. I know it must be really hard for him (her). Show _____ how beautiful he (she) is in Your sight. I thank You for the courage _____ showed by choosing to come to me for help. I pray You will enable him (her) with the strength he (she) needs to fight off the temptation that will come at him (her). I pray that You will instill hope . . .

# 8 RECOMMENDED RESOURCES

Davidson, Kimberly. *I'm Beautiful? Why Can't I See It?: Daily Encouragement to Promote Healthy Eating and Positive Self-Esteem.* Tate Publishing, 2006.

ICON Health. *Laxative Abuse: A 3-in-1 Medical Reference.* ICON Health Publications, 2004.

Jantz, Gregory, and Ann McMurray. *Hope, Help, and Healing for Eating Disorders: A Whole-Person Approach to Treatment of Anorexia, Bulimia, and Disordered Eating.* WaterBrook, 2010.

McClure, Cynthia Rowland. *The Monster Within: Facing an Eating Disorder.* Baker, 2002.

McGee, Robert S. *Rapha's 12-Step Program for Overcoming Eating Disorders: A New Biblically Integrated Approach to Recovery from the ABCs of Eating Disorders— Anorexia, Bulimia, and Compulsive Overeating.* Rapha/Word, 1990.

Mintle, Linda. *Making Peace with Your Thighs: Get Off the Scales and Get On with Your Life.* Thomas Nelson, 2006.

Mottram, David R. *Drugs in Sport.* 5th ed. Routledge, 2011.

Smalley, Gary. *Healthy Weight Loss.* Tyndale, 2007.

## Websites

Eating Disorders Treatment: www.eating-disorder.com/Eating-Treatment/Eating-Disorders/diuretic-abuse.htm

National Center for Biotechnology Information: www.ncbi.nlm.nih.gov/pmc/articles/PMC2962812/

National Eating Disorders Association: www.nationaleatingdisorders.org/

# 11 Hallucinogens

## 1 PORTRAITS

- Guy parked in the junior parking lot, like every other morning. He was about to walk across the lot to the building when a group of guys and girls got into a car next to his. He knew them but just barely. When he asked where they were going, they invited him along. He really didn't feel like going to school that day anyway, so without thinking, he jumped in. It turns out that these students had been skipping school every week to go party and use Ecstasy. They encouraged Guy to try the drug, and he had the time of his life. He started to skip school regularly and his grades dropped. Concerned, one of his teachers called his mother and asked if she knew of anything going on. After repeatedly denying that anything was wrong and fighting with his mom, Guy finally told her where he had been going.

- "Something was coming, I knew it was. I told my friends we had to go; we had to get back before midnight. Why? I don't know. All I knew is we needed to get out of this star-shaped field and get out of reach of the creatures. I ran as fast as I could while telling them to follow. There was a hole in front of me and I jumped over it. Did I make it?" Everything then went black. Cameron awoke to find himself in a hospital with his parents by his side. When his roommate called to see if he was at his parents' house, they knew something was wrong and went to look for him in his favorite field. He had broken his leg when he fell into a deep ravine in the woods down the street from his house. Cameron was high on LSD and couldn't judge the depth. It scared him a lot and he wants to get his life right. No more drugs and no more "bad trips."

- Anthony's zodiac sign is Scorpio and he desires to become one with his fate. He takes some magic mushrooms to become one with his sign and the universe. He cannot reach his full potential and experience his religion fully until he takes the drug. When he is high, everything makes sense and fits together and he feels he has become transcendent; his mind has opened up to things unseen by the normal human, making him special. Anthony decided to go to counseling, not for drug abuse but for the depression he experiences when he is not on the drug. He doesn't see his drug abuse as a problem and has threatened to leave if the counselor brings up the topic.

# DEFINITIONS AND KEY THOUGHTS : 2

- There are several *hallucinogens*, or *psychedelics*, used today including LSD, Ecstasy, PCP, peyote, ketamine, dextromethorphan, and mushrooms (psilocybin).
- Hallucinogens are known by their ability to upset the body's *serotonin levels, alter the brain's perception of stimuli*, and *trigger sounds or visions of things not based in reality*.
- These drugs have always been *associated with religious experiences and ceremonies, healing rituals, and predicting the future* (fortune-telling), experiences that include some kind of insight into the past as well as the present.
- The use of peyote has been associated with religion as far back as *four thousand years*.[1]
- In 2010 it was estimated that hallucinogens had been used in the preceding month by *1.2 million persons* in the United States(0.5 percent) aged 12 or older, including 695,000 (0.3 percent) who had used Ecstasy. These estimates were similar to estimates in 2009.[2]
- Hallucinogens reached their peak in popularity in the *sixties* and *early seventies* when the United States was involved in a war in Vietnam. This was during the rise of the hippie countercultural movement led by such icons as the Beatles.

## LSD

- *Lysergic acid diethylamide* is colloquially known as *acid, Lucy, Alice, boomers, blotter, cid, windowpanes, dots, hits, doses, tabs, yellow sunshine*, among other names.
- Currently, there is *no legal use of LSD in the United States*.
- Many abusers of LSD do so usually in connection with *religious beliefs*. The drug was first synthesized in a laboratory in 1938, and others like it are thought to bring about *insight through visions* (some hallucinogens have been used to that end for centuries).
- *In 2010* the number of preceding-year initiates of LSD aged 12 or older was *377,000*, which was *similar to the number in 2009* (337,000) but higher than the estimates from 2003 to 2007 (ranging from 200,000 to 270,000).[3]
- About *one in seven* (12.9 percent) *youths from ages thirteen to seventeen* indicated that LSD would be "fairly" or "very" easily available.[4]
- Highly absorbent *blotter paper* is *soaked in an LSD–distilled-water solution* (tap water contains chloride, which destroys LSD). Users stick the paper on their tongues, suck on it for five to ten minutes, and then most swallow the paper to get the maximum dose and effect.
- *Hallucinations or distortions of reality* happen three to sixty minutes after ingestion, and usually the effects last two to four hours, dissipating over the next eight to twelve hours.[5]
- *During a trip users report*:

- a sensation of having no boundaries, transcendent through time and space
- enhanced insight, intuitive "knowing," and a sense of awe
- awareness of sensory perceptions
- enhanced memory recall
- happiness, contentment, pure joy
- a sense of being "at one" with the universe

• The *negative effects* of LSD, as with any drug, are subjective, but the most common negative effects reported are:

- anxiety
- gastric distress
- rapid heart rate (tachycardia)
- increased blood pressure
- increased body temperature
- dilation of the pupils
- nausea
- muscle weakness, reflexes (hyperreflexia) and tremors
- dizziness

• The *negative effects usually begin* five to ten minutes after the dose is ingested.
• These effects are either interpreted as *bearable* or *unbearable*. If the latter is experienced, the user is said to have a *bad trip,* which is a panicked reaction to the drug's effects.
• The *tolerance level of LSD builds very quickly.* Often after just two to four days of continuous use, users typically have to wait several days before the same effects can be achieved again.[6]
• *Death by LSD* is virtually unheard of and only caused by accidents as *a result of perceptual distortions.* LSD overdose (typically defined as more than 60 micrograms at one time) is possible, but no lethal dose has ever been observed. Symptoms of overdose include *convulsions, hyperthermia,* and *exaggerated effects of the drug.* If you observe these reactions, get medical attention immediately.
• *Flashbacks* are periods of experiencing the effects of LSD without actually having taken the drug again. Normally heavy users who have abused LSD for a long time experience this phenomenon throughout the rest of their life. During a flashback, the individual experiences *perceptual distortions, flashes of light and color,* and *depersonalization.* Anywhere from 15 to 77 percent of LSD abusers will have at least one flashback.[7]

## Ecstasy (MDMA)

• *MDMA* or 3, 4-methylenedioxymethamphetamine is the drug commonly referred to today as *Ecstasy.* There are more than *150 street names* recorded for

Ecstasy. Some common ones are *X, E, XTC, hug drug, lover's speed, disco biscuit, Adam, beans,* and *Eve.*

- The drug was first introduced as an *appetite suppressant* and then the military was interested in it for *chemical warfare* in the 1950s. It became popular in the seventies and was then classified as illegal.

- Despite Ecstasy's being *illegal in the United States,* it is still *widely used,* evidenced by the *eight metric tons* or more that is manufactured each year.[8]

- It was estimated in 2008 that *nine million people* between the ages of five and sixty-four *had abused Ecstasy* in the preceding twelve months.[9]

- Most (59.2 percent) of the recent Ecstasy initiates in 2010 were *18 or older* at the time they first used the drug. Among past year initiates ages 12 to 49, the *average age* at initiation was *19.4* years.[10]

- Ecstasy's most popular venues are *dance clubs and raves,* putting it into the category of "club drugs," although it is used in other environments as well.

- The *effects begin within twenty minutes* of orally taking one dose and peak within one to four hours.

- MDMA was *experimented with as a drug to aid in psychotherapy* because it affects a person's openness, empathy, and introspection. Today it has gained popularity as the *"love drug"* because of its effects. The *perceived effects* are:

  — euphoria
  — increased empathy toward others
  — emotional openness
  — increased psychomotor energy
  — increased self-confidence
  — feelings of intimacy
  — increased desirability as sexual partner
  — belief of improved self-awareness
  — intense feelings
  — different state of mind or perceptions
  — sensitivity to colors and sound
  — heightened awareness of touch

- Several *side effects* occur with the use of Ecstasy, including:

  — nausea and/or vomiting
  — headaches
  — bruxism (grinding of the teeth)
  — hypertension and heart palpitations
  — sudden cardiac arrest
  — anorexia
  — urinary incontinence

— ataxia (lack of voluntary coordination of muscle movements), muscle tension

— blurred vision

— motor tics

— loss of consciousness

— hyperthermia or hypothermia

— seizures

— subarachnoid hemorrhage (bleeding in the brain)

— central venous sinus thrombosis (rare form of a stroke)

— increase in body temperature to dangerous levels (up to 117° F)

— dehydration and increased thirst

— "lockjaw" or "clamping"—the mouth becomes stiff and sore and a user finds relief sometimes by sucking on a lollipop, chewing gum, or smoking cigarettes. *This can be an easy identifier for Ecstasy abuse.*

- *Ecstasy abuse can be fatal.* The estimated *lethal dose* for humans is around 6,000 mg, which, depending on the potency of each of the tablets, is around 20 to 30 tablets. There have been reports of fatalities with *much lower doses* as well. *Mixing different chemicals and drugs with Ecstasy promotes an increased risk of death*, as well as taking higher doses.

## Phencyclidine (PCP)

- PCP is a *dissociative drug* originally of interest because of its *anesthetic* properties but not approved after the side effects were observed in clinical studies. It has also been used as a hog tranquilizer.

- Several street names exist, such as *angel dust, ozone, wack,* and *rocket fuel.*

- Currently the use of PCP is *waning* but is still used in combination with other drugs for enhancement purposes. Often it is *sold under another name* or *mixed with other drugs* and *accidental exposure* to PCP can occur to an unsuspecting user.

- It is believed that *less than 0.5 percent* of the total U.S. population has ever abused PCP.[11]

- It can be administered through *ingesting orally, intravenously, intranasally, or smoking.* Smoking PCP is most popular due to the level of control it offers on the amount taken. The user will add PCP to a leaf, such as cannabis, oregano, or mint, and smoke it.

- When smoked, PCP *starts to take effect in two to three minutes, reaches peak in fifteen to thirty minutes,* and *lasts for four to six hours* after a single dose.

- Under the influence of PCP *users experience*:

— fluctuations in level of consciousness

— hallucinations

— extreme anxiety

— disassociation

— euphoria

— decreased inhibitions

— a feeling of immense power

— analgesia (a deadening to the sense of pain)

— confusion and/or an altered sense of time

— loss of sensation (for example, feeling that body parts are no longer attached)

— paranoia

— depression and suicidal ideation

— irritability

— memory impairment

— seizures

— hypertension

— aggression

- Death can occur indirectly from PCP abuse. Either various health-related issues can cause death or *homicide and suicide may occur as users become aggressive and unpredictable.*

- *You cannot "talk down" an abuser of PCP* if he or she is in a state of drug-induced psychosis, as you can with LSD abusers. Often in difficult cases, *restraints or sedation are necessary to maintain control* of the individual until the episode passes.

## Peyote

- Peyote is a *small spineless cactus* that grows in northern Mexico and the southwestern United States. It has been used for thousands of years to aid in religious ceremonies to gain insight and see visions. Its principle ingredient is *mescaline.*

- Other common names for peyote include *devil's root, magic mushrooms, buttons, pellote,* and *sacred mushrooms.*

- The crown of the cactus (the part above the ground) produces *disc-shaped buttons that contain the psychoactive properties.* The buttons are either chewed or boiled in a tea and taken orally. Usually it is mixed in tea because of its very bitter taste.

- The *psychoactive dose* is about 0.3 to 0.5 grams and the effects usually *last up to twelve hours.*

- Peyote and mescaline are listed as Schedule 1 substances (i.e., have a high potential for abuse, no accepted medical use, and a lack of safety under medical supervision) and are *illegal* with the exception of use in *"bonafide religious ceremonies" by the Native American Church.*

- During an all-night religious ceremony, a member of the Native American church will consume anywhere from *ten to several dozen "buttons." The purpose of this is to communicate with God, fellow worshipers, and the self as well as to experience the healing of physical or spiritual illness.*[12]

- In some cases, the use of peyote in Native American culture is *seen as beneficial,* and some people advise its use every day. Some tribes will chew it up and *apply it to burns or snakebites* for healing.[13]

- In 2008, *7.8 percent of high school seniors had used hallucinogens other than LSD*—a group that includes peyote, psilocybin, and others—*at least once in their lifetime.* Use the previous year was reported to be 5.0 percent.[14]

- Of *eighty-nine clients, ten (11.2 percent) reported illicit use of peyote.* The vast majority of these youth (n = 8) reported using peyote only once or twice in their lifetime.[15]

- The *effects of peyote* include:

  — increased body temperature

  — increased heart rate

  — ataxia

  — sweating and flushing

  — headaches

  — dizziness

  — nausea

  — anxiety

  — paranoia and fear

- *Death* can be a result of peyote use by way of *suicide or homicide* brought on by the hallucinations.

## Ketamine

- Ketamine is a *dissociative anesthetic* that has hallucinogenic effects. It goes by several street names, such as *special K, vitamin K, cat valium, cat tranquilizer, jet, purple, super acid,* and *kit-kat.*

- Ketamine has earned its way into the *"club drug" category* because of its popularity among young adults in clubs, dances, and raves.

- Specific names are given to different experiences resulting from Ketamine. For instance, *"k-land"* refers to a mellow, colorful experience, and *"k-hole"* refers to an out-of-body, near-death experience. Other names for specific experiences are *"God"* and *"baby food."*

- The *effects of ketamine* are:

  — hallucinations

  — dissociation

  — sensitivity to light and sound

  — agitation

  — depression

  — cognitive difficulties

  — unconsciousness

— amnesia

— involuntarily rapid eye movement

— dilated pupils

— salivation

— tear secretions

— stiffening of the muscles

- As with LSD and PCP, users have reported *flashbacks*, experiencing the drug's effects after a long time without having taken the drug again.

- This drug is sometimes used as a way to facilitate *sexual assault,* as it incapacitates users, much like "roofies." For this reason, it is considered a *date-rape drug.*

- Most of the ketamine available for abuse comes from *legal shipments being diverted or stolen*, especially from veterinary clinics, where it is used to sedate animals.

## Dextromethorphan (DXM)

- DXM is a *cough suppressant* found in many OTC medicines. When taken in small, recommended amounts, it is a safe and helpful drug, but when abused and taken in large amounts, it can become problematic, even lethal.

- Beginning in the 1950s, *DXM started gradually to replace codeine* in all OTC cough medications because of the addictive qualities of codeine.

- It is obtained in many forms, such as *cough syrup, powder, capsules, or tablets.*

- It is known by names like *robotripping, robo, tussin, triple c, dex, skittles, velvet, drank, syrup, rome*, and *poor man's PCP.*

- Some *brand name cough medications* that contain DXM are Sudafed, Triaminic, Comtrex, Robitussin, Vicks, and Coricidin HBP.

- Abuse of DXM is popular among youth at *dance or rave parties,* as it heightens the senses to sounds and colors. Therefore it is a drug referred to as a *club drug.* Its growing popularity is attributed to its *availability* and also the *ease in which information about isolating the compound is found on the internet.*

- In a study done on more than 4,000 high school students in Dayton, Ohio, *4.9 percent of twelfth graders* reported lifetime use of DXM and *3.9 percent of eleventh graders* reported lifetime use of DXM.[16]

- The recommended amount of cough syrup with DXM is *15–30 mg up to 4 times a day*. The suppression of coughing lasts anywhere from 5 to 6 hours.[17]

- The drug begins to show its *psychoactive properties* when an individual ingests doses of five times more than the recommended amount.[18]

- The *side effects* of DXM abuse include:

— disassociation

— sensitivity to sounds and colors

— hallucinations

— agitation

- — paranoia
- — confusion
- — inappropriate laughing
- — overexcitability
- — lethargy
- — ataxia
- — slurred speech
- — sweating
- — hypertension
- — rapid eye movement

- When combined with other drugs, such as alcohol or antidepressants, the mixture *can be deadly.* Also, if the DXM is not isolated from other compounds included in the cough syrup, *the other chemicals have their own side effects* and can cause further complications and death.

## Mushrooms (Psilocybin)

- There are around 190 known types of mushrooms that contain *psilocybin and psyocyn,* which are *hallucinogenic compounds* abused for their psychedelic effects. Usually they are *indigenous to tropical to subtropical areas* of the United States, Mexico, and South America.[19]
- Usually mushrooms are *ingested orally* either brewed as a tea, covered in chocolate, or mixed with other food to mask the bitter taste. They are popular at dance parties or raves as a *club drug.*
- Mushrooms are commonly known as *shrooms, sacred mushrooms, God's flesh, silly putty, musk,* and other names.
- Psilocybin is currently *illegal* in the United States.
- According to a 1997 report, an estimated *5 percent of U.S. residents (10.2 million)* had tried psilocybin mushrooms.[20]
- *Side effects* include:

- — hallucinations
- — lightheadedness
- — euphoria
- — sensitivity to light and sound
- — nausea
- — cramping
- — vomiting
- — diarrhea
- — confusion of time
- — inability to discern reality
- — panic attack (a bad trip)

- The *effects* begin twenty minutes after ingestion and usually reach their peak in forty-five minutes.
- Some types of mushrooms are *toxic and poisonous to humans when eaten*. Some poisonous varieties look similar to the psychedelic types, so a misidentification can easily happen. If someone starts to feel ill after ingesting mushrooms, they should *seek medical attention immediately*.

## ASSESSMENT INTERVIEW 3

### Rule Out

*First, if someone is under the influence of a hallucinogen and they are having a "bad trip," you may need to call 911 if you cannot talk them down. The user often needs to be told the drug is causing them to feel the way they are and that the effects will eventually pass. However, if this does not work and they are a danger either to themselves or others, restraints or sedation may be utilized by emergency personnel until the episode passes.*

### General Questions

1. What drug or drugs do you use and how often?
2. Do you see your use of (the drug they use) as a problem?
3. Do you use the drug with someone in particular? Where do you generally go to use the drug? Why do you go to this place?
4. What are your religious beliefs? Do they have an influence on your drug use?
5. What have others in your life said about your drug use? Do they approve? Has your drug use developed any strains in your relationships with others?
6. While under the influence, have you ever done anything you later regretted? Have you ever been seriously injured or injured others while under the influence?
7. Have you ever broken the law while using your drug of choice?
8. Have you ever had a bad trip? What happened? In what situation were you when it occurred?
9. On a scale of 1 to 10, with 10 being the worst, how bad do you think your drug problem is?
10. How motivated are you to change? What obstacles do you think you will need to overcome if you want to change?
11. When off the drug, how do you feel?

## WISE COUNSEL 4

When compared to other drugs, hallucinogens are not extremely dangerous to the body, although there are risks to using them. And the effects they may have can be dangerous. Suicidal and homicidal behavior can result from the drug's influence as well as erratic and often unpredictable behavior. Many injuries occur when users run from an unseen threat or run to an unreal destination on dangerous terrain and are confused as to where they are. Also some users inflict damage on themselves because of certain religious beliefs or ideas that mandate it. If users start to see demons, creatures, or disturbing images of any kind, they may become violent, mistaking another person as a threat. Be careful to warn your clients about the risks involved with taking hallucinogens.

Most abusers of LSD, peyote, and other hallucinogens use the drug because of a strong connection to a religion. Peyote users are typically part of the Native American church, whereas LSD abusers can have a wide range of beliefs, sometimes appearing bizarre to others.

First, focus on the substance abuse problem and how it is negatively affecting the person's life. Once you have gained their trust and built up a healthy relationship, then address the religious beliefs. Often, when a client can see that you have helped him or her, there are opportunities for you to share your personal beliefs because the person is receptive.

It is always professional to become acclimated to other cultures different from your own. Do not assume anything about how your client thinks. Their values may be different from your own and you may need to approach certain topics differently than you normally would. Multicultural competence is a must when working with clients from other cultures.

# 5 ACTION STEPS

## 1. Assess the Situation

- Make an appointment with a professional counselor and talk through your experiences when you were under the influence of your drug of choice. With your counselor's help, assess the impact the drug has had on your life. Many times, we do not realize the negative effect something is having on us.
- Start to see the drugs you abuse as dangerous and hurtful substances rather than just a means to escape from problems or relax. Your perspective will change when you realize how the drug has stolen good things from you, whether your health, a relationship, or a goal never reached.

## 2. Make a Commitment

- Make the decision to get help with your drug use a top priority.
- Ask a friend to hold you accountable for sticking to your decision. Ask this person to help you get rid of your drugs. Some drug and rehab centers provide assistance with proper disposal, and many local police departments have anonymous drop-off boxes where the substances are then incinerated.

## 3. Learn How to Deal with Continuing Side Effects

- Often depression accompanies hallucinogen abuse, brought on by the drug's effects on the mind. Maybe the reason you abused hallucinogenic compounds is because of your depressive symptoms. Counseling can help you with those potential underlying problems.
- Because of the very nature of hallucinogenic drugs, which affect the mind, you may develop paranoia or anxiety. Flashbacks can leave you unnerved and unable to cope. Part of the counseling process is to work through these difficulties and learn effective coping strategies.

## 4. Find a New Activity

- Counseling will also guide you in replacing your drug abuse with something more constructive.
- Finding interesting ways to occupy your time will help you stay off the drug.
- Make sure your new activity helps you relax and find comfort and fulfillment. If it doesn't help relieve daily stressors, you may have a desire to return to your drug.

## 5. Guard against Relapse

- Keep tabs on yourself. If old feelings and habits creep back into your life, take steps to eliminate them as soon as possible.
- Pay attention to signs of relapse, such as not making your counseling meetings a priority, missing them, experiencing overwhelming stress, denying that you ever had a problem, and returning to old habits.
- If you see these warning signs, tell someone about them and implement new strategies to guard against relapse.

## BIBLICAL INSIGHTS 6

*In your relationships with one another, have the same mindset as Christ Jesus.*

*Philippians 2:5*

Hallucinogens distort the mind and perception. Christ's challenge to us is to be of like mind with Him. We should be striving to become more like Christ every day with our minds. This passage shows us how humble Christ was, even submitting to death on the cross (v. 8). Using drugs is a selfish act and not a humble act.

*So then, let us not be like others, who are asleep, but let us be awake and sober. For those who sleep, sleep at night, and those who get drunk, get drunk at night.*

*But since we belong to the day, let us be sober, putting on faith and love as a breastplate, and the hope of salvation as a helmet.*

*1 Thessalonians 5:6–8*

In earlier passages the apostle Paul talks about the end times. In these verses, Christians are admonished to be self-disciplined (sober), keeping in mind the great things to come (the rapture) and not being lethargic (apathetic), as the unsaved are. Those who are drunk or given over to drugs are not self-controlled, as other substances are controlling them, and this lack of control causes them to falter.

Just as a soldier suits up for battle, Christians should suit up with faith, love, and hope. The hope of salvation will help guard us against unwise thinking and keep us focused on things to come so we do not give our minds over to harmful substances.

*Therefore, with minds that are alert and fully sober, set your hope on the grace to be brought to you when Jesus Christ is revealed at his coming.*

*1 Peter 1:13*

There are three exhortations in this passage for Christians to bring on a new mind-set. The first says that we should prepare our minds for action. Be ready to make a decision to be obedient.

The second consists of self-control and being free of everything mentally debilitating, like drugs. Believers should be controlled by the Spirit, not drugs.

And the third exhortation is to set our hope on grace when Christ is revealed to us. This hope will produce determination and a positive attitude to carry on.

*Above all else, guard your heart, for everything you do flows from it.*

*Proverbs 4:23*

The Bible constantly repeats the need for Christians to be self-controlled and disciplined so they can make wise decisions. We are faced with temptations every day to compromise our beliefs. If a substance is interfering with our right state of mind, we are not in a strong position to ward off the attacks of the devil. Determine what your values are and guard your heart against compromising on those values.

## 7 PRAYER STARTER

Lord, we come before You today lifting up _____ and praying that You will intervene in his (her) life and capture his (her) heart. I pray that he (she) will lift up his (her) eyes to You and be so captivated that he (she) finds strength to put away the addiction. I thank You for _____'s courage to face this issue in his (her) life. He (she) wants to be free and I pray that You grant hope. Guide me as I guide him (her) . . .

# RECOMMENDED RESOURCES 8

Anderson, Neil T., Mike Quarles, and J. Quarles. *Freedom from Addiction: Breaking the Bondage of Addiction and Finding Freedom in Christ.* Gospel Light, 1997.

Clarke, David. *Converted on an LSD Trip.* Abshott, 2001.

Clinton, Tim. *Turn Your Life Around.* FaithWords, 2006.

Hurwitz, Ann Ricki, and S. Hurwitz. *Hallucinogens.* The Drug Abuse Prevention Library. Rosen, 1999.

Kuhar, Michael. *The Addicted Brain: Why We Abuse Drugs, Alcohol, and Nicotine.* Pearson Education, 2012.

Lookadoo, Justin. *The Dirt on Drugs.* Revell, 2008.

Murphey, Cecil. *When Someone You Love Abuses Drugs or Alcohol.* Beacon Hill Press, 2004.

## Websites

Encyclopedia of Mental Disorders: www.minddisorders.com/Flu-Inv/Hallucinogens-and-related-disorders.html

National Institute on Drug Abuse: www.drugabuse.gov/publications/drugfacts/hallucinogens-lsd-peyote-psilocybin-pcp; www.drugabuse.gov/publications/research-reports/hallucinogens-dissociative-drugs

# 12 Inhalants

## 1 PORTRAITS

- Jamie was bored and had nothing to do at home. She decided to go to the shopping center up the street. It was a favorite hangout spot for her friends in the area. When she got there, all her friends were sitting in a circle with butane bottles, sniffing them. They told her it was the "new cool thing to do," so she tried it. Immediately she felt great but then she came down fast. The next thought she had was to do it again. Eventually one of her friends sniffed another bottle, fell over, and never got back up. Scared to death, Jamie now wants to quit sniffing but doesn't know if she can. It feels so good. She starts going to church with someone who invited her and hopes she can find help there.

- *"Where am I? What happened?* Then it all comes back to me. I had just huffed some whippets and was walking along that brick retaining wall. I must have fallen off. Then I realize that the back of my head feels warm and wet. I reach back and touch my head—bloody. I wonder how bad it is. I decide to go to my friend's house to get him to look at it, but before I go, I make sure to take another hit. Man, that feels good. I get to his house and pass out again. Whether it was loss of blood or because of the last hit, I don't know. I wake up in my house with my parents standing over me telling me I have no choice. I am going in for treatment."

- One night, fourteen-year-old Kara was at a concert with her friends, one of whom was much older. While in the bathroom in the concourse, her friend pulled out a glue compound and offered it to her. They sniffed it and it felt great and they enjoyed the concert. The next day Kara asked her friend for more and she gave it to her. After the third bottle, her friend started asking for money. Kara was already hooked and couldn't say no, but one day her father caught her stealing money from his wallet.

## 2 DEFINITIONS AND KEY THOUGHTS

- Inhalants are *toxic substances* giving off *chemical vapors* that when sniffed, produce *an intoxicating effect.* They do not include chemicals inhaled after burning or heating, such as marijuana.

- The *long-term effects* of inhalants are still being researched, but a common conclusion speaks to the unpredictable and often dangerous consequences of their use and abuse.

- Inhaling these dangerous chemicals to get high is often referred to as *huffing*.
- There are specific *ways to abuse inhalants,* and they can be broken down into three categories:

  — *huffing:* soaking a rag in an inhalant and pressing the rag to your mouth
  — *sniffing:* inhaling or snorting fumes from an aerosol container
  — *bagging:* inhaling fumes from a product sprayed or poured into a plastic or paper bag

- Sniffing the cleaner for computers, such as Dust-off, is called *dusting.* Some abusers fill balloons and soda cans with the harmful substances and sniff them or heat up substances and inhale the fumes. *All of these ways of inhalation are extremely dangerous.*
- Some slang terms for inhalants include *air blast, bang, bullet bolt, buzz bomb, chroming, discorama, gluey, heart-on, high ball, hippie crack, huff, laughing gas, medusa, moon gas, oz, pearls, poppers, quicksilver, snotballs, spray, Texas shoe shine, snappers, whippets,* and *white out.*
- Most substances used as inhalants are *legal.* Some common inhalants are:[1]

  — *Adhesives*
    model airplane glue
    rubber cement
    PVC cement

  — *Solvents and gases*
    nail polish remover
    paint thinner
    paint remover
    correction fluid
    toxic magic markers
    pure toluene
    lighter fluid
    gasoline
    carburetor cleaner
    octane booster
    fuel gas
    air conditioning coolant (refrigerants)
    lighters
    fire extinguishers

  — *Aerosols*
    spray paint
    hairspray
    air freshener
    deodorant
    fabric protectors
    computer cleaner

— *Cleaning agents*
dry cleaning fluid
spot removers
degreaser

— *Food products*
cooking spray
aerosol-based whipped cream

— *Gases*
nitrous oxide
butane
propane
helium
ether
chloroform
halothane

- The abuse of inhalants *usually starts in adolescence* and is discontinued in adulthood. *Most individuals cease the abuse after a year or two.* But there are many adults each year who enter treatment for inhalant abuse.[2]

- It is estimated that around *4 percent* of inhalant abusers will go on to develop a *dependent pattern of abuse.*[3]

- Inhalant abuse is *worldwide.* In third world countries, however, the abuse is for a different purpose than recreational use. Many huff chemicals to dull the pangs of hunger or to get them through other forms of destitution (this can be seen, for example, in the street children of Brazil).

- Inhalants are viewed by some as a *gateway drug,* meaning that their use often encourages or leads to the abuse of other substances. In 2010, of the 3 million persons aged 12 or older who used illicit drugs for the first time within the preceding 12 months, a notable proportion reported using inhalants (9 percent) as their introduction.[4]

- Among persons age 12 to 49 in 2010, *the average age at first use* was 16.3 years for inhalants.[5]

- In 2010 there were *793,000 persons age 12 or older* who had used inhalants for the first time within the past 12 months, which was similar to the numbers in prior years since 2002.[6]

- In 2006, *10.3 percent* of persons treated for drug abuse in the United States were treated for inhalant abuse.[7]

- The *effects of inhalants* begin within seconds and will *usually last around forty-five minutes or less.* The effects include *euphoria, numbness, dizziness, loss of inhibitions,* and *mild hallucinations.*

- *Undesired side effects* of abuse include:

  — nausea

  — vomiting

— slurred speech
— excitement
— double vision
— ringing in ears
— agitation
— violence
— hangover feeling

- Inhalant abuse can be *lethal*. It is important to note that someone can die from the *first time an inhalant is abused or the two hundredth time;* it doesn't matter. Every sniff could be the last. Fifty percent of deaths associated with inhalants are caused by sudden *sniffing death syndrome* (SSDS) or a *cardiac arrhythmia* (ventricular fibrillation) SSDS occurs when an abuser is surprised or startled while sniffing or huffing. An especially exciting or frightening hallucination could also trigger the syndrome.[8]

- Many health concerns surface when inhalants are discussed. The *cardiopulmonary, respiratory, and central nervous systems* are all at risk when inhalants are abused. Several organs such as the *heart, lungs, kidneys, and liver* can all experience complications due to abuse. Other injuries such as *burns or damage to the body from falling or bumping* can result from inhalation of harmful substances. *Drug-induced psychosis* can surface and could possibly be permanent.

- *Depression* can be a consequence of inhalant abuse and because it is a risk factor for suicidal behavior, *suicide rates are higher among inhalant abusers* than among the general population. The greater the frequency and amount of drugs abused, the higher probability of suicide behavior being carried out.

# ASSESSMENT INTERVIEW 3

## Rule Out

Have you ever had harmful or violent thoughts toward yourself or others?

## General Questions

1. Think back to your first time using inhalants. Can you describe it for me?
2. What inhalants have you used or abused?
3. How often do you abuse chemicals and how much do you use?
4. On a scale from 1 to 10, 1 being not dangerous and 10 being very dangerous, how dangerous to your body are the chemicals you are using?
5. Have you consulted a medical doctor about this problem?
6. What comments have close friends or relatives, who are around you often, made to you about your actions? Have they changed in how they view you as a person? If so, why do you think that is?
7. Have you tried to stop using before? What happened?

8. When you are not high, how do you feel? What emotions surface?

9. What kind of environment are you in when you huff/sniff/bag? Are other people involved with you? Is there a favorite place you go?

10. Have you noticed that your use of chemicals has affected any part of your life in a negative way? Has your use affected your relationships or your ability to work at your job or school?

11. (*When counseling an adolescent*) How is your relationship with your parents or guardian? Describe to me how you interact with them.

# 4 : WISE COUNSEL

Always listen and pay attention to indicators of violence toward the client (self-harm) or others. Suicide is a risk with adolescents, especially ones who are abusing chemicals. Do not be afraid to address this issue if you see signs. Talking about it will not serve as a trigger to carry out harmful actions.

When possible, if you are dealing with an adolescent, involve parents in the counseling process. This will facilitate accountability and help keep the family engaged. Also, if there are issues in the family contributing to the teen acting out in this way, it will be helpful to counsel on these matters.

Do not lecture teenagers in a way that will make them think you are trying to control their lives. Before giving wisdom or instruction, win their trust and build a positive relationship with them. Show empathy, have compassion, and be understanding toward how hard their situation may be for them.

# 5 : ACTION STEPS

## 1. Tell Someone

- Find someone you really trust who is older and wiser than you and share your story with them. Tell them your struggles.

- Keeping your use of inhalants a secret only perpetuates the habit. Stop lying to people and let them help you.

## 2. Avoid Negative Influences

- You will have a hard time trying to stop using inhalants when everyone around you is doing it. Get away from people and places that encourage you to use.

- You might be able to resist peer pressure for a while, but it will eventually wear you down, and you will find yourself back in the same place where you started.

## 3. Get Help

- Once you have told someone about your use, allow them to assist you in getting the help you need to move beyond this difficult time. This proactive process helps facilitate change.
- You will need someone to coach you through the decisions that must be made to change your lifestyle and learn new coping mechanisms.

## 4. Sign a Contract

- Enter into some kind of written agreement with a counselor, parent, or pastor, saying you will not abuse inhalants anymore. This will give meaning and a sense of urgency to your decision to get clean. This provides for accountability.

## 5. Develop a Support System

- You cannot do this on your own. You need friends, family, and other resources to help keep you on the path to recovery. Report to them frequently about how you are doing.
- Guard against relapse. When you feel you are slipping back into your old habits, tell someone immediately and let them help you figure out a way to combat it.

# BIBLICAL INSIGHTS 6

*So I say, walk by the Spirit, and you will not gratify the desires of the flesh. For the flesh desires what is contrary to the Spirit, and the Spirit what is contrary to the flesh. They are in conflict with each other, so that you are not to do whatever you want.*

*Galatians 5:16–17*

A believer does not need to be held down by the power of addiction. The Holy Spirit, who lives in us, helps us experience victory over the desires of our flesh, which cause us to do things we do not want to do. It will not happen automatically, however. The Spirit waits to be called on before He will move to help.

Give control of your body over to the Holy Spirit. Pray and ask Him to take your desires away by His power when you are tempted.

*Do you not know that your bodies are temples of the Holy Spirit, who is in you, whom you have received from God? You are not your own; you were bought at a price. Therefore honor God with your bodies.*

*1 Corinthians 6:19–20*

If you are a believer, you are indwelt with the Holy Spirit. Your body has become a temple or residing place for God. Therefore your body is not your own because of Christ's sacrifice. This means you have a responsibility to live for Him and keep your body clean and free from harmful substances. Ask yourself, *Is it glorifying to God to sniff chemicals?*

*Plans fail for lack of counsel, but with many advisers they succeed.*

                                                              Proverbs 15:22

Sometimes you are not strong enough on your own to make a plan and stick to it. You need stronger people who care about you in your life to encourage you and lift you up to a place you could not achieve yourself.

*If we claim to be without sin, we deceive ourselves and the truth is not in us. If we confess our sins, he is faithful and just and will forgive us our sins and purify us from all unrighteousness.*

                                                              1 John 1:8–9

Be honest with God about your sins. All people who are trying to live a godly life struggle with relapse. That doesn't mean God will write you off. No matter how many times you fail, God will forgive. He is faithful. However, just as grace is not a license to sin, recovery is not a license to relapse.

# 7 PRAYER STARTER

Lord, we come before You today broken and needing Your grace. Please forgive us for our sins and cleanse us from all unrighteousness. Specifically, I want to pray for _____. Help him (her) realize the potential he (she) has and give him (her) the courage to fight for it. Empower him (her) with Your Holy Spirit and lead him (her) . . .

# 8 RECOMMENDED RESOURCES

Brotherton, M. *Buzz: A Graphic Reality Check for Teens Dealing with Drugs and Alcohol.* Multnomah, 2006.

Clinton, Tim. *Turn Your Life Around.* FaithWords, 2006.

Dobson, James C. *Preparing for Adolescence: How to Survive the Coming Years of Change.* Gospel Light, 2000.

Kuhar, Michael. *The Addicted Brain: Why We Abuse Drugs, Alcohol, and Nicotine.* Pearson Education, 2012.

Lobo, Ingrid A. *Inhalants: Drugs, the Straight Facts.* Chelsea House, 2004.

Lookadoo, Justin. *The Dirt on Drugs.* Revell, 2008.

Townsend, John. *Boundaries with Teens: When to Say Yes, How to Say No.* Zondervan, 2007.

## Websites

Inhalant Abuse Prevention: www.inhalant.org/inhalant-abuse/

Mayo Clinic: www.mayoclinic.com/health/inhalant-abuse/HQ00923

National Inhalant Prevention Coalition: www.inhalants.org/

National Institute on Drug Abuse: www.drugabuse.gov/publications/research-reports/
inhalant-abuse

## Other Resources

Poison Control Center: If you know of someone who has abused an inhalant, call
the Poison Control Center at 1-800-222-1222 or call the 800 number on the label
of the product.

# 13 Marijuana and Hashish

## 1 PORTRAITS

- Bret was used to going over to his friend's house almost every weekend to hang out. This particular time when he went over, he and his friend went to the backyard shed to get the four-wheeler to ride. While in the shed he saw a refrigerator; he was thirsty so he went to grab a drink. Instead he found what looked like marijuana. "Whoa, I wasn't expecting that," Bret said. His friend asked what he had said, but for some reason Bret shrugged it off, replying, "Never mind." That night, curiosity got the best of him and he went back to the shed and stole some of the marijuana. He looked up how to roll and smoke it and when he found time to himself, he did.

- Kelly was going to a senior class party with some friends. She heard Kent was going to be there and he was famous for being a pot supplier. She knew this party was going to be crazy with alcohol and weed. When she got to the party, she sought Kent out and asked him for some pot. She got enough for her friends. Darcy, Kelly's friend, was now faced with a choice—should she smoke her first joint? She didn't want to ruin the fun at the party and make this a big deal so she went along with it. That was the beginning of her declining grades, which caused her to fail two classes. As a result, she wasn't accepted into her preferred college.

## 2 DEFINITIONS AND KEY THOUGHTS

- Marijuana is a *plant* that is a member of the *Cannabis sativa* family. There are different kinds of cannabis and not all varieties have an abusive potential. Many kinds of cannabis are grown to harvest *hemp fiber*, which is used for stitching a variety of clothing or making paper, rope, jewelry, and canvas.
- Marijuana contains more than four hundred different compounds, but the *principle psychoactive drug*, among sixty other psychoactive compounds, is the lipid-soluble delta9-tetrahydrocannabinol (THC).
- Because THC is *lipid-soluble*, the most popular way to abuse the chemical is through *smoking* it. It is easily absorbed into the bloodstream through the lungs. It can also be abused other ways such as eating it.
- *Hashish* is the name for the *thick resin that comes from the flowers* of the plant. A popular way of abusing hashish is to *bake it into brownies* to mask its flavor. *Hash oil* is the oil the *Cannabis sativa* plant produces that contains anywhere

from 25 to 60 percent THC.[1] Often this oil is added to marijuana or hashish to make it more potent.

- The *current potency* of marijuana is unknown. Research conducted in 2004 said the concentration of THC in marijuana averaged at 9.6 percent, but currently there is so much variation between samples obtained that it is anyone's guess.[2]

- Marijuana was *first made an illegal substance in the United States in 1937* under the Marijuana Tax Act. It is a highly controversial drug and its legality is hotly debated, but *currently, as a substance of abuse, it is illegal to possess or abuse it.*

- Some states, including California, have decriminalization laws and medical marijuana laws. *In California it is legal for a patient and primary caregiver to possess and cultivate marijuana* (with a cap of six mature plants or twelve immature plants) *if it has been recommended by a physician* for medicinal purposes. However, it is still illegal to sell or distribute. Under federal law, marijuana is *illegal even with a prescription,* so patients *on federal property are subject to prosecution.* Medical marijuana is controversial, and many believe it is too easy to take advantage of the system.

- During the 2012 election cycle, the citizens of Washington State and Colorado voted to legalize the recreational use of marijuana, and another ten states are considering a move in the same direction.

- Marijuana is a hard drug to classify and there has been considerable debate over this. It acts as a *mild hallucinogen* but also produces *effects similar to depressants and stimulants.* In the United States, its official category is a *hallucinogenic.*

- There are many street names for marijuana, but here are the most popular used today: *blunt, chronic, dope, ganja, grass, herb, joint, bud, Mary Jane, MJ, kif, pot, reefer, green, trees, smoke, sinsemilla, skunk, weed, hash, tea, 420, hooch, ju-ju,* and *yerba.*

- A *blunt* is a cigar that has been emptied and filled with a marijuana and tobacco mix. A *joint* is a cigarette-size roll of marijuana that is smoked.

- *Marijuana is the most popular recreational, illicit drug in the United States,* still trailing the legal substances of alcohol and tobacco.

- *Marijuana is the biggest cash crop raised in the United States* at this time.[3]

- Worldwide marijuana use is estimated at *116 million abusers* over 15 years old.[4]

- It is estimated that *6,000 people per day try marijuana* for the first time and about *43 percent of people over 18 have abused or are currently abusing* the drug in the United States.[5]

- In 2010 there were *17.4 million users during the preceding month.* Between 2007 and 2010, the rate of use increased from 5.8 to 6.9 percent, and the number of users increased from 14.4 to 17.4 million.[6]

- The current rate of *abuse among youths ages 12–17* is 7.4 percent and is on the rise.[7]

- *Ninety-five percent of marijuana sold is smoked by 14 percent of abusers who do so daily.*[8]

- For years, many believed that marijuana was not addictive. However *10–20 percent of marijuana abusers go on to develop physical dependence on the drug,* especially due to greater potency levels of THC, the active ingredient in the drug. Countless more become psychologically addicted.[9]

- *Marijuana abuse is characterized by tolerance and withdrawal*—two criteria for addiction. Withdrawal from marijuana, however, is different from the common *withdrawal symptoms* experienced with other drugs. Withdrawal symptoms from marijuana include:

  — depression
  — anxiety
  — irritability
  — aggression
  — insomnia
  — sweating
  — nausea
  — tachycardia (rapid heart rate)
  — anorexia
  — vomiting
  — craving

- When marijuana is smoked, *it reaches the brain in seconds*, and peak amounts in the brain are seen in ten minutes[10]

- *Many abusers do not use marijuana exclusively.* They may also use cocaine or meth. No substantial research has been done as to the effects of mixing drugs. When drinking alcohol and smoking marijuana, a user could possibly be at *more risk of alcohol poisoning and overdose* because *marijuana is known to inhibit vomiting and nausea*. However, this is just a theory.

- There are *two phases of the marijuana high*. The *effects of the first phase* are reported to be:

  — mild anxiety
  — euphoria
  — relaxation
  — sensory distortions
  — altered perception of things
  — dysphoric experiences (intense feelings of depression)
  — laughter
  — talkativeness

- *Negative effects that come in the second phase include:*

  — anxiety
  — depression
  — ataxia (lack of voluntary coordination of muscle movements)
  — mood swings
  — hunger (known as the "munchies")

- These *effects last five to twelve hours* after a single dose.
- Marijuana is proven to *increase the heart rate by 20 to 100 percent within the first hour after smoking the drug*, which is more of a concern with older populations and those with known heart conditions.
- *Sidestream marijuana smoke* is shown to have *20 times more ammonia* in it than tobacco smoke. It also contains *carcinogenic compounds* that are an *irritant to the lungs.*
- Marijuana can also negatively affect *physical and mental health, memory, scholarship and academics, social life, family closeness,* and *career status.*
- *Long-term chronic use* of marijuana has been associated with *amotivational syndrome*, which is characterized by:

  — apathy
  — impaired judgment
  — loss of memory and concentration
  — no motivation, ambition, or interest in personal goals
  — distractibility
  — no interest in making plans beyond the present day

- Although this is seen in most long-term abusers of marijuana, *it could be the effects of the drug itself or the personality of people who seem to be drawn to the drug.* The very existence of amotivational syndrome is still in question.
- Marijuana has long been called a *gateway drug.* It is believed that users who are heavily addicted to harder drugs, such as cocaine and heroin, usually started with abusing marijuana. Thus the conclusion is that *marijuana encourages the use of other more dangerous drugs.* There is debate about whether this phenomenon actually exists or if people are drawing conclusions about relationships that are not necessarily real.
- Of the first-time users of an illicit drug in a preceding year, *61.8 percent reported that their first drug was marijuana.*[11]
- *Currently males abuse marijuana more than females.*[12]
- *Death as a result of marijuana abuse is rare but not unheard of,* specifically with people who have cardiac problems.

## ASSESSMENT INTERVIEW 3

1. How frequently do you abuse marijuana and how much do you use? How long have you sustained this pattern of abuse?
2. How old were you when you first tried the drug?
3. Think back to the first time you had an opportunity to use marijuana. What happened?
4. On a scale from 1 to 10, with 10 being very dangerous, how dangerous is your use of marijuana?

5. How has your use of marijuana affected your job, family, or relationships in general? Have you noticed a change in yourself, maybe in mood, attitude, or motivation?
6. Beyond the potential risks, how do you view your use of marijuana?
7. Have you ever done anything you later regretted while under the influence of marijuana? Have you ever broken the law or hurt someone you love (emotionally or physically)?
8. Is your motivation to change strong or weak?

# 4 WISE COUNSEL

Due to the way marijuana is viewed in our society, the current trend is to see it as a drug that is "not as bad as other drugs" or not even harmful at all. As a result, you may be faced with the challenge of having to convince a client of the potential risks associated with marijuana abuse. It is important to read current research articles and know the many risks involved with smoking marijuana (potency levels continue to increase). Especially with younger clients who may not have thought of the risks, it is important to know this information and be able to convey it to them.

Marijuana is a highly controversial drug and always has been. Clients may take advantage of this reality and voice their opinions about its legal uses and other issues when resistant to changing their behavior and wanting to justify their actions. Do not get into a power struggle with them over who is right and who is wrong. Stay focused on their desires for a better life and how marijuana is hindering that from happening.

Federal and state laws regarding marijuana and its uses are constantly being revised. It is important for you as a counselor to be up-to-date with the current legislation so you can speak with authority on these matters.

You must always adhere to confidentiality between you and your client. If a client confides in you and confesses to using an illegal substance currently, because of confidentiality you cannot contact the police without the possibility of being sued by your client for breaking confidentiality agreements. But if your client or others are in danger because of the drug abuse or for any other reason, you are required to report this. For example, if your client claims he will ingest enough drugs to kill himself, you are required to report that.

# 5 ACTION STEPS

## 1. Seek Help

- You will not be strong enough on your own to be able to make this change at first. By telling someone about your problem, you will have an added level of accountability that will motivate you and keep you serious about quitting.
- It is best to seek out a counselor or trained individual with the skills to be able to teach you coping mechanisms and guide you through this process.

## 2. Understand the Nature of Your Addiction

- You can be physically addicted to marijuana, so you will need to prepare for some physical discomfort resulting from withdrawal, and/or you can be addicted psychologically, used to being high. To break that cycle is your challenge. You need to be prepared for the physical battle, as well as the mental and spiritual battles, which may be even more challenging.
- It is helpful to know what you are up against, for this will determine an appropriate treatment plan to move you toward recovery.
- Have a plan. Be determined and exact in your approach to quitting. It will help you track your success and will guide you in the right direction if you should wander off the path of recovery.

## 3. Be Aware of Relapse Triggers

- Triggers are those things that remind you of smoking marijuana and may cause cravings. Triggers may be a certain place you used to smoke, people you smoked with, or an object associated with marijuana.
- It is best to remove triggers out of your life if possible. Sometimes this is not possible, so you must be aware of the effect triggers have on you and deploy distractions when you are tempted.
- Sometimes you may have to sever ties with friends to get clean, but the sacrifices made will be worth it in the end.
- It is definitely a good idea to get rid of all your gadgets or marijuana-related equipment that you used for smoking. Throw them away. You may want to destroy them as a symbol of your resolve.

## 4. Rearrange Your Schedule

- Depending on how often you smoked, when you stop, you will have a lot of free time on your hands. Fill that time with something productive so that you are not tempted to smoke again when idle.
- You may need to work on rearranging your schedule. Every action you take to cut down on the possibility of relapse will help in the long run.

## 5. Reduce Stress

- Many times stress can be an enemy to the recovering addict and can be the cause of a relapse in someone's life. It will be beneficial for you to have something in your life that helps you relax and is a healthier choice than marijuana. When you are stressed, rely on something healthy to get through it.
- This is best facilitated with the help of a trained professional, and it would be expedient to have a counselor work with you through recovery.

## 6 BIBLICAL INSIGHTS

*The acts of the flesh are obvious: sexual immorality, impurity and debauchery; idolatry and witchcraft; hatred, discord, jealousy, fits of rage, selfish ambition, dissensions, factions and envy; drunkenness, orgies, and the like. I warn you, as I did before, that those who live like this will not inherit the kingdom of God.*

*Galatians 5:19–21*

This verse condemns the use of drugs, asserting that their use is inappropriate for Christians. The word *witchcraft* in this verse translates to the Greek word *pharmakeia*, from which the English word *pharmacy* is derived.

By calling these things "acts of the flesh," the apostle Paul is showing how they originate from our sinful nature and not from the Holy Spirit. As Christians, we should act in ways that are pleasing to the Holy Spirit. Smoking marijuana is not a Spirit-filled activity.

*Do not get drunk on wine, which leads to debauchery. Instead, be filled with the Spirit.*

*Ephesians 5:18*

The Bible never specifically mentions marijuana abuse, but, as in this verse, it does speak to being high or intoxicated. In this verse it is clear that we Christians should be controlled by the Holy Spirit and not a substance such as marijuana.

*I have told you these things, so that in me you may have peace. In this world you will have trouble. But take heart! I have overcome the world.*

*John 16:33*

This is one of the most encouraging verses in all of Scripture. No matter what we face in this world or how desperate our situation, God is bigger and can help us through our problems.

Going into recovery, you can "take heart," be courageous, and hopeful of winning, because Christ has already defeated sin.

## 7 PRAYER STARTER

Lord, I pray for _____ as he (she) begins this journey to recovery from marijuana. I thank You for Your Word and how You promise to always be with us. We ask You now to be with _____ and give him (her) strength to resist the evil one and overcome his (her) problem with dependency. Place the right people in his (her) life who can encourage and uplift him (her). Guide my words and actions with wisdom and grace as I work with _____ . . .

# RECOMMENDED RESOURCES : 8

Anderson, Neil T., Mike Quarles, and Julia Quarles. *Freedom from Addiction: Breaking the Bondage of Addiction and Finding Freedom in Christ.* Gospel Light, 1997.

Clinton, Tim. *Turn Your Life Around.* FaithWords, 2006.

Kuhar, Michael. *The Addicted Brain: Why We Abuse Drugs, Alcohol, and Nicotine.* Pearson Education, 2012.

Lookadoo, Justin. *The Dirt on Drugs.* Revell, 2008.

Townsend, John. *Boundaries with Teens: When to Say Yes, How to Say No.* Zondervan, 2007.

## Websites

Narconon International: www.narconon.org/drug-abuse/signs-symptoms-hashish-use.html

National Institute on Drug Abuse: www.drugabuse.gov/publications/research-reports/marijuana-abuse

# 14 Narcotics and Opiates

## 1 PORTRAITS

- Mandy stares ahead as she drives, every now and then stealing a peek in the rearview mirror to look at her twenty-two-year-old son. Never in a million years did she think she would be driving him to a rehab center for heroin addiction. *My son an addict? Where did I go wrong?* she asks herself while trying to stay in her lane. Tears begin to make it hard to see. It was just a couple of days ago that she had found out about the addiction. Her son told her the whole story, that he had first tried marijuana and cocaine in middle school. He told her that nothing compared with the OxyContin pills he had gotten from a girl he dated in high school. Soon that led to other narcotics and mixing pills. Mandy blames herself for her son's condition because she didn't notice the signs and address the problem earlier, and she wonders if her divorce while he was in middle school was also a factor.

- Christina's story began when she was in a major car accident at age twenty-eight. She was on her way to work when it happened. The results were a back injury and a leg broken in five places. Needless to say, she was in tremendous pain and was prescribed Vicodin ES to help manage it during her recovery. After she was sent home with the medication, Christina realized she wasn't in any more pain. In fact, she felt great; euphoria flooded her senses. She still has no idea why she did what she did next but she took several more pills and felt even better. When she ran out of pills, she got more, and went through those in half the time they were prescribed for. Over the next year, she had been doctor shopping and lying about her pain to her family, husband, and doctors. When she could not find a doctor to write a prescription anymore, she attempted to write her own. She took it to the pharmacy and was detained. She spent two days in jail and decided she needed help.

- Amy is sitting by the phone with her hands pressed together. *It has been long enough. They should be getting back to me now,* she tells herself. Five more minutes pass and she bangs the desk with her fist, waking up her eight-year-old son who was asleep on the couch. Finally, the phone rings and her heroin supplier tells her where to meet and when. She tells her husband, and then the whole family gets in the car and goes to the deal. Amy gets the drugs and they can't even wait to get home. She and her husband shoot up in the car. She hates doing it in front of her boys but she can't help it. Her sons have seen her try to quit cold turkey before, only to end up screaming and hitting her husband for the heroin. They've also found their father passed out on the floor. This time when they get home, her husband shoots up again and passes out again. His arm is bloody, with a needle still sticking out of it. That's when Amy makes the decision and forces herself and her husband to go to a methadone clinic for the sake of their sons.

# DEFINITIONS AND KEY THOUGHTS 2

- The definition for the term *narcotic* has changed over the years and for the most part has been loosely applied. Originally the word was related to certain psychoactive compounds with sleep-inducing properties, but in some law enforcement circles it simply refers to any illegal or prohibited drug. However, for the purposes of this reference guide, a more widely accepted definition being used is that of narcotic analgesics described as *pain relievers and associated with opioids*.

- The word *opium* comes from the Greek word *opion* meaning "poppy juice." Opium refers to the dried latex that is obtained from scratching the seed pods of the opium poppy (Papaver somniferum).

- Some of the slang terms for opium are *O.P., china, hop, midnight oil, tar, dope, Big O, dopium, gum,* and *dreamer*.

- Pain is divided into three different categories: *acute pain, chronic pain, and cancer-induced pain*. Narcotics and opiates are drugs that treat all types of pain.

- Pain is something that everyone tries to avoid, and *this class of drugs is sometimes a solution to the problem of pain*. To help cut down on confusion, the classification of narcotics is needed. There are three different classes of compounds used to treat pain: *anesthetics* (results in a loss of consciousness), *local anesthetics*, and *compounds used to block awareness of pain* in the central nervous system (for example Novocain). *Narcotic analgesics* fall into this last category.

- Some *common narcotic analgesics* are morphine, meperidine (Demerol), methadone (Dolophine), fentanyl (Sublimaze), codeine, oxycodone (Perdocet, Oxy-Contin), and hydrocodone (Vicodin).

- Opiate compounds are divided into *three groups*: *natural opiates* (morphine, codeine), *semisynthetic opiates* (heroin), and *synthetic opiates* (methadone).

- It is estimated that 16.5 million (0.4 percent) people worldwide, ages 15–64, abuse opiates.[1]

- It is estimated that *Afghanistan produces 82 percent* of the world's supply of opium, all of which is going into the illicit drug market.[2]

- Opium is a highly produced drug, evidenced by the *global opium seizures amounting to 384 metric tons* in 2006.[3]

- In 2008, *5 percent of the U.S. population* was estimated to have taken an opioid in the previous 12 months.[4]

- Among persons aged 12 or older in 2009 and 2010 who had used pain relievers nonmedically in the past 12 months, 55 percent *obtained the drug they most recently used from a friend or relative for free*. Another 17.3 percent reported they got the drug *from one doctor*. Only 4.4 percent obtained pain relievers from a drug dealer or other stranger, and 0.4 percent bought them on the internet.

Among those who reported getting the pain reliever from a friend or relative for free, 79.4 percent reported in a follow-up question that the friend or relative had obtained the drugs from just one doctor.[5]

## Morphine

- *Morphine is the most abundant compound found in the resin of the opiate poppy*, with levels anywhere from 10 to 17 percent.[6]
- The compound was named after the Greek god *Morpheus* who was the god of dreams, and it was said that he could take any form and enter the dreams of those who slept.
- Morphine was first isolated as a compound in 1804 by Friedrich Sertürner.
- *It is used to treat moderate to severe pain* in patients.
- Morphine produces such *effects* as:

  — relief of pain
  — impairment of mental and physical performance
  — relief of fear and anxiety
  — euphoria
  — decrease in hunger
  — inhibiting the cough reflex

- Morphine is a *legal drug* but can only be obtained *with a prescription* and it is under severe government restrictions.
- Street names for morphine include *M, number 13, happy stuff, happy powder, white nurse, Red Cross, unkie, mojo, God's own medicine, vitamin M, Emma, Lady M, white lady, cube, morf, morph, white hop, white merchandise, uncle, Uncle Morphy, big M, Murphy, morphy, coby, cobics, gold dust, monkey dust,* and *needle candy.*
- *Within sixty minutes* after a single dose, peak blood levels of morphine are reached with *effects beginning around thirty minutes after dosage.* The analgesic effects will usually last four hours.[7]
- Morphine is highly *addictive* and can become habit-forming in a very short time. The *euphoric effects* can drive an individual to take *increasing amounts* and activate the *brain's reward system. Anticipating the euphoric effects, an individual can be driven to perpetual use.* When the brain has become accustomed to the high morphine levels *physiological dependence and tolerance develop.* When dosage is discontinued, the brain will have to function with depleted levels, and the *body craves more.* Often this craving produces a *preoccupation with the drug* in a person's life.
- Since morphine affects *the level of consciousness* in an individual, be aware that a person who is abusing morphine may not be fully aware of his or her surroundings or be able to think properly.

- When morphine is heavily abused, there is a *risk of overdose,* which can result in death. *Symptoms* of overdose include:

  — slow, shallow, or irregular breathing—can lead to respiratory failure
  — sleepiness
  — loss of consciousness
  — limp muscles
  — cold, clammy skin
  — small pupils
  — slow heartbeat
  — blurred vision
  — nausea
  — fainting

- If a person is addicted to morphine, they can expect withdrawal symptoms if dosing is discontinued. *Symptoms* include:

  — tearing
  — chills
  — yawning
  — nausea
  — sweating
  — sneezing
  — cramps
  — diarrhea
  — vomiting
  — muscle spasms
  — rhinorrhea (the nasal cavity is filled with mucous fluid)
  — increased body temperature
  — stroke
  — heart rate increase

- Babies who are born to a mother who abused morphine while pregnant *will go through withdrawal,* as *morphine can cross the placenta.*

## Codeine

- Codeine, like its chemical cousin morphine, is a *natural opiate* derived from the opium poppy seed. It is the second most abundant alkaloid found in the *Papaver somniferum* plant at 0.7 to 2.5 percent.
- It is used *to relieve mild to moderate pain* as it is estimated to have one-fifth the analgesic effect of morphine. It also has the ability to *suppress and reduce coughing.*

- Some street names for this drug and other compounds derived from it include *hydro*, *norco*, and *vikes*.
- *Peak levels in the bloodstream* can be observed from one to two hours after ingesting a single dose.[8]
- There are many *semisynthetic compounds* derived from the naturally occurring codeine, a few being *hydrocodone* or *hydromorphone and tramadol*.
- Codeine accounts for *10 percent of all drug-related deaths*.[9]
- *Hydrocodone is abused more* than any other illicit opioid.[10]
- When administered orally, *hydromorphone is thought to be five to seven times more potent than morphine*.[11]
- *Effects* of hydrocodone include:

  — drowsiness

  — dizziness

  — sedation

  — anxiety

  — nausea

  — constipation

  — urinary retention

  — depressed respiration

- *Withdrawal symptoms* include:

  — restlessness

  — muscle and bone pain

  — insomnia

  — diarrhea

  — vomiting

## Heroin

- Heroin is a *semisynthetic* opiate derived from morphine. Basically heroin is two morphine molecules joined together by an oxygen molecule creating diacetylmorphine.
- Some common street names, among hundreds, for heroin are *horse, brown sugar, Mexican black tar, dragon, dope, heron, herone, hero, hera, h, big h, white, China white, white nurse, white lady, white horse, white girl, white boy, white stuff, boy, he, black, black tar, black pearl, black stuff, black eagle, brown, brown crystal, brown tape, brown Rhine, chiba, chiva, chieva, Mexican brown, Mexican mud, Mexican horse, junk, tar, snow, snowball, smack, scag, scat, sack, skunk, number 3, number 4,* and *number 8*.
- *Consumption* of opiates and heroin in North America is said to be currently stable. However, *the numbers are still high*. The largest market is in the United

States with approximately 1.2 million heroin users or 0.6 percent of the population aged 15–64.[12]

- In 2010 there were *140,000 persons aged 12 or older* who had used heroin for the first time within the past 12 months.[13]

- *Heroin is twice as potent as morphine.*

- The chemists who first developed the compound used it on themselves and found that it *made them feel heroic*; therefore they named the compound heroin.

- Around the 1920s heroin users started financing their drug habit by selling scrap metal they had collected on construction sites to junk dealers, earning *their nickname "junkies."*

- Heroin can be introduced into the bloodstream *intranasally* and *intravenously*. When heroin is administered intravenously, it virtually has a *100 percent absorption rate*. It is important to note that often within the drug culture, those who inject heroin are seen as "lower on the totem pole" than those who abuse it intranasally. *Injecting heroin seems to be viewed conventionally as the very lowest one can sink into the drug culture.*

- The *flash* or *rush* is a phenomenon that heroin users often report. It lasts about one to two minutes and is *similar to the feeling of a sexual orgasm.*

- Other *effects* include:

  — warmth
  — dry mouth
  — nausea
  — heaviness in extremities
  — nasal congestion
  — sensation of floating
  — clouded mental functioning

- *Withdrawal from heroin is infamous for being a horrible experience.* Symptoms of withdrawal can start as little as *a few hours* after the last dose. Withdrawal is at its worst two to three days after the last dosage and can last for up to a week.

- *Symptoms* of heroin withdrawal include:

  — restlessness
  — agitation and moodiness
  — dilated pupils
  — insomnia
  — drug craving
  — diarrhea
  — muscle and bone pain
  — cold flashes with goose bumps
  — involuntary leg movements (kicking)

- During heroin withdrawal, diarrhea and vomiting can cause the individual to become severely *dehydrated*. As a result of this, *pulmonary aspiration* is also of concern.

## Methadone

- *Methadone* is a completely *synthetic drug* that is used to treat moderate to severe pain. It is also frequently used in treatment clinics as *part of detoxification programs* for those who are going through withdrawal.
- Two brand names for methadone are Dolophine and Methadose.
- Methadone can come in several forms such as tablets called Diskets, dispersible tablets, liquid solution, and an injection from a methadone clinic.
- Methadone is an *addictive drug and overdose can be lethal*. A 50 mg dose has been proven fatal for nontolerant adults, with doses as large as 180 mg per day used in treatment programs. Death caused by methadone overdose has been seen to occur within 24 hours after the overdose. Usually the dosage level starts low and the patient has to work up to the effective level of methadone.[14]
- Taken orally, methadone has an 80 percent absorption rate through the gastrointestinal track.[15]
- The effects begin in 30 to 60 minutes, peak in 2 to 4 hours, providing relief for 4 to 6 hours.[16]

## OxyContin

- OxyContin is a *fairly new drug* that was first introduced in 1995 as a way to alleviate long-term pain without having to have medication injected.
- OxyContin is a *trade name for the semisynthetic opioid oxycodone* and is strictly a time-released oral medication. However, *abusers will often defeat the time-release mechanism* through chewing the tablet, crushing it and dissolving it in water before injecting it into the veins, or taking larger dosages than recommended. Some users will heat the tablet on foil and then sniff the vapors.
- OxyContin is colloquially known as *oxycotton, OCs, oxy, ox, hillbilly heroin, pills, blue, kicker, 40* (40 mg tablet), and *80* (80 mg tablet), among other names.
- *Doctor shopping* is a term used to describe abusers who go from doctor to doctor feigning an injury to obtain a prescription drug, the most common being OxyContin and Valium.
- The term *pill ladies* is used for senior citizens who will sell their prescription drugs to abusers for quick cash.
- In 2010 the *number of new nonmedical users* of OxyContin aged 12 or older was 598,000, with an average age at first use of 22.8 years among those aged 12 to 49.[17]
- The *effects* of OxyContin may include:

  — euphoria
  — relaxation

— sedation

— respiratory depression

— constipation

— papillary constriction

— cough suppression

— liver damage

- *Overdose effects* have been shown to include:

    — extreme drowsiness

    — muscle weakness

    — confusion

    — cold and clammy skin

    — dilated pupils

    — shallow breathing

    — decreased heart rate

    — fainting

    — coma

    — death

- Legally, OxyContin is classified as a Schedule II drug (i.e., the substance has a high potential for abuse, a currently accepted medical use for treatment purposes, and may lead to dependence).

# ASSESSMENT INTERVIEW 3

1. How much and often do you abuse your drug of choice?
2. What situation were you in when you first abused your drug of choice? Did you have an injury that required pain relievers? What were the surroundings? Who was with you? What mood were you in?
3. What emotions and feelings are felt during and immediately after you abuse your drug of choice?
4. How does your abuse of this drug affect your performance at work, school, or at home? Do your family members or close friends comment on your abuse of the substance? What do they say?
5. Have you been doctor shopping, stolen from others, or broken the law in other ways to support your habit?
6. Have you tried to stop your use? What did you do? Why do you think it failed?
7. How much money do you spend to support your drug habit? What are the physical and emotional costs you have experienced as a result of your drug dependence?
8. Have you ever visited a methadone clinic? Are you currently going to one?
9. On a scale of 1 to 10, 10 being the worst, how bad do you see your level of abuse?

10. On a scale of 1 to 10, 10 being the most, how motivated are you to change and get rid of your drug habit?
11. On a scale of 1 to 10, 10 being the most, what level of control do you think you have over your decision to stop abusing drugs?

# 4 : WISE COUNSEL

Those who abuse drugs have become very good manipulators to support their habits. Some will lie and tell you they have an injury that requires pain killers and make up various stories. It is always prudent not to take their word at face value and, instead, consult with a client's physician. Also maintain your position of authority by not arguing or debating with them on anything; keep the conversation focused on them and their wanting to change.

Due to the nature of narcotic dependence, medical and professional attention will most likely be required for a safe and effective detoxification. The odds of relapse are high with this population, so it is important that you be prepared for the natural ups and downs of the journey. Strong accountability and multiple support systems are usually needed.

# 5 : ACTION STEPS

## 1. Seek Professional Help

- You will need structure, coaching, and support to overcome your addiction, and a professional counselor or a drug rehabilitation center can give you that.
- An inpatient drug rehabilitation center is the most effective means by which a heroin addict can be helped.
- Professionals will also be able to assist you through withdrawal and make it as comfortable for you as possible.

## 2. Appeal to God for Strength

- The decision to become sober and the journey you must take to accomplish it will not be easy. It will take strength, courage, and a steadfast resolve. Sometimes you will not have enough strength to stay the course. In those times you will need something bigger than yourself to aid you in your fight. Pray to God, who promises to be a help in time of need, and ask for His power to work in you.
- Become part of a 12-step group or a support group through a local church. This environment will be an encouragement to you and help give you strength.

## 3. Become Motivated

- Know that, to get sober, you will have to be willing to make sacrifices and do what it takes no matter what.
- Make a commitment to yourself and others to see this process through. Mentally prepare yourself by making a strong resolve that will last through the tough times.
- Write down your decisions in a contract, sign it, and keep it with you to remind you of the commitment you have made.

## 4. Educate Yourself

- Become familiar with the different treatment options and support groups around you.
- Know the possible harmful consequences to your body and spirit if you continue using your drug of choice.

## 5. Be Honest

- The very first step in recovery is realizing that you have a problem. Stop, slow down, and evaluate yourself. Ask others whom you can trust to be honest with you to describe how you are doing.
- For you to achieve and maintain recovery, you will have to dig deep and honestly face yourself, even if you don't like what you see.

# BIBLICAL INSIGHTS 6

*This is the confidence we have in approaching God: that if we ask anything according to his will, he hears us. And if we know that he hears us—whatever we ask—we know that we have what we asked of him.*

*1 John 5:14–15*

If you are a believer in Christ, then you can be confident that, when you pray, He hears you. As believers, we have the right to approach God freely and we can know that He will answer our prayers when they are according to His will. The Bible is very clear that our bodies are temples of the Holy Spirit (1 Cor. 6:19) and we should therefore demonstrate the fruit of self-control (Gal. 5:23). So if you ask for freedom and strength from God, you can be sure He will show up in your life and help you.

*God is our refuge and strength, an ever-present help in trouble. Therefore we will not fear, though the earth give way and the mountains fall into the heart of the sea.*

*Psalm 46:1–2*

**143**

This verse declares that God is our shelter from danger, a line of defense against any challenge we will face in this world. He promises to give us strength and be present in troubling times.

You do not need to fear withdrawal or the process of recovery. It will be a challenge, but there is a God who is all-powerful and promises to be with you. So do not fear! Step out with courage and start recovery.

*But God demonstrates his own love for us in this: While we were still sinners, Christ died for us.*

*Romans 5:8*

*Rather, clothe yourselves with the Lord Jesus Christ, and do not think about how to gratify the desires of the flesh.*

*Romans 13:14*

As soon as tempting thoughts surface, train yourself to think on godly things. When you realize you are making deliberate plans to relapse in the future, stop yourself and seek out your support system, telling them what you are thinking so they can keep you accountable.

*Submit yourselves, then, to God. Resist the devil, and he will flee from you.*

*James 4:7*

Submitting to God means to render obedience to Him. His commands in Scripture are to be followed and when you obey them, you have submitted your will to His will. Then make a stand against the devil and temptation, and, according to this verse, he will flee from you. By submitting to God and resisting the devil, you can come out from under the control of addiction.

# 7  PRAYER STARTER

Dear Lord, thank You for the privilege of being able to come to Your throne and for Your promise to us that You hear our prayers. We are grateful that Someone so powerful and able wants to hear from us and help. So Lord, we ask You to help right now in _____'s life. Give him (her) the strength and courage to fight this addiction and gain freedom from the strongholds it represents. Grant us grace and mercy as we go through this journey together . . .

# 8  RECOMMENDED RESOURCES

Anderson, Neil T., Mike Quarles, and Julia Quarles. *Freedom from Addiction: Breaking the Bondage of Addiction and Finding Freedom in Christ.* Gospel Light, 1997.
Clinton, Tim. *Turn Your Life Around.* FaithWords, 2006.

Kuhar, Michael. *The Addicted Brain: Why We Abuse Drugs, Alcohol, and Nicotine.* Pearson Education, 2012.

Lookadoo, Justin. *The Dirt on Drugs.* Revell, 2008.

McKeever, Bridget C. *Hidden Addictions: A Pastoral Response to the Abuse of Legal Drugs.* Haworth Press, 1998.

Nargi, Janice. *There is No Hero in Heroin.* Twin Feather, 2012.

Pullinger, Jackie. *Chasing the Dragon: One Woman's Struggle against the Darkness of Hong Kong's Drug Dens.* Rev. ed. Regal, 2001.

## Websites

Heroin Abuse: www.heroinabuse.us/

Narcotics Anonymous: www.na.org/

National Institute on Drug Abuse: www.drugabuse.gov/publications/drugfacts/heroin

Web MD: www.webmd.com/mental-health/abuse-of-prescription-drugs

# 15 Nicotine

## 1 PORTRAITS

- Frank was an ambitious and hardworking student through high school and college. He was captain of his basketball team and president of the Spanish club while in high school and was the president of student government and held other leadership roles in college. In addition to these achievements, Frank was also highly involved and active in his church since he got saved at age twelve. Due to his drive to succeed and accomplish great things, Frank began to feel overwhelmed by the tremendous pressure he placed on his shoulders as a result of all these responsibilities. One day after nearly suffering a breakdown, a friend encouraged him to smoke one cigarette to relieve his stress. Before long the use of cigarettes and other nicotine products turned into a full-blown addiction that has spiraled out of control.

- Trisha is an all-American teenage girl who grew up in a small town with her two younger brothers in a loving family. For as long as she can remember, her parents have smoked cigarettes, averaging a combined total of four-and-a-half packs a day. Since Trisha was not allowed to spend much time outdoors, she was always subjected to her parents' smoking habit. Now at eighteen, Trisha has been diagnosed with chronic bronchitis brought on by years of exposure to secondhand smoke. As a result of her experience, she constantly worries about the negative impact her parents' addiction to nicotine will have on her brothers, who are already showing signs of asthma.

- Kenny is a new believer in Christ and is learning to surrender all old bad habits to God and live life as a new creation. He has been able to give up most things so far. However, he is struggling with his addiction to nicotine, which has become a huge obstacle in his new walk of faith. Along with therapy and medication, Kenny has been seeking help from pastors at his local church.

## 2 DEFINITIONS AND KEY THOUGHTS

- *Nicotine is the drug produced in tobacco leaves.* It is also the substance in tobacco that is *addictive*. In its purest form, a single drop is enough to kill a person.[1]
- Common street names for nicotine cigarettes include *cigs, butts,* and *smokes.*[2]
- When a user chews, smokes, or inhales a tobacco product, *nicotine is delivered to the brain within 8 seconds.*[3]

- Even though there are 10 mg of nicotine present in a single cigarette, the user usually only *absorbs 1–2 mg*.[4]

- In spite of its numerous harmful effects, the addiction caused by nicotine keeps users strongly tied to this habit. *Of teens between the ages of 12 and 17, more than 3.5 million use nicotine*. In the American population in general, *66.5 million (29 percent) use nicotine in some form*.[5]

- Nicotine acts *like the neurotransmitter acetylcholine* and binds to its receptors, which cause rapid change to the brain and body. Additionally, nicotine causes *an increase in heart and breathing rates as well as a release of more blood sugar into the blood*, leading the user to feel very alert.[6]

- Nicotine also attaches to dopamine neurons and causes a huge release of these cells to create *a sense of pleasure*. Since the effect of nicotine soon wears off, continuous use helps maintain the high level of pleasure experienced.[7]

- Over time *the senses of smell and taste* of nicotine users is affected.[8]

- The *stamina of nicotine users is also reduced* when it comes to sports and exercise. Additionally, *the skin of smokers ages faster* than that of the average person. Heavily *discolored teeth* are also a consequence of nicotine use.[9]

- There have been *links found between nicotine use and agoraphobia*—the fear of going outside.[10]

- The ultimate harmful effect of nicotine is that it leads to death. Statistics show that about *five hundred thousand deaths every year* are caused by nicotine use. It is one of the top killers of Americans, accounting for one in six deaths.[11]

- *Quitting nicotine use is difficult* due to the withdrawal that follows. This leads to symptoms such as *anxiety, anger, depressed mood, difficulty concentrating*, and *an increased appetite for food and a craving for the drug*.[12]

- These *symptoms are, however, not permanent*. With the exception of increased appetite and the craving for more nicotine, these symptoms usually take about three to four weeks to overcome. The craving and increased hunger may remain for months.[13]

- Nicotine products contain other substances that can cause or increase the risk of contracting diseases, such as *coronary heart disease, ulcers, strokes,* and *various cancers associated with the lungs, larynx, esophagus, bladder, kidney, pancreas, stomach, and uterine cervix*.[14]

- *Pregnant women* who smoke have a higher risk of giving birth to *stillborn or premature babies*, as well as infants with low birth weight. They also risk having children who develop behavioral problems.[15]

- Addiction to nicotine can be described as a *chronic relapsing disorder* that can take years to overcome. Interventions that include *behavior therapies* and *medication treatments* have been found successful.[16]

- *Nicotine replacement therapy* is an effective way to help a smoker quit by giving the body enough nicotine to control withdrawal symptoms and yet avoid the jolt or rush associated with the addiction.[17]

- Four types of replacement therapy, which are found to be equally effective, are *gum, nicotine patches, nasal sprays,* and *nicotine inhalers.* The latter two are prescription therapies.[18]
- Other FDA approved medications for quitting include lozenges, which are available over the counter, as well as Zyban and Chantix, which are non-nicotine pills.[19]
- Nicotine *stimulates the release of adrenaline* also known as the fight-or-flight hormone. This increases the heart rate, reduces the flow of blood to the heart, and narrows the arteries, making smokers more likely to have *cardiovascular problems. However, the body begins to heal itself after a smoker quits the habit.*[20]
- *Secondhand smoke* accounts for more than three thousand lung cancer cases every year and an average of forty-six thousand heart-disease-related deaths in nonsmokers. It is also associated with increased asthma, colds, and ear infections in children and has been linked to sudden infant death syndrome (SIDS).[21]

# 3 ASSESSMENT INTERVIEW

One of the key characteristics of an addict is denial. To the substance user, there isn't a problem with his or her use. It is imperative for the counselor to break down this denial during the assessment.

When you conduct the interview, craft your questions around concrete circumstances, events, and symptoms. Usually the counselee will respond honestly if the counselor asks these questions in a nonjudgmental and nonthreatening way. The counselor should reframe the questions and use a similar approach when interviewing a family member of the substance user.

## Rule Outs

1. Has your use of nicotine products increased or decreased over the years? Has there ever been a time when you were free of using? *(The goal of these questions is to determine tolerance—the need for increasing amounts of the substance, to establish whether the use constitutes a problem or dependency. It is also important to assess strengths, including family strengths, as well as reasons for current treatment reliance. This information can be obtained from past histories of freedom from an addiction to nicotine.)*

2. Have you ever been treated for an addiction or been in counseling for any other reason? *(The purpose of this question is to determine the severity and the success or failure of prior treatment. It is also to assess whether a mental or dual disorder could be the underlying root of the use.)*

3. Has there ever been anyone, such as a family member, who has been hurt by or who has expressed concern about your nicotine use? Is your marriage or any romantic relationship being threatened by your nicotine addiction?

4. Has your use of nicotine landed you in any legal trouble? If so, what were the consequences of your actions?

## General Questions

1. At what age did you start using nicotine products? Can you remember why you tried them?
2. Have you ever been concerned about your use of nicotine? If so, why? Have there ever been any life-threatening events related to your use of nicotine? If so, was it your life or that of another person?
3. Would you encourage your closest friends and family members to use nicotine? Why or why not?
4. Do you ever try to hide your use of nicotine from your friends or family members by, for example, smoking far away from your home or limiting the frequency of your smoking when they are around? Would they be able to give an accurate description of your use?
5. Did anyone in your family use nicotine products heavily when you were growing up? Who is this person? How did you feel about his or her use while you were growing up?
6. What impact has your use of nicotine had on school, your job, or any other working conditions? Has the status of your employment been under threat due to your nicotine use?
7. Have you ever tried to quit using nicotine products? How successful has any attempt to quit been? Is there anyone in your life who could help you quit?
8. How would quitting affect your family?
9. If you are of strong faith, what role has your faith in God played in your desire to quit or in past attempts at quitting?

## WISE COUNSEL 4

It is important to first pay attention to any pressing medical matters that may have arisen due to the client's nicotine use. The first course of action will then be determined by the health of your client, particularly when an immediate health condition could be life-threatening. It is important never to overlook the potential health risks nicotine use can have on your client's body in spite of how he or she looks.

Be very mindful of your biases and assumptions about smokers. You may encounter clients who do not fit your stereotype of nicotine users, such as having discolored or missing teeth, scars, thin hair, or yellow fingers. Nicotine use is not identified with any particular group. People irrespective of race, status, or gender could be users. Be careful how you treat your clients if they are Christian, since their use of nicotine is frowned on in many Christian circles. Take time to reassure them of strict confidentiality and make your office a safe place to share and honestly talk about their problem.

Nicotine users who have developed an addiction are likely to be in denial about its severity. There may be some clients who will not admit to having a problem. Since an admission to having the problem connotes a need for change and therefore upsetting the norm, your client, along with family members, may be unwilling to take this step. It is important to be sensitive in your approach to handling this denial, but to still do so in a timely manner.

Interview the spouse and other family members who are old enough to understand the issue of your client's nicotine use to determine any challenging or enabling behavior on their part. Discuss alternative behaviors that are beneficial in encouraging the nicotine user to quit and get well.

# 5 ACTION STEPS

The following steps are directed to the counselor.

## 1. Encourage a Medical Checkup

- Going through a medical exam will help rule out any health problems associated with nicotine use.
- Treatment from a doctor is highly recommended in instances where the nicotine use has progressed to a disease state.
- A physician can also prescribe any medication that could help the user quit along with therapy.

## 2. Propose a Contract and Accountability

- Help the nicotine user commit to a system of accountability where they will agree to stop using the substance and seek help for their problem. They can reach this agreement by signing a contract with the counselor. If this contract is active for a period of time, it shows a high level of commitment and willingness to quit on the part of the client. However, in instances when a client is unwilling to commit to seeking help for the long term, shorter contracts of accountability can be used, in which the user commits to abstaining from use only until the next counseling session or for a few days, weeks, or months.
- Encourage your client to seek help through some type of Christian support program for recovering users of nicotine.

## 3. Arrange for Professional Help

- Encourage your client to be evaluated by a professional with expertise in chemical dependency to determine whether or not their use of nicotine constitutes an addiction. These types of assessments can be done at community mental health agencies, hospitals, and community abuse centers.
- A professional counselor would be helpful in treating the nicotine use if it is an addiction that is creating a gateway to other substance abuse or a dual disorder.

## 4. Encourage Quitting-Related Behaviors

- Encourage your client to engage in behaviors that promote quitting, such as removing all items related to nicotine use, like ashtrays and matches, from the home and car.
- Encourage your client to avoid being in smoking environments, spending more time in smoke-free surroundings.
- Help your client plan alternative activities to do in place of smoking.

## 5. Encourage Family Members to Seek Support

- Encourage the family members of your client to seek a Christ-centered support program for families of nicotine users. There are also 12-step programs for nicotine users that can be incorporated into treatment.

# BIBLICAL INSIGHTS : 6

*Do you not know that your bodies are temples of the Holy Spirit, who is in you, whom you have received from God? You are not your own; you were bought at a price. Therefore honor God with your bodies.*

*1 Corinthians 6:19–20*

As believers, we come to understand that our bodies do not belong to us but to the Lord. He has reserved our bodies as sanctuaries for His Holy Spirit. Therefore we need to care for our bodies in the best way possible to avoid causing them harm.

We are also meant to glorify God in everything we do with our bodies. Thus we must not do anything to harm them.

*Dear friend, I pray that you may enjoy good health and that all may go well with you, even as your soul is getting along well.*

*3 John 1:2*

It is the will of God that believers be healthy. The Word of God forms a connection between the healthiness of the soul and body. A healthy soul, one that belongs to Christ, needs to correspond to a healthy body. Nicotine use creates a disparity between the two and therefore hinders becoming a wholly healthy person.

*Therefore he is able to save completely those who come to God through him, because he always lives to intercede for them.*

*Hebrews 7:25*

The Lord Jesus died and rose to bring us closer to God. He bridged the gap between man and God by bringing us salvation. He continues to intercede on our behalf in any struggle or temptation we face. When we draw nearer to Him, we find all the healing we need.

*Do not be misled: "Bad company corrupts good character."*

*1 Corinthians 15:33*

Sometimes the environments we are in contribute to the decisions we make and what we do. It is important to surround ourselves with people who will encourage and keep us accountable in our journey to quit bad habits.

It is also important to avoid surroundings that will trigger old, poor habits and keep ourselves in the company of godly people who will encourage us to do what is right in the eyes of the Lord.

*Don't you know that when you offer yourselves to someone as obedient slaves, you are slaves of the one you obey—whether you are slaves to sin, which leads to death, or to obedience, which leads to righteousness?*

*Romans 6:16*

The Word of God shows us that we become slaves when we surrender ourselves to anything. Thus it is not surprising that addictions are hard to overcome. We become a slave to the substance we abuse. However, the good news is that we can surrender our will to the Lord Jesus, and He will become our new master whom we seek to obey and please.

# 7 PRAYER STARTER

Lord, I thank You for _____'s life and his (her) willingness to face this issue in his (her) life. It's not easy and I thank You for the bravery and courage _____ has shown. I pray that You will provide power over addiction and strength for _____ to see this process through to its end. Be with his (her) family and the people around; strengthen them and give them a spirit of support . . .

# 8 RECOMMENDED RESOURCES

Anderson, Neil T., Mike Quarles, and Julia Quarles. *Freedom from Addiction: Breaking the Bondage of Addiction and Finding Freedom in Christ.* Gospel Light, 1997.

Clinton, Tim. *Turn Your Life Around.* FaithWords, 2006.

Kuhar, Michael. *The Addicted Brain: Why We Abuse Drugs, Alcohol, and Nicotine.* Pearson Education, 2012.

May, Gerald G. *Addiction and Grace: Love and Spirituality in the Healing of Addiction.* HarperOne, 2006.

Moore, Beth. *Breaking Free: Discover the Victory of Total Surrender.* Broadman & Holman, 2007.

Welch, Edward T. *Addictions: A Banquet in the Grave: Finding Hope in the Power of the Gospel.* P&R, 2001.

## Websites

American Lung Association: www.lung.org/

Centers for Disease Control and Prevention: www.cdc.gov/tobacco/campaign/tips/

The Foundation for a Smokefree America: www.tobaccofree.org/?gclid=COiT242_q LACFUJo4AodVHGfSg

Mayo Clinic: www.mayoclinic.com/health/nicotine-dependence/DS00307

Medline Plus: www.nlm.nih.gov/medlineplus/ency/article/000953.htm

National Institute on Drug Abuse: www.drugabuse.gov/drugs-abuse/tobacco-addic tion-nicotine

Nicotine Anonymous: www.nicotine-anonymous.org/

# 16 Prescription Drugs

## 1 PORTRAITS

- Melanie loved sports and was an all-star athlete at her high school. One day during a game, she suffered a terrible fall, broke her arm, and fractured her foot. In spite of her injury her team won the match and qualified to play in the championship game that would take place two weeks later. Following surgery, her doctor prescribed strong pain medication to reduce the pain and help her recover quickly. Melanie had worked hard all her life to make it to her championship game, only to be placed on bed rest for a month while her injuries healed. Determined to make it and play in her championship game, Melanie took an unapproved extra dose of pain medication in an effort to numb the pain and speed up her rehabilitation process. Her efforts failed to convince her doctor. However, quitting the extra dose of prescription medication she had been taking felt worse, setting her on a path to abuse her medication.

- Due to his drunk driving, Jake was responsible for a fatal car accident that claimed the lives of an entire family. The memory of the horrible incident has haunted him for years and has affected his ability to sleep at night. His doctor recommended that he take a prescription sleep medication, which worked the first few times he tried it. However, Jake's insomnia returned a few weeks after he began taking his new sleep medication. He assumed his body had built a tolerance to the drug and decided to take more pills than prescribed. This new method seemed to help him sleep better and longer until one day he never woke up.

- Robert and Matthew were popular brothers at their high school. They hung out regularly and partied with their friends every week. One weekend they decided to throw a secret rave in an abandoned warehouse. To keep up with the high energy and excitement of the rave, they took their father's prescription pills for his narcolepsy, thinking it was safe because it was a legally prescribed drug.

## 2 DEFINITIONS AND KEY THOUGHTS

- Intentionally using any medication that can be legally prescribed *without first obtaining a prescription* is characterized as *prescription drug misuse or abuse. Using a prescribed drug in ways for which it was not meant to be used is also drug abuse.*[1]

- According to the National Survey on Drug Use and Health (NSDUH), approximately *seven million people* in the United States *abuse prescription medications every year*, accounting for nearly 3 percent of the population.[2]

- Following marijuana, prescription drugs are *the second most commonly abused drugs by young people.*[3]

- Most prescription drug abusers, approximately 70 percent, *obtain the medication from close friends or relatives.* About 5 percent, however, get them *from the internet or street drug dealers.*[4]

- *Caucasian men between the ages of twenty and sixty-four* are the highest abusers of prescription opioids.[5]

- About 12 percent of *active duty military servicemen* are also said to use prescription drugs nonmedically.[6]

- Although people with mental illnesses account for some reported prescription drug abuse, their use is overrepresented and exaggerated. Thus it is *not wise to assume that most abusers suffer from some mental illness.*[7]

- There are four main categories of prescription drugs that are abused. These are *pain relievers, tranquilizers, stimulants*, and *sedatives.*[8]

- The most commonly abused prescription drugs are *opioid analgesics,* which are mainly prescribed for pain.[9]

- *Opioid analgesics* are the *most heavily abused illicit drugs among high school seniors*, with one out of twelve high school seniors abusing Vicodin and one out of twenty abusing OxyContin. High school students who abuse these drugs are also at a higher risk of abusing other drugs and alcohol.[10]

- Often those who use prescription drugs for nonmedical purposes have *misconceptions about their dangers.* Since the drugs are legally prescribed by a doctor, these users assume they are safe, even though they affect the same parts of the brain as do illicit drugs when abused.[11]

- The *widespread availability* of such medications has also contributed to the increase in nonmedical use of these drugs. There has been a dramatic increase in the availability and frequency of prescribing such medications in recent years.[12]

- Some reasons for abusing these drugs include *getting high, regulating pain, reducing anxiety, and helping with sleep problems.*[13]

- There are *various risks* associated with commonly abused prescription medications. For example, an abuse of opioids, which are given to treat pain, can lead to a depressed respiratory system and eventual death.

- Since opioid analgesics can be injected, there is an *increased risk of contracting HIV/AIDS* through the use of unsterile needles.[14]

- The *abuse of central nervous system depressants* used to treat anxiety and sleep problems can lead to addiction and withdrawal symptoms, such as seizures. They can also depress the respiration system and lead to death.

- The *addiction to stimulants*, which are typically prescribed to treat ADHD or narcolepsy, can lead to unwanted consequences, such as seizures, cardiovascular problems, and psychosis.[15]

- The abuse of prescription drugs can be *effectively treated with therapy.*[16]

**155**

- One way to prevent the abuse of such drugs in the home is by limiting access with locked cabinets, as well as *safely and properly disposing of out-of-date prescriptions*.[17] The Federal Drug Administration (FDA) recommends utilizing community "take-back" programs, following disposal instructions for the medication, and mixing them with other trash items when throwing them away to minimize potential scavenging by animals or people.
- *More than twenty-seven thousand unintentional drug overdose deaths* in the United States every year are attributed to prescription drug abuse.[18]
- Physicians are becoming more sensitive to the pain of their patients. As a result, *some abusers have learned to exploit* this sensitivity to obtain higher doses.[19]
- *There can be risk in overprescribing* these medications when treating patients, especially with complex pain management cases.[20]

# 3 ASSESSMENT INTERVIEW

## Rule Outs

1. What medications have you been taking and for what problems are you taking them?
2. Have you ever been treated for an addiction or been in counseling for any other reason?
3. Has there ever been anyone, such as a family member, who has been hurt by or expressed concern about your dependence on prescription medication? Is your spouse threatening to leave you?
4. Has your use of prescription medication caused any legal trouble?

## General Questions

1. Have you combined your medication(s) with other drugs?
2. How long have you been taking this medication and what health conditions was it prescribed for?
3. Have you ever been concerned about your dependence on this drug? If so, why? Have there ever been any life-threatening events related to your taking this medication?
4. Do you ever try to hide your excessive use of your prescription medication from your friends or family members? Would they be able to give an accurate description of your use?
5. What impact has your use of this medication had on school, your job, or other working conditions? Have you ever lost a job due to your dependency on prescription drugs?
6. Have you ever tried to quit taking this medication? How successful has any attempt to quit been?
7. What role has your faith in God played in your desire to quit or your past attempts at quitting your dependence on this medication? Do you consider Him to be an essential part of your journey to become sober?

# WISE COUNSEL : 4

It is important to first check with the client's physician to learn if medications have been prescribed for any illnesses. It is also essential to verify the dosage to determine whether the client's dependency is due to the prescribed dosage or if it is a result of purposeful overdosing and abuse.

Since most likely the client obtained the prescription medication legally, they might be in denial about their addiction or dependency on the drug. They may justify their abuse as a legitimate medical use. They might even go further and attribute their abuse or overdose to an intensified medical problem they are suffering from and thus fail to take full responsibility for their abuse.

Even though your client could potentially be suffering from a mental illness, it is unsafe to assume this is the case since most prescription drug abusers do not fall under this category. However, it is wise to get a professional evaluation of your client's mental state to determine if a dual diagnosis is necessary.

If your clients are teens who use these medications nonmedically, talk to their parents and encourage them to learn ways of properly getting rid of old or leftover drugs from their homes to reduce their teens' access to them. Also encourage the parents to talk to and educate their teens on the dangers of such nonmedical drug use.

Interview spouses and other family members about your client's abuse of the prescription medication to determine if their behavior with the abuser is challenging or enabling.

# ACTION STEPS : 5

The following steps are directed to the counselor.

## 1. Obtain a Medical Report

- Obtaining your client's medical report with his or her consent will help you understand your client's medical conditions.
- It will also help explain the amount of medication prescribed to treat any medical condition.

## 2. Advise Getting Professional Help

- Encourage your client to see a professional with expertise in chemical dependency to determine whether his or her use of the prescription medication constitutes an addiction or abuse. You can obtain these types of assessments from community mental health agencies, hospitals, and community abuse centers.
- If it is found that the client is addicted, the services of a professional counselor who deals with prescription drug abuse would be helpful.
- Encourage your client to seek help through some type of Christian support program for recovering abusers of prescription medication.

### 3. Encourage Appropriate Behaviors

- To reduce the likelihood of abusing medications, encourage your client to remove excess or old prescription medication from the home and dispose of it properly.
- Help your client plan alternative activities to do instead of getting high.

### 4. Encourage Family Members to Seek Support

- Encourage the family members of your client to seek a Christ-centered support program for families of drug abusers.

## 6 BIBLICAL INSIGHTS

*"I have the right to do anything," you say—but not everything is beneficial. "I have the right to do anything"—but not everything is constructive.*

*1 Corinthians 10:23*

While your use of prescription medication might be legal, your misuse/abuse of the drug will not be beneficial in the long run. The legality of your use does not make it right before the Lord.

It is important to engage in things legally that align with your values and are beneficial in the long run.

*Be alert and of sober mind. Your enemy the devil prowls around like a roaring lion looking for someone to devour.*

*1 Peter 5:8*

Sobriety is God's standard for every believer. Being sober keeps you alert and watchful.

The devil is always on the lookout for those he can trap and harm. A drunken mind is an easier target for him. Therefore you could fall victim to his evil plans and schemes.

*Dear friend, I pray that you may enjoy good health and that all may go well with you, even as your soul is getting along well.*

*3 John 1:2*

It is the will of God for believers to be in good health. Medications for legitimate health conditions are not against His will.

The Word of God forms a connection between the healthiness of the soul and body. A healthy soul, one that belongs to Christ, needs to correspond to a healthy body. Prescription drug abuse creates a disparity between the two and hinders the process of becoming a wholly healthy person.

*Do you not know that your bodies are temples of the Holy Spirit, who is in you, whom you have received from God? You are not your own; you were bought at a price. Therefore honor God with your bodies.*

1 Corinthians 6: 19–20

As believers, we come to understand that our bodies do not belong to us but to the Lord. He has reserved our bodies as sanctuaries for His Holy Spirit. Therefore we need to care for our bodies in the best way possible to avoid causing them harm.

We are also meant to glorify God in everything we do with our bodies. Thus we ought to refrain from anything that harms them.

## PRAYER STARTER 7

Lord, I thank You for _____'s life and his (her) willingness to face this issue in his (her) life. It's not easy and I thank You for the bravery and courage _____ has shown. I pray that You will provide power over addiction and strength for him (her) to see this process through to its end. Be with his (her) family and the people around; strengthen them and give them a spirit of support . . .

## RECOMMENDED RESOURCES 8

Anderson, Neil T., Mike Quarles, and Julia Quarles. *Freedom from Addiction: Breaking the Bondage of Addiction and Finding Freedom in Christ*. Gospel Light, 1997.

Clinton, Tim. *Turn Your Life Around*. FaithWords, 2006.

Kuhar, Michael. *The Addicted Brain: Why We Abuse Drugs, Alcohol, and Nicotine*. Pearson Education, 2012.

McKeever, Bridget C. *Hidden Addictions: A Pastoral Response to the Abuse of Legal Drugs*. Haworth Press, 1998.

Minirth, Frank, Paul Meier, and Stephen Arterburn. *Miracle Drugs*. Thomas Nelson, 1996.

Welch, Edward T. *Addictions: A Banquet in the Grave: Finding Hope in the Power of the Gospel*. P&R, 2001.

### Websites

Centers for Disease Control: www.cdc.gov/mmwr/preview/mmwrhtml/mm6101a3. htm?s_cid=mm6101a3_w

Mayo Clinic: www.mayoclinic.com/health/prescription-drug-abuse/DS01079

National Center for Pain Medication Addiction: www.painmedicationaddiction.org/pain-relievers/commonly-abused-pain-relieverspainkillers?gclid=CPvb54K4y7AC FQYTNAodZHywVQ

National Institute on Drug Abuse: www.drugabuse.gov/drugs-abuse/prescription-drugs

Web MD: www.webmd.com/mental-health/abuse-of-prescription-drugs

# 17 Stimulants

## 1 PORTRAITS

- Andy had been having nightmares consistently for several months. Often he would hallucinate and hear voices that his parents would assure him did not exist. These nightmares became so intense that he had to sleep in his parents' room, an unusual choice for a seventeen-year-old. One day, while inspecting Andy's room for strange voices at his request, his mother discovered glass pipes, strange powders, lighters, and crystal-like substances stored under his bed. Her heart sank as she began to understand the root of her son's nightmares and hallucinations.

- Penelope's parents were going through a hard and bitter divorce at the beginning of her senior year in high school. Her dream of having the perfect senior year full of fun activities and experiences was quickly replaced with the nightmare and agony of enduring the unending fights between her parents and taking care of her ten-year-old sister. Unable to handle the pain of the reality she was living, Penelope resorted to abusing crystal meth and cocaine. On the night of her graduation, Penelope suffered cardiac arrest and was placed in the intensive care unit for four days.

- Soon after Sarah became pregnant, her boyfriend broke up with her and relocated to another state. Confronted with the harsh reality of being a single mother with an unstable job and the heartbreak of losing the love of her life, Sarah turned to the one source of comfort and pleasure she could count on—cocaine. A few months later she delivered a premature son who was half the recommended weight and needed various life-support machines to survive outside his mother's womb.

## 2 DEFINITIONS AND KEY THOUGHTS

- *Stimulants are types of drugs that increase energy and feelings of well-being and elevate the user's mood.*[1]
- Some examples of stimulants are *cocaine, methamphetamine, amphetamines, methylphenidate, nicotine,* and *MDMA* (better known as *Ecstasy*).
- There are *two types of cocaine*: powder made from the coca plant and crack, which is the smokable form of the drug heated to remove the hydrochloride it contains.[2]
- *Methamphetamines* come from the powerful amphetamine drug. It comes in two main forms, *crystals and powder*. This drug can be easily dissolved in water

or alcohol and as such may not be easily detected. Most methamphetamines used in the United States come from "super labs." However, it is also produced in small labs with cheap and often toxic ingredients, such as antifreeze, drain cleaner, and battery acid.[3]

- *Amphetamines* are usually prescribed medication by doctors and *used to treat problems such as attention deficit hyperactivity disorder (ADHD)*. They come mostly in the form of pills. One example is Adderall. This drug is usually crushed and snorted.[4]

- Like amphetamines, *methylphenidates,* such as Ritalin or Concerta, are often used as prescription medications to effectively treat attention deficit hyperactivity disorder.[5]

- Common names for *cocaine* include *coke, snow, flake, Charlie, candy*, and *rock*. *Crack* is the street name used to identify the *smokeable form of cocaine*. Cocaine combined with other drugs is a dangerous mixture. When combined with heroin, it is referred to as a *speedball*.

- Common names for *methamphetamines* include *meth, chalk, speed*, and *tina*. It is also called *ice, crystal, glass, fire*, and *go fast*.

- Some common street names for *amphetamines* include *bennies, crosses, truck drivers*, and *hearts*.

- Some street names for *methylphenidates* are *rits, west coast*, and *vitamin R*.[6]

- Stimulants are commonly swallowed, which does not have as much of an intense effect as injecting and smoking the drug, which is then quickly absorbed into the bloodstream.[7]

- A new report shows that of *adolescents* between the ages twelve and seventeen, more than *five hundred thousand* reported using stimulants for nonmedical purposes.[8]

- The above report shows that these users make up about 2 percent of their population. Seventy-one percent of users engaged in some form of *delinquent behavior* associated with their use of these drugs. These behaviors include serious fights, carrying a handgun, selling illicit drugs, and stealing. Twenty-three percent of them also had an episode of *depression*.[9]

- *Short-term effects of stimulants include feeling extremely joyful, increased alertness,* and a *decreased appetite*. Other short-term effects include being *anxious* and *irritable*; *increased heart rate, blood pressure, and body temperature; nausea; muscle spasms; blurred vision*; and *instances of confusion*.[10]

- The *long-term effects* of using stimulants include an *increase in craving* for the drug due to the body's increased tolerance. Other effects *include paranoia, aggressiveness, anorexia nervosa, hallucinations, delusions, dental problems, violent behavior, a chronic runny nose due to snorting*, and *potential risky sexual behavior,* which can lead to the spread of sexually transmitted infections such as HIV.[11]

- There are both physical and psychological side effects attributed to stimulant use. *Physical effects* include *dizziness, tremors, excessive sweating, flushed skin, chest pain with heart palpitations, vomiting, headaches,* and *abdominal cramps*.[12]

- *Psychological effects* include *paranoia, panic, suicidal/homicidal tendencies, hostility, aggression,* and *visual as well as auditory hallucinations.*[13]

- The use of these drugs can also be *fatal,* since they can lead to *heart conditions, hyperthermia,* and *convulsions.* These conditions can end in death if not given proper and early medical attention.[14]

- In case of an *overdose, high fever, convulsions, and heart failure* most commonly are experienced right before death.[15]

- Pregnant women who abuse stimulants stand the risk of delivering *babies with poor birth weight and body movements.* Children whose mothers abused these drugs while carrying them in the womb could also develop *attention problems* that could impair and hinder their performance in the classroom.[16]

- Stimulants work to *reverse the fatigue* brought on by both mental and physical tasks.[17]

- *Caffeine,* an active ingredient in coffee, tea, sodas, and over-the-counter medicines, is a popular stimulant.[18]

- Stimulants can be *helpful when used in moderation* because they promote alertness and help relieve illnesses. They help with obesity, which makes them popular weight-loss drugs, with narcolepsy, and in treating attention deficit disorders.[19]

- Even though stimulants promote alertness, they are used to *treat children with ADHD,* due to the calming effect they have on them.[20]

- Popular *psychostimulant treatments used for ADHD patients* include amphetamine-dextroamphetamine (Adderall), methylphenidate (Ritalin), and lisdexamfetamine (Vyvanse).[21]

- Some of the *reasons people abuse stimulants* is to enhance their self-esteem, improve mental and physical performance, reduce appetite for weight-loss purposes, and prolong wakefulness.[22]

- Stimulant *users can build high tolerance to these drugs very quickly,* which leads to physical and psychological dependence.[23]

- *Suddenly quitting* the use of this drug can result in depression, craving for the drug, anxiety, and extreme physical exhaustion, known as a *crash.*[24]

# 3 ASSESSMENT INTERVIEW

## Rule Outs

1. Has your use of any stimulant increased or decreased over the years? Has there ever been a time when you were free of using?
2. What medications have you been taking and for what conditions are you taking them?
3. Have you ever been treated for an addiction or been in counseling for any other reason?
4. Has a family member ever been hurt by or expressed concern about your stimulant use? Has your use placed a strain on your marriage? Has your use

of a stimulant landed you in any legal trouble? If so, what were the legal consequences of your actions?

## General Questions

1. What kind of stimulant do you typically use? Do you combine it with any other drugs?
2. At what age did you start using this stimulant? Can you remember why you tried it?
3. Have you ever been concerned about your use of this stimulant? Why or why not? Have there ever been any life-threatening events related to your use of this stimulant? Was it your own life or the life of another person?
4. Would you encourage your closest friends and family members to use this stimulant the way you do? Why or why not?
5. Do you ever try to hide your use of this stimulant from your friends or family members? Would they be able to give an accurate description of your use?
6. Did anyone in your family use this stimulant heavily while you were growing up? Who was it? How did you feel about his or her use while you were growing up?
7. What impact has your use of this drug had on your job, school, or other working conditions? Has your boss ever threatened dismissal due to your use?
8. Have you ever tried to stop using this drug? How successful has any attempt to quit been? Who could best help you quit? Do you have a good support system or would you try to do it by yourself?
9. How would quitting improve or impact your family?
10. Would you describe yourself as being of strong faith? If so, what role has your faith in God played in your desire to quit or in past attempts at quitting?

## WISE COUNSEL 4

The use of stimulants can lead to delusions and hallucinations so it is important to ask the client if he or she has experienced any of these. Additionally, check with the client's physician on whether the client has been placed on any stimulant medication for a legitimate health condition.

Keep in mind that stimulant users who have developed an addiction are likely to be in denial about the severity of their addiction. Your client may not admit to having a problem. Since such an admission connotes change and therefore upsetting the norm, your client, along with family members, may be unwilling to take this step. It is important to be sensitive in your approach to how you handle this denial. Also, since stimulants can be prescribed legally, some clients who abuse their medication may justify it as a legitimate use for medical purposes. They may attribute their abuse to an intensified medical problem they are suffering from and thus fail to take full responsibility for their abuse.

Interview spouses and other family members who are old enough to understand the issue of your client's stimulant use to determine any challenging or enabling behavior on their part. Discuss alternative behaviors that are beneficial and encourage the stimulant user to quit and get well.

# 5 ACTION STEPS

The following steps are directed to the counselor.

## 1. Advise Getting a Medical Checkup

- Going through a medical exam will help rule out any health problems associated with stimulant use.

## 2. Arrange for a Contract

- Help the stimulant user commit to a system of accountability in which he or she will agree to stop using the substance and seek help for the problem.
- After reaching an agreement, you or another counselor and the client should sign a written contract.

## 3. Advise Getting Professional Help

- Encourage your client to seek an exam from a professional with expertise in chemical dependency. This will help determine whether his or her use of the stimulant constitutes an addiction or abuse. Such assessments can be obtained from community mental health agencies, hospitals, and community drug abuse centers.
- A professional counselor would be helpful in treating the stimulant use if it is found to be an addiction or a dual disorder with a mental illness.
- Encourage your client to seek help through some type of Christian support program for recovering stimulant addicts.

## 4. Encourage Appropriate Behaviors

- Encourage your client to engage in behaviors that promote quitting, such as removing all items related to the use of the stimulant from their home.
- Encourage your client to avoid being in environments that promote the use of any stimulant, such as wild parties and raves.
- Help your client plan alternative activities to do when they get the urge to use the stimulant.

## 5. Encourage Family Members to Seek Support

- Encourage the family members of your client to seek a Christ-centered support program for families of stimulant abusers.

# BIBLICAL INSIGHTS : 6

*Do you not know that your bodies are temples of the Holy Spirit, who is in you, whom you have received from God? You are not your own; you were bought at a price. Therefore honor God with your bodies.*

*1 Corinthians 6:19–20*

As believers, we come to understand that our bodies do not belong to us but to the Lord. He has reserved our bodies as sanctuaries for His Holy Spirit. Therefore, we need to care for our bodies in the best way possible in order to avoid causing them harm.

We are also meant to glorify God in everything we do with our bodies. Thus we ought to refrain from anything that destroys them.

*Dear friend, I pray that you may enjoy good health and that all may go well with you, even as your soul is getting along well.*

*3 John 1:2*

It is the will of God that believers be in good health.

The Word of God forms a connection between the healthiness of the soul and body. A healthy soul, one that belongs to Christ, needs to correspond to a healthy body. Stimulant abuse creates a disparity between the two and therefore hinders becoming a wholly healthy person.

Stimulant abuse could also highlight a deeper problem of the soul, such as a loss of an emotional connection to God. It is important to also address this issue and help the client to restore, renew, or revitalize their faith in the Lord.

*Therefore he is able to save completely those who come to God through him, because he always lives to intercede for them.*

*Hebrews 7:25*

The Lord Jesus died and rose to bring us closer to God. He bridged the gap between man and God by bringing us salvation. He continues to intercede on our behalf in any struggle or temptation we face. When we draw nearer to Him, we find all the healing that we need.

*Do not be misled: "Bad company corrupts good character."*

*1 Corinthians 15:33*

Sometimes the environments we are in contribute to the decisions we make and what we do. It is important to surround ourselves with people who will encourage us and keep us accountable in our journey to quit bad habits.

It is important to avoid surroundings that will trigger old, poor habits and keep ourselves in the company of godly people who will encourage us to do what is right in the eyes of the Lord.

*Don't you know that when you offer yourselves to someone as obedient slaves, you are slaves of the one you obey—whether you are slaves to sin, which leads to death, or to obedience, which leads to righteousness?*

*Romans 6:16*

The Word of God shows us that when we surrender ourselves to anything, we become its slave. Thus it is not surprising that addictions are hard to overcome. The good news is that we can surrender our will to the Lord Jesus, and He will become our new master, whom we seek to obey and please.

*No temptation has overtaken you except what is common to mankind. And God is faithful; he will not let you be tempted beyond what you can bear. But when you are tempted, he will also provide a way out so that you can endure it.*

*1 Corinthians 10:13*

The Road to Recovery from an addiction is not easy. There will be temptations to relapse into the old habit of abusing the drug. The Lord assures the user who places his or her trust in Christ that He will walk with him or her throughout the Road to Recovery. He will strengthen him or her to be able to resist or endure the temptation without acting on it. God will not allow the user to suffer temptation beyond what he or she can handle. If the temptation is too great to endure, the Lord will always provide an avenue for escape to the recovering addict.

# 7 PRAYER STARTER

Lord, I thank You for _____'s life and his (her) willingness to address and face this addiction. It's not easy and I thank You for his (her) courage. I pray that You will provide power over the addiction and strength for _____ to see this process through to its end. Be with his (her) family, strengthen them, and give them a spirit of support. Surround _____ with people who will encourage him (her) throughout this difficult journey . . .

# 8 RECOMMENDED RESOURCES

Anderson, Neil T., Mike Quarles, and Julia Quarles. *Freedom from Addiction: Breaking the Bondage of Addiction and Finding Freedom in Christ.* Gospel Light, 1997.

Clinton, Tim. *Turn Your Life Around.* FaithWords, 2006.

Hedgcorth, Debra. *Mind over Meth.* Tate Publishing, 2008.

Kuhar, Michael. *The Addicted Brain: Why We Abuse Drugs, Alcohol, and Nicotine.* Pearson Education, 2012.

May, Gerald G. *Addiction and Grace: Love and Spirituality in the Healing of Addiction.* HarperOne, 2006.

Moore, Beth. *Breaking Free: Discover the Victory of Total Surrender.* Broadman & Holman, 2007.

Welch, Edward T. *Addictions: A Banquet in the Grave: Finding Hope in the Power of the Gospel.* P&R, 2001.

## Websites

National Center for Biotechnology Information: www.ncbi.nlm.nih.gov/books/NBK64333/

National Institute on Drug Abuse: www.drugabuse.gov/publications/drugfacts/stimulant-adhd-medications-methylphenidate-amphetamines

National Institute on Drug Abuse for Teens: www.teens.drugabuse.gov/facts/facts_stim1.php#what_are_they

Stimulant Abuse: www.stimulantabuse.net/

# PART 3

# Behavioral Addictions

This section provides a comprehensive look at important aspects of behavioral addictions and recovery.

Behavioral addictions are nonsubstance related and often include compulsive acts that are repeated over a sustained period of time. Furthermore, these behaviors typically result in serious and negative consequences that can impact the person across several domains (physical, mental, emotional, relational, and spiritual). The addict struggles with controlling his/her behavior in spite of the harm being caused toward self or others. Biblically based principles of care and counseling offer the opportunity for healing, wholeness, and restoration.

Remember the four basic steps that were presented in the introduction regarding the Road to Recovery:

1. *Recognize and admit:* the role of confession and breaking the power of the secret
2. *Clean out the infection:* the role of grieving and breaking the power of denial
3. *Renew the mind:* the role of truth and breaking the power of unbelief
4. *Exercise the will:* the role of accountability and breaking the power of fear

# 18 Bodybuilding and Body Image

## 1 PORTRAITS

- "What happened? I feel out of control." Joe has been bodybuilding since he was thirteen years old. "I love the way my muscles flex and the definition I see when I look in the mirror, but lately I just can't get the image of myself as a flabby guy out of my mind. I work out at the gym two hours every morning and night and just can't seem to shake the feeling that I'm inadequate and fat. My friends are saying they never see me anymore. I agree that I am spending a lot of time at the gym and it's getting pretty expensive to pay for two gym memberships—one near home and one near work."

- One day eleven-year-old Meagan said, "Mom, I'm going on your diet now and that means I can't eat my breakfast." Meagan's mother never realized her own poor self-image has affected her daughter's ideas about food. She thought her lack of satisfaction with her body, her feelings of being fat, and her aversion to looking in the mirror were her secret.

- Carly is just like any other sixteen-year-old. She is involved in youth group at church, acts in her high school theater program, and volunteers at the local animal shelter. However, Carly is keeping a secret from her parents. She hates the way she looks and constantly exercises, trying to change the image she sees in the mirror. She skips meals, barely eats, and is worried she won't fit into her costumes for her upcoming play. She is a size 8, and the director of her play says she looks fine, but Carly just can't believe it. She hates the way she looks and feels so out of control.

## 2 DEFINITIONS AND KEY THOUGHTS

- *Bodybuilding* or *body image addiction* is the *uncontrollable desire* or *urge to feel* the adrenaline that comes with overexercising or training or *obsessing* over one's appearance in a manner that hurts one's relationships with others, negatively impacts one's financial situation, and/or hurts one's health.

- Bodybuilding and body image addiction *can lead to eating disorders,* such as anorexia nervosa, bulimia nervosa, and binge eating.

- Multiple underlying *effects include a poor self-image, depression, anger,* and *compulsiveness.*

- Typically *stress hormones* help a person *cope* with an emergency situation. Adrenaline, cortisol, and other stress hormones are stimulants and *create a feeling of energy, excitement,* and *power or strength.* Bodybuilding, along with other sports, can leave a person wanting to exercise more to feel the rush of adrenaline. Often this leads to addiction—the overuse of exercise to keep feeling the rush.[1]

- *Post-adrenaline depression* occurs *when the effects of adrenaline wear off* after a workout, a sports event, a stressful day at work, and so on. One is left with feelings of depression, restlessness, nervousness, irritability, and aggravation.[2]

- *Withdrawal symptoms* occur *between periods of intense activity.* They are a result of low adrenaline levels and leave a craving for more exercise, activity, or intensity within a work or school environment.[3] This is what makes bodybuilding and overexercising so potentially addicting.

- Some research also indicates that the body's response to the stress of excessive exercise *releases beta-endorphins,* which are *addictive in nature, suppress the appetite, block anxiety,* and *result in a greater sense of euphoria.*

- In a study of teen women's magazines from the 1970s to the 1990s, 74 percent of the magazines cited *the primary reason to exercise was to look good,* and 51 percent suggested *it was to lose weight and burn calories.*[4]

## ASSESSMENT INTERVIEW 3

1. How much time do you spend looking in the mirror? Do you spend a lot of time thinking about the way you look, your body image?
2. When did you first start becoming dissatisfied with the way you look?
3. Do you work out more than once per day? Do you work out even when you are injured?
4. When was the last time you looked at yourself in the mirror and were happy with what you saw?
5. Does your desire to look good affect your relationships with others? Are your friends, family members, or co-workers aware of your behavior?
6. Do you compare yourself to others, those around you or those in the media? Is this comparison negative? If so, how does this affect your behavior? Do you overexercise, stop eating, or react in some other way?
7. If you were to change one thing about yourself, what would it be (body shape, chin, nose, fat, body proportions, muscle appearance, something else)? Do you think with that change, you would be happy with how you would look?
8. In light of how God views us, how do you think we should view ourselves?

## WISE COUNSEL 4

We live in an image-driven culture that is inundated with negative messages regarding our view of self. The media has multiple examples of what a man or woman should look like to appear popular, successful, and sexy. These messages may affect our way

**171**

of thinking and guide our goals, actions, and behaviors. When we focus too much on the physical, we can become blind to the spiritual. Remember what 1 Samuel 16:7 says, "Do not consider his appearance or his height, for I have rejected him. The LORD does not look at the things people look at. People look at the outward appearance, but the LORD looks at the heart."

Often the need to feel good about oneself comes from an inner need to avoid the pain of failure or rejection. As God's sons and daughters, we are loved and accepted. Our desire should be to please our Creator and understand that He is concerned about the heart and inward appearance of a person. When we are settled in our relationship with Christ and demonstrate a spirit of contentment with how we were made, then we can begin to look at ourselves as God sees us. This results in a greater capacity to understand the way we should view our physical appearance as well.

# 5 ACTION STEPS

## 1. Face How Your Behavior Affects Your Life

- If your bodybuilding, overexercising and training, or body image issues are affecting your relationships with your spouse, friends, and family or causing health issues, you need to accept that things have gotten out of control.
- Your focus on your body may be a financial burden as well. The costs of gym memberships, expensive diets, and excessive equipment, clothing, and gear may be a strain on your budget.

## 2. Acknowledge the Truth

- Understand that if you do not take steps to change your current behavior, things will not improve.
- When your overexercising or training is hurting your health and/or relationships, something must eventually give way.

## 3. Meditate on Being Made in God's Image

- God's desire is that you glorify Him in what you do. This responsibility comes before any efforts to look good or bodybuild.

## 4. Limit Exercise Time

- Spending only an hour or two each day exercising and devoting more time to family and serving God by helping others is a good way to divide up your time. Time for your relationships with God and with people is more important than spending three or more hours a day exercising.
- Exercise is a good thing, but too much of it, like anything else, will intrude on the more important priorities in life.

- Focusing on other activities can be just as beneficial when we see that it brings our lives and priorities back into balance.

## 5. Establish God-Honoring Values and Goals

- Place greater value on seeing God change your inside (heart, thought life, character) and spend less time and energy obsessing about the outside appearance.
- Seek to find a healthy balance between extrinsic and intrinsic motivations and pursuits.
- Decide on small measurable goals that will help you curb the time devoted to your body.
- Write down new goals for how you will spend your time.
- Make sure these goals represent areas of needed growth, such as quality time in relationships with family and friends; involvement in church, community, and school; and volunteering.

## 6. Be Consistent

- Just as you have been consistent with exercising and maintaining your outside appearance, work at achieving your new goals as part of a consistent lifestyle change.
- Strive for excellence in your spiritual life.

# BIBLICAL INSIGHTS 6

*I praise you because I am fearfully and wonderfully made; your works are wonderful, I know that full well. . . . How precious to me are your thoughts, God! How vast is the sum of them! Were I to count them, they would outnumber the grains of sand—when I awake, I am still with you.*

*Psalm 139:14, 17–18*

Our Creator loves us so intensely that His thoughts for us are more than the sand in the sea! When God created humans, He made us beautiful and amazing, with innate abilities and characteristics that give Him great joy! Our culture may tell us we will never look good enough, but God is pleased with the way He made each of us! We must never forget that our worth is in Christ; He loved us so much He gave up His life to save us.

*Charm is deceptive, and beauty is fleeting; but a woman who fears the LORD is to be praised.*

*Proverbs 31:30*

173

*Physical training is of some value, but godliness has value for all things, holding promise for both the present life and the life to come.*

*1 Timothy 4:8*

Exercise, fitness, and the desire to keep our bodies healthy are good things, but when we become too focused on our outer appearance, it can actually hurt the body, our relationships with others, and our relationship with Christ. Then we have to stop and reevaluate the reasons we are overexercising or looking so critically at our own image. We must understand that God looks first at our heart and motivations and does not put as much importance on our outward appearance. The body is temporary, but the soul is eternal. We should look at our bodies as tools to worship and serve our Creator, not as objects to be worshiped or obsessed over.

*Do you not know that your bodies are temples of the Holy Spirit, who is in you, whom you have received from God? You are not your own; you were bought at a price. Therefore honor God with your bodies.*

*1 Corinthians 6:19–20*

As Christians, we need to remember we were bought with a price—the shed blood of our Savior, Jesus Christ. We have been adopted into His family and now are children of the living God. We no longer belong to ourselves. Since we were redeemed by God, we belong to Him. Our bodies are His, and we must not misuse or devalue them.

*Therefore, I urge you, brothers and sisters, in view of God's mercy, to offer your bodies as a living sacrifice, holy and pleasing to God—this is your true and proper worship.*

*Romans 12:1*

Understanding our relationship with God and our standing as His children should help us accept responsibility regarding how we view our bodies. When we see how God wants to use our bodies to serve Him and His work instead of glorifying ourselves and our image in the mirror, then we will find our desires and compulsions will be less about us and more about Him. A healthy image of who we are in Christ will help guide us in how to regulate our compulsions regarding body image and exercise.

# 7 PRAYER STARTER

Dear heavenly Father, please help _____ to see his (her) worth the way You, our Creator, see each of us. Please open our eyes to help us see our value in the light of what You have done for us on the cross. Give _____ the strength to overcome any feelings and motivations that cause him (her) to spend too much time on his (her) body. Lord, help us live a balanced life that glorifies You! . . .

# RECOMMENDED RESOURCES 8

Graham, Michelle. *Wanting to Be Her: Body Image Secrets Victoria Won't Tell You.* InterVarsity, 2005.

Hart, Archibald D. *Healing Life's Hidden Addictions.* Servant, 1995.

———. *The Hidden Link between Adrenaline and Stress.* Thomas Nelson, 1995.

Hersh, Sharon A. *Mom, I Feel Fat: Becoming Your Daughter's Ally in Developing a Healthy Body Image.* Random House, 2001.

Newman, Deborah. *Comfortable in Your Own Skin: Making Peace with Your Body Image.* Focus on the Family, 2007.

Reall, Scott. *Journey to Healthy Eating: Freedom from Body Image and Food Issues.* Thomas Nelson, 2008.

TerKeurst, Lysa. *Made to Crave: Satisfying Your Deepest Desire with God, Not Food.* Zondervan, 2010.

## Websites

Diet Blog: www.diet-blog.com/06/bodybuilding_the_new_form_of_drug_abuse.php

# 19 Cutting and Self-Harm

## 1 PORTRAITS

- "I don't know why I do it!" says fourteen-year-old Sophie, trying to explain her actions. "I just want to *hurt myself* . . . the pain and anguish seem to come out when I cut." What most people do not know about Sophie is the shame she carries around every day from being sexually abused by an older cousin when she was twelve.

- Jack, a twenty-year-old college student, started smoking at sixteen. His stress in school and the feelings of inadequacy with peers make him do "crazy things," he says. "I put cigarettes out on my hands or wrists; it's my way of showing how I feel! Sometimes I just *get so mad* I punch the wall till my hand is bloody."

- Carrie's parents noticed that she has appeared to be very quiet and withdrawn lately. She gets extremely upset when they ask her how her day is going. They thought the black clothes, black eyeliner, and loud music were just a phase she was going through. One morning, as Carrie was leaving for school, her mother tried to ask her if there was anything she could do for her. Carrie said she was busy and started to leave. Her mother grabbed her arm and, when Carrie pulled away, it ripped the sleeve of her shirt. Her mother gasped in horror at the sight of many vertical cuts all the way down Carrie's arm. When her mother asked her why she had cut herself, Carrie said "Just leave me alone," and she ran out of the house.

## 2 DEFINITIONS AND KEY THOUGHTS

- *Cutting* is using a sharp instrument to slice the skin, causing the injury to bleed. At first glance, it may appear to be a suicide attempt. However, this type of *self-injurious behavior* is usually something different. The act of cutting is done to hurt oneself, thereby alleviating what is perceived as emotional pain.[1]

- According to a 2009 study, 44 percent of *emergency room visits* for patients aged 7–24 were for bodily self-harm.[2]

- Cutting and self-injurious behavior *impacts all cultures and socioeconomic groups.* Ninety percent begin during the teen years or younger (40 percent are males and nearly 50 percent have a history of childhood sexual abuse).[3]

- *Self-harm and self-mutilation* are defined as any behavior or act one does to *injure one's body on purpose.* It could be hitting, burning, scalding, scratching, cutting, piercing, bruising, banging or hitting body parts, pulling hair, and even swallowing poisonous or dangerous objects.[4]

- Cutting and self-harm are done to *provide a feeling of relief or create an emotional release from the stress, anger, pain, anxiety,* or *overwhelming pressure* felt by the person inflicting the harm.[5]

- Even though cutting and self-harm often result in a form of relief from emotional pain, *the effects are only temporary* and the *emotional feelings always flood back,* giving a greater desire to inflict even more physical pain.[6] This is the reason cutting and self-injurious behaviors can become addictive.

- Cutting and self-harm *can accompany other problems and diagnoses,* such as binge eating, binge drinking, depression, anxiety, post-traumatic stress disorder, schizophrenia, personality disorders (especially borderline personality disorder), and substance use disorders.

- Self-harm is typically seen as *nonsuicidal behavior,* although the risk for accidental death is elevated.

- These problems *may need the help of a qualified medical doctor.*

# ASSESSMENT INTERVIEW 3

1. How do you usually cope when you feel worried or distressed?
2. Do you ever use alcohol or drugs to help you cope? If so, under what circumstances and how much?
3. Have you ever harmed yourself before? If so, what was going on in your life that led to your feelings of distress?
4. In what ways have you harmed yourself before? Has this ever resulted in the need for medical attention?
5. Do you want to stop the self-harm? Have you tried before? Are you afraid to stop?
6. Could you commit to working with a counselor so that you could give up self-harm?
7. Do you have a personal relationship with Christ? Do you know that He loves you and wants to give you the strength to overcome this behavior?

# WISE COUNSEL 4

Self-harm and cutting are motivated by many different concerns:

- past traumatic experiences
- a way to express built-up feelings and emotions
- a way of releasing pressure, stress, and pain
- providing a feeling of control over one's body

Recovery from self-harm and cutting requires a social support system of friends and family, as well as counseling and strong accountability. It is important that the client have a desire and commitment to stop self-harm or cutting. It should be impressed on the client that they may relapse after beginning a treatment program. Explain that they must then confess what's going on, take responsibility, and renew their commitment to stop the behavior.

# 5 ACTION STEPS

## 1. Seek Professional Help

- Your counselor will help you find a competent professional who has been trained to assist you in working through any unresolved or underlying emotional and/or psychological issues so that you can stop the self-harm.

## 2. Understand Your Feelings

- Your feelings stem from pain and suffering. You need to address any areas of hurt, pain, and hopelessness in light of the fact that God loves you and wants to give you the strength to overcome these problems.

## 3. Find Appropriate Ways to Express Your Feelings

- Make a decision that overcoming the pain and finding relief through healthy alternatives to cutting or self-harm are priorities. Consider journaling, art, music, and other forms of appropriate expression that allow you to process your thoughts and emotions.

## 4. Set Boundaries

- Next, *set boundaries* that you will not cross (e.g., having a verbal and/or written contract with a counselor or accountability partner, cutting without first talking to someone, being alone with peers who cut or are encouraging the behavior, etc.).
- Choose a friend, relative, counselor, or youth leader as someone you can call when you have the urge to inflict self-harm or cut. They can help with accountability by checking in with you on a regular basis, praying with you for strength, and giving encouragement.

## 5. Allow God's Love to Motivate You

- Remember that you are of great value in the eyes of God and He loves you. He died on the cross for you! He wants you to have a life of hope, blessing, and peace.

- Find ways to be reminded daily of your importance to God. For example, read His Word, join a Bible study group, go to a Christian support group. Be assured that God's desire is for you to find healing and grow in your trust in Him.

## 6. Get Rid of Articles Used in Self-Harm

- Make an inventory with your accountability partner (friend, family member, counselor, youth leader, for example) of your personal belongings. Give items that you have used or that have contributed to self-harm or cutting behaviors (razor blades, needles, rubber gloves, tourniquets, sticks, knives, for example) to your accountability partner or throw them away.

## 7. Keep Track of Your Progress

- Keep a journal, write on a calendar, or use a diary for making notes about your progress, writing down your feelings, and keeping track of your journey toward freedom.

## 8. Develop a Close Relationship with God

- You cannot do this alone; the problems are bigger than you but are not too big for God to handle! Nothing is impossible for Him. Trust Him to work in your life and help you make important changes.
- Your relationship with God is important. Read your Bible every day, work through a devotional, and pray throughout the day. If you have an open heart and an open mind, God will work steadily in your life.

# BIBLICAL INSIGHTS 6

*Are not five sparrows sold for two pennies? Yet not one of them is forgotten by God. Indeed, the very hairs of your head are all numbered. Don't be afraid; you are worth more than many sparrows.*

*Luke 12:6–7*

Jesus said He knows and cares about little birds. How much more does He care for you! He counts how many hairs are on your head, and you are worth so much to Him.

*Cast all your anxiety on him because he cares for you.*

*1 Peter 5:7*

When we give our feelings of pain, anxiety, frustration, inferiority, rejection, hate, anger, and fear to God, He takes them and begins to work on our hearts, giving us grace and the strength to trust Him.

*He will cover you with his feathers, and under his wings you will find refuge; his faithfulness will be your shield and rampart.*

*Psalm 91:4*

The image of God in this verse is that He is a great, majestic eagle, with wings that cover and protect us, giving us peace and comfort. God wants us to take our problems to Him for the attention, grace, encouragement, and care that only He can give.

*. . . being strengthened with all power according to his glorious might so that you may have great endurance and patience.*

*Colossians 1:11*

When we are at our weakest moment, He is there with us, in the midst of our brokenness and pain, to give us all the power we need to resist the urge to hurt our bodies and the peace to overcome the temptation.

## 7 : PRAYER STARTER

Dear Jesus, I ask You to give _____ the strength to overcome this problem, knowing that You can bring true healing and forgiveness to wounded hearts. Help _____ understand that Your love and faithfulness are everlasting and that You will be with him (her) through every step of this journey. Thank You for Your hand of protection and safety always. Help _____ be faithful to give You every feeling of hurt, pain, anguish, and fear. May he (she) choose to value himself (herself) as You value him (her) . . .

## 8 : RECOMMENDED RESOURCES

Alcorn, Nancy. *Beyond the Cut: Real Stories, Real Freedom.* WinePress, 2008.
———. *Cut: Mercy for Self-Harm.* WinePress, 2007.
Hollander, Michael. *Helping Teens Who Cut: Understanding and Ending Self-Injury.* Guilford Press, 2008.
Levenkron, Steven. *Cutting: Understanding and Overcoming Self-Mutilation.* W. W. Norton, 1998.
McIntosh, Helen, B. *Messages to Myself: Overcoming a Distorted Self-Image.* Beacon Hill Press, 2009.
Robson, Abigail. *Secret Scars: One Woman's Story of Overcoming Self-Harm.* Biblica, 2007.
Rowell, Shannon. *Chains Be Broken: Finding Freedom from Cutting, Anxiety, Depression, Anorexia, and Suicide.* Covenant Media, 2010.
Scott, Sophie. *Crying Scarlet Tears: My Journey through Self-Harm.* Monarch, 2008.
Strong, Marilee. *A Bright Red Scream: Self-Mutilation and the Language of Pain.* Penguin, 1998.

Wilson, Jess. *The Cutting Edge: Clinging to God in the Face of Self-Harm.* Authentic Media, 2008.

## Websites

American Self-harm Information Clearinghouse: www.selfinjury.org

Focus on the Family: www.focusonthefamily.com/lifechallenges/abuse_and_addiction/conquering_cutting_and_other_forms_of_selfinjury.aspx

National Self-Harm Network: www.nshn.co.uk/

Youth Work Resources: www.youthworkresource.com/ready-to-use-session-plans/self-harm-session/

# 20 Eating Disorders

## 1 ｜ PORTRAITS

- Lucy has always looked good in the mirror; her husband, friends, and co-workers have always complimented her on how beautiful she is. However, what they never understood was that Lucy's self-image has been tied to other people's criticism and she has been exercising and then purging after dinner every night for years. Her secret is still hidden, even though she is never happy with what she sees in the mirror. Lucy has found that purging makes her feel more in control and she knows she can drop five or ten pounds very quickly. Lucy realizes she has a problem but does not know where or how to get help. What will her husband and friends think if they find out?

- Brianna is sixteen years old; she is actively involved in her youth group at church and with the drama department at school. She has the lead role in her high school play but wrestles with the way she looks. Worried about being thin enough for the part, Brianna has been taking laxatives on the weekends and starving herself. Her mother told her she really needs to start eating more, but Brianna feels fat and wants to make a big impression at her star debut. She does not think she has a problem but is rapidly progressing down a path all too familiar for many with an eating disorder.

- Erika's story is one of pain and abuse. "I met someone in a coffee shop two weeks ago who invited me to church. I had never attended a church in my life. They were all so very kind and accepting that I really felt for the first time there are actually people who care about me! I heard about Jesus and went forward at the end of the service. A sweet elderly woman took me by the hand and guided me to a place where we could sit. There she explained how to be saved. I told her that I am not worthy to be saved by God. I was abused as a child and have lived the last ten years with many different men. Some of them abused me as well, and I let them do it. I have always blamed and hated myself; starving, purging, and overexercising have been my only ways of dealing with my pain. My boyfriend says I am so skinny, but all I see is a fat pig. The woman who spoke with me explained that Jesus loves me so much He died for me. He wants to save me and help me through my fear and struggles. For the first time in my life I think there is hope!"

# DEFINITIONS AND KEY THOUGHTS : 2

- As many as *24 million people* of various ages and genders suffer from an eating disorder in the United States and the lifetime prevalence among 13- to 18-year-olds is 2.7 percent.[1]

- The *period between puberty and the early adult years* is the time of greatest risk for an eating disorder to develop, with more than 30 percent of "normal" dieters progressing to pathological dieting.[2]

- Almost 50 percent of people who are diagnosed with an eating disorder also have a *comorbid depression diagnosis*, resulting in the highest mortality rate of any mental illness (12 times higher for women than other disorders). It is the third most chronic illness among teens.[3]

- *Eating disorders* are a group of addictions comprised of *anorexia, bulimia,* and *binge eating.* All are associated with *abusing food* in an effort to deal with deep emotional, psychological and self-image problems.

- *Anorexia nervosa* is characterized by the obsession to be thin, resulting in *constant dieting, starvation, overexercise*; the *abuse of diuretics*; and *an unhealthy self-image*. Sufferers view themselves as overweight and unattractive no matter what they see in the mirror.

- *Signs of anorexia* are:[4]

  — extreme thinness
  — rapid weight loss
  — abnormal blood counts
  — irregular heartbeat
  — low or abnormal blood pressure
  — dizziness or fainting
  — light bluish color to fingers
  — soft, thin hair covering the body
  — thinning hair on the head that falls out
  — abnormal menses or no menstruation cycle
  — osteoporosis
  — swelling of the limbs
  — poor body self-image

- *Bulimia nervosa* is the addiction to controlling weight by binging on excess food and calories, then purging it by vomiting or taking diet pills and laxatives. Sufferers may also overexercise or starve themselves along with showing signs of anorexia or binge eating. Bulimia may be harder to identify than anorexia because the person's weight is usually closer to normal.

- *Signs of bulimia* are:[5]

  — swollen salivary glands
  — broken blood vessels in the eyes

**183**

— weight above or below average, due to excessive calorie intake and a purge cycle

— weight dramatically swinging from above average to below average

— dramatic changes in size, due to changes in water weight

— low self-esteem with critical and negative comments regarding appearance

- *Binge eating* is the process of overeating by consuming large amounts of food and calories. This may or may not be associated with bulimia and many times has little to do with self-image or a desire to be thin. Binge eating is an attempt to deal with emotional and physical pain by keeping oneself occupied with eating or the brief pleasure of enjoying food as a comfort and/or control tool.

- *Signs of binge eating* are:[6]

— excessive weight gain, usually above average weight

— a feeling or sense that one's eating is out of control

— signs of anxiety and depression (depression and eating disorders often go hand in hand)

— excessive eating when the person feels upset or anxious

— dieting, even when it is not related to an appropriate weight-loss program

— eating in secret or anxiety about people being present when eating or chewing food

# 3 ASSESSMENT INTERVIEW

1. Do you feel lonely? Are your relationships with family and friends unfulfilling?
2. Do you find it hard to get close to others or establish healthy relationships?
3. Are you often afraid that people are trying to control you? How do you feel about the authority figures in your life?
4. Do you believe you have value or worth as a person?
5. Have you or a close family member ever been abused (sexually, physically, verbally)?
6. Have you struggled with depression?
7. Are you uncomfortable in crowds? Do you hate for people to see you?
8. Speaking honestly, what do you see when you look in the mirror? Are you happy with your body and how you appear?
9. Have you dieted or exercised excessively in the past?
10. Have you ever binged while eating or purged after eating?
11. What were family meals like for you growing up? How have you viewed your eating habits in the past? What has changed recently that has led to your eating behaviors?
12. Where is God in your life? Can you describe your spiritual walk?

## WISE COUNSEL : 4

After asking various diagnostic questions related to a person's emotional, physical, and spiritual condition, discuss the underlying issues that may be present—lack of self-worth, poor self- or body image, and the improper use of food as a means of control. Explain how Christ values those who are His children. His value of us is our true value.

Explain clearly how unbalanced motives, fears, poor self-image, and destructive thinking (such as using food as a way of controlling pain and anxiety) are actually accomplishing the opposite of what the client wants and needs. Give examples of ways in which a person can replace the misuse or abuse of food by communicating his or her feelings to a counselor or loved one.

Explore steps to bring the client's life goals into a healthy balance, prioritizing them so that pursuing them is manageable and realistic. Make sure there is good accountability. Keep in touch, follow up, and provide encouragement and positive support. Also provide appropriate referrals to trained professionals.

## ACTION STEPS : 5

### 1. Depend on God

- There are many reasons why we abuse food—to look and feel good, to comfort ourselves, or feel in control of our lives or situation. Whether we starve or gorge on food, we are often masking the pain of a deep wound with a food "bandage" or a distorted self-image of the perfect person. The first step to recovery is admitting that this problem is bigger than you but is not beyond God's ability to handle. Don't feel hopeless or defeated. Look to God and ask for His help.

### 2. Get Professional Help

- Seek the advice and help of a medical doctor or dietician. A qualified health professional can assist with the physical aspects of your struggle, as well as prescribe a healthy meal plan.
- Get into therapy with a mental health practitioner who has training in eating disorders and begin working through any issues that have been buried or are unresolved.

### 3. Develop an Action Plan

- Develop an action plan regarding any positive steps that you must take to get control of your eating.
- Set a target weight that is realistic and healthy. Understand that the goal is to seek a balanced and healthy lifestyle. Do not confuse an unrealistic ideal or image of the perfect person with what is actually an attainable weight goal.

## 4. Depend on Your Support System

- Look for friends, family, church members, or small group individuals who can help encourage, support, and most importantly hold you accountable to keep your goals and follow the action plan your counselor and/or medical doctor has provided.

## 5. Be Prepared for Relapse Triggers

- Be aware of the warning signs and relapse triggers that may lead you back to bingeing, purging, or starving yourself.
- If you are having feelings of worthlessness or suicidal thoughts, tell a loved one or trusted friend immediately and contact your counselor or doctor.

# 6 BIBLICAL INSIGHTS

*But the LORD said to Samuel, "Do not consider his appearance or his height, for I have rejected him. The LORD does not look at the things people look at. People look at the outward appearance, but the LORD looks at the heart."*

*1 Samuel 16:7*

The heart of the matter is not the obsession concerning food. Food has become a misused tool applied to a hurting heart. A self-image problem is what is tearing at the soul of the person with an eating disorder. We must understand God does not view us according to what we see in the mirror. He looks straight at our hearts and sees the real us. We must make peace with who we are and start seeing ourselves as God does, beautifully created to spend eternity with Him.

*He heals the brokenhearted and binds up their wounds.*

*Psalm 147:3*

God is our healer and the one who mends our souls and broken hearts. There is nothing too difficult for Him, no burden too large for Him to carry. His shoulders are big enough; we need to give *all our burdens* to Him.

*I sought the LORD, and he answered me; he delivered me from all my fears.*

*Psalm 34:4*

Many times fear is the key reason we use food to soothe our pain. Sometimes we punish ourselves to pursue a visual standard in the mirror that we know deep down we can never attain. Yet Christ is with us and gives us strength and courage to walk humbly step-by-step in the journey of recovery from eating disorders.

*After all, no one ever hated their own body, but they feed and care for their body, just as Christ does the church—for we are members of his body.*

*Ephesians 5:29–30*

We should want to keep every part of our body healthy, to protect and value it, just as Jesus values all of us. As part of the church, we are also members of His body. We are valuable, worthwhile, and precious as part of His family. We should never devalue ourselves, hate ourselves, or mistreat our bodies. We are Christ's treasure and His bride.

## PRAYER STARTER 7

Dear Jesus, thank You that _____ is seeking help for the things he (she) is struggling with. I know that in You there is always hope, strength, and the courage needed to overcome these circumstances. Help _____ see himself (herself) as You do, wonderfully created to be in relationship with You. Guide his (her) every step and provide the peace that is needed to surrender all fears and anxious thoughts to You. Thank You for Your grace to yield control to the Holy Spirit . . .

## RECOMMENDED RESOURCES 8

Alcorn, Nancy. *Starved: Mercy for Eating Disorders*. WinePress, 2007.

Ayres, Desiree. *God Hunger: Breaking Addictions of Anorexia, Bulimia, and Compulsive Eating*. Creation House, 2006.

Cruise, Sheryle. *Thin Enough: My Spiritual Journey through the Living Death of an Eating Disorder*. New Hope, 2006.

Davidson, Kimberly. *I'm Beautiful? Why Can't I See It?: Daily Encouragement to Promote Healthy Eating and Positive Self-Esteem*. Tate Publishing, 2006.

Gerali, Steven. *What Do I Do When Teenagers Struggle with Eating Disorders?* Youth Specialty, 2010.

Jantz, Gregory L., and Ann McMurray. *Hope, Help, and Healing for Eating Disorders: A Whole-Person Approach to Treatment of Anorexia, Bulimia, and Disordered Eating*. WaterBrook, 2010.

McCoy, Shannon. *Help! I'm a Slave to Food*. Day One Christian Ministries, 2011.

Meacham, Gari. *Truly Fed: Finding Freedom from Disordered Eating*. Beacon Hill Press, 2009.

Morrow, Jena. *Hollow: An Unpolished Tale*. Moody, 2010.

Wierenga, Emily T. *Casing Silhouettes: How to Help a Loved One Battling an Eating Disorder*. Ampelon, 2012.

### Websites

Eating Disorder Hope: www.eatingdisorderhope.com/information/statistics-studies

National Association of Anorexia Nervosa and Associated Disorders: www.anad.org

National Eating Disorders Association: www.nationaleatingdisorders.org

National Institute of Mental Health: www.nimh.nih.gov/statistics/1EAT_CHILD.shtml

# 21 Fetishes and Bizarre Interests

## 1 PORTRAITS

- Rick always lied about where he was most afternoons after class, and Phil, his roommate, always wondered where he went. While looking for something in one of Rick's desk drawers in the dorm room, Phil came across a woman's lingerie top, bra, and panties. Phil thought maybe Rick's sister had somehow left some items in his roommate's luggage and they had been crammed into a desk drawer temporarily. However, over the next two months, Phil checked the desk drawer occasionally and noticed that sometimes the items were missing and sometimes they were moved around in the drawer. Phil began to suspect that something strange was going on and he did not know if he wanted to confront Rick about it.

- John is a deacon at his local church. Everyone sees him as a godly and responsible person. However, John's wife, Sarah, knows he seems to have a fetish with feet. At first, she thought it was just a weird quirk, but John is more focused on his wife's feet than being intimate with her. It has been a problem in their marriage over the past eight years. John even worked for years as a store manager in a shoe store just because he loved helping ladies try on shoes. John and Sarah are afraid to seek counseling because they would be so embarrassed if any of the pastors of their church found out. Yet Sarah is beginning to wonder how long she can go on without healthy love from her husband and how long John will let his fetish control him.

- Gary has been dealing with some difficult issues for a long time. He has a pornography addiction and a fetish for latex. Gary spends much of his time in chat rooms where most of his friends encourage their addictions. They call themselves "loonists" because of their latex fetish. Gary does not mention his fetish when dating women but he never stays in a relationship very long. He finds more fulfillment in his cyber world of self-gratification where there is no fear of rejection or failure, as there is in relationships with women in the real world.

## 2 DEFINITIONS AND KEY THOUGHTS

- *Fetishism* is the use of inanimate objects (for example, a female's intimate apparel) or a specific body part (for example, hair) for the purpose of sexual stimulation, either physically or mentally.[1]

- *Transvestic fetishism* usually involves a male wearing a female's clothing (cross-dressing) for physical and mental sexual stimulation.[2]
- Working in an environment that allows a person to be exposed to his fetish, such as working in a shoe store to come in contact with feet and pantyhose, often *intensifies the problem.*
- Usually fetishes are *rooted in a deep desire to fantasize* about one's idea of the most exciting and often unrealistic expectations of a sexual encounter. However, usually this fantasy never goes beyond the person's imagination. A deep inability to initiate and engage properly in a loving relationship causes the person to keep using inanimate objects as *a substitute for a relationship with a real person.*
- Usually fetishism *begins by adolescence*, even though the object of the fetish may have certain significance that emanated from an earlier period in childhood. Once the fetish becomes a pattern of behavior, it tends to become more *embedded and chronic.*[3]
- According to the DSM-IV-TR , the *criteria for fetishism* include:

  — lasting for more than six months and reoccurring fantasies that are sexually intense, involving urges and the use of nonliving objects (for example, women's underwear)
  — fantasies and sexual desires or behaviors resulting in significant problems or impairment in functioning in the social, occupational, or other areas of life
  — not limiting objects used to items of female clothing utilized in cross-dressing (as in transvestic fetishism) or items designed for the purpose of tactile genital stimulation (for example, a vibrator)

# ASSESSMENT INTERVIEW 3

1. Do you have any objects that you use when fantasizing about another person?
2. Would you consider what you do a fetish?
3. Have you used this object off and on for more than six months?
4. What are some of the earliest memories you have regarding your fetish? Are they more about the object or more about a particular person or experience in your past?
5. What were your parents like? Did they show you love and acceptance? How did they express their love verbally? Did they express their love by things they did for you?
6. What was your adolescence like? Did you have a lot of friends? Did you have a hard time expressing your opinions and feelings to others?
7. Did you masturbate daily as an adolescent? Do you still masturbate every day or nearly every day?
8. Is the idea of a relationship with a fantasized person more appealing than a relationship with your spouse or a potential future mate?
9. Has this fetish caused any problems in your life? Have you had to make any changes to accommodate this fetish?

# 4 WISE COUNSEL

Guard your initial reactions. It is very important not to react negatively or reject the client when they describe their fetish behaviors. We need to show care, respect, concern, and the love of Christ when dealing with these issues.

Offer guidance with sensitivity and concern but be careful about communicating to the client that his/her fetish behavior is necessarily permissible or healthy. Separating the person from the behavior is a helpful approach to take.

Get to the root of the issue. Feelings of shame and guilt are common in people with fetishes. They may also be somewhat defiant, asserting that the behavior is normal or accepted in our modern world. It is important that we confront immorality and express God's view of what healthy sexuality consists of within the context of marriage.[4]

Develop a plan of action. Accountability, regular visits, prayer, and biblical instruction can help guide a client down a healthy Road to Recovery.

# 5 ACTION STEPS

## 1. Look at the Past

- Childhood and adolescence experiences (especially trauma and abuse) may facilitate the formation of behaviors and addictions that affect current fetishes. Be willing to look back at your past to see if there were experiences that may have led to your fetish.

- The wounds of your past may be very painful. Allow your counselor to help you face them by talking through your memories, thoughts, and feelings about any significant or traumatic events.

- You may have an unmet spiritual need resulting from frequent sexual and emotional desires that the fetish has been feeding, usually unsuccessfully, and resulting in the addictive behavior. If this is the case, identify any false beliefs or distortions in your thinking or view of God. Replace them with truth and more balanced self-talk.

## 2. Receive the Truth

- What the world has taught people about love and relationships is not always healthy or factual. God has created marriage as a wonderful institution in which a man and a woman can experience genuine love, acceptance, and an intimacy worth developing and nurturing. Spend time learning about the rewards of operating within God's beautifully designed plan for intimacy. Get the help you need to go from "self-love" to a selfless love.

## 3. Be Accountable

- Ask a family member, friend, or Christian counselor to be your accountability partner.
- Work with your counselor to set up ground rules along with a framework that will guide your behaviors and choices and will incorporate accountability and feedback from others.

## 4. Trust God for Healing

- When we work toward our goals and trust God to give us strength, we can have hope that He will heal us. Persevere in your pursuit of a life that is pleasing to Christ. Spend time in prayer, asking God to teach you how to live a healthy life.

# BIBLICAL INSIGHTS : 6

*By the grace God has given me, I laid a foundation as a wise builder, and someone else is building on it. But each one should build with care. For no one can lay any foundation other than the one already laid, which is Jesus Christ. If anyone builds on this foundation using gold, silver, costly stones, wood, hay or straw, their work will be shown for what it is, because the Day will bring it to light. It will be revealed with fire, and the fire will test the quality of each person's work. If what has been built survives, the builder will receive a reward. If it is burned up, the builder will suffer loss but yet will be saved—even though only as one escaping through the flames.*

*1 Corinthians 3:10–15*

Just like the apostle Paul, we are building a life that is a temple of holiness to God. The foundation that we build on is the base of our life. If it represents sexual impurity, selfishness, greed, lust, and shame, then that becomes the foundation. Someday God will judge each of us by our works and the quality of the lives we have lived. He wants each of us to have a pure, holy, and victorious life.

*You have heard that it was said, "You shall not commit adultery." But I tell you that anyone who looks at a woman lustfully has already committed adultery with her in his heart.*

*Matthew 5:27–28*

Jesus makes an important correlation between the heart and the mind. Perhaps fetishes and bizarre interests are not always part of an adulterous act or part of sex outside of marriage. But it is important to understand that the very act of a fetish or some interest that leads to sexual immorality is an act of the heart and mind. To think and fantasize about someone other than one's spouse is lust in the heart and a sin of the mind. God views all lust as sin and so we must treat it as sin. The godly solution to sin is confession, repentance, and dependence on God for His grace and forgiveness.

*Because of this, God gave them over to shameful lusts. Even their women exchanged natural sexual relations for unnatural ones. In the same way the men also abandoned natural relations with women and were inflamed with lust for one another. Men committed shameful acts with other men, and received in themselves the due penalty for their error.*

*Romans 1:26–27*

An addiction such as a fetish is really just as much a heart problem as an addiction problem. When we can give God our hearts and minds, fully devoted to restoring our thinking to what is pleasing to God, then we are on our way to overcoming the addiction. We must be committed to healthy behavior and viewing others in the light of how God made us.

*Have nothing to do with the fruitless deeds of darkness, but rather expose them. It is shameful even to mention what the disobedient do in secret. But everything exposed by the light becomes visible—and everything that is illuminated becomes a light.*

*Ephesians 5:11–13*

We may ask what is acceptable within the bounds of marriage and what is not. When our deeds are pure and we are not hiding anything from our spouse, we can have a clear conscience before God. Keeping the marriage bed pure (see Heb. 13:4) is essential if we are to live in the light.

# 7 PRAYER STARTER

Lord, please guide _____, who has come for help with this addiction. We know that only You can give true peace, freedom, and healing. Give _____ the patience, strength, faith, and courage to see this through so he (she) can give You glory for the change in his (her) life. Thank You for a life that honors You in all things . . .

# 8 RECOMMENDED RESOURCES

Balswick, Judith, and Jack Balswick. *Authentic Human Sexuality: An Integrated Christian Approach.* IVP Academic, 2008.

Cloud, Henry, and John Townsend. *Boundaries.* Zondervan, 1992.

Dallas, Joe. *The Game Plan.* Thomas Nelson, 2005.

Gallagher, Steve. *At the Altar of Sexual Idolatry.* Pure Life Ministries, 2000.

Kern, Jan. *Eyes Online, Eyes on Life: A Journey Out of Online Obsession.* Standard, 2008.

Schaumburg, Harry W. *False Intimacy: Understanding the Struggle of Sexual Addiction.* NavPress, 1992.

# Food Addictions 22

## PORTRAITS 1

- Charlie has been overweight since he was seven years old. He used to drink an entire six-pack of Coke and eat several candy bars almost every day. He would hide the wrappers in each of the Coke cans and mix up the trash so his mother would not find them. Charlie does not only have a weight problem. He has spent the last eleven years telling himself that if he can only stick to this new diet, his problems will be over. Unfortunately, at 355 pounds, Charlie has an addiction to food. There is no stop button, no off switch, and he craves the smell and, taste and feeling of food in his hands.

- "Some think being addicted to food happens only to people who are genetically born that way, but I'm proof that this is not the case. My name is Sue, and all my pictures up until middle school were of a thin girl with dark brown hair smiling back in the photos. I thought I had a good childhood, that is until my parents divorced and our home was sold. My mom and I moved to Minnesota to live with my grandmother and that was the beginning of my problems. I had a hard time adjusting to our new life. I missed my dad, resented my mother, and found it difficult to find any friends. Eating was a comfort and still is to this day. I am forty-five-years old now, and I weigh 289 pounds. I have literally tried more than thirty different diets, as well as pills, laxatives, even purging. You name it and I have tried it. I think about food just like an alcoholic thinks about his next drink. Often I feel depressed and will order take-out food, for ten people sometimes, pretending I'm picking it up for a group. I know my problem is not just weight; it is an addiction of the mind. But how do I go about finding help?"

- Alex is thirty-six-years old and struggles with a food addiction. When he was a kid, he used to go to his neighbor's house to play with his best friend, Chris. Alex would tell Chris's mother that he had not eaten anything and would eat at their house and then go home and eat more. Alex has abused food most of his life. He goes to the drive-thru four or five times a day and often eats until he vomits. Alex has never had a girlfriend or developed any close emotional attachments. He is afraid of rejection but is also tired of losing out on so many things in life that are part of a family. His story is one that is familiar to many people because food addiction is such a prevalent problem. Alex wants to change but needs help.

# 2 DEFINITIONS AND KEY THOUGHTS

- There are many different eating disorders, obsessions, and compulsions. However, *food addiction* is different. It is defined as a *mental and physiological addiction to food.*
- *Food addiction* is the *uncontrollable and repeated use* of food to satisfy an individual's intense urge for emotional and cognitive pleasure.
- The DSM-IV-TR does not currently have a provision for food addiction, but it does have *a provision for out-of-control eating.*
- According to a March 2012 study in the *Journal of Psychoactive Drugs*, there is evidence to suggest that bingeing on *sugar-rich foods increases extracellular dopamine in the striatum* (strongly associated with emotional and motivational aspects of behavior) and therefore gives a particular food an addictive potential.[1]
- There is increasing research regarding the role of *fats and sugars* in the compulsive desire for certain foods.[2] This research has indicated some people may have an addiction to food for *physical or emotional reasons* that goes beyond mere misuse.
- Similar to other addictions, *tolerance dynamics* result in needing greater or more frequent amounts of food to be eaten *to achieve the positive effects* of stimulation from food.[3]
- When not eating, a person with a food addiction will show signs similar to a person with an alcohol or drug addiction—*obsessive thinking* or preoccupation with the addiction (food), remembering the sense of *pleasure or comfort* that the behavior brings, and an *overwhelming desire* from the senses (taste, touch, smell, feeling, and sight) regarding food.
- *Overeating* or *gorging* is not the only symptom of a food addiction. Other disorders may also be present, such as *bulimia, anorexia nervosa, bingeing, purging, excessive exercise,* or the *abuse of diet pills and laxatives.* The person with food addiction may also *diet*, even though they cannot stop thinking about food.

# 3 ASSESSMENT INTERVIEW

1. Do you find yourself obsessing about or preoccupied with thoughts of food? When you are not eating, are you thinking of food?
2. Do you become irritable, anxious, fearful, or tired when you are not eating?
3. Do you have a desire to eat even though you feel satiated and are not hungry?
4. Would you say eating is used to fulfill a longing or deep need in your life?
5. Have you made excuses, changed plans with family or friends, isolated yourself, or perhaps sacrificed opportunities so that you could satisfy your cravings?
6. Has your difficulty with food caused any problems in your relationships, at work or school, or in your social life?
7. Do you feel that along with any physical difficulties regarding food (e.g., diet restrictions due to obesity, diabetes, allergies, etc.), there may be a spiritual, emotional, or mental problem with food as well?

# WISE COUNSEL : 4

To properly treat a person with a food addiction, you may need the help of a family physician or dietician. They can address all of the concerns related to the physical issues.

As with many compulsions and obsessions, food can become a substitute for meeting emotional needs. It is important to address the underlying causes of the obsession, especially any areas of woundedness or trauma. Once any underlying pain from the past is sufficiently explored, as well as issues of fear and anger that may arise from these wounds, the rebuilding process can be initiated.

More than one session with the client will probably be necessary, along with an organized plan of action, which includes clear, obtainable goals and accountability partners. A social support system of encouraging family, friends, or church relationships will help keep progress on track. Clear communication of feelings and goals are critical to success.

Many people feel isolated in their struggle, showing signs of depression, low self-esteem, and a poor outlook on life. Helping them understand they are not alone is an important goal. According to the Centers for Disease Control, as of 2010, more than 35 percent of Americans are obese and 17 percent of all youth are obese.[4] With statistics this sobering, many feel the burden of dealing with a problem that affects thousands of people.

# ACTION STEPS : 5

## 1. Identify Underlying Factors

- To deal with your addiction to food, you will need to identify the reasons or triggers that cause you to crave food—fear, anxiety, depression, anger, low self-esteem, trauma, or distorted thinking. Your counselor with help you isolate these triggers.
- Identify the things that cause you pain and problems now, as well as the painful things in your past.
- Identify the types of food that you crave—sugar, fat, starch, flour, wheat, or other.
- *Refer to chapter 20 on Eating Disorders to identify any problems that may need additional help.*

## 2. Implement a Plan

- You and your counselor need to develop a plan to treat your addictive behaviors.
- You will need to see a physician and/or dietician for assessment and treatment of any physical problems you have. Your counselor will make referrals.
- Individual or group therapy, mentoring programs, weight-management programs, and residential treatment programs may also need to be considered.

- Recruit a support system of peers, family, church friends, and others who can serve as a social network and hold you accountable. An accountability partner whom you can contact whenever you need help and encouragement is essential throughout the process.
- Remember how much Christ loves you and values you as His child. He will provide you with strength, hope, and perseverance as you trust Him and pursue your goal of healing and victory, which He wants for you.

# 6 : BIBLICAL INSIGHTS

*Therefore, there is now no condemnation for those who are in Christ Jesus.*

*Romans 8:1*

As saved sons and daughters of the living God, we have been rescued, through Jesus's sacrifice for us, from the guilt, shame, and fear that once gripped us. There is safety, peace, and strength available for us to walk a path to true freedom that is without condemnation.

*Then Jesus was led by the Spirit into the wilderness to be tempted by the devil. After fasting forty days and forty nights, he was hungry. The tempter came to him and said, "If you are the Son of God, tell these stones to become bread." Jesus answered, "It is written: 'Man shall not live on bread alone, but on every word that comes from the mouth of God.'"*

*Matthew 4:1–4*

In everything we face, Jesus understands the temptation, pain, and anguish of the struggle. He is our example of how to live a victorious life and He wants to empower us to depend on Him and His Word.

*No temptation has overtaken you except what is common to mankind. And God is faithful; he will not let you be tempted beyond what you can bear. But when you are tempted, he will also provide a way out so that you can endure it.*

*1 Corinthians 10:13*

In every trial we face, through every addiction, regret, fear, pain, and time of loneliness, God is able to provide what we need to endure, overcome, or escape the difficult situation. God wants us to be victorious over our circumstances and He wants us to glorify Him through healthy and balanced decisions.

*When tempted, no one should say, "God is tempting me." For God cannot be tempted by evil, nor does he tempt anyone; but each person is tempted when they are dragged away by their own evil desire and enticed. Then, after desire has conceived, it gives birth to sin; and sin, when it is full-grown, gives birth to death. Don't be deceived, my dear brothers and sisters. Every good and perfect gift is from above, coming down from the Father of the heavenly lights, who does not change like shifting shadows. He chose to give us birth through the word of truth, that we might be a kind of firstfruits of all he created.*

*James 1:13–18*

We must remember that we live in a sinful world, filled with the broken and shattered remains of a once perfect creation. When sin entered the world, people fell from grace, but God did not let it stay that way without hope and redemption. Jesus wants to make us new on the inside. He promises rewards to those who do not give up but keep moving forward. Perseverance and surrendering to the will of God is a step-by-step journey. It is worth the struggle because a changed life awaits. No one needs to be a slave to food, but we must let God be our King!

*For everything in the world—the lust of the flesh, the lust of the eyes, and the pride of life—comes not from the Father but from the world.*

*1 John 2:16*

Sometimes we think we are in our struggle alone, that somehow no one can possibly understand the brokenness we feel. This is not true; our weaknesses are similar to those of everyone else. We all struggle with problems, and food cravings and obesity are two of the most common problems facing Americans today. The good news is that with Christ, freedom is always possible.

## PRAYER STARTER 7

Dear Jesus, thank You that _____ has come to the place where he (she) is ready to work on his (her) struggles with food. We know You want _____ to be able to give all the fear, pain, anxiety, and discouragement to You and that You alone can give the strength and courage to pursue a healthy path toward freedom. Fill _____ with Your Spirit and empower him (her) to be able to follow You completely with the hope that is laid before him (her) . . .

## RECOMMENDED RESOURCES 8

Fitzpatrick, Elyse. *Idols of the Heart: Learning to Long for God Alone.* P&R, 2002.
———. *Love to Eat, Hate to Eat: Overcoming the Bondage of Destructive Eating Habits.* Harvest House, 2005.
Maccaro, Janet. *Change Your Food, Change Your Mood.* Siloam, 2008.
Mercola, Joseph, and Ben Lerner. *Generation XL: Raising Healthy, Intelligent Kids in a High-Tech, Junk-Food World.* Thomas Nelson, 2007.
Morrone, Lisa. *Overcoming Overeating: It's Not What You Eat; It's What's Eating You!* Harvest House, 2009.

Sheppard, Kay. *Food Addiction: The Body Knows*. Rev. ed. Health Communications, 1993.

———. *From the First Bite: A Complete Guide to Recovery from Food Addiction.* Health Communications, 2000.

## Websites

All About Life Challenges: www.allaboutlifechallenges.org/food-addiction.htm

Food Addiction Institute: www.foodaddictioninstitute.org/?doing_wp_cron=1353 679461.8226640224456787109375

Food Addicts in Recovery Anonymous: www.foodaddicts.org/

Web MD: www.webmd.com/mental-health/mental-health-food-addiction

# Gambling 23

- Terry went out to the casino just for entertainment, to have a night out with the guys, and maybe to win a little money. His friends had said that gambling was fun, but after a long night, he finds himself struggling to break even and then realizes he has lost a considerable amount of money, the money that he had planned to use for an engagement ring for his girlfriend. Terry leaves the casino without the sense of fun and excitement his friends promised and now he has to explain his financial loss to his girlfriend and a possible delay on their engagement.

- Keith is a smart man and has been around awhile. He is good with numbers and has a decent job that should have been paying the bills, except nearly every day on his way home from work, he stops by the track to bet on horse races. There is this incredible drive in him to be the one to place the big bet on the highest odds and get the huge payoff. That would solve all of his financial problems at home and make sure he is financially secure for a long time. However, the money he wins is never enough; he always wants to win more and is never satisfied. Thousands of dollars keep coming and going like the wind.

- *This will be the one*, Susan told herself as she dragged her key across the lottery ticket to hopefully see winning numbers. She won fifty dollars! Susan was ecstatic and filled with a renewed sense of hope and anticipation. Maybe she could win more. Was this her lucky day? She must have been on a hot streak and she couldn't give up now. Susan went back into the gas station and purchased five more tickets, each for twenty dollars. Nothing good. Why couldn't she have just been happy with the fifty? Depressed and defeated she walked back to her car. *Tomorrow will be better,* she told herself.

- Steven loved the football season, and this was his best year yet for betting and winning. He bet on all the pro games, college football too. He even had a few bets on local high school teams. He knew everyone involved, the handlers, the bookies, everyone. Sometimes he found himself so stressed and tense waiting for the results that he couldn't even enjoy the game. What had the sport become? It was like work, work that he was rapidly losing control over.

# 2 DEFINITIONS AND KEY THOUGHTS

- *Gambling* takes place when something of material value, typically money, is risked with the possibility of winning more on an event with an uncertain outcome. Whether betting on a sporting event, playing a card game such as poker, buying a lottery ticket, or spinning a roulette wheel, one thing is certain: when it comes to gambling, the outcome is at least partly *decided by chance.*

- Typically all gambling games fall under one of two categories, *games of skill* and *games of chance.* Gambling may consist of *gaming or betting against the house* or it may be *peer-to-peer*, which is gambling against other individual participants.

- There are twice as many gamblers in the United States as cancer patients. Twenty-five percent of gamblers have made at least one *suicidal gesture.* Each gambler *costs the economy* an average of sixteen thousand dollars per year.[1]

- *More than 2.5 million people struggle with a gambling addiction* in this country with another 15 million who are at risk of developing the disorder. The gambling industry takes in more than *500 billion dollars* annually.[2]

- There are a number of reasons people give for gambling. These include *risk taking that provides an adrenaline rush, exotic or captivating locations connected to gambling experiences, hope for large monetary gains, the thrill of winning,* and *immersion into the casino atmosphere* that allows some to forget about everyday life.

- Frequently gambling leads to *financial difficulties* that may also increase the risk for compromising *moral*, and in some cases, *legal standards* to cover a debt.

- Often people use gambling as *a pathway to escape* their current circumstances, responsibilities, and pressures, much like those who turn to alcohol or another drug to dull their pain.

- *When gambling becomes a problem*, it can also *affect the people around the gambler*, including family members, friends, and relatives. Although it differs from country to country, on average, between 1 and 2 percent of any population who gamble have a problem and every gambler impacts those around him or her (usually in a negative way).[3]

- *Signs and symptoms* of a gambling addiction include but are not limited to the need to have more and more money to use for gambling, a preoccupation with planning a future gambling event or reveling in a past experience, multiple unsuccessful attempts to reduce the level of gambling, becoming easily irritated or uneasy when trying to cut back on gambling, and gambling to relieve stress, sadness, or anxiety.

- There are *no known specific causes* for developing a gambling addiction or pathological gambling behaviors; however, people with greater desires for thrill seeking and at-risk behavior and those who have grown up around gamblers are at higher risk.

- A national study conducted over the course of eight years to determine addictive gambling and alcoholism rates found that *3.5 percent of Americans are problem gamblers,* compared to 1.8 percent of Americans who are considered to be alcohol dependent. According to psychologist Dr. John Welte, after the age of twenty-one, problem gambling is more prevalent than alcoholism.[4]

- Around *2 to 5 percent of people are diagnosed with gambling addiction,* the majority of whom live in the United States. An interesting thing to note is that the demographic showing the *greatest increase in the disorder is among women,* who now comprise 25 percent of all individuals diagnosed as pathological gamblers.[5]
- Gambling has been found to have a *druglike effect on the brain* very similar to that of cocaine or morphine, impacting the prefrontal cortex as well as the blood flow to the brain.
- *Dopamine,* the pleasure inducing neurotransmitter in the brain, has been found to have a *direct link to gambling.* After a gambler wins, dopamine floods the brain, and levels drop during a losing cycle. This creates in the individual a greater desire to gamble and to find gambling opportunities, much like a drug addict experiencing withdrawal symptoms and needing the next "hit" to maintain the high.
- *Slot machines can often be the most addictive* to a gambler because of the surprise payouts that stimulate the dopamine neurons more than a somewhat expected win at a game of skill.

## ASSESSMENT INTERVIEW : 3

1. How much time in the last week or month would you say you spent gambling?
2. How much money would you say you have lost gambling? Have you ever had to borrow money to finance your gambling?
3. Have you ever sold or stolen something to finance your gambling?
4. As a result of your gambling, have you seen any disconnect from family members or others you have relationships with?
5. Do you find yourself with a great urge to go into a casino or to buy a lottery ticket simply because you are near locations where you can do these things?
6. Have you tried and failed to stop gambling and, if so, how many times?
7. Do you find yourself constantly thinking about the next big win or constantly reminiscing about previous winnings or losses?
8. Do you find yourself becoming irritated with those who talk to you about your gambling addiction?
9. Have you recently experienced disruptions in your sleep patterns and/or appetite or increased feelings of anxiety and depression?

## WISE COUNSEL : 4

It is important to understand that those who are addicted to gambling are experiencing a chemical rush in their brains that impacts the way they feel, act, think, and reason. Without the release of dopamine, gambling, as well as other high-risk behaviors, would lose a large degree of its luster. However, it is this release of dopamine that gives the gambler a high and keeps him or her coming back for more. The goal is not always necessarily about making money; instead it may have more to do with the experience and the "feeling" of winning. Certain depressants have been used to decrease dopamine levels in progressive gamblers (those who sink deeper into the addictive lifestyle over time), but this can be dangerous because these individuals may already be depressed due to substantial losses from their gambling behaviors. There is an enormous high for gamblers when they win, but that same high is often matched equally by the low that comes from losing and this low can be very dangerous. Gamblers can fall into a depressive state, trying desperately to dig their way out of the hole they now find themselves in. The gambler starts a downward spiral because, like others who wrestle with an addiction, he or she does not know when or how to quit.

More often than not, a gambling addict does not simply affect himself or herself, but family members, friends, and co-workers as well. Gambling can be very hard on those surrounded by the problem—causing financial, emotional, and sometimes even physical concerns. Gamblers may become dependent on the loans from loved ones and friends to support their habit, and this can lead to compounded problems. One important consideration for the family is to be actively supportive and help the gambler with their addiction without enabling them to continue. A gambling addiction is difficult to fight, but as with all addictions, there are some things that loved ones can do, such as setting appropriate boundaries.

Gambling needs financial resources to survive, and a compulsive gambler does not normally have the means to sustain the addiction indefinitely with his or her personal funds. Therefore it is important that family and friends manage their money well and not give in when the gambler asks, pleads, begs, or demands it.

The time of a recovering gambler should be filled with constructive activities to keep their mind off gambling as much as possible. They should stay away from gambling situations and the environments that normally result in craving.

# 5 ACTION STEPS

## 1. Admit There Is a Problem

- Many times compulsive gamblers and addicts will not admit there is a problem or that they are even gambling at all. You may claim you are not really losing money, are not depressed, and have not changed. It is important to acknowledge that something is wrong.

- It is time to accept responsibility for your gambling. This step is a reality check to help you and your counselor define the severity of the problem or to face the problems it has caused in your life.

## 2. Allow Someone to Hold You Accountable

- It may be critical for someone else to have control of your major financial assets until you can gain enough self-control to handle more autonomy. This is a hard but often a necessary step, especially if financial ruin is at the doorstep.

- This decision also means you need to let people be around you and hold you accountable to make sure you are not continuing to engage in gambling behaviors. They can help you fight those urges when they arise.

## 3. Replace Gambling with Healthier Habits

- Often gambling begins as an outlet for felt needs and so it is important to replace the habit with something healthier and to learn how to lead a more balanced life. A hobby, doing something creative, or getting involved in playing sports are types of activities that can be substituted for the gambling habit.
- For many gamblers, boredom is a trigger, because it allows the urge to gamble to return, which becomes increasingly difficult to resist. Trying to fill empty hours with the right kinds of activities is crucially important.

## 4. Join a Support Group

- This is a great time to realize you are not the only one struggling with this addiction and it is an opportunity to express how you feel to those who are empathetic and supportive and can understand your language.
- Rehab and support groups are also excellent sources for accountability. Gambling is situational and the urges are always more readily resisted in a small-group setting.
- Support groups, such as Gamblers Anonymous, have step-by-step programs that will help fight urges and move you closer toward sobriety and recovery.

# BIBLICAL INSIGHTS 6

*"I have the right to do anything," you say—but not everything is beneficial. "I have the right to do anything"—but I will not be mastered by anything.*

1 Corinthians 6:12

The Bible does not specifically say to avoid playing the slots or blackjack or other kinds of gambling; however, it does make note of the fact that we should do things that are beneficial to us and not detrimental. Gambling addictions can hurt us emotionally, financially. and spiritually. Even though there may appear to be some silence on the subject within the Scriptures, it is important to realize when the behavior is hurtful and destructive, indicating a need for change.

*They promise them freedom, while they themselves are slaves of depravity—for "people are slaves to whatever has mastered them."*

2 Peter 2:19

As with any addiction, gambling can have a strong hold over the mind and, in a very real way, can control an individual. The Bible says that we cannot serve two masters; man cannot serve God and money. Addictions consume individuals to the point where it is all they think about. Once this happens, people are enslaved to the behavior. God wants your time. He is a jealous God and He is jealous for you.

*For the love of money is a root of all kinds of evil. Some people, eager for money, have wandered from the faith and pierced themselves with many griefs.*

*1 Timothy 6:10*

At some level, every process gambler has an unhealthy and unbalanced love and desire for more money. There is a definite thrill-seeking mind-set for the high of winning, but ultimately there is also a desire for more wealth and the prestige that comes along with it. The money alone is not the problem; the love of money is ultimately the destructive force.

People who love money will never be satisfied. They will always crave more and there will never be enough. In the end, everything is meaningless under the sun except for God. God can help us focus on true kingdom priorities.

*Lazy hands make for poverty, but diligent hands bring wealth.*

*Proverbs 10:4*

People who gamble have the sense that a great deal of money can be made with little or no work involved. We must avoid a mentality that tells us we can have everything we want, how we want it, and when, without having to do anything for it. This is rarely the case.

The Bible instructs us to work and that idle people do more harm than good. Hard work is to be commended and will ultimately bring blessings. God gave us the ability to work not as a curse but as a gift. We should be cautious of trying to find the easy way out or the way to make a quick dollar. Diligence is a character quality to develop.

## 7 PRAYER STARTER

Lord, You are the restorer of lives and the breaker of chains. You can do anything, and I pray that You would break the addiction to gambling that is like a chain in _____'s life. He (she) has been struggling in this area and cannot fight the battle on his (her) own but needs You to carry the burden. You tell us to come to You if we are burdened and heavy-laden and You will carry our burdens for us. God, please surround _____ with Your love and grace and let him (her) know You are his (her) provider and sufficient for every need. Thank You that You care for us and love us . . .

# RECOMMENDED RESOURCES 8

Arterburn, Stephen, and David Stoop. *The Book of Life Recovery*. Tyndale, 2012.

Cleveland, Mike. *Higher Stakes: Freedom from Gambling and Betting*. Ingram, 2008.

June, Lee, and Sabrina D. Black. *Counseling for Seemingly Impossible Problems*. Zondervan, 2007.

McCown, William G., and William A. Howatt. *Treating Gambling Problems*. John Wiley, 2007.

Raabe, Tom. *House of Cards: Hope for Gamblers and Their Families*. Tyndale, 2001.

Shaw, Mark E. *The Heart of Addiction: A Biblical Perspective*. Focus, 2008.

———. *Hope and Help for Gambling*. Focus, 2010.

Welch, Edward T. *Addictions: A Banquet in the Grave: Finding Hope in the Power of the Gospel*. P&R, 2001.

Williams, Don. *12 Steps with Jesus*. Gospel Light, 2004.

## Websites

Gamblers Anonymous: www.gamblersanonymous.org/ga/

Gambling Addiction: www.gamblingaddiction.org

Mayo Clinic: www.mayoclinic.com/health/compulsive-gambling/DS00443

National Institutes of Health: www.nlm.nih.gov/medlineplus/compulsivegambling.html

No Gambling Addiction: www.nogamblingaddiction.com

# 24 Hoarding

## 1 PORTRAITS

- Henry calmly told Beth, "I think we should have a garage sale and get rid of some of these things. Some of our rooms are filled with stuff we never even use." Beth's hands began to sweat and her heart rate increased as she turned to her husband. "Well, what stuff are you talking about? So much of this is valuable to me. I don't think I could get rid of any of it." She started looking through a few of the piles and picked up an old lamp and a roll of packaging plastic. "Can't you see how valuable this is?" she asked.

- "Oscar, I can't open the door to this room. What's behind it?" Marie asked. She had just walked carefully along the foot-wide pathway in the hall that had stacks of boxes and items lining the walls. "Oh, those are all my clothes," Oscar responded. "They must have fallen over against the door. I don't remember there being that many piles in there though. I never know how much stuff I have anymore." Marie had sensed her brother was becoming a hoarder but did not know what to do about the situation.

- Gabe hated going to his aunt's house because it always smelled foul. The air was thick and there seemed to be several hundred cats running around. He hated cats and dreaded being dropped off there on weekends when his mother had to work. He walked up the sidewalk to the house. He could already smell it, but today the odor was worse. Gabe walked to the door and cracked it open. Two cats chased each other past him. Then the smell hit him harder, like a brick wall. When he looked inside, he saw two of the animals lying on the foyer floor, and they looked dead. Three more malnourished cats ran past him as he stepped inside and forty pairs of feline eyes stared right at him. *Where's Aunt Sara*, he wondered, *and why doesn't she do something about this?*

## 2 DEFINITIONS AND KEY THOUGHTS

- *Compulsive hoarding* (disposophobia) is the act of accumulating excessive amounts of both valuable and worthless items with an inability to use or discard any of them, regardless of space limitations, hazardous or unsanitary conditions, and financial gain from a sale or trade of the items.

- Hoarding has been studied as both an addiction and as a compulsive behavior and has been found to have *addictive tendencies* in what eventually becomes *a pathological compulsive disorder.* Approximately 5 percent of the population shows evidence of clinical hoarding and this rate is twice the rate of obsessive-compulsive disorder (OCD) and four times the rate of bipolar or schizophrenia disorders.[1]

- *Compulsions* are "repetitive behaviors or mental acts that the person feels driven to perform in response to an obsession."[2] They are *aimed at preventing or reducing stress, anxiety, pain*, or *masking an event or situation*, but are not necessarily related to the actual event, act, or pain that they are masking.

- *Addictions* are considered to be *compulsive and uncontrollable dependence on a substance or activity.* They *impact dopamine levels in the brain* and create a pathway for producing more of this desired chemical.

- Often those who suffer from *hoarding* do not experience any sort of pleasure release from the hoarding. In fact usually those who suffer from *OCD-based hoarding* do not want to hoard and experience an *extreme distaste for the behavior and stress* because of the amount of energy it takes to maintain it.

- Frequently hoarding is linked to OCD and somewhere between 18 to 40 percent of OCD patients indicate significant hoarding problems. However, there are some differences. With *most OCD sufferers, obsessions are often reported as intrusive and unwanted*, whereas *for many hoarders, the behavior can create pleasurable feelings of safety and comfort.*[3]

- OCD hoarding can occur through *four classic obsessions.* Among the most common of these are (1) *fears of contamination*—objects cannot be touched because they are contaminated and thus they accumulate on the floor or wherever they are dropped; (2) *superstitious thoughts*—unreasonable beliefs that throwing something away will result in a catastrophe of some kind; (3) *feelings of incompleteness*—symmetry obsessions (how objects are arranged or situated) fall in this category; and (4) *persistent avoidance of onerous compulsions*—not discarding to avoid endless checking before discarding can occur.[4]

- Often hoarding affects *middle-aged and older individuals* and can sometimes be related to *dementia, Alzheimer's disease*, and other conditions associated with aging. For younger age groups there is less hoarding or the hoarding tendencies have not fully manifested themselves yet.

- One of the common and more dangerous types of hoarding is *animal hoarding* (cats, rabbits, chickens, snakes, and so on). Individuals with the disorder will *hoard and constantly breed* these animals, sometimes into the hundreds.

- Collectively, evidence from neuropsychological testing and neuroimaging research suggests that compulsive hoarding is characterized by abnormal activity in areas of the frontal lobe, such as orbitofrontal cortex, ventromedial prefrontal cortex, and anterior cingulate cortex.[5] Most of the *dopamine-sensitive neurons are found in this area of the brain*, which also handles executive functioning (such as reasoning, logic, rational thinking, and cognitive processing).

- For many hoarders, the *process of sorting, deciding what to do with, and potentially discarding and getting rid of items* is an experience they avoid at all costs because it is *emotionally overwhelming* to them.

- People who hoard may have *emotional dysregulation* manifesting in *depression or anxiety*, as well as a *family history of hoarding and perfectionism*. They may experience difficulties with decision making, form intense emotional attachments to a wide variety of objects, experience personification of inanimate objects, and hold tightly to the belief of not wasting anything because of potential monetary and/or emotional value.

- Hoarders are quick *to assume unrealistic expectations* of what will happen if they throw or give away an item. They may think people will abandon them, they may have disturbing feelings, and they may feel lonely or lost.

- *The consequences of hoarding are especially dangerous for older persons* who have difficulty maneuvering through their home because of their clutter. One investigation found that 45 percent of hoarders could not use their refrigerator, 42 percent could not use their kitchen sink, 42 percent could not use their bathtub, 20 percent could not use their bathroom sink, and 10 percent could not use their toilet.[6]

- While both *individual and group therapy* are used to treat hoarders, responses to medications normally used for OCD patients have mixed results.

- A *new cognitive behavior therapy* has been developed using methods that combine elements of motivational interviewing, cognitive therapy, and behavioral practice for OCD and skills training. This treatment focuses on excessive acquisition, difficulty discarding possessions, and the disorganization that makes functioning problematic.

- *Group therapy* has proven effective because of the increased support, motivation, and accountability, often accompanied by reduced shame, guilt, and isolation associated with hoarding.

# 3 ASSESSMENT INTERVIEW

1. How much time would you say you have spent collecting items? When did this begin?
2. Do you obsess about the items you keep or feel compelled to do so?
3. Do you experience anxiety or find it difficult to imagine parting with any of your items?
4. Do you find yourself placing emotional value on any of the items you have collected?
5. Do you see yourself ever being able to stop collecting things?
6. Have you seen a decrease in your connection to and interaction with others?
7. Do you feel ashamed or guilty about your hoarding?
8. Do you see excessively bad things happening to you if you were to give away any of your items?
9. Does your hoarding frustrate you? Do you find yourself overwhelmed by the idea of sorting or discarding items? Do you stress frequently about having so much and having to deal with everything?
10. Have you ever sought any help to deal with your hoarding?

## WISE COUNSEL : 4

It is important to realize that hoarders may not actually want to hoard and that they also may not realize how much they have accumulated. Even though there can be some sense of pleasure, hoarding often masks a negative emotion or event, and the person engages in the behavior to avoid the unpleasant feelings. Usually hoarders struggle with a sense of abandonment, loneliness, isolation, and shame. These emotions are reinforced because of their behavior and because friends and family members find it difficult to cope with their hoarding and disconnect from them. It is reasonable to assume that a hoarder probably felt abandonment in childhood or has had a traumatic experience of some kind.

Hoarding is often a difficult disorder to treat because of the person's attachment style. He or she has a problem letting things go and in making decisions. It is common for hoarders to believe bad things will happen to them in regard to removing possessions, so it can be helpful to challenge this distorted thinking. For many the thoughts of organizing, sorting, and discarding can be overwhelming, and patience is needed when working through this step in the treatment process. Due to the complexity of this disorder, professional medical and therapeutic help may be necessary.

## ACTION STEPS : 5

### 1. Admit Hoarding Has Become a Problem

- Many times hoarders struggle to recognize that they have over-accumulated items with little or no real value and that keeping these things is pointless because of the clutter. It is important for you to admit that you could part with certain things or that some items are less important than others. This is an important stage in the recovery process. It will probably be a difficult step for you, because at this point you consider everything important. Talk with your counselor about the things you have and which ones you might be able to consider letting go.

### 2. Detach from Items

- It is normal for people to have certain emotional or sentimental attachments to items, such as trophies, memorabilia, or family heirlooms. However, it is abnormal for someone to have attachments to items such as ordinary newspapers or packaging materials. It is important for you to realize that letting go of these things will not cause anything disastrous to happen. Discuss with your counselor what terrible things you think may happen if you discard items.
- Take a step of giving away some small item. When the aftereffects have subsided, let your counselor know what you gave away and what feelings you had after giving it away. You will probably find that, once an item is out of sight, it loses some of its obsessive qualities and control. When you begin to realize this, you will slowly be able to get rid of additional items.

## 3. Reduce the Urge to Buy and Collect

- Merely getting rid of items is essentially pointless if you are simply going to buy and collect other things. Go shopping with your counselor and talk about how you do not need to buy the things you see. You may think you really need an item but notice how quickly you forget about it when you walk away from it.

## 4. Join a Support Group

- An effective treatment protocol is for individual therapy to be coordinated with a support group experience. It will be easier for you, who already struggles with isolation and shame, to be with other people who are working through the same issues. Knowing that you are not alone can be a powerful dynamic. Groups can be encouraging and motivating and can help you stay on track with the treatment plan that has been designed.

# 6 BIBLICAL INSIGHTS

*Do not store up for yourselves treasures on earth, where moths and vermin destroy, and where thieves break in and steal. But store up for yourselves treasures in heaven, where moths and vermin do not destroy, and where thieves do not break in and steal. For where your treasure is, there your heart will be also.*

*Matthew 6:19–21*

Hoarders build up their treasures on earth, and their emotions, well-being, and happiness are directly tied to the items they have acquired. However, the Bible says this should not be so and encourages us to invest in things with eternal significance.

*Then he said to them, "Watch out! Be on your guard against all kinds of greed; life does not consist in an abundance of possessions."*

*Luke 12:15*

God does not want everything we do and everything we think about to be focused on what can be collected or possessed in this world. Greed and things can become idols we put before God.

*Jesus answered, "If you want to be perfect, go, sell your possessions and give to the poor, and you will have treasure in heaven. Then come, follow me."*

*Matthew 19:21*

God wants us, as Christians, to be willing to give up whatever possesses and controls us just as He gave up everything for mankind. If we put too much of our heart in what we own, our treasure will only be in this world. Sometimes God may ask us to give up everything and follow Him.

## PRAYER STARTER  7

Lord, You are the creator of all things and You desire us more than anything else. I pray that You would open the eyes of _____ so he (she) can see that You are the greatest treasure anyone can have. Help _____ let go of any fears or anxious thoughts that are keeping him (her) in this bondage. He (she) has been holding on to material things and using them to cover up pain that only You can take away. Wrap Your arms around him (her). You are the true Comforter and the source of all grace. No amount of wealth or accumulation can replace You . . .

## RECOMMENDED RESOURCES  8

Collie, Robert. *Obsessive-Compulsive Disorder: A Guide for Family, Friends, and Pastors.* Haworth Press, 2005.

Emlet, Michael R. *OCD: Freedom for the Obsessive-Compulsive.* Resources for Changing Lives, 2004.

Johnson, William L., and Brad W. Johnson. *The Pastor's Guide to Psychological Disorders and Treatments.* Haworth Press, 2000.

Jones, Esther L. *Turning a Blind I: Christianity with OCD.* Crossbooks, 2011.

Peurifoy, Reneau Z. *Anxiety, Phobias, and Panic.* Rev. ed. Hachette, 2005.

### Websites

Anxiety and Depression Association of America: www.adaa.org/understanding-anxiety/obsessive-compulsive-disorder-ocd/hoarding-basics

Compulsive Hoarding Center: www.compulsivehoardingcenter.com/Compulsive_Hoarding.html

Help for Hoarding: www.helpforhoarding.net/hoarding-statistics-reveal-about-compulsive-hoarders/

Obsessive Compulsive Foundation: www.ocfoundation.org/hoarding/

# 25 Internet Use and Gaming

## 1 PORTRAITS

- "Sam, John just called to see if you want to go to the movies. What are your plans?" After passing on the message, Sam's mother heard a quick, "I'll be down in a couple of minutes." She shrugged and went back to vacuuming. Several hours later, Sam came down to the kitchen. "Where is everybody?" he asked. Sam's mother sighed. "It's been almost three hours since I called up to you. I'm sure John has already left. What were you doing?" "I was just finishing up an online quest on my MMORPG [Massively Multiplayer Online Role-playing Game]," he replied. "I didn't think it would take that long. Oh well, I guess I'll go start the next level if they've already gone."

- Henry is twelve years old and is allowed to play virtually any computer, video, or online game he desires, and he spends countless hours in front of computer screens and televisions. His games of choice have become more violent and promote pleasure killing and criminal behavior. Consequently Henry has begun to lash out more toward his parents and has developed a quick temper. His first response to handling situations seems to mirror that of several of the video games he constantly plays. His parents worry that the games are affecting his behavior.

- Susan's parents are worried about her because she spends countless hours on online virtual reality websites with her own personalized avatars (graphic representations of the online user), talking to people she knows only through these sites. Her parents have heard many bad things about this sort of online environment, especially regarding online predators and stalkers who use them to find and entice younger kids, only to abduct and abuse them. Could this be happening to their fourteen-year-old daughter?

## 2 DEFINITIONS AND KEY THOUGHTS

- The American Medical Association defines *heavy gaming usage* as *playing for an estimated two hours or more a day*.
- Studies have shown that only *10–15 percent* of gamers actually meet the criteria for a gaming addiction.[1]
- Among addicted gamers who were married, more than 50 percent of their spouses claimed to have a *stressed relationship* due to the addiction.[2]

- There are *physical, emotional, and social consequences* to having a gaming or internet addiction.
- Like most addictions, there is a *dopamine release* in the user's brain when the player is engaged online, which then drives the user to continue the behavior.
- According to the Entertainment Software Association, the *average gamer in the United States is now thirty years old* and more than 37 percent are above the age of thirty-six.[3]
- Studies show that 33 percent of gamers are playing *social games* and 15 percent play *online games*.[4]
- One of the reasons that an internet or gaming addiction can develop so easily is because of the *vast variety of opportunities* the internet offers, as well as the sense of safety and control it can give to the user.
- For younger teenagers who may be struggling with social interaction problems, the internet or gaming world becomes the best *source of relational connection.* They can create and project themselves however they desire while *avoiding face-to-face contact.*
- *Video and online games are addictive* in nature in much the same way as are casino games. They allow small wins that create emotional hooks to keep the user playing the game longer and longer.
- Several of the hooks include *the high score, beating the game, discovery, relationships,* and *role-playing*. Perhaps one of the most addicting factors is online role-play themes that have no ending. *The idea of becoming the greatest player in the game and moving to higher levels is one of the most provocative hooks* for a user.
- *Role-playing* allows the user to create *an emotional attachment* to the online characters, which can lead to the user actually feeling what the virtual reality character feels.
- Kids who are *easily bored* (especially males) *have poor relationships skills,* are more *impulsive,* have a higher level of *aggression,* are *outcasts at school,* or trend toward *seeking sensations* are more easily drawn into video game and internet addiction.[5]
- *Therapy* for gaming and internet addiction, for the most part, follows the *same protocols* as with any addiction because the symptoms are similar. There is increased activity with gaming, increased thoughts about the game, neglect of relationships, and neglect of other priorities in life, even hygiene.
- It may be difficult to treat a gaming addiction because of *the poor and underdeveloped social skills of the addicted person*. If the majority of social interaction comes via an internet or gaming device, face-to-face dialogue is more awkward and less functional.
- Another complicating factor in treating a gaming or internet addiction is that *the devices/systems used by the addict are the very things he or she depends on for other uses,* such as homework and television viewing. Attempting interventions with an internet addict without the ability to remove him or her from the source of temptation would essentially be like telling an alcoholic to stop drinking but still letting him or her go to bars.

- There has been some success with weaning an addict off video games by *progressively limiting hours of play*, but there are also *therapeutic camps*, such as wilderness camps and team environments that completely remove the addicted person from all sources of the addiction.

# 3 ASSESSMENT INTERVIEW

1. Do you feel preoccupied with being on the internet?
2. How much time in the past week would you say you have spent gaming?
3. Do you have strong negative emotions (for example, moodiness, depression, irritability) when you have not been able to play a game or be online for extended periods of time?
4. Do you use gaming or the internet as a form of escape?
5. Do you neglect sleep or stay up much later than you planned to play a game or be online?
6. Do you find that the closest relationships you have are the ones online?
7. Do you find your thoughts and emotions correlated to the release of a new popular video game or online gaming environment?
8. Do you try to downplay how much you play on the internet or video game console?
9. Have you tried to stop playing video games but found yourself unable to do so on your own?
10. Have you found yourself losing already developed friendships because of the amount of time you spend online?

# 4 WISE COUNSEL

As with any addiction, one of the primary reasons for participating in the behavior is the pleasure-inducing chemicals—the endorphins and dopamine—that are poured into the brain and create a euphoric feeling. Video and internet games can produce many of the same reactions that gambling, bungee jumping, or other risk-taking behaviors do by using a different reward system. There is a certain mystery and anticipation about a new video game that can easily entice a player to complete the game no matter the number of levels or necessary time commitment. The graphics and special effects are important, but the most enticing part for a player is the story line and the mystery and anticipation of what is going to happen next. A video game can completely immerse a user so that he or she is thinking of nothing else but what is happening in the game. This is the reason people talk about different levels and gameplay even when the user is offline. The excitement of the unknown takes control of the thought process.

It is becoming increasingly important to address MMORPGs and online gaming societies because of the interactive, social, and relational dynamics that are affiliated with them. The internet allows access to millions of people in the gaming realm, especially in games like *World of Warcraft*, which is easily the most addicting MMORPG in existence. Usually these groups of players or societies are great escapes for youth and adults to create their own controllable environment. Online societies allow the user to be shy and adventurous all at the same time by keeping the individual free from face-to-face conversation. Ultimately, as much as gamers may argue to the contrary, they are losing positive and healthy social interactive skills.

Treatment for gaming addictions on the internet or on video game consoles starts with the removal of the device in question. This can be hard because a computer or Xbox is used for activities other than gaming. However, it is important to create some space between the addict and the source of the addiction. Interactions in real time with real people allow addicted gamers to develop their own personality as opposed to creating artificial personas online.

# ACTION STEPS 5

## 1. Admit There Is a Problem

- It may be very difficult for you to admit you have a gaming addiction because the games seem situational. You may think, *I will stop playing so much when I beat this game* or *I only play* this *game a lot, not all of them.* What you fail to understand is that whenever a new game comes out, you will be drawn to seek the next thrill from it, just as much as you did with the previous one, and it will dominate your thoughts and your time.
- Be realistic about how much time and thought you spend on gaming and admit you have a problem. This is an important first step to recovery.

## 2. Begin Regulating Game Usage

- Trying to regulate your game playing is another difficult step because you may not be aware of exactly how much time you spend immersed in the game or in cyberspace. However, beginning to regulate usage will help you wean yourself off games to a point where life is more manageable and playing games is not consuming so many hours of every day. Try limiting yourself to an hour or two of playing per day.
- The challenge in setting limits is that it will always seem you are at the most crucial point of the game when it's time to quit. You may be tempted to promise that you will stop right after the next level, but resist this urge and stop the game when the time you have set for yourself is up.

## 3. Remove the Video Game or Computer Entirely

- Complete abstinence is a stronger measure than trying to cut back, but if the other steps are followed, it should be doable. You may wonder how this would be possible, but if you have already limited online or gaming activity to an hour or two per day, removing a device for a week or so at a time should be reasonably successful.

- When computer use is required for work or school, you can still remove the video game from the hard drive and/or make yourself accountable to another person in terms of online gaming.

## 4. Have Positive Peer Interaction

- At this point in your recovery you need to use your free time to rekindle relationships or develop new ones. Participate in activities that encourage social interaction. This may be awkward at first. Be patient with yourself as you acquire new skills in interacting with friends and family.

# 6 BIBLICAL INSIGHTS

*Finally, brothers and sisters, whatever is true, whatever is noble, whatever is right, whatever is pure, whatever is lovely, whatever is admirable—if anything is excellent or praiseworthy—think about such things.*

*Philippians 4:8*

People who are constantly playing video games or are online find that their thoughts, their emotions, and everything about them are consumed by the experience. The Bible says that we should not be consumed with the things of this world because they pale in comparison to the things that are heavenly.

*But if we walk in the light, as he is in the light, we have fellowship with one another, and the blood of Jesus, his Son, purifies us from all sin.*

*1 John 1:7*

The Bible calls us as Christians to have fellowship with others in Christ and grow in our understanding of salvation through fellowship with them, as well as through the Bible. It is difficult if not impossible to do this when all of our time is spent in front of a computer or video game console. The Lord wants us to interact with other people and to fellowship with one another face-to-face and in the congregation.

*As iron sharpens iron, so one person sharpens another.*

*Proverbs 27:17*

There is value in welcoming and allowing others to disciple us and help us grow together. Interacting with real people, especially other believers, is the best way to stay sharp in life. A video game system or online website will not do this for us.

*Like a city whose walls are broken through is a person who lacks self-control.*

*Proverbs 25:28*

Often people who are addicted to video games or the internet do not realize how much time they are spending on these activities and are not exercising the necessary self-control to stop playing and do something else. God wants us to have self-control—one of the fruits of the Spirit given in Galatians 5—because without it, we are destined to fall and remain broken.

## PRAYER STARTER : 7

Lord, You are the master of our time and You desire to have first place in our heart and life. There is no greater reward than spending time with You, and so I pray You would take away from _____ the addiction to gaming or the internet so that he (she) may know You more intimately. It is not good for man to be alone or for us to have no fellowship outside our home. God, may You bring people into _____'s life to encourage and strengthen him (her) and may You fill his (her) thoughts with Your words and love. You care for us and love us. Thank You for the freedom we can experience in You . . .

## RECOMMENDED RESOURCES : 8

Careaga, Andrew. *Hooked on the Net.* Kregel, 2002.

Cash, Hilarie, Kim McDaniel, and Ken Lucas. *Video Games and Your Kids: How Parents Stay In Control.* Issues Press, 2008.

Clark, Neils, and Shavaun P. Scott. *Game Addiction: The Experience and the Effects.* McFarland, 2009.

Kern, Jan. *Eyes Online, Eyes on Life: A Journey Out of Online Obsession.* Standard, 2008.

Roberts, Kevin. *Cyber Junkie: Escaping the Gaming and Internet Trap.* Hazelden, 2010.

Shaw, Mark E. *Hope and Help for Video Game, TV, and Internet Addictions.* Focus, 2010.

Young, Kimberly S. *Internet Addiction: A Handbook and Guide to Evaluation and Treatment.* John Wiley, 2011.

### Websites

Net Addiction: www.netaddiction.com/index.php?option=com_content&view =article&id=18&Itemid=79

Online Gamers Anonymous: www.olganon.org/

Tech Addiction: www.techaddiction.ca/gaming-addictionstatistics.html#.ULAY kqPWqJU

Videogame Addiction: www.video-game-addiction.org/social-consequences.html

# 26 Kleptomania and Stealing

## 1 PORTRAITS

- Nancy comes from a wealthy family of five. Throughout her life she has lacked nothing she ever wanted. Although Nancy has all the money she needs, a very full closet, and generous parents, she struggles with a powerful urge that has taken control over her life. She finds herself bringing home items from stores and campus buildings every day that she did not pay for. She is overcome by guilt and anxious about being caught, but the behavior continues anyway. Her parents are unaware of Nancy's habit. She is afraid to tell them and seek help for fear of being arrested and bringing shame to the family name.

- Raul is a junior at a large inner-city high school. He has big dreams of becoming a petroleum engineer who will help his family move to a nice neighborhood and provide all their needs for them. He needs to attend college to realize his dreams. Unfortunately Raul's family cannot afford to send him to college right after high school. Desperate to achieve his goals as fast as possible, Raul joins a local, violent gang in an attempt to earn money fast. For initiation into the gang, Raul is forced to steal various items from an electronics shop. His attempt does not end well when he is caught, arrested, and sent to juvenile detention shortly thereafter.

- Jacob is an award-winning professor of neurobiology at one of the nation's most prestigious universities. His research has gained him widespread fame in the scientific community, and he has several resource books to his credit. He has the admiration of his colleagues as well as his family. Behind the mask of fame, glory, and success, however, lies a dark secret that Jacob has kept for more than twenty years. He suffers from an incessant need to steal items that are of no value to him. He even stole his son's rattle from his crib when he was a baby. No matter how hard he tries, the urges do not disappear but increase every time he resists the temptation to steal. Jacob's problem has gotten out of hand to the point where those around him are beginning to get suspicious.

# DEFINITIONS AND KEY THOUGHTS : 2

## Kleptomania

- *Kleptomania* is characterized by the *incessant need and psychological urge to steal* items of little to no value to the individual.
- Studies have indicated that less *than 1 percent of the general population* have this disorder, with a higher prevalence among those diagnosed with obsessive-compulsive disorder (7 percent) and bulimia (65 percent).[1]
- According to the DSM-IV-TR, the items stolen *are not taken as a result of need or financial lack,* but typically can be afforded by the individual.
- It is still *unclear whether kleptomania is in itself a psychological disorder* or a manifestation of an underlying psychological issue.[2]
- The DSM-IV-TR outlines *the following criteria* for arriving at a kleptomania diagnosis:[3]

  — The individual continually fails to resist the urge and temptation to engage in theft of items that are of little value to and not needed by the individual.
  — The individual experiences tension before stealing.
  — The tension is relieved by the act of stealing.
  — The theft is not due to any of the following: anger, revenge, delusions, hallucinations, or impaired judgment due to mental retardation, dementia, alcohol intoxication, and drug intoxication.

- While kleptomania is not a widespread problem in the general population, accurate forecasting can prove to be elusive due to the shame often attributed to the act of stealing. *Few people would be willing to admit* they struggle with this issue because of the shame and a fear of being turned in to authorities.
- Studies have shown *an estimated 5–10 percent of psychiatric cases* involve kleptomania. The disorder is more prevalent among women than men and typically begins during the late teens and early twenties.[4]
- Kleptomaniacs do not always enter a place with the intent to steal. *The behavior is often unplanned and spontaneous.* They also do not limit their theft to stores and public environments; they steal from friends and family members as well.[5]
- Kleptomania has been characterized as an *impulse-control disorder,* like pathological gambling or chronic hair-pulling. Typically it *occurs with other disorders* such as obsessive-compulsive, personality, and mood disorders.
- Although there is no consensus or conclusion regarding the causes of kleptomania, neuroscientists researching the issue believe it is *a problem associated with the frontal lobe area of the brain and the limbic system,* which controls moods and emotions. Kleptomania acts like other addictive behaviors that share similar neurotransmitters and pathways in the brain. The primary neurotransmitter suspected to be affected is *serotonin,* which is found in low levels in such conditions.[6]

- Research attributes some cases of kleptomania to *head trauma or brain injuries* suffered by the individual.[7]

- Kleptomania is usually *treated with a combination of medications and psychotherapy*. Medications used for treatment include *antidepressants*—selective serotonin reuptake inhibitors (SSRIs), such as Prozac; mood stabilizers, such as lithium-based Lithobid; antiseizure medication, such as Topamax and Depakene; and addiction medication, such as Revia and Vivitrol.[8]

- In counseling, *cognitive-behavioral therapy* is the preferred method used to treat kleptomania. Some techniques through this method include *covert sensitization* in which the kleptomaniac imagines facing the negative consequences of stealing until the urges subside.[9]

- Another technique sometimes used is *aversion therapy*, in which the kleptomaniac practices *mildly painful techniques,* such as holding his or her breath to create discomfort whenever there is the urge to steal. This then leads the individual to associate pain and discomfort with the urge to steal and reduces the impulse.[10]

- *Systematic desensitization* is used to cognitively treat kleptomania. In this approach the individual practices *relaxation techniques* and also pictures himself or herself controlling and overcoming the urge to steal.[11]

## Stealing

- Engaging in theft does not necessarily mean the individual is a kleptomaniac. Unlike kleptomania, *stealing is a broader problem* that may be engaged in for *various reasons*, including anger and antisocial behaviors.[12]

- One reason why people steal is an actual need for an item that they cannot afford. This is different from the impulse dynamics found in kleptomania. This stealing becomes a *means of survival*.

- People can steal *to maintain a drug addiction habit* that has diminished other resources. They steal to obtain the drugs they are addicted to and sustain the high associated with continued use.

- Stealing is also *part of organized crime*, which typically involves gangs who engage in the crime for a profit or initiation rituals.

## 3 ASSESSMENT INTERVIEW

1. How long have you been struggling with your intense urge to steal? At what age did you identify this urge?
2. Why do you steal? Do you do it because you need the items you take or are they typically items of little or no value to you?
3. Have you gone through financial hardship over the years?
4. Have you ever suffered from a brain injury?
5. Have you been placed on medications as a result of your brain injury? What are they and how often do you take them?

6. Have you ever been treated for an addiction or been in counseling for any other reason?
7. Has anyone, such as a family member, ever been hurt or expressed concern about your urge to steal or the act of stealing itself? Have your actions placed a strain on your marriage?
8. Do you use any type of illicit drug before you engage in stealing?
9. Have you ever been concerned about your stealing? Why or why not?
10. Are there other family members or close friends who regularly steal or struggle constantly with the urge to steal? Was this something you regularly observed while growing up?
11. Do you ever try to hide your tendency to steal from those around you?
12. Have you ever stolen from close friends or family?
13. What do you typically do with the items that you steal? Do you keep them, throw them away, give them as gifts?
14. Do you steal to support a drug habit or have you been involved with a gang?
15. Have you ever been caught stealing? What legal consequences did you face as a result?
16. What impact has your stealing had on your job or schoolwork? Have you been threatened to be dismissed by your boss due to your actions?
17. Have you ever tried to quit stealing? How successful has any attempt to quit been? Is there anyone who could help you quit?
18. Do you have a good support system or do you try to manage your problems by yourself?
19. How would quitting your habit of stealing improve or impact your family or significant relationships?
20. Would you describe yourself as being of strong faith? If so, what role has your faith in God played in your desire to quit or past attempts at quitting?

# WISE COUNSEL 4

Kleptomania and stealing are not the same thing. While both involve theft, kleptomania is a compulsive disorder that goes beyond the act of stealing. Keep in mind that incidents of stealing do not automatically define a client as a kleptomaniac. The client may not readily admit to having a problem or engaging in theft for fear of being turned in to law enforcement authorities. For this reason it is important to develop a trusting relationship with your client.

Unlike casual stealing, kleptomania is not necessarily a condition the client decided to have or can simply stop. This is due to the psychological or mental factors that may be involved. Kleptomania is more of a compulsive behavior disorder that can develop autonomously, while stealing involves more intentional planning and engagement in the act for some form of gain.

Do not make an immediate character judgment about the client. Kleptomania is not a respecter of persons and can affect people of any race, gender, and socioeconomic status. Since the disorder typically involves stealing items of little to no value, it is unlikely that the client steals for profit. Also keep in mind there may be an underlying brain injury that set the client on the path of kleptomania.

Interview the client's spouse and other family members who are old enough to understand the issues surrounding the client's stealing to help assess any challenging and enabling behavior on their part. This process also assists in determining the strength of available support systems. Discuss alternative behaviors that are beneficial in challenging and encouraging the client to refrain from stealing or greatly reduce his or her urge to steal.

# 5 ACTION STEPS

## 1. Get a Medical Checkup

- Going through a medical exam will help determine whether or not your kleptomania was brought on by any trauma to the brain.
- A thorough examination may determine whether medications might have a beneficial impact on your behavior.

## 2. Sign a Contract

- Working with your counselor, commit to a system of accountability, which includes your agreement to seek the help of a professional counselor when you have an uncontrollable urge to steal. *The success of this step will depend on the severity of your client's kleptomania.*
- Sign a contract with your counselor that states you agree to the system of accountability the two of you have worked out.

## 3. Get Professional Help

- If you have not had a brain injury, a professional counselor will be helpful in treating your kleptomania, especially if your stealing is related to an addiction or is the result of a dual disorder with a mental illness.
- Seeking help through a Christian program for recovering kleptomaniacs or addicts will be very helpful.

## 4. Adopt Quitting-Related Behaviors

- Commit yourself to behaviors and activities that help reduce your urge to steal, especially activities that limit your access to items you might want to steal. Plan certain activities to do when you feel a strong urge to steal, such as taking a walk, playing a sport, or talking to someone on the phone.
- Avoid any environments that make stealing easy, such as department stores, malls, and any shops with many items on display.

## 5. Encourage Family Members to Seek Support

- *Encourage family members of the client to seek a Christ-centered support program for families of kleptomaniacs or compulsive stealers.*

# BIBLICAL INSIGHTS 6

*Anyone who has been stealing must steal no longer, but must work, doing something useful with their own hands, that they may have something to share with those in need.*

*Ephesians 4:28*

According to this Scripture, the Lord desires everyone to engage in honest work that provides what is needed to live and function. The Lord equates stealing with dishonesty.

Even when profit is made honestly, God encourages us to remember those in need and share a portion with them. Being able to bless others in this manner is a rewarding experience.

*The commandments, "You shall not commit adultery," "You shall not murder," "You shall not steal," "You shall not covet," and whatever other command there may be, are summed up in this one command: "Love your neighbor as yourself."*

*Romans 13:9*

The Lord makes it clear that stealing shows a lack of love or regard for others. One manifestation of a healthy self-identity or God-esteem is the ability to show love toward others as people who are created in the image of God.

*Do not steal. Do not lie. Do not deceive one another.*

*Leviticus 19:11*

According to God's standard, stealing not only involves the act of taking something that does not belong to us but is also associated with dealing falsely and lying to others. Thus stealing leads a person to commit more than one sin before God.

The act of stealing not only impacts our relationship with God but also affects our relationships with others.

*Do not trust in extortion or put vain hopes in stolen goods; though your riches increase, do not set your heart on them.*

*Psalm 62:10*

Placing our trust in riches gained from stealing or robbery amounts to nothing in the end. It will ultimately result in separation from God.

When our hearts are set on riches and materialistic gain, we leave little room for God to dwell in and operate. He wants us to give our whole hearts to Him first and place our trust in Him above anything else that competes for our attention.

*For the love of money is a root of all kinds of evil. Some people, eager for money, have wandered from the faith and pierced themselves with many griefs.*

*1 Timothy 6:10*

Loving money in place of loving God leads to various problems including stealing. The problems derived from loving money first can cause tremendous pain and suffering to ourselves and those around us.

Our faith in Christ is also affected when we engage in acts of theft as a result of our love for money. We become more distant in our walk with God and lose the passion and love we have for Him.

*No temptation has overtaken you except what is common to mankind. And God is faithful; he will not let you be tempted beyond what you can bear. But when you are tempted, he will also provide a way out so that you can endure it.*

*1 Corinthians 10:13*

There is no temptation that catches God by surprise. He understands the complexities of kleptomania and all other temptations better than any person could ever hope to understand. He will always help you through the temptation and provide a way of escape when it becomes more than you can bear.

*But he was pierced for our transgressions, he was crushed for our iniquities; the punishment that brought us peace was on him, and by his wounds we are healed.*

*Isaiah 53:5*

No issue or problem is too hard for the Lord to handle. No sin is too great for Him to forgive. He suffered the brutality of the cross and rose in victory to heal our suffering, bring us peace, and ultimately reconcile us with the Father. He took all the suffering, sin, and problems we face on Himself when He surrendered to the cross. Thus, if we steal or suffer from kleptomania, the Lord can bring us healing. Even though it may not be instantaneous, He will always lead and guide us to become well in Him.

# 7 PRAYER STARTER

Lord, I thank You for _____'s life and his (her) willingness to address and face this issue. It is not easy to admit to having a problem, and I thank You for the courage _____ has shown. I pray that You will provide him (her) strength to resist the urge to steal and to see this healing and recovery process to its end. Be with his (her) family and those involved; comfort them and give them a spirit of support. Surround _____ with people who will encourage him (her) throughout this difficult journey . . .

# RECOMMENDED RESOURCES 8

Berg, Jim. *Welcome to Freedom That Lasts.* Journeyforth, 2011.

Clinton, Tim. *Turn Your Life Around.* FaithWords, 2006.

Cupchick, Will. *Why Honest People Shoplift or Commit Other Acts of Theft: Assessment and Treatment of "Atypical Theft Offenders"—A Comprehensive Resource for Professionals and Laypersons.* Booklocker.com, 2002.

Goldman, Marcus J. *Kleptomania: The Compulsion to Steal—What Can Be Done?* New Horizon, 1997.

Grant, John, S. W. Kim, and Gregory Fricchione. *Stop Me Because I Can't Stop Myself: Taking Control of Impulse Behavior.* McGraw-Hill, 2004.

Shulman, Terrence Daryl. *Something for Nothing: Shoplifting Addiction and Recovery.* InfinityPublishing.com, 2004.

## Websites

Kleptomaniacs Anonymous: www.kleptomaniacsanonymous.com/

Mayo Clinic: www.mayoclinic.com/health/kleptomania/DS01034

National Institutes of Health: www.ncbi.nlm.nih.gov/pmc/articles/PMC535651/

Shoplifters Anonymous: www.shopliftingprevention.org/saredirect2/

# 27 Pornography and Sexual Addiction

## 1 PORTRAITS

- John is a thirty-year-old father of two children, married six years to his wonderful wife, Cassie, and is the owner of a thriving small business. He is also a small group leader in his church and a respected civic leader in the community. Outwardly John's life seems perfect, but Cassie caught him looking at pornography on the internet yesterday. After a heated discussion, the truth behind the lies finally came out. John has been wrestling with an addiction to pornography since he was twelve years old. He used to look at his father's *Playboy* magazines stashed in the garage tool bin and has been looking at porn his entire adult life. His wife never knew until now. When John was on the computer, Cassie always thought he was working. John has known for a long time that he has a problem and has tried to stop more times than he can count. He does not want to hurt his family, but the addiction is more than he can handle.

- Henry was raised in a godly Christian home, attended church faithfully for the eighteen years he was under his parents' roof, and vowed to keep his virginity until marriage. Before Henry left home for college, he never really wanted to look at pornography, let alone live a promiscuous lifestyle. However, during his freshman year at a local state university with non-Christian roommates, Henry found himself immersed in a dorm room filled with computers displaying pornographic websites, X-rated magazines, and roommates who slept around with any girl they could. The exposure to this sexual immorality created a lust that increasingly consumed Henry's thought life and behavior. By his senior year in college, he had stopped going to class and was a full-blown sex addict. He has tried to hide his behavior from his parents, but they have already seen the change in him. Henry does not like the path his life has taken but does not know where to turn. How can he get his life back on track? To whom should he turn for help?

- Sally started innocently enough looking at pornography with some of her girl-friends. She wanted to know what the big attraction was for the guys. Things progressed and before long, she began experimenting with some of the acts she was watching, knowing she was trying to fill an empty void in her life. Sally grew up in a broken home and was sexually abused by her stepfather when she was eleven. Now, ten years later, she is promiscuous and constantly fights her growing sense of shame and guilt but has been drawn into the emotional and physical high of stretching her sexual boundaries. She has had two abortions and has been treated for a sexually transmitted disease several times. Sally is beginning to wonder if suicide is the only way to be free of her torment.

# DEFINITIONS AND KEY THOUGHTS  2

- Approximately *forty million people* in the United States use the internet to *view pornography.*[1]
- Of all search engine requests, *25 percent are pornography related.*[2]
- *Seventy-two million internet users* per year visit pornography sites.[3]
- In 2003 more than *50 percent of all online purchases were related to sexual activity,* with 30 million users logging on to pornographic websites on a daily basis. Nearly 25 million Americans access pornographic sites 1–10 hours per day and another 4.7 million spend in excess of 11 hours every day viewing pornography.[4]
- There are nearly *5 million pornographic websites* with more than 300 million pages (20 percent of which are related to child pornography). The porn industry takes in *more than 15 billion dollars every year* with more than 1 billion dollars in DVD rentals (55 percent from hotel viewers). Almost 10 percent of the U.S. population is sexually addicted with 28 percent of this group being women.[5]
- *Sexual addiction* affects as many as *20 to 30 million people* in the United States alone.[6]
- *Sexual addiction* is a *physical, cognitive, emotional, spiritual, relational, and behavioral problem* that is grounded in compulsive behavior. In this addiction *pornography, prostitution, masturbation*, and *deviant sex acts* are used to fill a deep craving for intimacy and emotional needs in an improper way.[7]
- Some types of sexual addictions are *pornography, cybersex, excessive masturbation, prostitution, serial affairs, strip clubs, massage parlors*, and *fantasy.*[8]
- One element of sexual addiction is *risk taking*. There is often the emotional/physical thrill involved in *trying to get away with extramarital affairs, pornography, prostitution*, and *other sexual acts*.
- Sexual addictions and pornography are sometimes *used to mask pain* from both the past and present. Understanding the warning signs can help identify sexually addictive behavior.
- Sexual addiction in extreme cases *can lead to exhibitionism, child molestation, sexual deviancy, abuse, and rape*. These extreme cases are not the norm.[9]
- Most people who struggle with sexual addiction are not necessarily deviant but are *trapped in a cycle of dysfunctional behaviors and thought processes*.

# ASSESSMENT INTERVIEW  3

1. Is your pornography or sexual addiction a secret from others (including a spouse or loved one)?
2. What forms does your sexual addiction take?
3. Have you ever engaged in child pornography or child sexual abuse? Note: if the counselor is licensed by a state regulatory agency or is mandated by the state in his or her capacity, a report may need to be filed with local Child Protective Services.

4. Do you have a personal history of childhood sexual abuse?

5. Do you masturbate, watch pornography, or commit other sexual acts to make you feel better when you are depressed, lonely, feeling unloved, or hiding pain?

6. Do you avoid sex with your spouse or any other forms of friendship and meaningful relationships to masturbate or watch pornography? Do your sexual acts keep you from caring for others' needs?

7. Do you think about watching pornography, masturbating, or other sexual acts on a continual basis? Do these thoughts dominate your thought life?

8. Has pornography caused you a financial, time, or relationship strain?

9. Do you often tell yourself you will stop and never watch pornography again only to go right back to it?

10. Are you willing to commit to actions and accountability that will help you defeat your addiction?

11. Do you have a personal relationship with Jesus Christ? If you do not, would you like to know how to have the peace and strength that only God can give?

12. If you have professed Christ as your Lord and Savior, will you commit to daily Bible reading and prayer for strength and support from God?[10]

# 4 WISE COUNSEL

Understand that every form of sexual activity comes with strong addictive tendencies. Even a sexual relationship in marriage can become addictive. Fantasy is often the base for sexual addiction because thoughts create sexual arousal and result in a neurochemical high.[11] Pornography and masturbation are the most common types of acting out behavior.

When assessing behavior, look at past history and present actions for clues of:[12]

- uncontrollability and compulsiveness
- high or low tolerances for sexual thoughts, actions, and images
- an escalating pattern of inappropriate sexual behavior
- poor self-image or feelings of inadequacy
- childhood sexual experiences and/or abuse

Appropriate treatments may include:[13]

- accountability partners who call, text, and keep in touch
- abstinence from any form of sex for a period of time (for example, ninety days)
- personal therapy through one-on-one counseling
- group therapy through a 12-step or other group therapy program
- developing alternative methods for gaining self-control and replacing the addiction with something healthy and balanced
- spiritual counseling and biblically based spiritual direction
- marriage counseling with both husband and wife participating in marital therapy

There are no easy fixes, as sexual addictions develop over time. Repair, forgiveness, and true healing will take place progressively. The client must be dedicated to working through this over the course of his or her life.

## ACTION STEPS 5

### 1. Stop the Behavior

- Stop the behavior by establishing barriers that prevent or limit access to pornography. Load pornography-blocking software on your computers and give the password to an accountability partner.
- Be resolute and make no room for sexual addiction in your life. If the sexual addiction includes strip clubs or prostitutes, avoid the areas of town where these are available, especially when there is no one else with you.
- Do not allow yourself to be alone for long periods of time.
- Remove identifying information from your phone regarding people or businesses that are part of your addiction and delete all pornographic information from your computer hard drive.

### 2. Get Professional Counseling

- To work through the hidden feelings and triggers from the past that have fueled your sexual addiction and behaviors, you may need to see a counselor who is trained to handle sexual addictions.

### 3. Develop an Action Plan

- Your counselor will help you make a plan of action that will start the rebuilding process.
- Name one or more accountability partners and keep in daily contact with them about your routine, habits, temptations, and any relapses.
- Find encouragement from church, family, friends, or an addiction support group.
- Know what triggers your desires and work to put something healthy in their place.
- Know when you are vulnerable and need to call for help; do not be afraid to leave a situation of temptation, even if it means confusion or embarrassment.

### 4. Develop a New Identity

- Develop a new identity based on God's truth in your life and the knowledge that He loves you and you are complete in Him.
- Your habits, patterns, and lifestyle have been established and molded around your addiction. Now that you have left that lifestyle behind, you must replace your old schedule and mind-set regarding day-to-day living with a new schedule

of safe activities, patterns, and lifestyle choices that encourage healthy relational and spiritual growth.

## 5. Maintain Your New Way of Life

- Develop habits that will maintain treatment gains and newly acquired skills, sustaining ongoing growth.
- Scripture memory, healthy new relationships, avoiding places of temptation, and making the daily choice not to return to your addiction all aid in a culture of freedom.
- Do not stop working with your counselors or therapy groups unless you are discharged from their care. You may think you are over your addiction, but just one mistake can pull you back into a spiral of disaster. You must be committed to this new lifestyle for the rest of your life.

# 6 BIBLICAL INSIGHTS

*For all have sinned and fall short of the glory of God, and all are justified freely by his grace through the redemption that came by Christ Jesus.*

*Romans 3:23–24*

We are all sinners and have committed wrong. The first step is to admit our sin before a holy God and realize Jesus offers forgiveness and freedom from sin entirely through His grace.

*You have heard that it was said, "You shall not commit adultery." But I tell you that anyone who looks at a woman lustfully has already committed adultery with her in his heart.*

*Matthew 5:27–28*

Jesus teaches that heart attitudes are just as important as our actions. Thinking lustfully is just as sinful as committing adultery, because in our minds we have already committed the act. Jesus teaches us to separate ourselves and our minds from the evil, to keep away from it so it does not eventually destroy us!

*So I find this law at work: Although I want to do good, evil is right there with me. For in my inner being I delight in God's law; but I see another law at work in me, waging war against the law of my mind and making me a prisoner of the law of sin at work within me. What a wretched man I am! Who will rescue me from this body that is subject to death? Thanks be to God, who delivers me through Jesus Christ our Lord!*

*Romans 7:21–25*

The apostle Paul says that the spiritual nature inside of us wants to do the right things before God, but the sinful nature in us is constantly fighting within us to do wrong. Our sinful nature wants to keep us slaves and prisoners of sin. However, we do not have to live that way. Jesus rescued us from that prison, and we are now free to serve Him.

*You will keep in perfect peace those whose minds are steadfast, because they trust in you. Trust in the LORD forever, for the LORD, the LORD himself, is the Rock eternal.*

*Isaiah 26:3–4*

Our real battle is over the mind and thought life. If we keep our minds focused on God's truth and promises, only then can we have God's perfect peace. He alone provides the ability to stay focused on good things, rather than the negative.

*But each person is tempted when they are dragged away by their own evil desire and enticed.*

*James 1:14*

Everyone is presented with choices that may seem good on the surface but only feed fleshly or evil desires. If we are tempted, we must be careful of letting evil desires grow unchecked, breeding lust and discontent in our hearts.

*No temptation has overtaken you except what is common to mankind. And God is faithful; he will not let you be tempted beyond what you can bear. But when you are tempted, he will also provide a way out so that you can endure it.*

*1 Corinthians 10:13*

There is nothing new out there that someone else has not already been tempted with, but God always give us the ability either to leave it behind and run away from the sin or to resist the temptation. The choice is always ours to do either right or wrong.

## PRAYER STARTER 7

Dear Jesus, please give strength, comfort, and determination to _____ to experience true deliverance when temptation comes and the ability to repent and turn back to You. Help _____ put godly and healthy relationships in the place of sexual addictions. Give him (her) the ability to trust You and to stay active in using accountability partners. Thank You for freedom from guilt, shame, and other harmful emotions . . .

# 8 RECOMMENDED RESOURCES

Arterburn, Stephen, and Fred Stoeker. *Every Man's Battle*. WaterBrook, 2000.

———. *Every Young Man's Battle*. WaterBrook, 2009.

Carnes, Patrick *Out of the Shadows: Understanding Sexual Addiction*. Hazelden, 2001.

Carnes, Patrick, David L. Delmonico, and Elizabeth Griffin. *In the Shadows of the Net: Breaking Free of Compulsive Online Sexual Behavior*. Hazelden, 2001.

Clinton, Tim, and Mark Laaser. *The Quick-Reference Guide to Sexuality and Relationship Counseling*. Baker, 2010.

Crosse, Clay, Renee Crosse, and Mark Tabb. *I Surrender All: Rebuilding a Marriage Broken by Pornography*. NavPress, 2005.

Dann, Bucky. *Addiction: Pastoral Responses*. Abingdon, 2002.

Earle, Ralph H., and Mark Laaser. *The Pornography Trap: Setting Pastors and Lay Persons Free from Sexual Addiction*. Beacon Hill Press, 2002.

Ethridge, Shannon, and Stephen Arterburn. *Every Woman's Battle*. WaterBrook Press, 2003.

Frederick, Dennis. *Conquering Pornography: Overcoming the Addiction*. Pleasant Word, 2007.

Harley, Willard F., and Jennifer H. Chalmers. *Surviving an Affair*. Baker, 1998.

Hart, Archibald D. *The Sexual Man: Masculinity without Guilt*. Word, 1994.

Laaser, Debra. *Shattered Vows*. Zondervan, 2012.

Laaser, Mark. *Becoming a Man of Valor*. Beacon Hill Press, 2011.

———. *Healing Wounds of Sexual Addiction*. Zondervan, 2004.

———. *7 Principles of Highly Accountable Men*. Beacon Hill Press, 2011.

———. *Taking Every Thought Captive*. Beacon Hill Press, 1997.

Laaser, Mark, and Debra Laaser. *The Seven Desires of Every Heart*. Zondervan, 2008.

Laaser, Mark, and R. Earle. *Pornography: A Resource for Ministry Leaders*. Beacon Hill Press, 2012.

Means, Marsha. *Living with Your Husband's Secret Wars*. Baker, 1999.

Schaumburg, Harry W. *False Intimacy: Understanding the Struggle of Sexual Addiction*. NavPress, 1992.

Stoeker, Fred, and Brenda Stoeker. *Every Heart Restored: A Wife's Guide to Healing in the Wake of a Husband's Sexual Sin*. WaterBrook, 2011.

Weaver, Andrew J., Charlene Hosenfeld, and Harold G. Koenig. *Counseling Persons with Addictions and Compulsions: A Handbook for Clergy and Other Helping Professionals*. Pilgrim, 2007.

Wilson, Meg. *Hope after Betrayal: Healing When Sexual Addiction Invades Your Marriage*. Monarch, 2007.

## Websites

Faithful and True Ministries: www.faithfulandtrue.com/

New Life: Every Man's Battle: www.newlife.com/emb/

Sex Addicts Anonymous: www.saa-recovery.org/

The Society for the Advancement of Sexual Health: www.sash.net/sexual-addiction

Web MD: www.webmd.com/sexual-conditions/guide/sexual-addiction

# Shopping and Excessive Collecting 28

PORTRAITS 1

- Beth said she was just window shopping, moving from store to store and looking at the deals on sale. She had been good with her money and only purchased a few small items, that is until she came to a store where almost everything was on clearance. Beth went inside and all she could think about were the great deals she did not want to miss and how much she would save. At the end of the day, she had spent several hundred dollars and walked shamefully out of the store with three bags of clothes, three more than she had planned on buying. This was rapidly becoming a common theme, and the resulting arguments with her husband were growing more tense every week as they tried to manage their budget.

- Nate opened the door carefully and slowly walked into the guest room. He did not want to knock over any of the model cars that filled the entire room. Years of buying every imaginable kind of collectible car was taking its toll. Nate had one more to put in place but as he stood there and looked around the room, it seemed that there was nowhere to put it. He shrugged and yelled down the hall to his wife, "Hon, we are going to need another room for the cars!"

- Ruth would always get depressed after going shopping. She did not really understand it but every time she returned with a bag or two full of clothes, jewelry, or other items she "absolutely needed," she always felt embarrassed by how much she had just spent. It was probably a good thing no one ever went shopping with her, but the shame and guilt grew to the point where she began to shop more and more online because it felt less awkward. Unfortunately she started spending even more than before. Sometimes Ruth would stay up late into the night and watch the infomercial programs, unable to resist buying from the sales that were being promoted. She knew she had a problem but did not seem able to control her buying habits. She just wanted the anxiety to go away and it always seemed that buying something would help; in the end it just produced more negative feelings.

## DEFINITIONS AND KEY THOUGHTS 2

- *Compulsive-buying disorder* (better known as CBD or *oniomania*) is characterized by excessive shopping cognitions and buying behaviors that lead to distress or

233

impairment. While some of the symptoms may be related to bipolar disorder, they are not limited to manic or hypomanic episodes.

- *Excessive collecting* is defined as the need to continue to collect a certain type of item for its intrinsic worth and/or for the purpose of simply having the largest collection.

- CBD is linked to a number of different problems, such as *anxiety disorders, substance-use disorders,* and *eating disorders.* It is also affiliated with *impulse-control disorders.*[1]

- According to the research, *CBD affects 5–8 percent of the U.S. population,* and *80–95 percent* of people affected by CBD are *women.*[2]

- CBD is difficult to classify because of the *comorbidity* associated with the disorder. It has been *linked to obsessive-compulsive disorder and mood disorders,* as well as *impulse-control disorders.*

- *Excessive collecting* has often been associated with hoarding, but there are several differences between the two. Excessive collecting involves the *collecting of a single item or type of item,* whereas hoarding rarely has a specified range in terms of objects.

- Eventually hoarding begins to impair daily functioning and limits an individual's ability to live a normal life, while *excessive collecting may simply take up a room in the house.*

- Excessive collecting and compulsive shopping fall under a similar category of *obsessive-compulsive disorder.*

- Excessive collecting is different from hoarding in the sense that the *excessive collectors are usually very neat* and take good care of their collection. Hoarders continue to randomly pile up more and more items with no sense of order or care.

- Hoarders also differ from collectors in the sense that they feel shame or embarrassment when confronted with their hoarding problem, but *collectors are often proud of their collections* and revel in the chance to share them with fellow collectors.

- Both CBD and excessive collecting are related to *impulse control issues* in that both groups *cannot help buying the items in question* and both *receive an emotional and/or psychological release* with each purchase.

- The *onset* of CBD appears to be in the *late teens and early twenties.*[3]

- There is some evidence that CBD *runs in families* that struggle with *substance abuse disorders, anxiety disorders,* and *major depression.*[4]

- *Symptoms* of CBD include an *obsessive preoccupation with shopping and spending* and devoting large amounts of time to those behaviors. It is a continuous problem not a seasonal one, such as a Christmas shopping spree.

- Studies have shown there are *four distinct phases* to CBD: *anticipation, preparation, shopping,* and *spending.*[5]

- Often those suffering from CBD *shop alone and are embarrassed* by their actions.

- *Causes* of CBD range from *cultural influences* to *neurobiological theories* centering on disruptions in neurotransmission with the serotonergic, dopaminergic, or opioid systems.

- *Treatment* for both CBD and excessive collecting, due to their impulse disorder components, have included *the use of selective serotonin reuptake inhibitors (SSRIs)* to balance the neurotransmission.
- *Cognitive-behavioral therapies* have also been used in conjunction with a medication regimen to treat both excessive collecting and CBD. The most successful were those using *group treatments*, while self-help books and psychopharmacologic treatment studies have yielded mixed results.[6]

# ASSESSMENT INTERVIEW : 3

1. Do you feel overly preoccupied with your shopping, collecting, or spending habits?
2. Do you feel out of control when you are shopping or collecting?
3. Do you feel anxious or depressed until you actually purchase the item you are considering? Do you shop to relieve stress or feelings of anger and disappointment?
4. Do you experience a sense of shame or guilt related to your shopping or collecting habits?
5. How often do you buy items on credit that you normally would not purchase?
6. Have you had to juggle your budget or have you experienced a debt crisis related to your shopping or collecting behaviors?
7. Have you tried to control your shopping and spending or collecting before but have been unsuccessful?
8. How much money would you say you have spent on your collecting?
9. Can you think of any negative feelings or consequences that have come as a result of your collecting, shopping, and spending?
10. Has your excessive shopping or collecting negatively impacted your relationships?

# WISE COUNSEL : 4

Shopping and excessive collecting are frequently categorized as obsessive-compulsive disorders because of their behavioral orientation and therefore are not always viewed as addictions. Behaviors can be modified, and this offers hope for treatment outcomes. Excessive collecting can be a precursor to hoarding and is often linked with that disorder; however, collecting itself is not the problem. Many times collectors will invest their sense of identity and well-being into collecting instead of focusing on other priorities in life. They may not be able to manage the obsessive-compulsive dynamics and therefore collect to ease their anxiety or stress. It is important to explain that possessions will never provide ultimate fulfillment and self-identity needs to be affirmed through a vibrant relationship with Christ.

Shopping is a normal pastime for many people; however, it can also lead to financial ruin for a lot of individuals. Compulsive buying disorder manifests when a person cannot resist the urge to buy something because of the anxiety he or she is experiencing. For individuals like this, support and accountability are necessary. Often they are ashamed and feel guilty for their behavior and would like to stop if they could. Nevertheless, the shopping addiction may also point to other problems and more deeply rooted issues, such as problems with self-image, low self-esteem, family problems, or untreated anxiety.

# 5 ACTION STEPS

## 1. Admit There Is a Problem

- It is important to admit that you have a problem and that you cannot resist the urge to buy. Whether it is the urge to buy whenever you go shopping or the urge to buy the items you are collecting, your behavior is causing problems in life and needs to be addressed. Recognizing and admitting the problem is the first step you must take before you will be able to address adequately the underlying issues.

## 2. Destroy Credit Cards

- Destroy credit cards if you use them to buy more than you should, and set up an accountability system that oversees your bank and checking accounts. These actions can help significantly because people often use quick and easily accessible funds without full awareness of the eventual consequences that the misuse of monetary assets or credit can cause. It is always easy to use a credit card for a purchase without thinking about where the money will eventually come from.

## 3. Shop with a Friend or Family Member

- It is also usually easier to withstand and resist the urge or temptation to spend money when you have someone there to talk you out of impulse buying. Someone with CBD is less likely to buy an item when others are present, watching you make the purchase. Accountability to others brings a more balanced perspective.

## 4. Find Other Enjoyable Pastimes

- Collecting and shopping are two activities that can literally take up an entire day. Whether or not it is sitting online and surfing on eBay, for example, or going to the mall and roaming for hours, these are time-consuming activities. Filling time with more constructive experiences can be beneficial and productive. When you decide to give up destructive or dysfunctional habits, you must replace them with healthier ones so you aren't tempted to return to the activities you gave up.

# BIBLICAL INSIGHTS : 6

*Do not store up for yourselves treasures on earth, where moths and vermin destroy, and where thieves break in and steal. But store up for yourselves treasures in heaven, where moths and vermin do not destroy, and where thieves do not break in and steal. For where your treasure is, there your heart will be also.*

*Matthew 6:19–21*

People who compulsively buy or collect excessively may base their self-worth on possessions versus finding their treasures in heaven. They are putting everything they have, their heart, soul, and mind, as well as their time, into things that will not last in eternity with them. God does not desire these things as much as He desires relationship with His creation.

*She considers a field and buys it; out of her earnings she plants a vineyard. She sets about her work vigorously; her arms are strong for her tasks. She sees that her trading is profitable, and her lamp does not go out at night.*

*Proverbs 31:16–18*

The Bible recognizes the wise behavior of balanced stewardship. Individuals who have a shopping addiction struggle with saying no to impulsive buying regardless of the cost or what sort of financial problems may result from the decision. This Scripture speaks to the process of weighing the cost and not acting imprudently.

*No temptation has overtaken you except what is common to mankind. And God is faithful; he will not let you be tempted beyond what you can bear. But when you are tempted, he will also provide a way out so that you can endure it.*

*1 Corinthians 10:13*

God will not leave us without a means of escape regarding temptation. If the urge to buy or collect something is overwhelming, leaving us helpless to resist, God will provide a way out. His desire is that we experience freedom from addiction.

*"I have the right to do anything," you say—but not everything is beneficial. "I have the right to do anything"—but I will not be mastered by anything.*

*1 Corinthians 6:12*

Compulsive shoppers and collectors are enslaved by their behavior. While shopping and collecting are not inherently bad and we are no longer under the law, God does not want us to be a slave to anything of this world. Self-control is a fruit of the Holy Spirit and brings with it true freedom in Christ.

## 7 PRAYER STARTER

Lord, You desire for us to value the things of heaven and to be good stewards of our financial resources. We ask that You break the chains of compulsive shopping (excessive collecting) in _____'s life. He (she) has been unable to stop on his (her) own, but with Your grace and guidance You will do mighty works beyond anything we can ever ask or think. Remove every anxious thought from _____. Help him (her) treasure You above all else and experience the freedom that comes from trusting You completely in all things . . .

## 8 RECOMMENDED RESOURCES

Grayson, Jonathan. *Freedom from Obsessive Compulsion.* Berkley, 2004.

Hawkins, David. *Breaking Everyday Addictions: Finding Freedom from the Things That Trip Us Up.* Harvest House, 2008.

Osbron, Ian. *Can Christianity Cure Obsessive Compulsive Disorder?* Brazos, 2007.

Weaver, Andrew J. *Counseling Persons with Addictions and Compulsions.* Pilgrim, 2007.

### Websites

About.com: www.addictions.about.com/od/lesserknownaddictions/a/shoppingadd.htm

National Institutes of Health: www.ncbi.nlm.nih.gov/pmc/articles/PMC1805733/

Web MD: www.webmd.com/mental-health/features/shopping-spree-addiction

# Technology and Social Networking 29

- Susan and her parents were driving to a ski resort in the Rockies for the week and they were about four hours into the trip. The vacation was supposed to be a relaxing experience when the family would have a chance to connect and fellowship with one another. However, the battery in Susan's phone died, and she did not bring her laptop because she thought her cell phone would be sufficient. Now she had no way of contacting her friends and being on Facebook, Twitter, or texting. She became nervous, anxious, and jittery and started to complain about "surviving" the rest of the drive. She knew her friends needed to know what she was doing and she could not communicate with them!

- David was scheduled to go to a movie at 6:30 p.m. with his friends but before he could leave to meet the group, one of his friends on Facebook sent him a new interactive game request. The next thing David remembered was his parents coming in to tell him good night. He had skipped dinner and the half dozen text messages from his friends wondering why he wasn't at the movie. He was completely absorbed in this new virtual world and even though it was pure fantasy, it was still intoxicating.

- Mary could never imagine not having social media to stay connected with the outside world. Checking Facebook was almost always the first thing she did when she got up in the morning and the last thing before she went to bed. Her biggest thrill was adding names to her Twitter and Facebook accounts. It was a fierce competition among many of her peers to have the most contacts. Recently Mary was scrolling through her friends list on Facebook, feeling good about how many names were displayed. She stared at some of the newer faces. Then it dawned on her that she had more than 1,500 Facebook friends but did not know most of them personally!

## DEFINITIONS AND KEY THOUGHTS 2

- *Internet addiction disorder* (IAD) is the condition of someone who uses the internet obsessively to the point of experiencing an emotional high similar to that of gambling or other highly addictive behaviors.

- *Facebook addiction disorder* (FAD) is a more recent term used to describe excessive hours spent on Facebook, representing so much time that an individual's life is drastically affected and there is little sense of a healthy balance in the person's life.

- Both of these terms are relatively new (within the past ten years) but have been added to the addiction lexicon due to the explosion of *time-consuming social media sites* such as Facebook, MySpace, and Twitter.

- Recent studies have shown that Facebook and Twitter are *more addictive than tobacco and alcohol,* and, as for someone trying to quit these substances, when someone quits using the social media sites they may experience *emotional and psychological withdrawal symptoms.*

- Facebook users tend to be more *extraverted and narcissistic* compared to infrequent or nonusers and have a *lower self-esteem* than the general population.[1]

- As of 2011 there were over *500 million active Facebook users* (1 out of every 13 persons in the world); 28 percent check their accounts on a cell phone before getting out of bed in the morning and 61 percent must check at least once per day; the fastest growing dynamic is Millennials—the generation following Generation X—(with a 74 percent growth rate in a one-year period); more than 70 percent of U.S. citizens use Facebook and each person has an average of 130 friends; 57 percent of people talk more frequently online than in face-to-face communication; 19 percent of Facebook users identify themselves as having an addiction; 69 percent of Facebook gamers are women; and 53 percent of women routinely participate in social media on a weekly basis.[2]

- There are *five key symptoms of Facebook addiction*: (1) withdrawal symptoms when trying to quit, (2) virtual dates—telling someone to be online at a certain time instead of going and meeting somewhere face-to-face, (3) fake friends, (4) a reduction of normal social/recreational activities, and (5) tolerance, which means the individual can no longer function normally without stimulation from Facebook.

- Facebook, Twitter, and MySpace *appeal to the relational needs of many people*; however, these social media sites greatly devalue and change the concept of intimacy, as well as the dynamics of close and personal relationships.

- The University of Maryland's International Center for Media and the Public Agenda completed a study in which they found four in five students had *significant mental and physical distress, panic, confusion, and extreme isolation* when forced to unplug from their technology sources for an entire day.[3]

- A "clear majority" of almost 1,000 university students, interviewed at 12 campuses in 10 countries, including Britain, America, and China, were *unable to voluntarily avoid their gadgets* for one full day.[4]

- Eight to 18-year-olds devote an average of *14.5 hours each week using entertainment media,* a large portion of which is through social networking sites.[5]

- The *age group that dominates social networking sites is 35–44-year-olds,* followed by Millennials (18–28 years old), with only 3 percent being 65 years old or older.[6]

- Social networking and the rate at which people use the internet is *changing the dynamics of how the brain processes information.* There are an increasing number of problems associated with using books and articles and processing linear information because of the constant bombardment of information and data overload.

- People are beginning to depend on social networking websites for the purpose of *relationship building* and *information acquisition* instead of using traditional formats.
- Of those using social networking sites, *26 percent are under the age of 24.*
- Of *Twitter* users, *64 percent are 35 years or older, whereas 61 percent of Facebook users are 35 or older.*[7]
- Social networking, while having positive qualities, can also easily become *addictive* as people begin to depend on this medium for information and connection, even though *the connection with people is seen as both artificial and superficial.*
- *Treatment* for people addicted to social networking includes *complete abstinence,* which is often complemented by positive reinforcement, *cognitive-behavioral therapy,* and *antidepressant medications.* Some approaches are similar to dieting—the user is *gradually weaned off social networking sites.*

## ASSESSMENT INTERVIEW 3

1. How much time do you spend on social networking sites each day?
2. Do you set your cell phone to receive audible alerts whenever anything is happening in your social networking accounts?
3. How often do you check your "level of influence" on social networking sites?
4. Do you frequently interrupt your activities and your conversations on the phone or in person to read or send a text message?
5. Is it easier for you to interact with people in online chat rooms and sites or in person?
6. Do you feel a pressing need to find out what is going on in people's lives via social networking sites and vice versa?
7. Do you use social networking sites as an escape from the real world?
8. Have you created online personas, fictitious characterizations, and/or avatars online? How much time do you spend in virtual communities?
9. Do you take pride in how many friends you have or how many followers you have on your social sites?
10. Do you often lose track of time when you are on social networking sites and miss important events or appointments?
11. Have you neglected work, school, and/or interaction with peers and family members as a result of excessive social networking? Has work or school performance suffered due to this behavior?
12. Have you experienced increasing levels of depression, anxiety, restlessness, moodiness, or sleep disturbance?
13. Have you tried to quit using social networking sites excessively before but had problems trying to do this on your own?

# 4 WISE COUNSEL

In today's world, with iPhones, iPads, iTouches, laptops, and all of the other various devices that keep us connected and informed, it is hard to imagine people functioning without all the available technology. However, this rapidly changing, fast-paced, push-button, and instant-everything culture is turning society into a virtual generation, and even the older population is now being affected. As a whole, we are devaluing the worth of actual conversations or communicating via a handwritten letter. Social networking sites make it easy for people to know *about* others versus *actually knowing them* on a personal basis. Real relationships and genuine fellowship require a face-to-face component instead of being entirely online.

The reasoning behind this is that when people sit in front of their computer screen they can avoid being genuine, transparent, or vulnerable. This can create an artificial persona and emotional walls that are rarely penetrated. Networking is not inherently destructive and being able to stay connected can be beneficial. However, it is vitally important to overall mental, emotional, and spiritual well-being to do more than just say hello on a Facebook wall and tweet a friend. This hardly compares to a personal phone call, letter, or meaningful time spent with another individual. People who are addicted to social networking need to be lovingly confronted and helped. Are they using the internet to cope with unresolved issues? Are they addicted to the high of having so many friends or to the information flow that comes through social networking websites? Social networking addiction can lead to increased levels of depression and anxiety, procrastination, poor impulse control, lower productivity, avoidance of family members, escapism, and in extreme cases, dissociation.

# 5 ACTION STEPS

## 1. Admit There Is a Problem

The first step to recovery is admitting that you are spending an excessive amount of time on the internet, checking Facebook, texting, and tweeting. Talk with your counselor about the amount of time you spend online and the events you have missed because of being involved in various online activities.

## 2. Regulate Usage

Decide on time limits that you will place on your internet social networking. You may decide on restricting your usage to a certain number of minutes per day and determine certain times of the day when you will not go online. You may find it beneficial to give yourself some emotional space after a day at work or school before going online. This will help you decompress instead of jumping right onto your social networking sites.

## 3. Use Other Communication Tools

Many of the websites used for social networking offer a number of organizational and scheduling tools that make it easy to keep track of dates and times of upcoming events. To help you limit your use of these sites, start using a physical planner. Limit text messaging by calling people on a land or cell phone. Handwrite personal notes and letters, which can be very meaningful to the recipient. These alternative forms of communication can lead to effective relationship building.

## 4. See a Professional Counselor

If you are experiencing any underlying causes of internet and/or social networking addiction, especially depression, anxiety, or other comorbid conditions, ask your counselor for a referral to a qualified professional therapist.

## BIBLICAL INSIGHTS 6

*To Timothy, my dear son: Grace, mercy and peace from God the Father and Christ Jesus our Lord. . . . Recalling your tears, I long to see you, so that I may be filled with joy.*

*2 Timothy 1:2, 4*

In this passage, the apostle Paul is talking to Timothy by way of a letter. He addresses his son in the faith fervently and expresses his great desire to have Timothy come and meet him face-to-face because he wishes to be lifted up by his visit. To Paul, the presence of Timothy with him in the flesh was the most important thing. It was not so much about passing a message via Facebook or Twitter—granted those did not exist in the first century—but about face time that was far more beneficial.

*They devoted themselves to the apostles' teaching and to fellowship, to the breaking of bread and to prayer.*

*Acts 2:42*

The disciples devoted themselves to spending time together and being in each other's fellowship. They did not write back and forth to one another, but instead fellowshipped in one place together. Again, this shows the importance of being with people face-to-face instead of on the computer or only through text messaging.

*For now we see only a reflection as in a mirror; then we shall see face to face.*

*1 Corinthians 13:12*

One day we will enjoy pure and unbroken fellowship with the Lord. There will be no barriers or hindrances. He who knows our every waking thought, every desire of the heart, every prayer request and burden that we carry will speak and communicate with us in the intimate and personal language of relationship.

*Those who live according to the flesh have their minds set on what the flesh desires; but those who live in accordance with the Spirit have their minds set on what the Spirit desires. The mind governed by the flesh is death, but the mind governed by the Spirit is life and peace.*

*Romans 8:5–6*

People who are addicted to social networking put all of their excitement, desires, and energy into the wrong things and in the wrong places. God wants us to put our efforts into building true relationships with our spiritual brothers and sisters, as well as with Him. We are to set our minds on the things of the Spirit and not on things that can so easily be taken away.

## 7 PRAYER STARTER

Lord, You desire for us to have fellowship with one another because You designed us for deeply meaningful relationships. True relationships are one of the greatest gifts You have given, so right now I ask that You help _____ and take away his (her) addiction to social networking. Give him (her) an abiding awareness of Your presence and a fresh revelation of what it means to be in a personal relationship with the King of the universe. May _____ be able to build the relationships You desire. Thank You for Your provision and grace . . .

## 8 RECOMMENDED RESOURCES

Careaga, Andrew. *Hooked on the Net*. Kregel, 2002.

Friesen, Dwight J. *Thy Kingdom Connected: What the Church Can Learn from Facebook, the Internet, and Other Networks*. Baker, 2009.

Jantz, Gregory L. *Hooked: The Pitfalls of Media, Technology, and Social Networking*. Siloam, 2012.

Kern, Jan. *Eyes Online, Eyes on Life: A Journey Out of Online Obsession*. Standard, 2008.

Nesdahl, Melissa, and Pam Stenzel. *Who's in Your Social Network?* Regal, 2009.

Rosen, Larry D. *iDisorder: Understanding Our Obsession with Technology and Overcoming Its Hold on Us*. Palgrave Macmillan, 2012.

Young, Kimberly S. *Internet Addiction: A Handbook and Guide to Evaluation and Treatment*. John Wiley, 2011.

## Websites

Help Guide: www.helpguide.org/mental/internet_cybersex_addiction.htm

Internet Addiction Cure: www.internetaddictioncure.com/index.html

Net Addiction: www.netaddiction.com/

Safety Web: www.safetyweb.com/internet-addiction

Tech Addiction: www.techaddiction.ca/facebook-addiction-statistics.html#.ULJU
  g6PWqJU

# 30 Voyeurism and Exhibitionism

## 1 : PORTRAITS

- John has been interested in photography since high school and has won awards for his pictures and freelance work for weddings and special events. He is fairly shy and does not date or socialize much with girls at the local college where he attends. One thing people do not know about John is that he is deep into voyeurism. He sits in the car outside his apartment complex at night and takes pictures of girls undressing and changing clothes with the use of a high-powered telephoto lens. He gets excited and thrilled at the thought of posting these pictures on a local chat room website where he frequently talks to other guys who share his addiction for catching women naked on camera. John is fairly confident no one really knows about his behavior but he does become anxious at the thought of being caught.

- Carol and Denise just moved into a new warehouse apartment in a thriving downtown metropolitan neighborhood. They have been moving their belongings in all day and did not think other people could see them through the window while they were changing clothes. However, that evening Carol looked outside and saw a man sitting on the rooftop of the apartments across the street. He had binoculars and seemed to be looking in the direction of the apartment! She screamed and closed the blinds, yelling out to Denise that someone was on the roof watching them. Denise called the police. They came to the apartment building but told them that because the police did not see the act, they could do nothing. Carol and Denise were frightened and angry. How could someone be so disgusting and invade their privacy that way?

- Rod has a new job; actually this is his fifth job in the past few years because he cannot seem to stay employed for more than six or seven months at a time. He has a number of personal problems and is in and out of dating relationships all the time. Rod has an overly expressive personality and is frequently known as the life of the party, but most people don't know that Rod is an exhibitionist. He loves crowded places where he can flash his nude body at people for a quick thrill. He has been caught only once and had to pay a small fine. Secretly he struggles with depression and anxiety and at home cries constantly because of the pervasive sense of loneliness that dominates his life. Rod is addicted to attention but he has no idea how to conduct himself in public or how to have a proper conversation, especially with a woman. The real question is how long can Rod live this roller-coaster life before he looks for help?

# DEFINITIONS AND KEY THOUGHTS ⋮ 2

- *Voyeurism* is a psychosexual disorder or *paraphilia* that involves the act of observing a person who is undressing, naked, or engaged in sexual activity without their knowing. Secretly watching someone under these conditions arouses in the voyeur sexual fantasies or behaviors.[1]

- The person being observed is usually *a stranger* to the voyeur. He or she may fantasize about sexual activity with the one being observed, but this *rarely moves beyond the fantasy*.[2]

- *Research, which is somewhat lacking in this area,* seems to indicate more *voyeurs are men* and that the onset of the behavior begins around fifteen years of age.[3]

- According to the DSM-IV-TR, *to be diagnosed as a voyeur* one must have one of the following conditions:

  — *Experience six months or more* of intense, recurring, sexually arousing urges, fantasies, and behaviors that include observing an unsuspecting person who is undressing, naked, or engaged in sexual activity.[4]

  — *Have sexual urges, fantasies,* and *behaviors* that cause social or occupational impairment or other important functioning difficulties that are clinically significant.[5]

- *Online cameras and chat rooms* on pornographic sites have allowed voyeurs to watch others privately or in voyeuristic websites where the activity is staged by active participants. This has allowed many voyeurs to be able to keep their behavior secret, find others who share their addiction, and avoid criminal prosecution.

- Today's media culture has *increased its orientation and comfort level for voyeurism and exhibitionism* with numerous reality television shows and movies that push the boundaries of sexual promiscuity and decency.

- Another form of voyeurism is *listening to erotic conversations* (known as telephone sex) or *to other people involved in sexual activity.*

- *Exhibitionism* is the exposure of private body parts (genitals) to complete strangers (sometimes with an overt sexual suggestion) to receive a sexual thrill from the experience.[6]

- Also known as *Lady Godiva Syndrome, flashing, or apodysophilia*, exhibitionism seeks sexual fulfillment from being observed by others, often with the secondary desire for others to engage in sexual activities with them.

- Now a large percentage of exhibitionist behavior *takes place online in chat rooms, on websites,* and through *texting* and *emailing pictures.* This has caused exhibitionists to stay in online social circles and not so much in more public environments.

- Exhibitionism has also become *common in adolescent circles*—called *sexting.* Teens use cell phones with camera capabilities and send nude pictures of themselves or certain body parts to friends, classmates, a boyfriend or girlfriend, and even complete strangers.[7] Sexting can be deemed *felony child abuse* when the sharing or distribution of pornographic images *involves a minor.*

- *Fifteen percent of teens* say they have received a nearly nude or sexually explicit nude picture in a text from someone they know.[8]
- *Voyeurism is the opposite of exhibitionism.* The exhibitionist becomes aroused from exposing him or herself sexually, while the voyeur gets sexual gratification from observing others secretly. While they appear to be a compulsive behavior disorder, *neither usually involve violence.* However, both behaviors are typically *nonconsensual* and therefore, by definition, "forced" on the unsuspecting person.
- Many voyeurs and exhibitionists *masturbate* while watching others or exposing themselves. Both behaviors *can result in criminal fines, incarceration*, and *court-ordered counseling.*
- While research is still fairly limited when it comes to voyeurism and exhibitionism, there are some indications they can be *the result of childhood trauma and/ or frequent exposure to or observation of sexual acts, higher than normal levels of testosterone, traumatic brain injury*, and *a tendency toward poor impulse control and/or obsessive-compulsive disorder.*[9]
- The very nature of the *pornography industry* so prevalent on the internet caters expressly to voyeurs and exhibitionists.
- International, state, and local laws differ from country, region or state, and municipality, but laws range from *misdemeanors* to *felonies* and can result in *fines and imprisonment*, as well as *registration as a convicted sex offender.*
- Rarely do voyeurs and exhibitionists seek help on their own and often they enter treatment only *following legal action and court-mandated counseling.*

# 3 ASSESSMENT INTERVIEW

## Interviewing the Exhibitionist

1. What exhibitionist acts are you currently involved in? How much time goes by between exhibitionist acts? How does your exhibition usually occur? Is there a process you go through and a preferred location?
2. Explain when you first recall exposing yourself or had a desire to expose yourself. How old were you at that time? Were there any other people involved? How does that experience differ from current activities?
3. Do you masturbate when you expose yourself? Have you masturbated since childhood? When was the first time you remember seeing nude or sexual images?
4. When you expose yourself, do you want sexual contact with the person viewing you or do you want some other form of gratification? Have you ever tried to contact or talk with the people to whom you have exposed yourself?
5. Have you ever been caught? Were there criminal or civil charges brought against you? Are you a registered sex offender?
6. Have you tried to quit in the past? How long did your abstinence from exhibitionism last? Do you watch pornographic films or websites, visit exhibitionist chat rooms and websites, participate in erotic webcam activities, and participate

in other interactive sexual practices? Are there any financial difficulties tied to this behavior?

7. Are you currently in a relationship or married? Have you ever been divorced? Did exhibitionism play any role in the divorce? Is exhibitionism affecting your relationships with others? How is your sex life? Would you rather masturbate, expose yourself, or engage in pornographic or online webcam activity or social chat environments instead of engaging in sex with your spouse?

8. Are there any other habits or addictions you have or are currently dealing with in addition to your exhibitionist tendencies? Do you feel that giving up exhibitionism will improve your life? How, why, and in what way? Are you fully prepared to commit to counseling and any other means necessary to free yourself of this addiction?

9. Has anyone ever helped you with this problem in the past? What methods did they use?

## Interviewing the Voyeur

1. What voyeuristic acts are you currently involved in? How long have you gone between spying on and watching others? How do you go about spying on someone? Do you have a method, technology, or favorite place for your voyeurism?

2. When was the earliest time in your life you remember the urge to spy on someone who was naked or engaging in sexual activity? How did that encounter feel? Did you masturbate? Were you looking at pornography?

3. Do you currently masturbate, view pornography, engage in sexual webcam activities and chat sites, or participate in other sexual behaviors?

4. Are their certain locations or environments you find more appealing for voyeurism? Do you know or live near the people you spy on? Have you ever tried to contact the people you spy on?

5. Have you ever been caught? Were there criminal or civil charges brought against you? Are you a registered sex offender?

6. Are you married, divorced, or in a relationship currently? Have your voyeuristic tendencies caused any relational, financial, or emotional problems?

7. Have you ever tried to quit your voyeurism? How long did it last? Did you feel better during this time or did you feel worse? Why? Would your life be better if you could leave voyeurism and/or other addictions behind?

8. Has anyone ever helped you with this problem in the past? What methods did they use? If you are to continue counseling, are you committed to giving 100 percent effort to the process and will you follow the treatment plan?

## WISE COUNSEL 4

Voyeurism and exhibitionism affect not only the person with the disorder but the target of the behavior as well. A sexual desire or urge can become an addiction when the urges and desires are acted on and continually persist. Acting out can have criminal and civil consequences.

The causes of voyeurism and exhibitionism have been researched, and several theories have been proposed (e.g., random or accidental observation of an unsuspecting person that was stimulating, successive repetitions of the behavior, the inability to filter intrusive thoughts and images having strong sexual content, early childhood exposure to strong sexual content, etc.).

Circumstances under which voyeuristic behavior is triggered include:[10]

- excessive and unstructured free time
- feeling alone or isolated from people
- depression
- stress, turmoil, and traumatic life events
- poor communication skills
- accidentally coming across someone with whom you are infatuated or obsessed while they are naked and/or engaging in sexual activity
- pornographic or erotic websites, strip clubs, movies, and materials with strong sexual themes
- periods of significant sexual arousal due to high testosterone levels

Circumstances under which exhibitionist behavior is triggered include:[11]

- traumatic sexual encounters in the past (childhood abuse)
- a lack of relational boundaries regarding sexual behavior
- periods of significant sexual arousal due to high testosterone levels
- stress, turmoil, and traumatic life events
- previous brain injury

*Note:* Not all people with voyeuristic or exhibitionist tendencies are full-blown addicts and many do not have criminal records. Just like any addiction, there are stages of progression from desire to fulfillment to continual habitual behaviors.

# 5 ACTION STEPS

## 1. Acknowledge Your Problem

The first step toward recovery is admitting you have a problem that you cannot deal with on your own.

## 2. Seek Professional Help

Due to the complexity of the disorder and potential underlying causes, your counselor will help you find a trained mental health professional who can work with you effectively.

## 3. Agree to a Treatment Plan

Your counselor will help you work out a targeted treatment plan of goals and objectives with a schedule of counseling times and dates.

## 4. Find Accountability Partners

Meet regularly with others who can journey with you, checking with you daily to help monitor your activities and determine your motivation level, noting any weaknesses in behavior or possible relapses.

## 5. Commit to the Counseling Process

Make a commitment to apply 100 percent of your energy and focus to accomplishing the goals and treatment plan laid out by your counselor. See this through to the end. The worst thing you could do is let yourself think you are free from an addiction only to give in to temptation a few months later and start the behavior all over again. Being free from addiction for life is the goal. Consider finding a support group where you can get involved.

# BIBLICAL INSIGHTS 6

*Can a man scoop fire into his lap without his clothes being burned? Can a man walk on hot coals without his feet being scorched?*

*Proverbs 6:27–28*

Our actions do not affect ourselves only but also others around us, including friends and family members. Often sinful choices damage us and our relationships, shackle our minds and hearts, and make us slaves to lust. It is hard to break free from such an addiction, and only with God's help, strength, the accountability of others, and a good counselor or pastor, can our slavery from addiction be broken.

*You have heard that it was said, "You shall not commit adultery." But I tell you that anyone who looks at a woman lustfully has already committed adultery with her in his heart.*

*Matthew 5:27–28*

Jesus teaches us that sins of the heart are wrong, regardless of whether we commit the act physically. A voyeur or exhibitionist may think that because a sexual act has not been committed with another person, he or she has not sinned. However, in these verses we see that our thoughts can be just as sinful as the lustful act of adultery itself. We must admit we are sinning and that our actions hurt others, including ourselves.

*Love must be sincere. Hate what is evil; cling to what is good. Be devoted to one another in love. Honor one another above yourselves. Never be lacking in zeal, but keep your spiritual fervor, serving the Lord. Be joyful in hope, patient in affliction, faithful in prayer. Share with the Lord's people who are in need. Practice hospitality.*

*Romans 12:9–13*

We must understand that to show genuine and godly love the concept of agape needs to be embraced, along with a changed life. When we are more concerned about other people and their needs and place them above our own wants and desires, then we are demonstrating godly love. We must put away selfish and lustful desires. Exposing oneself or spying is wrong. When we become more concerned for the safety and welfare of others, hating what is evil, then we are walking in a manner that pleases God.

*Let your eyes look straight ahead; fix your gaze directly before you. Give careful thought to the paths for your feet and be steadfast in all your ways. Do not turn to the right or the left; keep your foot from evil.*

*Proverbs 4:25–27*

One key to proper accountability and a life of right choices is to learn to be focused on the things of God—fixing our eyes, mind, heart, and goals on a path straight ahead and not changing our mind or losing motivation. This is paramount to recovery from any addiction, and it is a biblical principle taught in these verses. If we remain focused on our goals, and our heart is committed to trusting completely in God's grace, we will keep from evil and honor Him in our behavior.

# 7 PRAYER STARTER

Dear Lord, I want to thank You for bringing _____ here for counseling. It requires a lot of courage and humility to take this crucial step and seek help for an addiction such as this. Jesus, I ask that You give _____ the strength to resist temptation, the courage to seek accountability and stick with a treatment plan, and the faith to trust that You will finish the good work You have begun in his (her) life. Thank You for Your hand of grace and protection over _____ as we journey together toward freedom . . .

# 8 RECOMMENDED RESOURCES

Arterburn, Stephen, Fred Stoeker, and Mike Yorkey. *Every Man's Battle: Workbook—Winning the War on Sexual Temptation One Victory at a Time.* Random House, 2009.

Dann, Bucky. *Addiction: Pastoral Responses.* Abingdon, 2002.

Gallagher, Steve. *At the Altar of Sexual Idolatry.* Book and workbook. Pure Life Ministries, 2000.

Hart, Archibald D. *The Sexual Man: Masculinity without Guilt.* Word, 1994.

Laaser, Mark R. *Healing the Wounds of Sexual Addiction.* Zondervan, 2004.

Schaumburg, Harry W. *False Intimacy: Understanding the Struggle of Sexual Addiction.* NavPress, 1992.

Stoeker, Fred, Brenda Stoeker, and Mike Yorkey. *Every Heart Restored: A Wife's Guide to Healing in the Wake of a Husband's Sexual Sin.* WaterBrook, 2010.

Weaver, Andrew J., Charlene Hosenfeld, and Harold G. Koenig. *Counseling Persons with Addictions and Compulsions: A Handbook for Clergy and Other Helping Professionals.* Pilgrim, 2007.

Welton, Jonathan. *Eyes of Honor: Training Men for Purity and Righteousness.* Destiny Image, 2012.

## Websites

Behave Net: www.behavenet.com

Encyclopedia of Mental Disorders: www.minddisorders.com/Del-Fi/Exhibitionism.html

Sexual Recovery Institute: www.sexualrecovery.com/voyeurism-exhibitionism.php

# PART 4

# Process Addictions

This section provides a comprehensive look at important aspects of process addiction and recovery.

Process addictions are similar to behavioral addictions, and the two terms are sometimes used interchangeably. As such, they are often overshadowed by chemical/substance addictions even though they too are marked by compulsive and dependent behaviors. Some of the features in this last category include personality orientation, internal beliefs, and unmet emotional and relational needs. A healthy and vibrant relationship with God is essential for helping individuals move beyond the dysfunctional behavior patterns to find freedom and restoration.

Remember the four steps that were presented in the introduction regarding the Road to Recovery:

1. *Recognize and admit:* the role of confession and breaking the power of the secret
2. *Clean out the infection:* the role of grieving and breaking the power of denial
3. *Renew the mind:* the role of truth and breaking the power of unbelief
4. *Exercise the will:* the role of accountability and breaking the power of fear

# 31 Adrenaline and Thrill Seeking

## 1 PORTRAITS

- "I want to go sky diving," John said as he left work. His co-workers were amazed that he was so brave as to be willing to jump out of an airplane. He says that the thrill of "risking it all" is what keeps him motivated. He cannot be persuaded that it is too dangerous, mainly because the more dangerous the activity the more interested he becomes. John finds that most life events for him are boring. When he is at home alone, all he can think of is how bored he is. However, at the root of his thoughts is a sense of loneliness. He has been unable to experience deep relationships for various reasons. He seeks out thrills just to feel alive, but the moment is so fleeting he is unable to have any kind of sustained happiness. John is an adrenaline addict.

- Anna is a thirty-two-year-old stock trader living in the heart of Manhattan. She has worked tirelessly to rise in position and influence and has finally reached her goal of being recognized on Wall Street. Anna spends countless hours at work, analyzing stocks and determining the next big hit. She has few friends and finds herself thinking about work even when she is away from the hustle and bustle. On a recent trip out of the city to her family's home in Albany, Anna was on edge and struggled to rest despite her time away from work. She was irritable and complained of boredom. Her mother mentioned she had not seemed like herself lately and was too consumed with work. However, Anna ignored her mother's observations and was eager to return to work after the weekend away was over.

- Josh was formerly involved in Special Operations in the United States Navy. He has recently returned to his small hometown from his third and final deployment. He was hired for a relatively stress-free job in sales and was ready to begin to maintain a more settled lifestyle than the military would provide. After just a few months back home, Josh now feels bored and uninterested in the slow pace of civilian life. He longs for the camaraderie and excitement he once experienced in the military. In an attempt to have this back, Josh joined a contracting company and has chosen to deploy to Iraq to work a private security job. Because of the location, Josh is sure he will experience possible combat situations that will provide him the rush that he has found so fulfilling.

# DEFINITIONS AND KEY THOUGHTS : 2

- *Adrenaline* is the familiar term for the hormone *epinephrine,* which is released in the body through the adrenal glands in response to stress. As a *stimulant*, it is used to treat conditions such as cardiac arrest, anaphylaxis (allergic reactions), asthma, and croup. *Adrenaline increases heart rate, blood pressure, and other bodily responses to external stressors.*

- Adrenaline is also a *neurotransmitter* that is a critical component of the fight or flight response of the sympathetic nervous system.[1]

- *Slang terms* for an addict to adrenaline include *thrill seeker, adrenaline junkie,* and *thriving on pressure.*

- *Participating in dangerous or high-risk activities*, such as mountain climbing, sky diving, high-speed driving, and gambling, can provide an adrenaline rush. *Sensation seeking*, also called *excitement seeking*, refers to the pursuit of sensory pleasures by those who desire excitement for its own sake, regardless of the particular activity or environment.[2]

- A more subtle cause for adrenaline addiction arises out of *common life stressors*. Many people disguise their adrenaline addiction by appearing busy. Some individuals need the pressure of going from place to place or doing one activity after another to feel a sense of vitality. Businessmen and women who overwork and skip lunch breaks and vacation days may have an adrenaline addiction. Resting is not an option for them.[3]

- Frequently adrenaline addicts exhibit *certain habits*, such as *pacing, leg kicking, fast gum chewing, restlessness*, and *finger drumming.*[4]

- These addicts have an *obsession with what has not been done or the feeling of wanting to do something.*[5]

- Often they are preoccupied with *feelings of guilt* if goals are not accomplished, resulting in greater *irritability* and *aggressiveness.*[6]

- *Withdrawal* periods can be defined by a sense of *depression* or *anxiety.* This is the result of the chemical reduction, which is a natural process the body goes through after a stressful situation.[7]

- Some adrenaline addicts experience *more significant physical symptoms*, such as heart problems, heart attacks, and panic attacks or even a lack of adrenaline after a significant release from the adrenal glands.[8]

- Adrenaline addiction can be *particularly difficult to overcome* for two basic reasons. First, adrenaline is a *naturally occurring hormone of the body* that needs to be activated in times of real stress. If one is in recovery from the addiction, a sudden accident or life stressor may actually *rekindle the desire* to continue certain behaviors. Second, having the addiction can actually be *viewed as a positive characteristic* in certain environments, particularly in the business world. The same stigma found with other forms of addiction is not always applied to this problem.[9]

- Some addicts use adrenaline *to keep unresolved feelings of loss, abandonment, and disconnection repressed.*[10]

- Some are more concerned with the intensity adrenaline offers rather than living a life of quality that has natural highs and lows. The addiction for these individuals is not based on repressed feelings but in *avoiding the lack of feelings.*[11]
- The addict will *often not see his or her addiction as problematic* and may even revel in or brag about his or her adrenaline-seeking lifestyle.
- Family members, co-workers, and friends will often be *unaware* that an actual addiction is present, and those who risk confronting the addict are often met with great *resistance.*[12]

# 3 ASSESSMENT INTERVIEW

1. Describe your typical day and what motivates you. (*Take special note of any action that requires adrenaline to complete.*)
2. After the day is complete, how do you feel?
3. Throughout the day, do you often feel tired, distracted, or overwhelmed? What do you do in those moments?
4. What tends to stress you out?
5. Do you often take risks that others do not or will not take?
6. What do you consider to be a good vacation or relaxation activity? (*Note that an adrenaline addict will likely choose a thrilling, adventurous activity.*)
7. How would it make you feel to go an entire day without using your technology devices (phone, computer, iPad, and so on)? How would you feel if you did not go to work?
8. When in your life did you start to feel an unnatural amount of stress?
9. During the times that you slow down, do you feel irritable or anxious?

# 4 WISE COUNSEL

A normal function of the body is producing adrenaline. God has designed our bodies to react appropriately in times of stress as a way to protect us from danger. Because this hormone occurs naturally in the body, recovery from an addiction to it is somewhat complicated, particularly because it has chemical properties similar to other stimulant drugs. It is impossible to shut down epinephrine in the system. However, the continual misuse of adrenaline to experience a high can damage the body over time if untreated.

A crucial aspect of working with the individual is to assess the underlying reasons for the addiction. Is something in the person's life increasing adrenaline levels and being used to overcome certain thoughts or feelings? As stated before, this tendency may be due to a sense of loss, disconnection, and abandonment. Anxiety is often at the root of most adrenaline addictions. Some have anxiety about job loss, so they work hard to prove their worth. Others experience anxiety because they feel disconnected in their relationships or even from themselves; therefore, they thrill seek to find meaning in life. Adrenaline addiction is a complex phenomenon that can easily go unnoticed. Initially the caregiver may need to proceed on the notion that the individual is not even aware of the problem.

Take note of the client's demeanor during your meeting. If he or she has a sense of urgency, seems restless or anxious, or is constantly checking the phone, he or she may be addicted to adrenaline. Keep in mind the key characteristics of an adrenaline addict. It can be difficult to convince the client of the problem. It may be revealing to discuss relaxation. If the person expresses guilt, anxiety, or despondency over an impending lull in activity, root issues may actually surface. This can be an ideal opportunity for further self-exploration and in changing behaviors.

# ACTION STEPS 5

## 1. Recognize the Problem

- One of the essential goals is to recognize you have a problem. You may not be aware that the addiction to adrenaline can actually exacerbate ongoing stress, as well as cause other harm to your body.
- Once the problem is acknowledged, you can better understand how the addiction is influencing your life. Accepting the truth about the problem provides a foundation on which to build a recovery process.

## 2. Let Others Know about the Problem

- Begin by telling close friends and family members about the addiction. Make it clear about its impact and that you are seeking to address the core issues involved. These individuals can become an important part of a support and accountability system.
- If the adrenaline-based issues are tied to your work, you may consider talking with co-workers and supervisors about your problem. This can be a difficult step for an adrenaline addict whose core issue is often a need for value in the workplace. Taking steps in this direction may bring some backlash, but explaining the health benefits of proper rest and pacing, as well as the value of setting boundaries, can enhance the work environment.
- A special note for those who do not have a traditional job (stay-at-home moms, small business owners, or students) and who do not have co-workers or supervisors: ensure that you have others who can serve as accountability partners, whether a spouse, roommate, or close friend. Make sure they are checking on your progress and encouraging moments of rest and relaxation.

## 3. Understand the Core Issue

- Most adrenaline addicts have one or more core issues that cause them to seek out the use of their natural adrenaline to help cope. Know what your issues are.

- If the adrenaline addiction is the result of something deeply rooted, such as anxiety or depression, be sure to seek the proper help. See a counselor regularly, read self-help books and articles, or attend a support group.
- Replacing adrenaline use with other over-stimulating activities is not the goal. You must keep in mind patience is necessary in breaking a habit that has been a natural part of life. You will still feel adrenaline, but maintaining a healthy balance will keep the overuse from occurring so frequently.
- Getting the rest and relaxation you need is probably going to expose the core issues to you. It is important to understand that facing and overcoming these issues will help you relax and unwind after very stressful situations. Your body and mind need the recovery time.[13]

## 4. Incorporate Lifestyle Changes

- Find activities that make you happy without stressing out your body with the overuse of adrenaline. You can experience joy, happiness, and other sensations apart from thrill seeking and adventure.
- Boredom is not the only other option in life. There is an entire spectrum of activities and experiences that are not stressful or overly life-threatening. Begin trying new things that are relaxing and pleasurable.
- Interventions to reduce stress and adrenaline include exercise, relaxation techniques, and getting enough sleep.[14]

# 6 BIBLICAL INSIGHTS

*What do people get for all the toil and anxious striving with which they labor under the sun? All their days their work is grief and pain; even at night their minds do not rest. This too is meaningless. A person can do nothing better than to eat and drink and find satisfaction in their own toil. This too, I see, is from the hand of God, for without him, who can eat or find enjoyment?*

*Ecclesiastes 2:22–25*

The book of Ecclesiastes is all about the nature of our lives being short moments in comparison to the measure of eternity. It is important to realize we have only a short time on earth. Spending our days working so aggressively will only result in further dissatisfaction in life. A healthy balance between work and pleasure in life is important. God has designed us to be in that balanced life.

*And do not set your heart on what you will eat or drink; do not worry about it. For the pagan world runs after all such things, and your Father knows that you need them. But seek his kingdom, and these things will be given to you as well.*

*Luke 12:29–31*

Jesus is speaking about those who worry over the various things in life, including what they will eat and drink. Everyday worries such as these often lead to greater stress in life and we may use them as reasons for working so hard. Jesus talks about the nations of the world that are seeking after all the things of the world. As a Christian, the focus should be on seeking the kingdom of God. Focusing on His plans and goals is going to make the anxiety less necessary. Knowing God will provide our every need is a key aspect of overcoming stress and adrenaline addiction.

*Do not be anxious about anything, but in every situation, by prayer and petition, with thanksgiving, present your requests to God. And the peace of God, which transcends all understanding, will guard your hearts and your minds in Christ Jesus.*

*Philippians 4:6–7*

The apostle Paul writes to the Philippians in a time when anxiety-fueled adrenaline may have been threatening to overcome his life. He was in Roman possession under house arrest, likely chained to a guard. He had every reason for an increase in his stress levels but he tells the Philippians not to be anxious. He even gives guidelines for addressing the anxiety of life. He says to pray and let God in on our troubles and to acknowledge His work in our life with thanks. In return, God will give us peace, which is beyond all understanding. Even when times are stressful and overwhelming, God's unfathomable peace is given to guard us from the temptation to let adrenaline run our life.

## PRAYER STARTER 7

Today, we come to You, God, and ask that You give us peace, joy, and rest. Help us place our trust completely in You. I ask that You would help _____ to stop letting all of life's stressors control his (her) thoughts and plans. Make him (her) aware of the damage being done to his (her) body, which is the temple of the Holy Spirit. Please relieve _____ from the unhealthy grip that adrenaline has on him (her). Help him (her) find rest in Your presence and protection from falling into the temptation of letting adrenaline control his (her) life. Facing this alone is not easy; give him (her) others to make the journey alongside him (her), encouraging him (her) to live in a way that pleases You. Keep his (her) focus on You and remind him (her) daily of Your provision . . .

## RECOMMENDED RESOURCES 8

Church, Matt. *Adrenaline Junkies and Serotonin Seekers: Balance Your Brain Chemistry to Maximize Energy, Stamina, Mental Sharpness, and Emotional Well-Being.* Ulysses Press, 2004.

Hart, Archibald D. *Adrenaline and Stress: The Exciting New Breakthrough That Helps You Overcome Stress Damage.* Thomas Nelson, 1995.

————. *The Anxiety Cure.* Thomas Nelson, 2001.

————. *The Hidden Link between Adrenaline and Stress.* Thomas Nelson, 1995.

————. *Thrilled to Death: How the Endless Pursuit of Pleasure Is Leaving Us Numb.* Thomas Nelson, 2007.

## Websites

About.com: stress.about.com/od/situationalstress/a/adrenaline0528.htm

Adrenaline Addicts Anonymous: www.adrenalineaddicts.org/

American Heart Association: www.heart.org/HEARTORG/

American Institute of Stress: www.stress.org/

National Institute of Mental Health: www.nimh.nih.gov/health/topics/anxiety-disorders/index.shtml

National Institutes of Health: www.ncbi.nlm.nih.gov/pmc/articles/PMC2396566/

# Anger and Rage 32

- Rob is a sixteen-year-old high school student. Recently his parents have noticed he has been hanging out with the wrong crowd at school and is beginning to fail his classes. Most obviously, though, his parents are concerned about the growing anger he is beginning to display with them at home. He often lashes out when he does not get his way, throwing household items, screaming, cursing, and threatening his parents and others. Rob's parents have consulted their senior pastor, Rob's youth pastor, and several teachers, without any success. They have come for counseling, desperate to both understand and help their raging teenager.

- Mary, a mother of two, is married to a deacon in her small Baptist church and is seeking counseling because she is afraid of her husband, Brad. She has always known Brad had a temper, but with the recent cut in his hours at work, he has begun to rage at both her and the children. He has made threats about what he is capable of doing to Mary and has even challenged her by saying that because of his position in the church and his status in the community, no one would believe that he is capable of harming his family. Last night Brad hit Mary for the first time in a fit of rage. Though afterward he apologized over and over, begging her to keep it a secret, Mary packed up what she could and took their children to her mother's home. Now she is secretly seeking help to know how to get out of her dark situation.

- Chris is the president and CEO of a Fortune 500 company. Though he has been very successful in launching and maintaining his business, he is notorious for his anger. Most of his employees complain about his temper, stating that the only reason they remain with the company is for the benefits and just having a job. In the public eye, Chris is a charmer and a visionary; however, to those with whom he works most closely, he is a tyrant with a short fuse. He has married and divorced four times, and emotional and physical abuse have been suspected in at least two of his marriages.

## DEFINITIONS AND KEY THOUGHTS 2

- "*Anger* is an emotion characterized by antagonism toward someone or something you feel has deliberately done you wrong."[1]
- *Rage* is the amassing of unexpressed anger and perceived ill-mannered reactions that flow to the surface in some form of expression.[2]

- In *a spiritual sense, anger* is described this way: It is "both a divine and human emotion which is aimed at the rectification of wrong and must be wisely expressed and carefully monitored."[3]

- Anger is *not necessarily good or bad, healthy or unhealthy*, but has the *potential to move in either direction*. Anger is simply an emotion that, when acted on, can have good or bad consequences. For example, after hearing about a woman who has been assaulted in the local park, anger can be good if it causes changes to be made, such as better security in the park at night. An adverse reaction might be that on hearing of the same assault, an individual seeks out the offender and repays him in a form of vigilante justice. The *consequences* of expressing the emotion of anger are what make it good or bad.[4]

- Anger becomes *toxic* when it is *allowed to linger* for an extended period of time, if it is a *frequent response* to life events, or when it is the *result of inappropriate behavior*. Often the emotion manifests when someone has done something wrong and is confronted with his or her behavior.[5]

- While *anger is a universal and normal emotion, its expression is unique and individual*; each person expresses anger in his or her own way. Those with more extroverted personalities will typically be more open and less restricted when communicating displeasure with someone or over something, while introverted personalities are more likely to hold in their anger. Circumstances, however, do play a key role in how anger will be expressed.[6]

- Each person has a *"style" of anger expression*. The manifestation of anger can be categorized in many ways. Here are three that include most of them:

  — *Vocalization*—verbally expressing the emotion directly to the object of anger. This can be done *without control* when the individual allows anger to direct what is said. When anger is vocalized *with control*, it is expressed with a consideration for time or place and with the purpose of manipulating the object of the anger.[7]

  — *Internalization*—trying to keep the emotion from ever coming to the surface of consciousness. Anger can be *repressed* (the psychological process of repelling one's desires and impulses toward pleasurable instincts)—the person does not accept his or her anger and loses touch with emotions. It can also be *suppressed* (the conscious choice not to indulge in a particular thought, feeling, or action), with the person denying they have anger.[8]

  — *Slow expression*—nonverbal or behavioral expression. The ultimate goal of this expression of anger is to exact revenge on the object of anger and is often seen in the form of slander, gossip, or passive-aggressive behavior.[9]

- Many people use their *heritage and family background* as an excuse for their anger and expression of anger. Furthermore, many *blame other disorders* (such as ADD, ADHD, personality disorders) to justify the behavior. However, anger is often rooted in past trauma, lost control, hurt feelings, or an emotional sense of injustice. No matter the source, there is still a need to deal with anger and its expression.[10]

- Anger *becomes rage in a variety of settings and for different reasons.* It is often the result of several factors that tend to build up to a point where expression becomes haphazard and overtakes rational and calm thinking. Many people find that in moments of rage and shortly thereafter, they cannot explain why they acted in the way they did, even though at the core, a sense of hurt and injustice has likely occurred sometime in their life.[11]

- *Intermittent explosive disorder* (IED), an *impulse-control disorder*, goes beyond normal anger and includes *violent outbursts* that are aggressive, impulsive, and disproportionate to whatever is taking place in the moment.[12] Frequent episodes of road rage, domestic violence, and temper tantrums are all examples. As many as sixteen million American adults may have IED.[13]

- Anger is often considered a *secondary emotion,* emanating from a deep need. It can be an expression used to *avoid and suppress* such things as guilt, abandonment, fear, anxiety, embarrassment, and insecurity. The anger serves to communicate the underlying emotion or thought that needs some measure of resolution. To address the anger, it becomes necessary to deal with the root emotion at its source.[14]

- A more subtle form of anger is known as *passive-aggressive* behavior or the process of expressing and *dealing with underlying anger indirectly*. Examples include resentment, oppositional behaviors, constant complaining, procrastination, unusual stubbornness, sullenness, irritability, and a cynical or hostile demeanor.[15]

## ASSESSMENT INTERVIEW 3

The following assessment questions are drawn from *Overcoming Emotions that Destroy* by Ingram and Johnson.[16]

1. Have you ever experienced a strong sense of anger or rage (*explain the difference if necessary*)?
2. Explain a time when you overreacted in anger to something and regretted your behavior later. Afterward, did you feel as though it was difficult to explain or even understand your actions?
3. Have you ever said something when you were angry you wish you could take back?
4. When you were angry, did you ever come to realize that you had made a bad decision? Explain an instance.
5. Have you ever ruined a friendship, marriage, family relationship, ministry, or business relationship because of anger? What kind of effect did that have on the other person? How did it affect you?
6. Have you ever seen a person hurt because of someone's anger—physically, emotionally, or psychologically?
7. Have you ever experienced road rage or perpetrated an act of violence on someone?
8. What triggers your anger?
9. Are there any unresolved events in your life that manifest in angry responses?

10. Are there people in your life you need to forgive? If so, can you describe the events related to the unforgiveness?

# 4 : WISE COUNSEL

Anger is a difficult emotion to work with. God has given man anger for using righteously. When used properly, anger can drive an individual to seek justice on behalf of others, as well as show love and compassion to hurting victims from tragedy and trauma. However, anger, being a strong emotion, can easily move to improper and unbalanced expression.

In Genesis 4 there is a description of the very first murder in human history. Two brothers, Cain and Abel, both loved God and wanted to please him. Abel was a shepherd, and Cain tended the gardens. When it came time to offer a sacrifice to God, Abel offered the lamb, while Cain offered his first fruits. The offering was to be made for sin, therefore it required a blood sacrifice. So Cain's sacrifice was unacceptable to God. Cain was angry with God and Abel because his brother's sacrifice was accepted, and his anger drove him to do the unthinkable—in a rage Cain killed Abel. Before this time murder was not even known. Cain presents a sobering picture of someone with an unresolved anger problem.

Cain was disappointed that God did not accept his sacrifice and those hurt feelings, while not necessarily justified, were still there. Then his disappointment turned to anger because he felt he had been treated unfairly. The anger in Cain's heart became infected until it boiled over with rage and he killed his brother. Now Cain was left to face the consequences of his sinful actions.

While the person you are counseling may not have the same strength of anger to kill as Cain did, they may be angry enough to wrestle with deep bitterness and hatred. In 1 John 3:15 it says, "Anyone who hates a brother or sister is a murderer, and you know that no murderer has eternal life residing in him." The heart and spirit of the individual are what God is most concerned with; hatred or deep anger buried in one's heart must be addressed.

Anger does not normally surface without reason, just cause, or a precipitating event. At the core of most anger is a sense of injustice that has impacted an individual. That anger is not necessarily expressed directly to the person who is actually the source of the hurt. It may take time and considerable prodding to find the reasons behind the anger, depending on how deeply rooted and internalized the person's thoughts and emotions have become. Recognize that the anger may be just as much a mystery to the person as it is to you; discernment is often needed to see what the source is.

Family members and support group peers are often necessary and helpful with people who have anger problems. Years of unexpressed or poorly expressed anger may lie in their hearts, and there will likely be new events that cause anger to be further exacerbated. A family approach to anger in some cases may be a better option if it represents a safe environment. Staying calm, laying down ground rules, and sticking to them are important considerations because anger can quickly escalate if not handled properly. Keep pursuing underlying causes because anger will only resolve itself when it is released at the source.

# ACTION STEPS 5

## 1. Take Ownership of the Anger

- An important step in the recovery of all addictions is to realize that you have a problem. Take note of the anger that you have in your heart, accept it, and begin working on changing it. Be solution-focused rather than merely venting strong emotion.

## 2. Slow Down and Give Yourself a Time-Out

- Take time to carefully think through your words and actions before you say or do anything. Think about the possible consequences. If in the middle of an interaction you feel angry, get somewhere alone for a few minutes if necessary.
- Anger can cause us to react impulsively rather than respond calmly to a situation. This can sometimes be the result of miscommunication, when you have not listened carefully or have misunderstood the situation. Jumping to conclusions is usually not an effective approach to problem resolution. It is healthier to rest and de-stress because this can diminish the anger that you are experiencing. A few slow, deep breaths may be helpful.

## 3. Use Physical Activity

- Sometimes physical activity can help relieve stress and dissipate energy, especially if it stems from negative and bottled-up emotion.

## 4. Keep a Journal

- Pay attention to the times when you become angry and then write down what made you angry and how you responded. Find the common patterns related to your anger and begin taking steps to be more alert when those things are about to happen.
- Journaling can also be an effective means of expressing emotions, helping you get them out without causing distress or harm to others.

## 5. Seek Help

- Do not think that your anger is something that you can control on your own. Continue to meet with your counselor or pastor to develop increased understanding of the anger you are experiencing.
- Ask a friend to be your accountability partner. This person can check with you on a regular basis and you can express to them how anger makes you feel.

## 6. Seek Forgiveness

- Seek healing and restoration (where appropriate) of any relationships you have damaged. Your counselor can help you know how to approach this.
- Accepting responsibility for your anger may help others respond in kind. Admitting your faults and mistakes to others is challenging, but they need to know you are trying to change your behavior.

# 6 BIBLICAL INSIGHTS

*Tremble [be angry] and do not sin; when you are on your beds, search your hearts and be silent.*

*Psalm 4:4*

This passage is a great example of the nature of anger. It is neither good nor bad but something that must be addressed and expressed in a way that does not promote sin. If anger is causing sin in your life or another's, then you must take into consideration how your anger could be handled better. It also speaks of meditating, literally taking time to think through what the day has brought. Consider your anger and let it rest in your heart, as you allow the Lord to help you deal with it in a way that is healthy. Finally, it says to be still, having a sense of peace with your anger and a willingness to take the necessary steps to resolve whatever is going on. Being still is a peaceful attitude that requires deep trust in God.

*And do not grieve the Holy Spirit of God, with whom you were sealed for the day of redemption. Get rid of all bitterness, rage and anger, brawling and slander, along with every form of malice. Be kind and compassionate to one another, forgiving each other, just as in Christ God forgave you.*

*Ephesians 4:30–32*

Another aspect of anger is that when it is sinful, it puts you at odds with the Holy Spirit. The apostle Paul encourages us not to work against the Holy Spirit and he lists many ways we may do that. The bitterness that anger and rage produce is to be done away with. Wrath from trying to exact revenge on those who hurt you and anger toward another must be removed so the Spirit can work within you. Speaking evil about others and having hatred are sure signs of anger in the heart. Laying these things down before God will enhance and improve your relationship with Him.

For the Christian, there is no room for intense hatred and anger; it should be replaced with kindness toward others, being open and tender, listening to what they have to say. We can forgive others easier when we grasp just how much Christ has forgiven us—a much greater debt than anyone owes us. Learn to be a person who walks in the Spirit, and anger will be harder to hold on to.

*My dear brothers and sisters, take note of this: Everyone should be quick to listen, slow to speak and slow to become angry, because human anger does not produce the righteousness that God desires.*

*James 1:19–20*

James was a practical man. His entire epistle is filled with practical suggestions for living the Christian life. Here he gives the formula for avoiding anger. First he says to be "quick to listen," which is to say, be a listener. Be the person who listens first rather than immediately offering an elevated opinion or a response of anger. Second, we are encouraged to be "slow to speak," which is to say, do not talk unless appropriate. Part of any healthy relationship is to express oneself, but when we are working through a problem or difficulty that might bring anger, we need to slow down, talking less and listening more. Third, we must be "slow to become angry," not just jumping to a default position of anger. Take the time to listen and talk through a matter to find the right solution that does not cause anger to spill over and damage the relationship. If anger is appropriate, it should come only after a discussion that is pleasing to God. There is a purpose in all this because wrath leads only to unrighteousness.

## PRAYER STARTER : 7

God, I come to You today on behalf of _____. Please help him (her) realize what he (she) really needs is for You to be in control. Help him (her) resolve past hurts and bring healing and restoration wherever it is needed. I ask that as _____ allows You to work out his (her) anger issues, You would provide the fruit of self-control, which only comes from Your Spirit. Guard his (her) life when it comes to the dangers of anger. Make a way for him (her) to break free from reacting in anger and rage. You have called us to be people of righteousness, and we know our anger and hatred do not bring You glory. Lord, I ask that You help us find the source of anger and that You would be glorified throughout this whole process . . .

## RECOMMENDED RESOURCES : 8

Arterburn, Stephen, and David Stoop. *Boiling Point: Understanding Men and Anger.* W Publishing, 1991.

Carter, Les, and Frank Minirth. *The Anger Trap: Free Yourself from the Frustrations That Sabotage Your Life.* Jossey-Bass, 2003.

Chapman, Annie. *Putting Anger in Its Place: A Woman's Guide to Getting Emotions under Control.* Harvest House, 2000.

Chapman, Gary. *Angry: Handling a Powerful Emotion in a Healthy Way.* Northfield, 2007.

Dobson, James. *Emotions: Can You Trust Them?* Regal, 1980.

Ingram, Chip, and Becca Johnson. *Overcoming Emotions That Destroy: Practical Help for Those Angry Feelings That Ruin Relationships.* Baker, 2009.

Jones, Robert D. *Uprooting Anger*. Northfield, 2005.

LaHaye, Tim, and Bob Phillips. *Anger Is a Choice*. Zondervan, 1982.

Potter-Efron, Ronald. *Rage: A Step-by-Step Guide to Overcoming Explosive Anger*. New Harbinger, 2007.

Stanley, Charles F. *Surviving in an Angry World: Finding Your Way to Personal Peace*. Howard, 2010.

## Websites

American Psychological Association: www.apa.org/topics/anger/index.aspx

Anger Alternatives: www.anger.org/

Psychology Today: www.psychologytoday.com/basics/anger

# Anxiety and Worry **33**

- Addie is a homemaker and a mother of four. She and her husband, Sam, decided that she should homeschool her children through the eighth grade until they were ready to enter high school at fifteen. Two of her children have now been successful in the public school system, maintaining above average grades and receiving praise from teachers. However, Addie worries incessantly about the possibilities of their getting into trouble, failing morally, or getting hurt in an accident. She refuses to let her teens go to after-school functions for fear they will begin to hang with the wrong crowd. They are not allowed to drive after five o'clock in the afternoon because she believes most wrecks happen at night. Other than church activities, the teens are not able to hang out with friends outside of school, and Addie constantly questions if they are lying to her.

- Constance was recently in a terrible car accident with her cousin who, after being airlifted from the scene of the crash, died in the hospital. Constance has sought counseling because she cannot stop reliving the events of that night. Most debilitating, though, is the anxiety she feels about having another loved one die. She is constantly calling, texting, and checking in with her close friends and family members. She cannot go to bed at night without knowing they are all safe at home. She finds herself losing time at work, absorbed by the fear of re-experiencing the loss of someone close to her. Her supervisor has complained about her recent lack of productivity, and her friends and family members are becoming irritated by her unnecessary worry for their safety.

- Devin could not leave his home today. Once again, he called in sick to work, much to his boss's frustration. One year ago Devin became dehydrated after having a stomach virus. The symptoms, including heart palpitations, confusion, and dizziness, which led Devin to the emergency room, were incredibly scary to him. Since that hospital visit, Devin has grown increasingly fearful of getting sick and has begun to avoid any environment that may cause him to catch a virus. His girlfriend has broken up with him, he is having difficulties at work, and his friends and family have complained of his no longer being interested in maintaining relationships with them. Though Devin longs to feel normal, his fear and constant worry about getting that sick again cripple his efforts to move on with his life.

271

# 2 : DEFINITIONS AND KEY THOUGHTS

- *Worry and anxiety are basically two sides of the same coin.* Worry is the thinking part of the anxious mind.[1] "Anxiety is a painful or apprehensive uneasiness of mind tied into some impending event."[2]
- Many terms have been used to describe *anxiety*, including *worry* and *fear*. Each of these conditions represents a different level that could be viewed on the same continuum.
- There are different types of *anxiety disorders*: generalized anxiety disorder (GAD), panic disorder, post-traumatic stress disorder (PTSD), social anxiety disorder, obsessive-compulsive disorder (OCD), and specific phobias.[3]

  — *Generalized Anxiety Disorder*—The disorder is characterized by chronic and excessive worry that seems invasive and persistent and can focus on any number of issues or concerns, often accompanied by physical symptoms. It tends to manifest during adolescence and young adulthood and can impair daily functioning. The diagnosis is made after at least six continuous months of almost daily and debilitating worry. GAD affects about 6.8 million American adults (3.1 percent of the population), with women twice as likely to be diagnosed as men.

  — *Post-Traumatic Stress Disorder*—This is an extreme anxiety disorder that usually develops as the result of severe trauma and/or a life-threatening event. It can have the look and feel of a continual panic attack with symptoms that include flashbacks, hypervigilence, an agitated startle response, nightmares, and avoidance of stimuli that remind the person of the event. PTSD impacts approximately 7.7 million people (3.5 percent of the general population), with women more likely to be affected than men. Sexual trauma (childhood sexual abuse and rape) and more recently, combat-related trauma are significant causes of PTSD.

  — *Social Anxiety Disorder*—Also known as social phobia, this disorder is characterized by an extreme shyness and the fear of rejection, shame, and failure in public. Performance anxiety or "stage fright" would be a common example. The disorder impacts about 15 million people (6.8 percent of the general population) and affects both men and women equally.

  — *Obsessive-Compulsive Disorder*—The primary symptoms of this disorder are intrusive and unwanted thoughts (obsessions) and behaviors (compulsions) that feel impossible to control or stop. This may include excessive hand washing, the need to order or arrange items, recurring worry over forgetting something, and so on. Approximately 2.2 million people (1.0 percent of the general population) are diagnosed with OCD, and the disorder affects men and women equally.

  — *Phobias*—These are unrealistic and/or exaggerated fears of a specific object, activity, or situation that in reality presents little or no danger. Some of the more common phobias include the fear of certain animals (snakes or spiders, for example), fear of flying, fear of public speaking, fear of heights. Phobias affect around 19 million people (8.7 percent of the general population), with women twice as likely to be diagnosed as men.

- *Anxiety and depression* can go hand in hand and are believed to originate from the same biological and genetic roots. Anxiety can exacerbate depression and vice versa, which is why both conditions usually need to be assessed for treatment purposes.

- *Low levels of anxiety can be beneficial* in terms of alertness, increased focus and concentration, and perceiving harm; however, *persistent, excessive, and uncontrollable anxiety can overwhelm and incapacitate a person.* An estimated forty million people eighteen and older in the United States (18 percent of the adult population) suffer from an anxiety-related disorder. Anxiety disorders are the *most common mental illness* in this country, representing more than forty-two billion dollars in annual health costs.[4]

- Individuals who are diagnosed with an *anxiety disorder* are three to five times more likely to *see a doctor* for the condition and six times more likely to be *admitted to a hospital* for psychiatric treatment than the general population.[5]

- There is also a *physical reaction* in response to worry or anxiety. The release of hormones causes such responses as muscles tensing up, heart and breathing rates to increase, dry mouth, and heightened eyesight and hearing, thereby increasing awareness.[6]

- Other *symptoms of chronic anxiety and worry* include feelings of panic and fear, uncontrollable obsessive thoughts, sleep disturbances, muscle tension, physical weakness, poor memory, sweaty hands, fear or confusion, the inability to relax, constant worry, shortness of breath, dizziness, numbness or tingling in the hands and feet, heart palpitations, an upset stomach or nausea, and poor concentration.[7] In more severe cases, this can include recurring night terrors, flashbacks, emotional numbing, and panic attacks.

- Due to the physical reactions associated with anxiety, a *cycle of heightened fear responses* begins to develop. When a fear response occurs, the body needs to recover through rest or relaxation. However, many begin to gravitate toward anxious reactions because of the release of adrenaline and other hormones and may ingest caffeine or other stimulant-based substances to maintain the "high." This does not allow the body to properly rest and recover from the initial fear reaction.[8]

- *Personality traits* also play a key role in the development of anxiety and worry. Many Type A personalities, those who constantly pursue perfection, allow this desire to impact all areas of life, creating general feelings of dissatisfaction, insufficiency, and failure. This in turn feeds the anxiety-based reaction to always be perfect while simultaneously worrying about how to make that happen.[9]

- Fears and phobias can occur *throughout our developmental stages* in life. Over the course of our life span and especially in the early and formative years, we begin to develop irrational and illogical fears based on a number of factors. For example, babies have a natural fear of abandonment or stranger anxiety, but if that fear is never addressed by loving and attentive parents, then this may develop into abandonment and attachment issues later in life.[10]

- Anxious people may have a profile that includes *tired eyes, a depressed mood, a lack of motivation, having negative self-talk, a poor self-image,* and other signs that look like general fatigue or a lack of sleep.
- Fear is often present in *spiritual warfare.* Spiritual problems are enhanced by the presence of fear and anxiety. These are usually guilt- or shame-based and can indicate a *fear of failure, rejection,* and/or *condemnation.* Essentially, fear brings a Christian down and keeps him or her from serving God.[11]

# 3 : ASSESSMENT INTERVIEW

1. What are some of the things that cause you to worry or be anxious?
2. What are some of the symptoms you experience when you feel anxious?
3. Are you constantly tense, worried, or feeling on edge?
4. Do you wrestle with feelings of apprehension and dread?
5. Have you experienced sudden and unexpected attacks of heart-pounding panic?
6. How do you deal with the anxiety or worry you are feeling?
7. Do you have any fears? Why do you fear these things? Are any of your fears irrational?
8. Do you feel anxious when others are watching or observing you?
9. To what degree do you struggle with the fear of failure or rejection?
10. How much sleep do you get? Do you sleep well?
11. Is there anything from your past that you think about often or obsess about?
12. Have anxiety and worry had a negative impact on work, school, or life at home?

# 4 : WISE COUNSEL

Anxiety and worry are two of the most common problems that people face. They can emerge from any number of life experiences and/or genetic factors. The person wrestling with excessive anxiety and stress sometimes feeds off the pressure but is often unaware of the damage this causes him or her and others. The obsessive nature of the thought patterns in those who are anxious creates a wave of emotional and physical responses. Many people become anxious over small things that do not actually affect or endanger them as much as they believed they would. These then grow as irrational fears because they are based outside of reality. While there may be some degree of possibility or truth related to the fear, what is feared is still highly unlikely to occur. Usually the irrational nature of fear needs to be addressed.

For others, their anxiety originates almost entirely in the form of thoughts. They are constantly thinking about what makes them anxious. To challenge these cognitions is to encourage more balanced, healthy, and rational thinking. Many individuals obsess over a particular thought or action regarding something they have either done or do not want to do. Changing thought patterns can help address the underlying anxiety.

Finally, many are overly self-conscious. The goal is to first gain a positive and godly self-identity rather than being too preoccupied with how one appears to others. The desire to be perceived by others as competent and happy can create a sense of lack in some area, which causes the person to obsess or worry about the resulting impact. They tend to focus on their weaknesses rather than their strengths. Encourage individuals like this to put their trust and confidence in God and not dwell on the negatives. Many anxieties that are harmful lie within a framework of false thinking or negative self-talk.

# ACTION STEPS 5

## 1. Search Your Thoughts

- When you begin to worry, take a moment to step back and control your thoughts. Think about the things in your life that demonstrate God's presence and love.
- If the thought is logical and results in an anxious reaction, then respond accordingly and in a balanced manner. Allow the anxiety to motivate rather than debilitate your ability to do what needs to be done.
- If the thought is irrational or simply fear-based, then attempt to move on. Try to stop obsessing about it. This may be easier said than done, but when you begin to create a habit of putting away thoughts that do not operate on logic, it becomes easier and less likely to occur. Your counselor can teach you how to do this.
- Accept the fact that life is sometimes filled with uncertainty; excessive worry will not change a situation or result.

## 2. Take Care of Yourself

- Exercise regularly, as this is a natural stress reliever.
- Make sure you are getting enough sleep and adopt healthy eating habits.
- Consider reducing the intake of nicotine and alcohol, as they can exacerbate symptoms.
- One of the best ways to relieve anxious thoughts is to learn specific relaxation techniques that address breathing and reducing muscle tension. These techniques are used to cause your mind and body to stay calm, not letting your anxious thoughts dominate, sending the wrong signals to the body.
- Various techniques can be used to help you relax quickly. Your counselor will help you find someone who can teach them to you. Use them when you feel overcome by anxiety and are in need of immediate relief. Longer form techniques can be used periodically to just help you find rest from a worrying mind.

### 3. Pray and Meditate on God's Word

- When you are facing a multitude of worrisome thoughts and anxiety, just stop and pray for God to release you from them. Give Him the opportunity to order your steps in the moment. He knows your inner thoughts and He can bring calm and peace to your mind.
- Select passages of Scripture that speak to the issues of worry, fear, and anxiety. Allow the truth of God's Word to bring you peace and freedom.

### 4. Adjust Your Schedule

- First, if you do not have a calendar, consider getting one or use some mechanism to track your schedule and activities.
- If your schedule is too full, start making priorities, deciding what needs to be done and what is just optional. Delete some of the optional activities to give yourself more time for the necessary tasks. Creating space in your schedule not only frees up time but it can free up the mind and be de-stressing.
- The more events and activities you are involved in, the greater the potential stress and the feeling of being overwhelmed. This can start an avalanche of worry and anxiety, so set reasonable boundaries for yourself and limit your activities.

### 5. Seek Professional Help

- You may be suffering from an anxiety disorder that requires the attention of a medical doctor and other trained professionals who can assess the possible need for medication and/or therapy. Certain trauma or biologically based anxiety is not a condition that can be resolved only by sheer willpower.

## 6 BIBLICAL INSIGHTS

*Do not be anxious about anything, but in every situation, by prayer and petition, with thanksgiving, present your requests to God. And the peace of God, which transcends all understanding, will guard your hearts and your minds in Christ Jesus.*

*Philippians 4:6–7*

God encourages us to trust in Him for every circumstance and situation. Any difficulty we may be facing is never bigger than our God. Even in times of legitimate anxiety, He tells us to take our requests to Him in prayer, but with an attitude of expectant thanksgiving. In response He will give us a supernatural peace that will guard our minds and hearts. The Lord is always reaching down to help us through our anxious moments.

*Then Jesus said to his disciples, "Therefore I tell you, do not worry about your life, what you will eat; or about your body, what you will wear. For life is more than food, and the body more than clothes. Consider the ravens: They do not sow or reap, they have no storeroom or barn; yet God feeds them. And how much more valuable you are than birds! Who of you by worrying can add a single hour to your life? Since you cannot do this very little thing, why do you worry about the rest? Consider how the wild flowers grow. They do not labor or spin. Yet I tell you, not even Solomon in all his splendor was dressed like one of these. If that is how God clothes the grass of the field, which is here today, and tomorrow is thrown into the fire, how much more will he clothe you—you of little faith! And do not set your heart on what you will eat or drink; do not worry about it. For the pagan world runs after all such things, and your Father knows that you need them."*

*Luke 12:22–30*

Jesus is clear in His words to His disciples that they should not worry or be stressed about their daily needs. God will provide food, health, and clothing. Life should not be consumed with worry, but we should focus on how to honor and serve Him. He is able to supply all our needs and will receive glory when we cry out to Him for help in our difficult circumstances. We become a living testimony to the love He has for His creation. Once we gain this perspective, it will not necessarily eradicate every fear and anxiety in our lives, but the abiding sense of peace will sustain us nevertheless.

*Anxiety weighs down the heart, but a kind word cheers it up.*

*Proverbs 12:25*

Anxiety that builds up in our hearts becomes like a heavy weight that drags us down into fear, worry, and depression. Anxiety can cause hopelessness, but a good or kind word makes us glad. One way to overcome anxiety is to be filled with encouraging words. This may require that we correct our self-talk and meditate on God's faithfulness. When we do this, the spirit within us rejoices and is lifted up with gladness.

*Cast all your anxiety on him because he cares for you.*

*1 Peter 5:7*

Every thought or circumstance that causes our hearts to be anxious should be given to God. We need to throw or cast these things away and we have the freedom to do this because He loves and cares for us. His desire is that we be free from worry. The more we trust in His grace, the more peace we will experience in our daily lives.

*For you were once darkness, but now you are light in the Lord. Live as children of light (for the fruit of the light consists in all goodness, righteousness and truth). . . . But everything exposed by the light becomes visible—and everything that is illuminated becomes a light.*

*Ephesians 5:8–9, 13*

Fear is like a darkroom that develops all our negatives! Those things that are fear- and worry-based create the dark and negative places in our hearts and lives. The one thing that will stop a developing photograph in its tracks is light. This is because light penetrates and overcomes the darkness. We must allow the light of God's Word to shine in our minds, hearts, and spirits—to illuminate us with truth so His peace will reign in us instead of anxiety and fear.

## 7 PRAYER STARTER

Lord, Your Word says that we are to be anxious for nothing, but in everything, through prayer, we must make our requests known to You. I am asking now that You remove every worry, fear, and anxiety in _____'s life. I pray that he (she) would focus on what You are doing in and through him (her). You have provided everything _____ needs to be fulfilled in You. Please keep his (her) heart in perfect peace, a peace that the world could never give; it comes only from Your Holy Spirit . . .

## 8 RECOMMENDED RESOURCES

Dobbins, Richard D. *Your Feelings: Friend or Foe?* VMI, 2003.

Evans, Tony. *Let It Go: Breaking Free from Fear and Anxiety.* Moody, 2005.

Fitzpatrick, Elyse. *Overcoming Fear, Worry, and Anxiety.* Harvest House, 2001.

Hart, Archibald D. *The Anxiety Cure.* Thomas Nelson, 2001.

Jantz, Gregory L., and Ann McMurray. *Overcoming Anxiety, Worry, and Fear: Practical Ways to Find Peace.* Revell, 2011.

Meyer, Joyce. *21 Ways to Finding Peace and Happiness: Overcoming Anxiety, Fear, and Discontentment Every Day.* FaithWords, 2007.

Miller, Randolph C. *Be Not Anxious.* Seabury, 1952.

Mintle, Linda. *Letting Go of Worry: God's Plan for Finding Peace and Contentment.* Harvest House, 2011.

Nichols, Ken. *Harnessing the Power of Fear.* Alive Ministries, 1996.

Phillips, Bob. *Overcoming Anxiety and Depression.* Harvest House, 2007.

Welch, Edward T. *When I Am Afraid: A Step-by-Step Guide away from Fear and Anxiety.* New Growth, 2009.

Wright, H. Norman. *Winning over Your Emotions.* Harvest House, 1998.

### Websites

Anxiety and Depression Association of America: www.adaa.org/

Help Guide: www.helpguide.org/mental/anxiety_types_symptoms_treatment.htm

National Institute of Mental Health: www.nimh.nih.gov/health/topics/anxiety-disorders/index.shtml

Web MD: www.webmd.com/anxiety-panic/guide/mental-health-anxiety-disorders

# Chronic Stress and Self-Imposed Pressure 34

## PORTRAITS 1

- Joy is an overachieving college senior who is trying to get into a major medical school. She has excelled in school and has always dreamed of becoming a doctor. Recently, however, she feels lost in the stress of it all and feels as though she is caving under the pressure. Though her parents never say anything, she believes they will be disappointed with her if she fails to continue on her current path of success. Joy's parents have spent thousands of dollars on her education, and she is desperate not to let them down. Due to the stress, she is having difficulty sleeping and is incredibly unhappy in her present situation.

- Troy is a floor manager at a local factory. Recently his boss has notified him that the company will begin downsizing and moving work to other states. Troy has a wife and three children and is desperate to maintain his midmanagement position. He has begun taking on more work and has been logging a lot of overtime hours. His wife has been complaining about his absence from home and his increasingly grumpy mood. Troy, however, feels that she doesn't understand the burden he carries when it comes to taking care of the family. Overwhelmed by the stress of waiting to see what happens, Troy feels as though he is losing control and losing his family.

- Christy's father passed away two years ago, and her mother was diagnosed with Alzheimer's disease soon after his death. Because of the stress and uncertainty that her mother was facing, Christy decided to move back home to take care of her. After two years of caring for her mother, who is slowly deteriorating, Christy is overwhelmed by the pressure of it all. She is happy to care for her mother and does not want to force her into a nursing home facility, but she feels alone and completely overwhelmed. None of her siblings are able to assist.

## DEFINITIONS AND KEY THOUGHTS 2

- *Stress* can be seen as "a state of mental and physical tension or the conditions that induce the tension."[1]
- The nature of stress is determined as *positive or negative* based on its outcome for the person. If it causes problems in daily life, then it is considered negative; if it is beneficial or motivates us to produce a change in our situation, then it is considered positive.[2]

- *Eustress:* the stress of everyday normal living, which is seen as positive and beneficial.
- *Distress:* the stress caused by strain, overexertion, exhaustion, suffering, or some kind of pain.
- *Burnout versus stress.*[3]

  — *Burnout* is a defense mechanism characterized by *disengagement.*
  — *Stress* is characterized by *over-engagement.*
  — In *burnout* the emotions become *blunted.*
  — In *stress* the emotions become *overactive.*
  — In *burnout* the *emotional* damage is primary.
  — In *stress* the *physical* damage is primary.
  — The exhaustion of *burnout* affects *motivation and drive.*
  — The exhaustion of *stress* affects *physical energy.*
  — *Burnout* produces *demoralization.*
  — *Stress* produces *disintegration.*
  — *Burnout* can best be understood as a loss of *ideals and hope.*
  — *Stress* can best be understood as a loss of *fuel and energy.*
  — *Burnout* produces a sense of *helplessness and hopelessness.*
  — *Stress* produces a sense of *urgency and hyperactivity.*
  — *Burnout* produces *paranoia, depersonalization,* and *detachment.*
  — *Stress* produces *panic, phobias,* and *anxiety disorders.*
  — *Burnout may never kill you,* but your long life may not seem worth living.
  — *Stress may kill you prematurely,* and you won't have enough time to finish what you started.

- Dr. Hans Selye, a Canadian endocrinologist who is called the father of stress research, used the term *general adaptation syndrome* and defined stress as the "non-specific response of the body to any demand."[4]
- "*Stress becomes dangerous when it interferes with your ability to live a normal life for an extended period of time.* You may feel 'out of control' and have no idea of what to do, even if the cause is relatively minor. This in turn may result in you feeling continually fatigued, unable to concentrate, or irritable in otherwise re-laxed situations. Prolonged stress may also compound any emotional problems stemming from sudden events, such as traumatic experiences in your past, and increase thoughts of suicide."[5]
- "Stress can also *affect your physical health* because of the human body's built-in response mechanisms. You may have found yourself sweating at the thought of an important date, or felt your heartbeat pick up speed while watching a scary movie. These reactions are caused by hormones."[6]
- "The longer your mind feels stressed, however, the longer your physical reaction systems remain activated. This can lead to *more serious health issues.* . . . Extended reactions to stress can alter the body's immune system in ways that

are associated with other 'aging' conditions such as frailty, functional decline, cardiovascular disease, osteoporosis, inflammatory arthritis, type 2 diabetes, and certain cancers. Research also suggests that stress impairs the brain's ability to block certain toxins and other large, potentially harmful molecules."[7]

- Of all visits to the doctor, 80–90 percent are stress related. Stress releases *adrenaline* and *cortisol* into the bloodstream with the potential for *harmful effects over time*:[8]

  — a narrowing of the capillaries and other blood vessels leading in and out of the heart
  — a decrease in the flexibility and dilation properties of blood vessels and their endothelium linings
  — a decrease in the body's ability to flush excessive LDL cholesterol out of its system
  — a decrease of up to 50 percent in certain cognitive processes
  — an increase in the production of blood cholesterol (especially LDL)
  — an increase in the blood's tendency to clot
  — an increase in the depositing of plaque on the walls of the arteries
  — an increase in heart, breathing, and glycogen conversion rates
  — an increase for risk of cardiovascular disease, high blood pressure, stroke, and a compromise of the body's immune system

- More than *fifty million* Americans suffer from high blood pressure and nearly *sixty million* suffer from some form of cardiovascular disease, resulting in *more than one million deaths* each year (two out of every five who die, or one every thirty-two seconds). Heart disease has been the *leading cause of death* in the United States every year since 1900 (except 1918) and crosses all racial, gender, socioeconomic, and age barriers.[9]

- "Feelings of despair that accompany stress can easily worsen into chronic depression."[10]

- A variety of factors *contribute to the development of stress*, including work stress, environmental stress, aggravators, major life events, relational stress, and personal stress.[11]

- Those who are severely stressed will exhibit certain signs:

  — *Emotional signs* include apathy, irritability, overcompensation or denial, grandiosity (overemphasizing and exaggeration of one's achievements), anxiety, mental fatigue (preoccupation, concentration problems).
  — *Behavioral signs* include avoidance of stress-inducing behavior, extreme actions such as gambling or alcohol use, administrative problems like poor attendance, poor hygiene, accidents, and legal troubles.
  — *Physical signs* include phobias about frequent illnesses, exhaustion, self-medication, and other ailments such as headaches, insomnia, nausea, diarrhea, sexual dysfunction, body aches, and pains.[12]

- *Stress results from several different things in a person's life*. Many individuals are stressed because of self-imposed standards and pressure. This can result from many things, but at its core, it is likely the result of perfectionism. *Perfectionism* is a "tendency to set extremely high standards."[13]

- There is a scale or spectrum on which perfectionism is placed.[14] *Not all people are completely perfectionistic in every aspect of their lives.* In fact they are more likely to be driven in one or two main areas, while the other areas suffer.

- There are essentially *three levels* of the spectrum that someone can fall under. They are as follows:

  — *Normal or healthy perfectionism.* These are *balanced* individuals and those who generally show a *positive approach* to life. They are interested in success and often do well. They do not have obsessive thoughts about their work, they focus on what is required, and they rarely let work impinge on their time with family, friends, or for leisure activities.

  — *Neurotic or unhealthy perfectionism.* These individuals have a hurried demeanor. They *seem constantly stressed*, which is normally rooted in their desire for perfection or at least their perceived perfection. They find their *self-worth* in setting and achieving unrealistic goals and are often *disappointed in themselves and unhappy* with their progress on assigned tasks and projects.

  — *Nonperfectionism.* These individuals will likely *appear lazy and unmotivated.* They are lacking in any desire to accomplish or even set goals. They can be neurotic about the fact they do not want to do anything and even proud about their lack of motivation or drive. They are happy to be unproductive, often never expecting anything from anyone including themselves.[15]

- *Self-imposed pressure* is another form of perfectionism and it can come from *false perceptions*, particularly in relationship-oriented stress. Individuals who struggle with this dynamic think others are disappointed or mad at them, thereby creating pressure to change dramatically and fit a certain mold to make people happy. *Pressure from within* is usually characteristically unwarranted or even irrational.

## 3 ASSESSMENT INTERVIEW

1. Describe the amount of stress you experience in the workplace. Do you find that your stress comes from the environment you work in or from job performance?
2. How much control do you have over your work setting? How much control do you have at school or at home? Do you feel that you have too little or too much control?
3. What are some of the goals you are currently working toward? Describe in detail how you might react to a problem that comes up in an effort to achieve these goals.
4. Is there a relationship in your life that causes you stress? Explain.

5. How are your communication skills in your relationships?
6. Do you feel as if you are understood and accepted in your significant relationships?
7. Describe your weekly schedule.
8. What are some things that annoy you and why?
9. Describe some ways that you like to relax. Do you find it difficult to relax?
10. Have you ever tried to slow down and enjoy life more?
11. When you are stressed, do you ever say or do something you later regret? Explain.
12. Are you experiencing any physical symptoms related to stress, such as gastro-intestinal pain, constipation, unusual fatigue or exhaustion, tension headaches, muscle tension (especially in the back, neck, or jaw), decreased libido, high blood pressure, or a weaker immune system?
13. Are you experiencing sleep disturbances, recent weight gain or loss, excessive anxiety and panic, or periods of emotional eating?

# WISE COUNSEL : 4

Stress is a natural part of life and a major reason why this particular process addiction can be so difficult for people to break free from or even be aware of. When individuals have negative feelings toward their stress, they may think life would be better if the stress just went away. However, when the stress finally does diminish, they find themselves bored or just simply unhappy. They thrive on an adrenaline-fueled existence and believe purpose comes from being busy, having a full calendar, being accepted by others, and performing and experiencing higher and higher levels of success.

One factor regarding stress is that people will frequently involve themselves in multiple activities. Many will use alcohol and other substances as a means to break away from the stress in an attempt to keep exhaustion, burnout, and regret at a distance. A common theme for those buried in stress is the reality of being so busy reaching for the future that the person fails to enjoy the present and cannot remember the past. In these situations, they end up looking back on life and wondering why so much time was spent on work or worrying about the next promotion. Then they may lament and grieve over lost time and opportunities with family members and close friends or the failure to simply enjoy life.

Those facing stress-related problems are likely coming for help because they are overwhelmed by life and are running on empty from an emotional and physical standpoint. They may want to maintain their current lifestyle because they feel this is necessary. Effective caregiving means confronting the dysfunction and presenting alternatives worth considering. Taking steps to change can be hard, but expectations must be adjusted. A person with excessive stress may be struggling with one or more fears, as well as faulty patterns of thinking.

If you are working with individuals who are putting unnecessary pressure on themselves, you may have to address some denial and minimization. At the source of the pressure is a false belief that they must meet certain standards to feel okay about who they are. These are probably deeply ingrained thoughts that have either been taught or come from certain life experiences. Patience is needed because perfectionistic ideals related to life, work, school, relationships, etc., frequently surface during the counseling process.

# 5 ACTION STEPS

## 1. Identify the Stressors

- Take note of the stressors in your life. If you find that work stresses you out, for example, take some time and look at the specifics of what is so stressful. There is strength in knowing what bothers you.
- What are your pet peeves and what tends to annoy you? Learn that you cannot always control the behavior of others or change people. However, if possible, be sure you avoid those situations and/or individuals that constantly annoy you. Set appropriate boundaries when needed.
- Explore the reasons you are stressed. Are there work-related issues, financial concerns, or relational difficulties? Could it be a self-confidence issue, attachment problems, or even validation concerns? Find the deep-rooted causes that result in stress.

## 2. Monitor Your Moods

- Take your emotional pulse from time to time and learn how to respond versus react in situations. Sometimes overreacting to an event or person is not worth the secondary stress it produces.
- If you get stressed, think through what is going on internally with your mood at that moment. The stressor, when combined with the accompanying mood, can create a dynamic that only heightens the stress further.
- Reframe negatives into positives and apply faith to whatever is causing stress in your life. For example, instead of saying, "I always freeze up and lose my train of thought when I speak in public," a client can say, "I know I'm not the only person who ever gets anxious about this. God is able to take the things that are weak in my life and turn them into strengths so He can be glorified in the process."

## 3. Make Time to Relax

- If you get stressed, find an activity you enjoy. Exercise and other physical activity are great for releasing stress from the body.
- Massages, spa days, manicures, baseball games, playing with your children, running, reading, listening to music, doing something creative, and enjoying a hobby are some examples of activities that help lower stress.
- Make one or two health-related commitments to take better care of yourself (for example, improving your sleep or eating habits, exercising more often, cutting

down on caffeine intake). People who are chronically stressed often suffer from inadequate sleep and in some cases suffer from stress-induced insomnia.

## 4. Analyze Your Schedule

- Take time to closely examine your schedule. Find times that are filled with activities that are not necessarily priorities. If it means cutting back at work or in other areas, make an effort toward change. Manage your time, or your calendar will control you. Ask yourself if the negative consequences of being consumed by a schedule are worth risking your health and significant relationships.
- Set appropriate limits on your various projects and commitments, especially those where you feel the most overwhelmed. Stop taking on extra responsibility in areas that are not priorities.
- Learn to triage (assess and prioritize) your daily and life events.
- Make yourself accountable to others regarding your schedule and be open to the feedback you receive from them.

## 5. Seek Professional Help

- Untreated chronic stress can result in serious complications physically, emotionally, mentally, spiritually, and relationally. Consider getting a complete physical checkup to make sure every system in your body is functioning optimally. A therapist or life coach can work with you to develop an individualized stress prevention plan. These steps will also increase both support and accountability in your life.

# BIBLICAL INSIGHTS 6

*Therefore, there is now no condemnation for those who are in Christ Jesus, because through Christ Jesus the law of the Spirit who gives life has set you free from the law of sin and death. For what the law was powerless to do because it was weakened by the flesh, God did by sending his own Son in the likeness of sinful flesh to be a sin offering. And so he condemned sin in the flesh, in order that the righteous requirement of the law might be fully met in us, who do not live according to the flesh but according to the Spirit. Those who live according to the flesh have their minds set on what the flesh desires; but those who live in accordance with the Spirit have their minds set on what the Spirit desires. The mind governed by the flesh is death, but the mind governed by the Spirit is life and peace. The mind governed by the flesh is hostile to God; it does not submit to God's law, nor can it do so. Those who are in the realm of the flesh cannot please God.*

*Romans 8:1–8*

The apostle Paul encourages the Romans to realize that following the law without the Holy Spirit living in and through us is impossible. Christ became the final sacrifice that covered sin and fulfilled every requirement of the law for all time. His work on the cross freed us from the law and the penalty of sin.

When we are constantly stressing, we may be trying to live in the flesh and completely through our own self-effort, believing the law is more important than the Spirit. When we seek to be holy and righteous in our own strength, this leads to spiritual stress because we are trying to live a life that is perfect and without blame, but it is impossible. Stepping beyond this approach to life brings freedom and we are no longer under condemnation. Trusting and resting in God will bring peace and greater joy for those choosing to leave their stressful lifestyle behind.

*Peace I leave with you; my peace I give you. I do not give to you as the world gives. Do not let your hearts be troubled and do not be afraid.*

*John 14:27*

The peace of God is an amazing thing. It goes beyond the understanding of what the world can offer and stands in stark contrast. One of the many reasons stress is a part of life is that the world promises empty fulfillment by offering materialistic pursuits that will never bring lasting peace or joy. God, however, brings peace to give us rest and it far surpasses understanding and what is expected. In a life of difficult circumstances, His peace is a refreshing alternative to the chaos of life.

*Cast your cares on the LORD and he will sustain you; he will never let the righteous be shaken.*

*Psalm 55:22*

Many times, the stress we have is a natural outcome of living in a broken and fallen world. We worry about the things that need to get done, work hard to accomplish our goals, and strive to provide for ourselves and our families. Stress can be a natural motivator but it can eventually overwhelm us so completely we start shutting down in many areas of life. However, God has given a promise that if we cast our burdens or stress on Him, He will sustain us and bring stability into our lives and circumstances.

When we feel weary and heavy laden, Jesus invites us to give Him the things that burden us (see Matt. 11:25–30). He is not angry, demanding, or punitive in doing this, but "gentle and humble of heart." When we yoke up with Christ, He carries the load while we have the blessing of walking alongside Him.

*Be still, and know that I am God.*

*Psalm 46:10*

Learn to be silent and learn to be still. Scripture tells us that Jesus would often go to a quiet place to be alone with His Father (Luke 5:16). What is it about life that compels us to try to do more than Jesus did? We must develop an attitude and habit of intentionally slowing down, settling our hearts and minds and spirits, and listening for God's still, small voice.

## PRAYER STARTER : 7

Lord, today we praise You for Your every provision. Too often we forget about what You have done and continue to do in our lives. I ask You to help _____ and relieve the stress he (she) is experiencing. You have said in Your Word that if we cast our burdens on You, You will take care of them. Give _____ the confidence to give up his (her) stress and the pressures that take him (her) away from You. Help him (her) see the world through Your eyes. Stress has been a master in his (her) life, and I pray that You would have Your rightful place and take control in every area that is causing stress. Forgive us for the times we have failed to trust in Your grace . . .

## RECOMMENDED RESOURCES : 8

Colbert, Don. *The Biblical Cure for Stress*. Siloam, 2002.

Coty, Debora. *Too Blessed to Be Stressed: Inspiration for Climbing Out of Life's Stress-Pool*. Barbour, 2011.

Hagar, W. David, and Linda C. Hagar. *Stress and the Woman's Body*. Revell, 1996.

Hart, Archibald D. *Adrenaline and Stress: The Exciting New Breakthrough That Helps You Overcome Stress Damage*. Thomas Nelson, 1995.

Jantz, Gregory. *How to De-stress Your Life*. Revell, 2008.

McGee, Robert. *The Search for Significance*. Thomas Nelson, 2003.

Meyer, Joyce. *Straight Talk on Stress*. Hachette, 2003.

Pierce, Pam, and Chuck D. Pierce. *The Rewards of Simplicity: A Practical and Spiritual Approach*. Baker, 2009.

Powlison, David. *Stress: Peace amid Pressure*. Resources for Changing Lives, 2004.

Ronsisvalle, Mike. *Stress Relief for Life: Practical Solutions to Help You Relax and Live Better*. Siloam, 2011.

Whiteman, Thomas, and Randy Petersen. *Stress Test: A Quick Guide to Finding and Improving Your Stress Quotient*. Pinon, 2000.

Winter, Richard. *Perfecting Ourselves to Death: The Pursuit of Excellence and the Perils of Perfectionism*. InterVarsity, 2005.

### Websites

About.com: www.stress.about.com/od/stressmanagementglossary/g/Chronicstress.htm

American Psychological Association: www.apa.org/helpcenter/understanding-chronic-stress.aspx

Mayo Clinic: www.mayoclinic.com/health/stress/AN01286

# 35 Co-dependency and Toxic Relationships

## 1 PORTRAITS

- Julie has had it. Once again she was up all night waiting on her alcoholic boyfriend, Derrick, to make it home safely. "This is it," she exclaimed when he finally walked through the door at 5:00 a.m.; "I am through with the worrying and caretaking! Our relationship is over!" Julie packed up what she could and left for a friend's house, promising herself she would no longer return to the relationship. Three days later, Derrick called Julie after being picked up by the police for his third DUI offense. He promised to change his ways and enter rehab once again if she would come bail him out. Julie feels responsible for him and goes to the jail to pick him up against her friend's advice. Despite her frustration and doubts, Julie finds herself getting excited about being a part of his promised recovery.

- Amy has never gone longer than four weeks without a boyfriend. Her most recent relationship with Joe, an attractive businessman, has ended after three months of wild excitement, followed by a terrible breakup. She had convinced herself she was in love this time—in love like she had never been before. However, as the reality of a single life sets in, Amy's longings for Joe are quickly extinguished by the deep loneliness she wishes to stifle. Once again Amy goes out on the town, looking for someone, anyone, to fill her deep desire for relationship and intimacy.

- Bill is a hardworking father of two. Ten years ago he and his ex-wife went through a tumultuous divorce. Three years after the divorce, Bill fell head over heels in love with Diana, a previous high school fling with whom he rekindled a relationship after a class reunion. Their marriage started off great, and Bill swore he would never go through another divorce. However, over the past several months, Bill has watched Diana spiral out of control due to the overuse of prescription drugs and alcohol. He never knew she had such a problem until it started wreaking havoc in the marriage. Diana refuses to go to counseling or rehab, though she has lost her job and many relationships due to her continued addictions. Bill fears for the safety of his children and wonders how he ever got into another relationship that seems doomed to fail. Instead of seeking help, though, Bill continues to bail his wife out, gives her money, and believes her when she promises to do better.

# DEFINITIONS AND KEY THOUGHTS : 2

- "Although the term was first developed in the substance abuse treatment arena, specifically referring to the wives of men who abuse alcohol, *co-dependency* has more recently been used almost generically to describe *a dysfunctional style of relating to others.*"[1]

- "An *essential characteristic* of someone who is co-dependent is that they *continually invest their self-esteem in the ability to control and influence behavior and feelings in others*, as well as in themselves, even when faced with adverse consequences such as feelings of inadequacy after failure."[2]

- Co-dependency is *when one person is trying to make the relationship work and the other party is not.*

- A co-dependent relationship is one where the *needs of the individuals are met in a dysfunctional way.*[3]

- *Forty million Americans* are labeled as co-dependents, with the majority being women.[4]

- At its core, co-dependency relates to an unbalanced need to *rescue* and/or *fix.* Co-dependents reason that if they can rescue others from a given situation or fix their problems, then they are needed. Since there is often a strong accompanying need to be accepted and wanted, then the co-dependent *continues in the dysfunctional cycle.*

- Often co-dependency has a *source in family relationships.* These family systems are characterized by the suppression of feelings, desires, and needs, when keeping these issues hidden helps the family survive ongoing problems. In this kind of family environment, *abuse and addiction can thrive* and members begin having feelings of anger, shame, and fear that go unaddressed.

- *Enmeshment* can occur within this population. The term is defined as "[using] an individual for our identity, sense of value, worth, well-being, safety, purpose and security. Instead of two [healthy individuals], we become one identity . . . our sense of wholeness comes from the other person."[5] Personal boundaries are permeable and vaguely defined.

- Co-dependency is not necessarily a disease, but rather *an addictive behavioral pattern* that works much like a drug to create dependency, but in this case the dependency is on a relationship.

- *Personal boundaries are essentially nonexistent* for the co-dependent. A significant component is that the person is anxious about the thought of being alone, so he or she will do anything to avoid this. Sexual, personal, financial, and emotional favors or requests are almost always met with willingness.

- The co-dependent has a need to gain self-worth from the approval of others (typically a central person in his or her life) and is obsessed with being able to control this person's behavior.[6]

- Since co-dependency tends to be *a learned behavioral pattern*, children of co-dependents are at a greater risk to continue the habit of becoming a co-dependent later in life, even though they often notice their parent's co-dependent tendencies.[7]

- The co-dependent may be characterized as having *physical and psychosomatic issues* that are related to stress, such as anxiety, stomach problems, heart related concerns, and fatigue.[8]
- Often the co-dependent lives by *three rules*: Don't talk. Don't feel. Don't trust.[9]
- Some *characteristics* of co-dependent individuals include:[10]

  — an exaggerated sense of responsibility for the actions of others
  — low self-esteem and poorly developed self-identity
  — a tendency to confuse love and pity, since they love those they can rescue
  — the pressure to do more than their share all of the time
  — being people pleasers
  — obsessive thinking caused by dependency, anxieties, and fears
  — feeling hurt and reactive when their efforts are not recognized
  — a propensity to hold on to relationships at all costs to avoid abandonment
  — experiencing guilt when they assert themselves
  — a compelling need to be in control and to control others to feel safe and secure
  — lack of trust in self and others
  — difficulty identifying personal feelings
  — rigidity and difficulty in reacting to change
  — lacking boundaries and struggling with intimacy
  — chronic anger, lying, and dishonesty
  — poor and dysfunctional communication skills
  — indecisiveness
  — denial about their behavior and the problem

- *Toxic relationships* include those involving people who are manipulative, narcissistic, excessively negative, judgmental or critical, dream killers, insincere, disrespectful, and never satisfied.[11]

# 3 ASSESSMENT INTERVIEW

1. Tell me about your experiences in relationships. Have you ever lived with or been in a relationship with someone with a drug, alcohol, or other addiction problem?
2. What was your family environment like growing up?
3. Do you ever find yourself trying to fix someone else's problems or rescue them from their circumstances? Do you feel obligated to help others at all costs?
4. Do you find it difficult to say no or to set boundaries in your life and relationships?
5. Do you have trouble expressing your feelings or opinions? Do you stay quiet to avoid arguments?

6. Describe your personal identity. (*Note if he or she uses others to help define self.*)

7. Do you become preoccupied with what others think about you?

8. Do you feel overly self-conscious, inadequate, or like a bad person whenever you make a mistake?

9. Have you ever had trouble asserting yourself? Did you feel selfish or guilty for doing so?

10. Do you have trouble asking for help?

11. How do you feel when you make a mistake? Do you think others view you negatively or positively when you do?

12. Do you feel stuck in any relationship in your life? If so, what feelings are most prominent in your interactions with that person? What would your life be like if that person were no longer in your life?

13. Are you overly compliant in your relationships, even when doing so may bring you harm?

14. Do you suppress your thoughts and feelings to avoid a sense of vulnerability?

15. Do you avoid intimacy (emotional, physical, spiritual, or sexual) as a way to protect yourself and maintain distance from others?

16. Is it difficult to make decisions?

17. Where do you see yourself in five years? What do you expect your life to be like then? (*Look for signs of confusion or insecurity about personal identity.*)

# WISE COUNSEL 4

Co-dependency is not considered a disease but rather an addictive and dysfunctional pattern of behavior. It cannot be cured with medicine or rehab but needs to be addressed with appropriate intervention, yet with caution because of its pervasive nature and its potentially negative impact on relationships. Symptoms of the problem may create a unique challenge. Individuals will exhibit their co-dependency in a variety of means, but two basic ways tend to emerge—helping and enabling. If the co-dependent is primarily a helper, he or she will constantly be concerned with meeting the other person's needs. If the co-dependent is primarily an enabler, he or she will allow others to continue in harmful behaviors, with the goal of protecting those addictive behaviors.

The co-dependent is probably not going to change overnight because he or she developed these learned behaviors over a period of time, most likely in childhood. Patterns in life have been impacted by family environments that promoted co-dependency. Therefore it is important to be patient with the process. Since co-dependents find purpose in their relationships with others and feed off their need to rescue and fix, it is difficult to remove the reward system that stems from these dynamics. Careful confrontation as to the unhealthy aspects of co-dependency is necessary for change to take place.

Co-dependents must learn how to find their identity and sense of purpose in God. It is important that they build on the solid foundation of God's love for them. He wants them to be healthy in their relationships, and co-dependency, in some respects, can be like idol worship because it substitutes the relationship for God.

# 5 ACTION STEPS

## 1. Ground Your Identity in Jesus

- This is the first and most essential step. Part of the problem with co-dependency is that it makes you rely on others for your identity and worth, but in Christ your identity is secure. You do not have to worry about where you stand in Christ; He accepts you completely and is consistent and faithful in His love for you.
- Study God's Word and find out who God says you are, rather than defining yourself by others or even by your own accomplishments. Understand that He is the source for healing issues of failure, shame, and rejection in your life.
- Avoid finding your identity from within because we are all sinners before God and in need of His forgiveness, mercy, and grace. God has created you in His perfect image in which you can live and be fulfilled. He formed you in your mother's womb and knows you intimately, both inwardly and outwardly.

## 2. Refuse to Be an Enabler

- You must identify the areas in which you enable others to have toxic relationships with you. Take a stand and walk away from those behaviors, which are toxic in your life.
- If you are in a relationship that is toxic, seek help on how to break free from the dysfunction. Unless the dynamics of the relationship move toward a healthy and balanced orientation, you will continue to experience negative consequences.
- Stop living as a victim and move beyond that as a survivor. Tough love is saying no to the continual dysfunction, and it is never wrong to say no when saying yes leads only to abusive behavior against you and greater co-dependency.

## 3. Set Healthy Boundaries

- Being co-dependent requires establishing strong boundaries, particularly at the beginning of a relationship. Stating clearly and assertively the things you are going to be responsible for and those you are not will help mediate the tendency to become co-dependent in the relationship.
- Understand that no matter how deeply involved you become in a relationship, no one person will ever satisfy the deepest longings of your heart. You must realize you have been idolizing people and it may be difficult to let go of those perceptions.
- Boundaries are going to be difficult at first, and they may even make you feel lost, without an identity. Refocus when it gets tough, realizing your identity and confidence lie in God's view of who you are.

## 4. Find Accountability Partners

- Talk with your counselor to explore family or origin issues that may have contributed to your co-dependent behaviors.
- Find a support group and find accountability partners to take the journey with you.

# BIBLICAL INSIGHTS : 6

*You shall have no other gods before me.*

*Exodus 20:3*

*They exchanged the truth about God for a lie, and worshiped and served created things rather than the Creator—who is forever praised. Amen.*

*Romans 1:25*

The Exodus verse is the first commandment God gave to Moses, and while it may seem as though it does not apply to the topic at hand, it is perhaps the most important thing to know as a co-dependent. The act of idolatry occurs almost without consciousness. The co-dependent's god has become the relationship or person he or she is co-dependent on. It is not unusual for fallen human nature to seek out something to worship and give attention to rather than God. Even people in healthy relationships can find they are putting their relationships with others before God.

*Then you will know the truth, and the truth will set you free.*

*John 8:32*

Frequently truth for co-dependents is hidden. They use blinders to ignore the abuse and mistreatment they receive, but consequently, they are also blinded to their own value and self-worth that comes from God. They feel shameful and guilty about many things and live in bondage to the lie that identity is best found in others.

In reality God is concerned and cares about your personal identity. He wants to show you the truth of His love and mercy, to cover your sins, and set you free from the burden of insecurity. He has died for you, to give you an opportunity to fully experience Him in relationship. Your desire will be to be seen as He sees you. God will never abuse you, neglect you, abandon you, or lie to you. Nothing will ever separate you from His love (see Rom. 8:31–39).

*Am I now trying to win the approval of human beings, or of God? Or am I trying to please people? If I were still trying to please people, I would not be a servant of Christ.*

*Galatians 1:10*

One of the key aspects of being a co-dependent person is that acceptance and approval in life can come only from the person you are co-dependent on. Constantly seeking his or her approval can make the other person like a god in your life. The apostle Paul speaks here of his deep commitment to proclaiming the gospel. He is being ridiculed in Galatia at a church he actually started. These false teachers had come in and begun to turn the Galatians away from Paul. Paul is assuring them he is not out to please men and conform to their methods or message. Co-dependency changes one's mission and message in life from what God intended to what another person desires. You must continue, like Paul, to please God and not man. God's plans for us will always fulfill our ultimate purpose in life.

# 7 PRAYER STARTER

Dear Lord, I pray today for _____, asking that You be the Lord of his (her) life and direct his (her) paths. God, we thank You for the relationships You have given us and acknowledge that You created us for relationship, in relationship, and through relationship. Bring balance now to every one of _____'s relationships. Help him (her) set any needed boundaries and have a greater sense of Your love and acceptance. Give him (her) the confidence to make the necessary changes in his (her) relationships. We know that Your approval is what we should seek in life . . .

# 8 RECOMMENDED RESOURCES

Arterburn, Stephen, and David Stoop. *The Book of Life Recovery*. Tyndale, 2012.

Cloud, Henry, and John Townsend. *Boundaries*. Zondervan, 1992.

———. *Boundaries in Marriage*. Zondervan, 2000.

Engelmann, Kim V. *Running in Circles: How False Spirituality Traps Us in Unhealthy Relationships*. InterVarsity, 2007.

Groom, Nancy. *From Bondage to Bonding: Escaping Codependency, Embracing Biblical Love*. NavPress, 1991.

Hawkins, David *When Pleasing Others Is Hurting You*. Harvest House, 2010.

Hemfelt, Robert, Frank Minirth, and Paul Meier. *Love Is a Choice: Recovery for Co-dependent Relationships*. Thomas Nelson, 1991.

Ramey, Mary. *Adult Children, Adult Choices: Outgrowing Co-dependency*. Sheed and Ward, 1992.

Vernick, Leslie. *The Emotionally Destructive Relationship: Seeing It, Stopping It, Surviving It*. Harvest House, 2007.

Welch, Edward T. *When People Are Big and God Is Small: Overcoming Peer Pressure, Co-dependency, and the Fear of Man*. P&R, 1997.

## Websites

Adult Children of Alcoholics: www.adultchildren.org/

Celebrate Recovery: www.celebraterecovery.com/

Codependents Anonymous: www.coda.org/

Mental Health America: www.mentalhealthamerica.net/go/codependency

Recovery Connection: www.recoveryconnection.org/addiction-codependency
   -treatment/

# 36 Cults and the Occult

## 1 PORTRAITS

- Marshall is an eighteen-year-old who was raised as a Scientologist. He has recently begun college at a state university and his friend and roommate introduced him to Christianity. Though he had never questioned his parents' beliefs and practice of Scientology, he is beginning to see contradictions in their doctrines. Marshall asks his Christian friend a lot of questions about his faith and is struggling with what he grew up to believe and what he sees lived out by his Christian friend. With the biblical principles he is learning, he feels more freedom and certainty. However, he is afraid that his parents will disown him if he chooses to leave the Church of Scientology.

- Sue is a thirty-three-year-old mother of two who is struggling to raise her children. She grew up in the David Koresh compound in Waco, Texas, where false beliefs and twisted doctrines permeated her and her family's thinking. Though Sue escaped the confines of the Davidian compound prior to the federal siege and eventual fire, which killed both of her parents and one of her siblings, she still wrestles to function normally in relationships and as a parent and she feels she has no one in her life who truly understands her difficulty.

- Max grew up in a strictly religious family. Though he often questioned his parents' beliefs, he never sought to challenge them. When he was nineteen, he met Jared, an incredibly intelligent yet isolated young adult whose involvement in the occult sparked Max's curiosity. What Max learned from Jared and the other members of his coven made him feel as though he fit in and answered a lot of his questions. Where his parents' strict religious practices made him feel different, this coven involvement gave him a sense of belonging and satisfaction. Soon Max was participating in satanic rituals with Jared and the other members and had no interest in participating in activities outside of the group.

## 2 DEFINITIONS AND KEY THOUGHTS

### Cults

- "A *cult* is often understood as a religious group with strange beliefs *out of the cultural mainstream*."[1]
- Some of the most *common cults today* are Mormonism, Jehovah's Witness, Scientology, and Unitarian churches.

- Typically people who belong to a cult are not there because they wanted to join a cult. *They felt the group was legitimate and healthy.* People join these groups with a desire to find meaning in life, be a part of social change, and experience fulfillment or happiness.[2]

- Cults convey a message that the world is bad or evil and that they are good and pure. They encourage others to become a part of their group because they offer the good and pure things. While many mainstream religious groups hold this view also, *cults often use intense methods to strike fear in their members and ensure adherence to their strict codes.*[3]

- Most cults have distinct methods that are used to *control their members.* Some of these include "coercion, intimidation, threats, physical and verbal abuse, manipulation, dishonesty (by leadership), sexual bullying, isolation, separation from friends and family, and forfeiture of personal finances."[4]

- *Techniques of psychological manipulation often found in cults:*[5]

  — *Isolation*: a loss of reality is induced by physical separation from society and all rational references.

  — *Mind control*: a state of high suggestibility is created through a thinly disguised form of meditation.

  — *Peer-group pressure*: the suppression of doubt and resistance to new ideas is achieved by exploiting the natural need to belong.

  — *Love bombing*: a false sense of family and belonging is contrived through hugging, kissing, touching, and flattery.

  — *Lack of privacy*: a loss of the ability to evaluate is achieved by preventing private contemplation.

  — *Sleep deprivation and fatigue*: disorientation and vulnerability are created by prolonged mental and physical activity and by withholding adequate rest and sleep.

  — *Games*: the need for direction when playing games with obscure rules is used to increase dependence on the group.

  — *Meta communication*: subliminal messages are implanted by stressing certain key words or phrases in long, confusing lectures.

  — *No questions*: an automatic acceptance of beliefs is accomplished by discouraging all questions or challenges to authority.

  — *Confusing doctrine*: complex lectures on an incomprehensible doctrine are used to encourage blind acceptance and rejection of logic.

  — *Rejection of old values*: acceptance of a new lifestyle is accelerated by constantly denouncing former values and beliefs.

  — *Confession*: destruction of personal egos, increased vulnerability to new teachings, and the recruits' weaknesses are revealed through sharing innermost secrets and fears.

  — *Guilt*: teachings of eternal salvation are reinforced by exaggerating the sins of the former lifestyle.

— *Fear*: loyalty and obedience to the group are maintained by threatening soul, life, or limb for the slightest "negative" thought, word, or deed.

— *Chanting and singing*: non-cult input is screened out by demanding repetition of mind-narrowing chants or phrases when faced with non-cult ideas.

— *Lack of inhibition*: abdication of adult responsibility is encouraged by orchestrating childlike behavior.

— *Change of diet*: disorientation and increased susceptibility to emotional arousal is achieved by depriving the central nervous system of necessary nutrients through the use of low-protein diets.

— *Controlled approval*: vulnerability and confusion is maintained by alternating between rewarding and punishing similar actions.

— *Dress*: individuality is removed by demanding conformity to the group dress code.

— *Flaunting hierarchy*: acceptance of cult authority is produced by promising advancement, power, favor, and salvation.

— *Finger pointing*: a false sense of righteousness is created by pointing to the shortcomings of the outside world and other groups.

— *Replacement of relationships*: pre-cult family relationships are destroyed by arranging cult marriages and "families" and by restricting contact and communication with the outside world.

— *Financial commitment*: an increased dependence on the group is achieved by "burning bridges" to the past through the donation of all assets to the group.

- *Types of cults*[6]

— *Religious cults*: these groups utilize a common belief system that may use certain rituals and ceremonies, but all incorporate various forms of mind control and have a devoted attachment to or extravagant worship of a particular person or idea.

— *Commercial cults*: these groups, often referred to as "cults of greed," promise certain benefits (such as success, power, influence, financial reward) if you follow their ideas or programs. Mind control techniques are used.

— *Self-help cults*: these groups often target business people and organizations, offer courses and seminars, and specialize in creating powerful emotional and cathartic experiences. Concepts are shared with religious undertones and delivered through a seemingly endless succession of events, books, and videos.

— *Political cults*: these groups use political rhetoric, unrest, and creative concepts to implement mind control on a large scale to recruit members and influence culture. Often they work through various media outlets to accomplish their goals. Nazi Germany and Stalinist Russia would be examples of such cults achieving power.

— *Pagan religions*: these groups are polytheistic and indigenous to certain cultures and people groups and are broadly defined as either "heathen," non-Christian, or outside the faith traditions of the Abrahamic-based religions (Judaism, Christianity, and Islam). *WICCA* (Witches International Coven Council Association), for example, is one of the best known entities of this type. They represent a diverse pagan religion, and their adherents practice witchcraft, sorcery, rituals, and the use of ceremonial "magick."

- Another distinction between cults and mainstream groups is that the *results are different*. People do not necessarily find everything that they are looking for in the mainstream groups and may leave and look elsewhere. However, cults have more damaging track records. A common trait of those leaving cults is that they are *far worse than they were before joining the group*.[7]

- There are several *reasons a person ends up leaving a cult*. The following are four factors that have been observed:[8]

  — The member in some way *breaks away from the isolation* imposed on the group.
  — The member becomes *connected with an instructional or teaching relationship with another group or with another person*. This creates a confusion as to which group or person deserves their loyalty.
  — The member becomes aware that the group has not or *will not create any social change*.
  — The member sees *inconsistency in the leader's ideals and actions*.

- "Bromley [a professor of sociology at Virginia Commonwealth University in Richmond, Virginia] divided the *disaffiliation process* into three stages: *disaffection, precipitating event, and separation*. Disaffection is characterized by doubts that are managed by repression or avoidance, but refuse to go away. Individuals at this stage may begin to pull away or distance themselves from the activities of the group. The incident or precipitating event that triggers a definite action may seem trivial to other members of the group; however, it crystallizes unresolved discontent and provides a reason to formally withdraw from the group."[9]

- Cult members who have left may display a *dissociated personality*. They will be disconnected to the person they once were before joining the cult.[10]

- Family *counseling and relationship building* will likely be necessary for the individual. It is likely that right before involvement with the cult the person had closed all communication off with the family. It is important to deal with the family issues from before the cult involvement, and because of the cult involvement, the issues that have developed will also need to be addressed.[11]

- There are often *deep feelings of anger* toward the cult and its leaders.[12]

## The Occult

- The term *occult* comes from the Latin word *occultus* and means "hidden."[13]
- "Occultism is a *belief in supernatural sciences or powers*, such as magic, astrology, alchemy, theosophy, and spiritism, either for the purpose of enlarging man's powers, of protecting him from evil forces, or of predicting the future."[14]

- Today's occultism is concerned with learning *secret knowledge and rites* used by ancient societies.[15]
- Since occultism is typically viewed as satanic, the *nature of the enemy* must also be considered. Before his fall, Satan was called *Lucifer,* which signifies light and great beauty. He was the "morning star, son of the dawn" (Isa. 14:12) until his pride caused him to desire being greater than God. God had created him and adorned him with every jewel. He was full of wisdom and had the "seal of perfection." He was "anointed as a guardian cherub" (Ezek. 28:14). The following are some of his names:

  — *Satan* (Matt. 12:26)—a Hebrew word meaning "the resistor or adversary"
  — *Devil* (John 8:44; Heb. 2:14; James 3:15–16; 1 Pet. 5:8)—a Greek word meaning "the accuser and slanderer"
  — *Tempter* (Matt. 4:3; 1 Thess. 3:5)
  — *Father of lies* (John 8:44)
  — *Lord of death* (Heb. 2:14)—he has the power of death because he can accuse sinful man
  — *Beelzebul* (Mark 3:22–23)—means "lord of the dunghill" or "the lord of the flies"
  — *Belial* (2 Cor. 6:15)—literally means "worthlessness"
  — *Evil one* (Eph. 6:16; 1 John 2:13)
  — *Prince of this world* (John 14:30)—also referred to as "the god of this age" (2 Cor. 4:4)
  — *Ruler of the kingdom of the air* (Eph. 2:1–2)—indicates Satan's domain goes beyond the confines of the earth
  — *Great enemy and a roaring lion* (1 Pet. 5:8)
  — *Angel of light* (2 Cor. 11:14)—with the ability to deceive
  — *Serpent* (Gen. 3:1–14)—indicates cunning, deception, and lies

- *Satan's hierarchy*: "For our struggle is not against flesh and blood, but against the *rulers*, against the *authorities*, against the *powers* of this dark world and against the *spiritual forces* of evil in the heavenly realms" (Eph. 6:12).

  — *Rulers/principalities* comes from the Greek word *archai* and denotes a high level of satanic prince set over nations and regions of the earth (as in Dan. 10:13, 20 where it talks of the "Prince of Persia" and the "Prince of Greece").
  — *Authorities* comes from the Greek word *exousia* and carries the connotation of both supernatural and natural government.
  — *Powers/world forces* comes from the Greek word *dunamis*, and many biblical scholars believe the words refer to evil forces that, while not over a country or region, operate within it to influence culture and certain aspects of life.

— *Spiritual forces* comes from the Greek word *kosmokratoras* and refers to many types of evil spirits that commonly oppress people through lust, envy, pride, greed, rebellion, and so on.

- *Levels of warfare*

  — *Cosmic conflict* is the ongoing conflict between the Creator and His faithful angels on the one side and the rebellious hierarchy of evil forces under Satan on the other side.

  — *Against the redeemed.* God told the serpent in the garden: "I will put enmity between you and the woman, and between your offspring and hers" (Gen. 3:15). This warfare can be direct in that we personally come under attack (for example, the flaming arrows in Ephesians 6:16), or it can be indirect (as we acknowledge the devil can have broad influence over the affairs of life).

  — *Against the lost.* The apostle Paul tells us in 2 Corinthians 4:4: "The god of this age has blinded the minds of unbelievers, so that they cannot see the light of the gospel that displays the glory of Christ." This battle is on the cutting edge of all spiritual warfare because Satan has already been defeated.

- *Important occultic numbers:*

  — 1 equates with primal chaos.
  — 3 designates triple repetitions and is seen as effective in incantations and rituals.
  — 5 symbolizes justice.
  — 7 in occultic rites possesses mystic implications.
  — 13 is the number of members in a coven, the members being associated with thirteen lunar moons.
  — 4 x 4 in Talmudic computations is the devil's own number.
  — 7 + 9—multiples of these numbers are believed to possess magical potency; the odd numbers are seen as lucky and triple repetitions are characteristically used in rituals.
  — 666 is the sign of the Beast or Antichrist; the Roman letters used for numbers interestingly add up to this total:

  $$
  \begin{array}{rcr}
  D & = & 500 \\
  C & = & 100 \\
  L & = & 50 \\
  X & = & 10 \\
  V & = & 5 \\
  I & = & 1 \\
  \hline
    &   & 666
  \end{array}
  $$

- *Important occultic dates:*
  — September 22—Autumn equinox
  — June 21—Summer solstice

- March 20—Spring equinox
- December 21—Winter solstice
- February 2—Candlemas
- April 30—Walpurgisnacht
- October 31—Samhian (Hallows Eve)
- November 1—Festival of Hecate

- *Important occultic colors:*
  - *Candles*: black for unbinding or death; red for sexual rituals; purple or lavender for conjuring or summoning
  - *Robes*: white for initiation rituals or the object of the sacrifice; red for sexual ritual; skyclad is naked; black for all other activities

- *Satanism defined.* It is the *darkest side of the occult and the complete antithesis of Christianity.* The black mass, black magic, facets of the drug culture, sexual orgies, and blood sacrifice are all part of this religion. *Lucifer is worshiped* as a personal and powerful devil. Although satanic witchcraft exists, many if not most witches claim that they do not personally worship Satan. Pleasure seeking is a key aspect of its philosophy.

- *Self-styled Satanists* are often teenagers who read books, watch movies, or listen to records that view sex, violence, drug use, and Satanism as marketable commodities. This group will often attempt to imitate their favorite writer, actor, or rock star and *create their own versions of Satanism.* Many may not actually believe in or worship Satan.

- *Religious Satanists* are *members of the Church of Satan,* founded by Anton LaVey on April 30, 1966, in San Francisco. He wrote the *Satanic Bible,* which has sold more than a million copies, *The Complete Witch,* and *The Satanic Rituals.* The Church of Satan does not actively seek members and carefully screens those who want to join. For LaVey, Satan was only a symbol. He said that he "neither believed in God nor Satan." He rejected the supernatural, an afterlife, heaven, and hell. The basic theme of his religion is *self-assertion, self-indulgence, antiestablishment,* and the *gratification of one's physical and mental nature.* He believed that each person should live according to his or her own set of rules.

- *Satanic cults.* While there has been controversy about the existence and scope of these groups, it is alleged that Satanists are involved in criminal activities such as *drug trafficking, kidnapping, pornography, and various forms of sacrifice.* They tend to be the least visible regarding their activities and their affiliation with other cult members.

  - The *typical profile* includes those who have above average intelligence, are usually creative and curious, may be using drugs, are possibly underachievers, are usually males, frequently begin as teenagers or young adults, come from middle or upper-middle class families, have a low self-esteem, have difficulty in relating to peers, and are loners and isolated.

— *Signs of active involvement* include an obsession with fantasy and role-playing games; an obsession with heavy metal, black metal, or thrash metal rock; books on magic, witchcraft, paganism, Satanism, and grimoires; objects used for spells or rituals; candles (tapered or in the shape of a human figure); candle holders; incense; knives; pentagrams; inverted pentagram; inverted cross and the number 666; symbolic jewelry; drug use (incense is a common cover-up for the odor of some drugs); unexplained paranoia or fear of the world; a preoccupation with the color black and/or death themes; extremely secretive (refuses to talk about anything, hides things, seems unresponsive); a fear of discussing involvement due to the belief that others in the group will know psychically or otherwise.

- *Ritualistic abuse* is a brutal form of abuse of children, adolescents, and adults, consisting of physical, sexual, emotional, and psychological abuse involving the use of rituals. "Ritual" as used here does not necessarily mean Satanists. However, many survivors state that they were ritually abused as *part of satanic worship and for the purpose of indoctrinating them* into satanic beliefs and practices. Ritual abuse rarely involves a single episode but is usually repeated abuse over an extended period of time. The physical abuse is severe, *sometimes including torture and killing*. The *sexual abuse* is usually painful, sadistic, and humiliating, intended as a means of gaining dominance over the victim. The *psychological abuse* is devastating and involves the use of ritual and indoctrination, which includes mind-control techniques, mind-altering drugs, and intimidation to convey profound terror of the cult members or the evil spirits they believe cult members can command.

  — *Common beliefs of victims*: there is no escape, the cult completely controls me, I am incapable of protecting myself, the cult is my only "true" family, memories are dangerous, disclosures are dangerous, Satan is stronger than God, God does not love me, God wants to punish me, my life is controlled by Satan, my life is dedicated to Satan.

## ASSESSMENT INTERVIEW 3

1. Describe some of the rules that were used by the group.
2. What are some things that you enjoyed doing before joining the group that you wish you could still do?
3. Since leaving the group, have you felt any type of strong emotion, such as anger, fear, anxiety, or sadness?
4. When you joined the group, what was it about that group that made you want to become a part of it?
5. Are there any relationships you would like to have back that you lost because of your involvement with the group?
6. What form of psychological or emotional manipulation were you subjected to?

7. Tell me about your beliefs regarding God, Christianity, the death and resurrection of Christ, eternity, angels and demons, and the Bible.
8. Have you ever participated in an occult group or activities? If so, describe your experiences.
9. Have you ever been abused? Have you ever abused or violated another person?
10. Have you ever renounced past behaviors that were part of your being involved with a cult or the occult? Have you repented of any sins committed as part of a group, asked for God's forgiveness and for Him to cover your sins?
11. Have you found a good church to attend? Do they teach from the Bible? Are you fellowshipping with other believers?

# 4 : WISE COUNSEL

One thing to note is if you are working with someone who has issues with a cult or the occult, he or she is likely trying to leave or has already left. People still trapped within the cult will not be interested in seeing you for help because they believe that is what the group is there for. Furthermore, they would not have permission to see you even if they wanted to. Be cautious about using terms such as *cult* and *Satanism*, minimizing or invalidating their experiences, or accusing them of certain behaviors. The client may already be wary of anyone in authority and also be hypervigilant, so these things can cause them not to trust you. Many come to reality on their own timetables and when they are ready to accept their experiences as being part of a false cult.

People join cults for different reasons; however, a common thread among cult members is significant unmet needs for belonging and feeling unwelcome or unaccepted in their social support systems. They may have had few friends or felt they did not fit in with their family or normal peer groups. Obviously there are exceptions to this, but it is important to realize that some sort of hurt and insecurity is behind their behaviors and choices. Therefore during your sessions and interactions, family issues will often play an important role in the counseling process. Be careful to avoid any intensification of these issues. The feelings that led the person to the cult can come out in a way that is more volatile than desired or expected. Anxiousness as a result of psychological manipulation can increase the likelihood of relapse back into "group-think" behaviors.

A major issue associated with cults is that participation with the group strips away the individual's identity and freedom. Cult leaders strive to have complete authoritarian leadership over their followers' lives. They remove individual freedom through intimidation, rules that are incredibly difficult to follow, and severe consequences for violating them. Clients must be given an appropriate amount of freedom and self-determination in counseling to re-establish a sense of control of their life. As you progress and the client regains a measure of independence, the new freedom will be helpful in developing a more balanced and accurate worldview.

In moving through the counseling sessions, there should be a noticeable reduction in the degree of group-think because the oppression that has limited their lives is diminished and their own personalities will re-emerge. Cult members have been indoctrinated into believing everyone in the group must conform to the same standards, look, and beliefs. However, God has created us all different and with unique personalities.

# ACTION STEPS : 5

## 1. Accept Responsibility and Choose Grace

- One of the things that many cult and occult survivors feel is that they were completely to blame for believing false doctrines and teaching and for allowing themselves to be deceived. While this may be true, accepting that you cannot change the past is essential to moving on. Many survivors were led to believe they had crossed the line with God and could never be forgiven or turn back. This is another lie. There is no sin so deep that God's grace is not deeper still. Confession, repentance, forgiveness, and restitution, however, are all important processes that you may need to pursue. Since many cultic groups have a works-oriented mind-set, you need to learn a balanced understanding of grace.

## 2. Move toward Healthy Self-Control

- As a member of a cult, you likely did not have much power over your decisions and if you did, you faced considerable punishment, guilt, shame, and anguish over independent choices. Take the time to realize you have a measure of control back in your life and can make many of your own decisions now. Ask yourself what you like and what you do not like.
- Choose life over death, freedom over bondage, peace over fear, forgiveness over condemnation, and grace over false works.
- Replacing the control of group-think with the spiritual fruit of self-control (Galatians 5) is essential to recovery.

## 3. Reconnect with Loved Ones and Friends

- You probably have severed relationships with family members and old friends as a result of your involvement in the group. Reconnecting can be a difficult step because it requires you to be open and transparent about your issues. However, there is a trade-off for doing this. You will regain important relationships that can help redefine who you are apart from the group. In many cases, family and friends have been concerned for your safety and well-being. They may have felt that they lost you forever and are now hopeful once again and open to repairing any damage that has been caused.

## 4. Pray

- You should pray to God about anything, but be specific about your needs.
- Ask God for forgiveness, discernment, peace, and His grace and direction in your life. Ask Him to help you develop a balanced understanding of your personal identity. Ask Him to heal your mind and heart and to provide for your needs, and talk to Him about your struggles. He wants to hear from you about all these things and reveal His love to you in a new way.

## 5. Read the Bible

- Due to the nature of your cult involvement, a balanced, healthy, and biblical knowledge of who God is and what His Word really teaches is critical to your overall recovery. Take the time to talk with people, especially respected and trusted Bible teachers, and learn from them.
- Read your Bible, commentaries, and other works on the major doctrines of Christianity. There are many excellent commentaries and resources available to help you learn and grow. Your counselor will suggest some for you to read. Above all, do not be afraid to ask questions.

## 6. Fellowship with Other Believers

- Because you were associated with an unhealthy and ungodly group of people, spending time with Christians in worship, Bible study, fellowship, and social activities is important.
- Find a church where you feel safe and one where the Bible is taught regularly and Christ is honored.

## 7. Get Professional Help

- Due to the depth of deception, abuse, mind-control techniques, and other experiences, you will most likely need to work with a professional therapist and others who have expertise in cult deprogramming. It is essential that you connect with Bible-believing counselors and experts who can bring the truth of God's Word into the recovery process. If you are attending a church, be sure to ask your pastor for help as well.

## 8. Find Accountability Partners

- There is a network of other Christians who have left cults and the occult. Your counselor will help you find reputable organizations and resources that provide accountability and support for ex-cult members. They can help you discern and understand what the best options and next steps are for you.

# 6 BIBLICAL INSIGHTS

*Dear friends, do not believe every spirit, but test the spirits to see whether they are from God, because many false prophets have gone out into the world.*

*1 John 4:1*

One of the major purposes of 1 John is to expose and denounce false teachers. It was of considerable concern then and it still is today. John calls on believers to test the spirits, to think, and to have discernment when listening to those who preach or teach a doctrine. God, through the Holy Spirit, will reveal whether or not their message is true. If you are going to discern between the spirits, then it requires you to be a student of God's Word. There exist numerous ideas and teachings in the world because there are so many false prophets and teachers.

*The person without the Spirit does not accept the things that come from the Spirit of God but considers them foolishness, and cannot understand them because they are discerned only through the Spirit.*

*1 Corinthians 2:14*

The apostle Paul expounds on the nature of discernment. The context for this passage discusses how a person who is unsaved finds it difficult to understand that Christ died for our sins, that He has risen from the dead, or how we can have a personal relationship with Him. Some things about the gospel cannot be understood until a person is born again and has the Holy Spirit to give them understanding.

When there are things about God's Word that are difficult to understand, the deceptive teachings of a false cult can become attractive, even to someone who professes to be a Christian. This is because all religious error has an element of truth contained within it. However, often these groups mask themselves under the guise of Christianity and declare themselves to have extra revelation or be more enlightened. They are deceiving others into thinking they know more than what the Bible says. Everything we need to know about God and His interactions with the world, He has given us in His Word, the Bible. Trust in the Holy Spirit's ability to show you the truth.

*Therefore, there is now no condemnation for those who are in Christ Jesus, because through Christ Jesus the law of the Spirit who gives life has set you free from the law of sin and death.*

*Romans 8:1–2*

More often than not, when people have been in a cult, they feel as if they crossed a threshold to the point where Christ's death cannot cover their sin. The good news is that salvation through His love covers a multitude of sins and the repentant is no longer condemned in God's eyes. If a person is living and walking according to the Spirit, then they have been set free and given power over the sins that they committed. Following the Spirit brings freedom and joy and never leads to bondage and depression. Christ does not condemn us. Our freedom is found in Him.

*We also have the prophetic message as something completely reliable, and you will do well to pay attention to it, as to a light shining in a dark place, until the day dawns and the morning star rises in your hearts. Above all, you must understand that no prophecy of Scripture came about by the prophet's own interpretation of things. For prophecy never had its origin in the human will, but prophets, though human, spoke from God as they were carried along by the Holy Spirit.*

*2 Peter 1:19–21*

One of the key features of cults is that they take scriptural concepts and interpret them improperly. Some cults even have their own set of religious texts that they consider to be inspired by God. What Scripture says is that there is not one element of prophecy or truth that came directly from a man or any private interpretation that was put into the Word of God. Only what the Holy Spirit prompted in a person was spoken or written. This is an important principle to keep in mind, as many cults base their structure on a member's level of knowledge concerning spiritual doctrines. God is not hiding Himself from the world; He desires to be known by all people. Cults build impenetrable barriers for their members and use techniques that convince members they are not worthy enough to know the full truth. This mind-set maintains the leader's power and control over cult members. Yet God is not that way; He has revealed all we need to know Him deeply and intimately.

*What, then, shall we say in response to these things? If God is for us, who can be against us? He who did not spare his own Son, but gave him up for us all—how will he not also, along with him, graciously give us all things? Who will bring any charge against those whom God has chosen? It is God who justifies. Who then is the one who condemns? No one. Christ Jesus who died—more than that, who was raised to life—is at the right hand of God and is also interceding for us. Who shall separate us from the love of Christ? Shall trouble or hardship or persecution or famine or nakedness or danger or sword? As it is written: "For your sake we face death all day long; we are considered as sheep to be slaughtered." No, in all these things we are more than conquerors through him who loved us. For I am convinced that neither death nor life, neither angels nor demons, neither the present nor the future, nor any powers, neither height nor depth, nor anything else in all creation, will be able to separate us from the love of God that is in Christ Jesus our Lord.*

*Romans 8:31–39*

When we come to Christ in humble confession and brokenness to receive His gift of salvation, nothing can separate us from His love and grace. Cults and occult groups try to convince followers that the leader, the group, Satan, or his demons are more powerful and influential than God. Nothing could be further from the truth. In Christ we are able to conquer all things—our fears, our sin, deception, and the lies of the enemy. The battle in the spiritual realm is not between a good and all-powerful God fighting against a bad, but equally all-powerful Satan. The battle is one in which the Creator of the universe and the King of Kings has already defeated sin at the cross of Calvary, the created one (Satan), and his followers, and now has the keys of hell and of death in His possession. One day, He will return to reclaim the earth to rule and reign with those who are fully His.

## PRAYER STARTER : 7

Dear Lord, I lift up _____ before Your throne of grace. I know You care deeply for him (her). I pray that You heal and restore him (her) to bring balance and truth to his (her) thinking and understanding of spiritual things. You tell us in Your Word that You want us to know You intimately. Help _____ know that You are the source of all truth and true fulfillment. Thank You for revealing Yourself and showing _____ he (she) has been searching in all the wrong places for enlightenment and meaning. I pray You will give _____ redemption and freedom. Place a shield of protection around him (her) and guard his (her) mind and spirit as we move forward in this process . . .

## RECOMMENDED RESOURCES : 8

Carden, Paul, ed. *Christianity, Cults, and Religions*. Rose, 2008.

Geisler, Norman L., and Ron Rhodes. *Correcting the Cults: Expert Responses to Their Scripture Twisting*. Baker, 2005.

Jackson, Andrew. *Mormonism Explained: What Latter-Day Saints Teach and Practice*. Crossway, 2008.

Martin, Walter, Jill Martin Rische, and Kurt Van Gorden. *The Kingdom of the Occult*. Thomas Nelson, 2008.

Martin, Walter, and Ravi Zacharias. *The Kingdom of the Cults*. Bethany, 2003.

Mather, George A., Larry A. Nichols, and Alvin J. Schmidt, eds. *Encyclopedia Dictionary of Cults, Sects, and World Religions*. Zondervan, 2006.

Murphy, Ed. *The Handbook for Spiritual Warfare*. Thomas Nelson, 2003.

Schnoebelen, William. *Romancing Death: A True Story of Vampirism, Death, the Occult, and Deliverance*. Destiny Image, 2012.

Sire, James W. *Twisting Scripture: 20 Ways the Cults Misread the Bible*. InterVarsity, 1980.

Woods, Bonnie. *Deceived: One Woman's Stand against the Church of Scientology*. Roperpenberthy, 2009.

### Websites

All About the Occult: www.allabouttheoccult.org/

Cult FAQ: www.cultfaq.org/

How Cults Work: www.howcultswork.com/

Spiritual Abuse Awareness: www.spiritualabuseawareness.com/

Spiritual Research Network: www.spiritual-research-network.com/home.html

Watchman Fellowship: www.watchman.org/index-of-cults-and-religions/

# 37 Narcissism and Attention Seeking

## 1 PORTRAITS

- Carl is forty-six and supervises twenty-five employees in a major company. Though he is highly productive and has helped the company succeed in a number of key projects, Carl is known for his arrogance and is extremely disliked by his colleagues and those he supervises. He constantly brags about his many accomplishments, is self-centered, has an inflated sense of entitlement, and frequently takes credit for the work that others do. He has few friends, and those who do tolerate his behavior often talk behind his back about his irritating demeanor and the unrealistic expectations he puts on others.

- Shelia is a bright and attractive eighteen-year-old. Throughout her life she has strived to be perfect and has been pretty successful. Because of her involvement in school clubs, soccer, church, and pageants, Shelia is well-known in her small community. Most people, however, do not know the frustration and hurt she carries around because of her alcoholic mother and abusive father. Rather than succumbing to the pain, though, Shelia continues to excel and be involved. She thrives on the attention she receives and feels important because of this involvement. This has increasingly caused her to seek out opportunities and environments where she can draw attention to herself.

- Tanner is the star quarterback on his college football team. As a child he excelled in sports; his family and high school coaches were certain he would be equally successful as he entered his college career. All Tanner has ever known is the praise of others. He excels regardless of adversity and feels empowered as he carries his teammates to victory week after week. He feels special—different from the rest of his peers and teammates—and confident of the power he holds on the team and in social circles. In relationships Tanner is manipulating and overpowering, often belittling others with sarcastic, arrogant, and judgmental statements. Many around him put up with this behavior, though, because of the status he holds and the popularity he maintains.

## 2 DEFINITIONS AND KEY THOUGHTS

- *Narcissism* is characterized by an inflated sense of self-importance, a deep need for approval and admiration, a belief of being superior to anyone else, and little interest in the lives of others.[1]

- The word *narcissism* comes *from a Greek myth* in which a handsome young man named Narcissus sees his reflection in a pool of water and falls in love with it. This gives rise to the perception that narcissists have a grandiose sense of self-importance.

- Underlying the image of a superior person and his or her projected self-importance, the individual is *usually vulnerable to even the slightest criticism because of a weakened self-esteem.*[2]

- Narcissism can come across as positive self-esteem and self-confidence, but it goes far beyond that. It is *displayed as a lack of care or value in other people.*[3]

- *Narcissistic personality disorder symptoms* may include: [4]

  — believing that you are better than others
  — fantasizing about your power, success, and attractiveness
  — exaggerating your achievements or talents
  — expecting constant praise and admiration
  — believing that you are special and acting accordingly
  — failing to recognize other people's emotions and feelings
  — expecting others to go along with your ideas and plans
  — taking advantage of others
  — expressing disdain for those you feel are inferior to you
  — being jealous and envious of others
  — believing that others are jealous of you
  — trouble maintaining healthy relationships
  — setting unrealistic goals
  — being easily hurt and rejected
  — having a fragile self-esteem
  — appearing tough-minded or unemotional

- The narcissistic person is going to have *significant areas of personality impairment.* Those areas include: [5]

  — *Self-functioning*

    1. They have *difficulty with their sense of identity* and often seek to put others down to improve their own image. They must inflate and exaggerate the self to accept who they are. Often their emotions reflect the fluctuations in their self-esteem.
    2. They are *unable to direct themselves.* They do things and set goals according to the approval and praise of others. They lack their own motivation because of a sense of entitlement but can have standards that far exceed practicality.

  — *Interpersonal functioning*

    1. They have *difficulty with empathy* or showing compassion because of an inability to identify with the problems of others. They can be very

**311**

perceptive concerning a person's reactions and his or her feelings, but only to the degree that they relate directly back to them.

2. They have an *extreme desire for attention* and want to be the focus of others' interest.

- The narcissist can become *impatient and very antagonistic* toward others because of his or her grandiosity and attention-seeking behaviors.[6]
- The *etiology* of the personality disorder is not always readily apparent because each situation has a unique set of circumstances. A common cause is *a dysfunctional childhood*, which included pampering, high expectations, or abuse.[7]
- There are *several types of narcissistic people* such as the following:[8]

  — *Normal.* By nature the person is *competitive and self-assured* and believes in him- or herself. *Charming, clever, confident,* and *ambitious,* such a person often becomes an effective and successful leader.

  — *Unprincipled.* The person is *fraudulent, exploitative, deceptive,* and *unscrupulous.* Although people displaying this type of narcissism are usually successful in society and manage to keep their activities within the accepted norms, they can also be found in drug rehabilitation programs, jails, and prisons.

  — *Amorous.* This person is *erotic, exhibitionistic, seductive, aloof, charming, exploitative,* and *reluctant to become involved* in deep, mutual, intimate relationships.

  — *Compensatory.* This person has *illusions of superiority* and an image of high self-worth, but with an underlying emptiness, insecurity, and weakness. This type is sensitive to others' reactions and *prone to feeling ashamed, anxious, and humiliated.*

  — *Elitist.* A person with an excessively inflated self-image who is a social climber, admiration seeker, self-promoter, bragger, and empowered by social success.

  — *Fanatic.* A *severely narcissistically wounded* individual who usually has major paranoid tendencies, holding on to an *illusion of omnipotence.* These people are fighting the reality of their insignificance and lost value and are trying to reestablish their self-esteem through grandiose fantasies and self-reinforcement.

- Individuals who are *at risk for developing narcissism* typically experienced one or more of the following as children:[9]

  — Their *needs and fears were viewed as unimportant* or they were even hated by their parents.

  — They were *not given appropriate praise and attention.*

  — They were *neglected* or emotionally or verbally *abused.*

  — They were given *excessive praise* and were *overindulged* by their parents.

  — They were *spoiled.*

  — They *learned manipulative behaviors* from their parents.

- *Untreated narcissists* can also face substance and alcohol abuse, depression, suicidal thoughts or behavior, relationship difficulties, and problems at work or school.[10]
- Treatment typically centers around *cognitive-behavioral therapy*, *family therapy*, and *group therapy*.[11]

# ASSESSMENT INTERVIEW 3

1. Who are the most important people in your life? Describe them as best as possible. *If clients cannot seem to relate beyond themselves, they may struggle with narcissism.*
2. Describe your childhood. Were you allowed to do certain things your peers were not doing? Did you grow up with strict or lenient parents?
3. When someone criticizes you, what is your normal reaction?
4. At social or family gatherings, do you try to make people notice you? What are some of the behaviors you do to get attention at these functions?
5. Have you ever been turned down for something you deserved? Why did you think you deserved it?
6. Do you view yourself as better than others?
7. Do you have difficulty identifying with the feelings, needs, and viewpoints of others?
8. Do you set unrealistic goals for others around you?
9. Do you ever exaggerate your talents or achievements?
10. What are your future plans?
11. What do you believe others think about you? Are you hypersensitive to criticism?

# WISE COUNSEL 4

Narcissists can be a very difficult population to work with. In fact, because of their narcissism, most will not seek help. A breakdown or significant conflict at work or home usually leads them into counseling. As a result of the conflict, they may be more receptive and emotionally vulnerable than under normal circumstances. The one issue that keeps them from appearing sufficient (the capacity for empathy and compassion) is now more likely to be addressed. Role modeling empathy on your part (e.g., showing concern, being attentive and a good listener, reflecting feelings, etc.) may be helpful in working toward changed behavior patterns. Other times, balanced but appropriate confrontation may be indicated.

Understanding which type of narcissist you are counseling (from the list above) is important. Each type will have different behavioral traits, and you must consider how the narcissism manifests in their everyday life. This can help in breaking through different barriers to find root causes for the disorder. However, they may try to resist addressing the more difficult aspects of their upbringing or interpersonal relationships.

Many narcissists view their behavior as normal because personality disorders are usually identified by thought processes that do not violate a person's conscience or make him or her feel bad. They simply view the world and their relational style with others as natural, even though they may be unaware of how negative the perception is of them. This general lack of awareness and/or concern for others takes place on a continuum. There is a level of narcissism in all of us, but when this orientation becomes a lifestyle and interferes with the ability to develop healthy interpersonal relationships, it can become a significant problem for the person.

# 5 ACTION STEPS

## 1. Take Responsibility

- It is time to take ownership of your problems. You must realize you have an inflated sense of self that needs to be addressed. The source of your problem lies with a sinful heart that seeks only to please itself. Rely on the presence of the Holy Spirit to remind you daily of your responsibility to give God first place in all areas of your life and then to serve others.

## 2. Learn about the Issue

- In seeking recovery for anything, education is a helpful step. Read about narcissism and narcissistic personality disorder. Learn from various sources, from books to the internet.
- Ask your counselor to refer you to a psychologist who understands your disorder and can work with you on changing your thoughts, attitudes, and behaviors.

## 3. Find Accountability Partners

- Find trusted individuals you can rely on, people who truly care about you and have your best interests at heart, who will be your accountability partners. Give them permission to confront you lovingly whenever you are behaving in a narcissistic manner. Open yourself up to their constructive feedback and do not shut down when they point out your shortcomings. The goal is not necessarily to feel good but to change.

## 4. Keep Working on Change

- Change, even desired and sought-after, is never automatic or easy. Diligence and focus will be required. Due to the nature of fallen man and the universality of selfishness in our world, it can be easy to feel frustrated or envious. Frustration may come when you fail in some way or because you have done something driven by your narcissism. You may feel jealous when you don't get your way or another person receives or experiences something you think you deserve instead.

- Don't let your missteps discourage you. Stand firm and recommit yourself to your goals every time you falter.

## 5. Take Time to Be with God

- Spend time each day in prayer, asking God for guidance, confessing sin, and reaffirming your trust in Him.
- Center yourself at the beginning of each day by spending time refocusing on who you are according to God's Word. Remember that He is the source of all good things and has given every gift and ability that you possess or need in life.
- Meditate on appropriate Bible verses (your counselor can direct you to them) and ask God to change your heart, transform your character, and make you more Christlike.

## BIBLICAL INSIGHTS : 6

*Jesus replied: "'Love the Lord your God with all your heart and with all your soul and with all your mind.' This is the first and greatest commandment. And the second is like it: 'Love your neighbor as yourself.' All the Law and the Prophets hang on these two commandments."*

*Matthew 22:37–40*

Jesus clarifies the basis for the entire law—loving worship of God and loving service to others. When we think too highly of ourselves and think of others as less important, we compromise His precepts. Loving others takes different forms and many of the commandments and exhortations in Scripture relate to how this is accomplished. Take time to be with God so He can give you the same mind-set He has toward all people and teach you how to love them.

*And he died for all, that those who live should no longer live for themselves but for him who died for them and was raised again.*

*2 Corinthians 5:15*

Jesus is our greatest example of what it means to love someone selflessly and sacrificially. He loved His creation so much that He was willing to be crucified for us, and we should endeavor to be living testimonies of that same love. Because He has died for us, we should no longer live selfishly, but live for Him and pursue His desires.

*Do nothing out of selfish ambition or vain conceit. Rather, in humility value others above yourselves, not looking to your own interests but each of you to the interests of the others. In your relationships with one another, have the same mindset as Christ Jesus: Who, being in very nature God, did not consider equality with God something to be used to his own advantage; rather, he made himself nothing by taking the very nature of a servant, being made in human likeness. And being found in appearance as a man, he humbled himself by becoming obedient to death—even death on a cross!*

*Philippians 2:3–8*

Jesus epitomizes humility, grace, and what it means to have a servant's heart. He laid down everything and took the lowest place, so that in due time His Father could exalt Him to His right hand. The character of Christ and His humility are in direct opposition to the behaviors of a narcissist. He is our example and the One to model our lives after.

*Love is patient, love is kind. It does not envy, it does not boast, it is not proud. It does not dishonor others, it is not self-seeking, it is not easily angered, it keeps no record of wrongs. Love does not delight in evil but rejoices with the truth. It always protects, always trusts, always hopes, always perseveres.*

*1 Corinthians 13:4–7*

In the great chapter on love, 1 Corinthians 13, we see how love is to be selfless and not self-seeking. These verses tell us what love is and what it is not. God is love and He embodies the construct in every imaginable way. Love is not just something that is felt, though it involves the emotions. Love is also an act of the will and a decision to show through our outward behavior the results of an inward transformation.

# 7 PRAYER STARTER

Lord, I ask right now that You come and empower _____ to live a life that is pleasing to You. Help him (her) put on a mantle of love and, with a servant's heart, think of others first and more highly than himself (herself). I pray that he (she) will be committed to working through any selfishness and narcissism. Please be a source of strength and encouragement. This is a battle that we all face, and You have the ability to transform our thoughts, our attitudes, and our behaviors to align with Your will. Help us see others with Your eyes, speak to them with Your words, and love them the way You would . . .

# 8 RECOMMENDED RESOURCES

Behary, Wendy T. *Disarming the Narcissist: Surviving and Thriving with the Self-Absorbed.* New Harbinger, 2008.

Chan, Francis. *A Selfless Pursuit of God*: Parts 1 and 2. Focus on the Family Radio Broadcast, 2011.

Hotchkiss, Sandy, and James F. Masterson. *Why Is It Always about You?: The Seven Deadly Sins of Narcissism.* Free Press, 2002.

King, Patricia. *Overcoming the Spirit of Narcissism: Breaking the Destructive Patterns of Self-Idolatry and Self-Exaltation*. XP, 2010.

Lerner, Rokelle. *The Object of My Affection Is in My Reflection: Coping with Narcissists*. Health Communications, 2009.

Meier, Paul, Cynthia Munz, and Lisa Charlebois. *You Might Be a Narcissist If . . . : How to Identify Narcissism in Ourselves and Others and What We Can Do about It*. Langdon Street Press, 2009.

Nouwen, Henri. *The Selfless Way of Christ: Downward Mobility and the Spiritual Life*. Orbis, 2012.

Priolo, Lou. *Selfishness: From Loving Yourself to Loving Others*. P&R, 2010.

Twenge, Jean M., and W. Keith Campbell. *The Narcissism Epidemic: Living in the Age of Enlightenment*. Simon & Schuster, 2010.

## Websites

Psych Central: www.psychcentral.com/blog/archives/2008/08/04/how-to-spot-a-narcissist/

*Psychology Today*: www.psychologytoday.com/basics/narcissism

# 38 Obsessions and Compulsions

## 1 PORTRAITS

- Elaine woke up at 6:24 a.m. sharp and sprung to her feet so as to not get out of bed at 6:25, an odd number. She walked to her bathroom, opened and closed the door four times, and then walked into the bathroom to get ready. It was time for breakfast, and just as Elaine had done for the past seven years, she poured her glass of orange juice exactly to the red line on her glass cup, buttered her toast with exactly four swipes of butter, and picked up four napkins, then put back two of them. Before she headed out for work, she touched the door handle four times to make sure she would not leave the door unlocked.

- Jeanne felt a pang of embarrassment as another person took an extended look at her chapped, cracked, and bloody hands. She knew it was unreasonable, but she could not stop herself from washing her hands for twenty-seven seconds under piping hot water so as to cleanse herself of the contamination she may have contracted after picking up the office phone. She tried to reason herself out of her "germ fear," but every time she encountered a contamination threat, she could not bring herself to calm down until she had completed her washing ritual.

- Jeremy had just finished straightening up the area around his desk at work for the fourth time that day. He knew it was completely irrational to be so concerned with the neatness and order of his space, as co-workers often reminded him, but every time he saw an uneven stack of papers, a drawer partially open instead of fully closed, loose paper clips lying around, or a book out of alphabetical order, his agitation and obsessing about these things drove him to organize and reorganize until everything reflected perfection.

## 2 DEFINITIONS AND KEY THOUGHTS

- *Obsessive-compulsive disorder* (OCD) is distinguished by *obsessions* (the unwanted and intrusive domination of one's thoughts or feelings by a persistent idea, image, or desire) that provoke anxiety or distress in the individual and/or *compulsions* (the irresistible and persistent impulse to perform a certain act) that exist to counteract these negative emotions.[1]
- *Statistics* concerning OCD include the following:[2]

— OCD affects approximately *2.2 million American adults* every year.

— People with OCD may go *several years without being diagnosed or treated* for the disorder.

— The *total annual costs* associated with OCD are estimated to be about 8.4 billion dollars.

— *Lifetime prevalence for developing OCD* among people aged 18–45 years in the United States is 2.0–2.3 percent (approximately 1 in 40 adults).

- Usually when individuals are obsessing or acting on a compulsion, they *do not realize their behaviors or thoughts are unreasonable.* However, they generally recognize the dysfunction when their thinking is not clouded with the obsession or compulsion.

- Individuals who suffer from OCD feel that their compulsions are *necessary for survival*, and in the process of their actions, the chemicals in their body are prepared to either fight or flee.

- Some *basic components* of OCD are *obsessions, compulsions, intrusive thoughts, anxiety, thought-action fusion,* and *scrupulosity.*

## Obsessions

- There is *no specific set of thoughts* marking an obsession, but all obsessions are unwanted; they are repetitious thoughts that cause anxiety or distress. While individuals know these thoughts come out of their mind, they also feel that the thoughts do not necessarily originate in themselves and *they feel powerless to control these intrusive ideas.*[3]

- *Common obsessions* include the following:

— *contamination*—body fluids, germs/disease, environmental contaminants, household chemicals/solvents, dirt

— *unwanted sexual thoughts*—forbidden or perverse acts and images, homosexuality, those that involve children or incest, aggressive sexual behavior

— *losing control*—fear of self-harm, fear of harming others, fear of violent or horrific images, fear of blurting out obscenities, fear of stealing things

— *scrupulosity*—concern about offending God, blasphemy, excessive worry about morality or right and wrong

— *harm*—fear of being responsible for an accident or tragedy, fear of harming others due to carelessness or a lack of vigilance

— *perfectionism*—concern about evenness or exactness, concern with the need to know or remember something, fear of losing or forgetting important information, an inability to discard things

## Compulsions

- Compulsions are *repetitive behaviors or mental acts that create an outlet to alleviate the anxiety produced by an obsession.* For example, when persons with OCD ruminate about whether they locked the door (obsession), they will go to the door to make sure they did indeed lock the door (compulsion) and therefore relieve the anxiety from their questioning minds. A compulsion can also display itself through rituals (for example, taking a shower in the exact same progression or time frame to purify oneself from contamination).[4]

- *Common compulsions* include the following:

  — *washing and cleaning*—excessive hand washing or washing only in a certain way, excessive showering or bathing or teeth brushing or grooming or toilet routines, excessively cleaning household items or other objects, doing other things to prevent or remove contact with contaminant

  — *mental compulsions*—excessive reviewing of events to prevent harm, praying to prevent harm to oneself or others, counting while performing a task and ending on a particular word or number, "canceling" or "undoing" (for example, replacing a bad word with a good one)

  — *checking*—checking that you did not/will not harm others, checking that you did not/will not harm yourself, checking that nothing terrible happened, checking that you did not make a mistake, checking some part of your physical condition or body

  — *repeating*—rereading or rewriting something, repeating routine activities (locking doors, turning stove off, checking that iron is unplugged, for example), repeating body movements (such as tapping, touching, blinking), repeating activities in certain multiples

  — *miscellaneous compulsions*—collecting items that result in significant clutter or hoarding, putting things in order or arranging things until it "feels" right, telling or asking or confessing to get reassurance from someone on a matter

- *Anxiety* is an *abstract sense of foreboding.* We all experience anxiety, but only those who suffer from OCD experience an *intense anxiety or angst* that carries with it a sense of *imminent foreboding or tragedy.*

- Insecurity tells the individual's brain and body to speed up, and the body prepares to respond as if the individual were truly in an emergency. Due to a *perceived severity of the situation*, the individual *overanalyzes* what is going on in the moment because of all of the options and possibilities he or she sees.

- *Intrusive thoughts* are much like acid reflux and knee-jerk reactions; they are *unwanted and unexpected ideas or images.* The thoughts are unwanted because they most often *center on themes of blasphemy, danger, undesirable consequences, violence, or contamination.* They are unexpected because they *do not originate with a conscious thought, but with an emotion.* Before the thought interrupts consciousness, the individual will feel *alarm and panic.* Then the individual attempts to interpret the accompanying feelings of angst. Since the thought originates in a feeling, it *cannot be explained*, and a superstition or irrational belief (such as, "I caught a disease," "My thought caused reality," "The germs will kill me") arises *to provide a rationale for the idea*.

- *Thought-action fusion* (TAF) is a term used in treating OCD that describes a *confusing interplay between thoughts and events in the mind of the individual*. The first way TAF shows up in OCD is in an individual's belief *that thinking about something disturbing or improper will predispose the individual to commit the action.* ("The more I think about harming someone I love, the more likely I will be to do it.") The second way TAF exposes itself is in the *fear that an unacceptable, intrusive thought is just as sinful as acting on that thought.* ("The thoughts of harming someone I love are practically just as sinful as if I were actually to harm them.") Many have suggested that TAF is connected to the common feelings of over-responsibility in individuals diagnosed with OCD.[5]

- *Scrupulosity* is defined as *seeing sin where there is no sin*. It is an extreme form of religiosity in which the individual is frantically trying to achieve greater and greater perfection of integrity and character. Scrupulosity is described as *a defective conscience or an intense focus on a small scruple* (a feeling of doubt or hesitation with regard to the morality or propriety of a course of action), while severely neglecting the broader principle the scruple was meant to uphold. *Scrupulosity is a strict adherence to rules while being blinded to overarching principles.*[6]

## Criteria for OCD

- The following criteria for OCD are from the DSM-IV-TR:[7]

  — *Criteria A and C:* Recurrent obsessions or compulsions that are severe enough to be time-consuming (i.e., they take more than one hour per day) or cause marked distress or significant impairment.

  — *Criterion B:* At some point during the course of the disorder, the person has recognized that the obsessions or compulsions are excessive or unreasonable.

  — *Criterion D:* If another Axis I disorder is present (major mental disorders, developmental disorders, and learning disabilities), the content of the obsessions or compulsions is not restricted to it.

  — *Criterion E:* The disturbance is not due to the direct physiological effects of a substance (e.g., a drug of abuse, a medication) or a general medical condition.

## Causes of OCD

- It has been suggested that OCD is a *chemical imbalance issue*; however, researchers are conducting ongoing projects that will give more understanding of the origin of OCD. Individuals may have certain quirks and one event, especially if it involves trauma of some kind, can trigger an onrush of obsessive or compulsive behavior. Some women, when faced with common hormonal fluctuations associated with childbirth, may experience a chemically based shift that can lead to OCD and fantasies of harming her child. For the most part, however, there are *no certain events that activate obsessive or compulsive behaviors*. In the same vein, there is *no one neurobiological basis for the development* of OCD either.

- On average, OCD *emerges in the late teens for men and early twenties for women*. On rare occasions OCD may emerge as early as six months or as late as in one's sixties. If OCD is noticed at a very early age, it is most likely that the child has a close relative with OCD as well.

- Obsessive/compulsive tendencies *increase during times of stress or life change*. It has been suggested by some that for new mothers, OCD may be as common as postpartum depression.

## 3 : ASSESSMENT INTERVIEW

The key components to look for are recurring thoughts that cause anxiety and an action (mental or physical) that serves to neutralize that anxiety.

### Rule Outs

1. Do you have another Axis I disorder? (The content of the obsessions or compulsions is not restricted to it.)
2. Are you taking any medications or are you using or abusing any drugs?
3. Could these thoughts be the result of another general medical condition?
4. Do any of your relatives suffer from an anxiety disorder or OCD? (*An interesting correlation has been found between childhood OCD and a close relative also having OCD.*)
5. Do you remember any obsessive or compulsive behaviors as a child or teenager? (*The majority of adults with OCD remember obsessive/compulsive tendencies during childhood, although a negative response is not a complete rule out.*)
6. Are the thoughts you are having related to real-life issues, for example concerns about job security, family functioning, or grades in school? (*Generally, OCD thoughts are unrelated to real-life concerns.*)

### General Questions

1. Are you concerned about the possibility of having an OCD diagnosis?
2. Are there unwanted thoughts that cause you anxiety?
3. Do you want these thoughts to go away but cannot seem to get them out of your head?
4. Do the thoughts you are having disturb you?

5. Do the thoughts you are having go against what you really value, believe, and cherish? (*Usually obsessions go against the individual's values, so obsessive thoughts would cause confusion and distress in the person.*)

6. Do you initiate an activity to neutralize the stress of these thoughts? (*These actions would be classified as the compulsions.*)

7. Do you think that your thoughts (*obsessions*) or reactions to these thoughts (*compulsions*) are irrational or extreme?

8. Do the thoughts you are having take up more than an hour during your day or impair your normal daily routine, social interactions and relationships, or functioning at work or school? (*Obsessive thoughts must consume more than an hour each day and significantly alter one's regular functioning to be considered for OCD.*)

9. Do you avoid situations in which the thoughts or actions agitate you?

# WISE COUNSEL : 4

As a counselor of an individual with OCD, be intentional about instilling hope. Despite the anxiety produced within those who suffer from OCD, it is a very treatable disorder. However, these individuals must be willing to confront the brain's messages of panic and courageously live with the uncertainty as to whether there really is a crisis at hand.

Help the individual realize that intrusive thoughts are not inherently sinful. In cases when obsessions violate cherished values, remind the client that sin is when a person "knows the good they ought to do and doesn't do it" (James 4:17). These cases generally are the result of thought-action fusion (previously discussed) and it is important to help the individual differentiate between an obsessive thought and his or her own thoughts. Ask the person if this disturbing thought is something that he or she desires to do. (Ask, for example, "Do you want to harm your child?") This may help the individual separate an obsessive thought from something they would actually choose to do of their own volition—having an intrusive thought about harming someone he or she loves does not make him or her an abuser at heart. Another example is that experiencing an intrusive, disturbing image of committing adultery, with no desire to commit the act, does not make the person an adulterer.

Encourage individuals to choose not to meditate on the intrusive thoughts, even though it may be extremely difficult. The more they meditate on the thoughts, the stronger the obsessions will become. Also encourage the individual not to submit to the desire to act on the compulsion. Acting on the compulsion reinforces the obsession because it creates an allowance for the obsession by providing a "way out" or an "escape" mechanism to alleviate the anxiety if the individual continues to obsess.

It would be easy to consider the struggles of those with OCD as simply quirky or odd. Most individuals know that their angst is irrationally over the top and they probably condemn themselves for it. In some cases, honestly admitting the struggle helps the sufferer deal more properly with the issue he or she is facing. However, this takes a lot of courage since many individuals are aware that their obsessions and compulsions are irrational. When they do confess, remember that they may not be able to overcome their struggle through encouragement alone—they need community, support, and, most likely, medical and/or professional counseling as they battle their own mind.

# 5 : ACTION STEPS

## 1. Reframe the Thought

- Try not to give too much weight or significance to the obsessive thoughts you have. When individuals feel obsessions emerge, it is helpful to reframe the intrusive thought and replace it with truth, especially biblical truth whenever and wherever it is appropriate. Healthy self-talk can help reduce overall anxiety. It is important for you to understand that with OCD, the compulsion to neutralize the anxiety from the obsessive though is a retreat from negative emotion (although the negative emotion may seem irrational).

- Decide prior to an OCD episode what you believe about your fear. Write it down and put your note in a place where you will remember to look when you are struggling. Try to endure the anxiety and pain of the obsessive thought and turn your mind to something else (find a distraction, such as picturing a big red stop sign), rather than acting on the compulsion. When you realize that everything is still all right, even thought you didn't act on the obsessive thought, the less likely you will be disturbed by it in the future. Expect this to be an extended process, with ups and downs. It will require determination and focus on your part.

## 2. Move toward God's Grace

- *Pastors have seen symptoms of OCD decrease as an individual becomes more acquainted with the grace of God. This is especially true in cases of scrupulosity. With this in mind, guide the individual into a deeper knowledge of the extent of the grace that God gives to those who come to Him with humble hearts and empty hands.*

- Spend time reading God's Word and focusing on appropriate passages that deal with God's grace, which is available to you as His child. Your counselor will direct you to passages for reading and meditation.

## 3. Distinguish Obsessions and Compulsions from Reality

- It is important to be able to differentiate between what is you and what is your OCD. Your counselor will help you formulate practical and tangible ways to identify and externalize obsessive thinking.

- Naming the OCD thoughts out loud may help you identify them. You can learn to externalize obsessive thoughts by identifying them or using related terms for them, such as "obsessive thinking," "anxiety," or "doubt." (*OCD was originally termed "the doubting disease."*) For example, when you are having an obsessive thought, try telling yourself, "This is just me being anxious, but everything is really OK. I don't need to act on it."

- *This step is especially good for children who may not have all the developmental tools they need to process what is going on internally. For example, a child suffering with OCD once called her obsessive thoughts "Worry Bugs," and when they would come, she made sure she "stomped" on them. Other names are "Agent Worry," "Mr. Worrier," and "My worrywart thinking."*

## 4. Pay Attention to Diet and Nutrition

- It has been observed by some psychologists that OCD demands a strict diet. Because chemicals influence OCD, it makes sense to be aware of and keep watch over the chemicals entering your body through food. Food influences anxiety levels directly, so you should decrease caffeine intake and increase vitamins and minerals, such as iron, B vitamins, calcium, phosphorus, and potassium, which all correlate with a reduction of anxiety levels.
- Another practical tip is to control carbohydrate intake, which causes serotonin levels to spike and then dramatically decrease, resulting in stress and difficulties regulating emotion.
- Make an appointment with a registered dietician or nutritionist for consultation.

## 5. Consult a Physician

- A number of medications, primarily antidepressants, have been specifically approved by the Food and Drug Administration (FDA) for the treatment of OCD because they boost serotonin levels, producing positive results.
- You may need to consult a medical doctor who can determine the right medication or combination of medications for you and the correct dosage levels that will provide effective symptom relief.
- *Antidepressants that have been found effective include clomipramine (Anafranil), fluvoxamine (Luvox), fluoxetine (Prozac), paroxetine (Paxil), and sertraline (Zoloft).*

## 6. See a Professional Counselor

- It may be beneficial for you to meet with a therapist who has had experience using cognitive-behavioral therapy (CBT) with people who have OCD. Be prepared to work at retraining your thinking so that you are not controlled by your obsessions and compulsions. Small steps are important in the beginning.
- *The goal of CBT is to gradually expose the individual to his or her fears and obsessions until he or she no longer turns to the compulsion or ritual for relief but is able to respond peacefully. For example, a good exercise for an individual dealing with perfectionism may be drawing a picture that is intentionally imperfect, while simultaneously being coached to reframe thoughts, such as that art with mistakes provides opportunities for richer growth and creativity. For an individual who panics when driving over bumps because they think they have driven over a person,*

*an assignment to intentionally drive on a rough dirt road for a few minutes every day for two weeks can help to reframe thoughts.*

# 6 BIBLICAL INSIGHTS

*But I trust in you, LORD; I say, "You are my God." My times are in your hands; deliver me from the hands of my enemies, from those who pursue me.*

*Psalm 31:14–15*

Martin Buber, a Jewish theologian and author of the book *Two Types of Faith*, makes a clear distinction in belief: believing in a person or merely believing a thing to be true. OCD sufferers are convinced of the facts of their circumstances and truly struggle to accept a truth that is contrary to their obsession. Their belief is grounded in how they feel about a situation. In Psalm 31 David is fleeing from the murderous intentions of his own son yet makes the declaration that he is trusting in the Lord, Jehovah, and that the outcome depends on God. The individual who desires to be freed from OCD must not rely on facts or compulsions to soothe themselves. Instead, they must trust God and transfer the responsibility of their worry over to him. For example, the individual who anxiously wonders if they locked the door must give responsibility to God over the security of their house. For the individual who dreadfully fears contamination, they must give responsibility for their health to God.

*Come to me, all you who are weary and burdened, and I will give you rest. Take my yoke upon you and learn from me, for I am gentle and humble in heart, and you will find rest for your souls. For my yoke is easy and my burden is light.*

*Matthew 11:28–30*

We serve a God who offers freedom from the anxiety and fears associated with OCD. He desires for His children to have an abundant life. OCD is not a value issue—struggling with obsessive thinking does not make someone less precious to the heart of God. He promises to come alongside us and carry whatever burden is weighing us down. Our response should be to let go and give it to Him.

*Do not be anxious about anything, but in every situation, by prayer and petition, with thanksgiving, present your requests to God. And the peace of God, which transcends all understanding, will guard your hearts and your minds in Christ Jesus.*

*Philippians 4:6–7*

God encourages us to trust Him for every circumstance and situation. Any difficulty we may be facing is never bigger than our God. Whether in times of legitimate anxiety or obsessive thinking, He tells us to bring our requests to Him in prayer, but with an attitude of expectant thanksgiving. In response He will give us a supernatural peace that will guard our mind and heart. The Lord is always reaching down to help us through our anxious moments.

*Cast all your anxiety on him because he cares for you.*

*1 Peter 5:7*

Every thought or circumstance that causes our heart to be anxious should be given to God. We need to throw or cast these things away and we have the freedom to do this because He loves and cares for us. His desire is that we be free from worry. The more we trust in His grace, the more peace we will experience in our daily lives.

*You will keep in perfect peace those whose minds are steadfast, because they trust in you. Trust in the LORD forever, for the LORD, the LORD himself, is the Rock eternal.*

*Isaiah 26:3–4*

Meditating on God and His Word helps keep our thoughts focused, peaceful, and less anxious. When intrusive thoughts and compulsive behaviors cause our heart to be anxious, we can trust Him for help and believe that He is with us as we journey toward recovery. If we do, we will experience His peace.

## PRAYER STARTER 7

Lord, Your Word says that we are to be anxious for nothing but in everything with prayer we must make our requests known to You. I am asking now that You remove every worry, fear, and anxiety in _____'s mind. I pray that he (she) would experience freedom from unwanted thoughts and compulsive behaviors. We know that the person the Son sets free is free indeed! Help _____ trust You more completely with these issues. Thank You for Your promise to keep his (her) heart in perfect peace, in a peace that the world could never give, a peace that comes only from Your Holy Spirit . . .

## RECOMMENDED RESOURCES 8

Baer, Lee. *Getting Control: Overcoming Your Obsessions and Compulsions*. Plume, 2012.

Ciarrocchi, Joseph W. *The Doubting Disease: Help for Scrupulosity and Religious Compulsions*. Paulist Press, 1995.

Hyman, Bruce, and Cherry Pedrick. *The OCD Workbook: Your Guide to Breaking Free from Obsessive-Compulsive Disorder*. New Harbinger, 1999.

Osborn, Ian. *Can Christianity Cure Obsessive-Compulsive Disorder? A Psychiatrist Explores the Role of Faith in Treatment*. Brazos, 2008.

Penzel, Fred, *Obsessive-Compulsive Disorders: A Complete Guide to Getting Well and Staying Well*. Oxford University Press, 2000.

## Websites

Beyond OCD: www.beyondocd.org/ocd-facts/

Help Guide: www.helpguide.org/mental/obsessive_compulsive_disorder_ocd.htm

International OCD Foundation: www.ocfoundation.org/whatisocd.aspx

National Institute of Mental Health: www.nimh.nih.gov/health/topics/obsessive-compulsive-disorder-ocd/index.shtml

OCD and Christianity: www.ocdandchristianity.com

OCD Center: www.ocdcenter.org/about-ocd/ocd-statistics.php

# Religious Addiction and Toxic Faith  **39**

- MaryAnn had just experienced another disturbing flashback from being sexually abused as a child and she immediately called her new church mentor, Mrs. Sherman, to seek comfort. She explained her pain in detail and waited for Mrs. Sherman's response. "Dear heart, you just have to give it to the Lord. You do not have to deal with the pain—it is the Lord's. Perhaps He is trying to show you an area of sin in your life. Just keep praying and have faith and He will take away these flashbacks. Freedom will come soon enough. It's wrong to doubt and be afraid."

- It was Sunday morning, and Sherri was so excited to go to church. Her husband, Dan, worked long hours to provide for the family, and it had been a tiring week of her attending to the little ones alone. She thirsted for the refreshment of being overwhelmed with a euphoric connection to the supernatural. Worship time at church was the only "Sherri" time when she finally had a chance to escape reality and enter into heavenly realms. She eagerly attended every service, conference event, Bible study, and prayer meeting. Sherri felt like less of a believer if she did not make every effort to be available to God this way.

- "Submit to your spiritual authority, brother!" The words rang in Kenny's ears and even before he had the chance to get his bearings, Jason, the senior pastor, started yelling at him in anger and throwing out Bible verses about being disobedient. "Now read your Bible and stop complaining, especially if you want to stay in leadership around here—you know that God puts us under authority in life. Don't ever question the counsel we give you again. We're here for your own spiritual well-being and protection."

## DEFINITIONS AND KEY THOUGHTS : 2

- Frequently *religious addicts and victims of spiritual abuse* think they are the only ones who hurt, doubt, or wrestle with their spirituality (when, in reality, we all face times of confusion and pain). This explains why, when a call for "healing" comes (for example, made by a religious guru who claims peace and to have answers), they respond with unchallenged acceptance.

- An individual with a *toxic faith* has *developed a relationship with rules and religious practices in exchange for a relationship with the true God*. Toxic faith is

329

seen around the world in the absence of religion (atheism), as well as among different religions (Christianity, Judaism, Islam, Buddhism, and others). Instead of worshiping Christ, the "toxic faithful" sometimes *create their own image of God,* one that excuses them from the realities of life and permits them to abuse self or mistreat people, be isolated from healthy relationships, and ignore problems. These actions further separate individuals from having a personal relationship with God.

- Individuals who grew up in *homes with rigid rules*, have experienced *past traumatic disappointment or abuse*, or have *low self-esteem* are especially *susceptible* to developing a toxic faith. This orientation typically requires a works and performance-based existence, as rituals and rules ensure the individual's connection to the "god" that medicates their pain. Toxic faith may escalate into *addiction* so that individuals turn again and again to find solace in their religion, even if its practice becomes harmful.

- *Symptoms of religious addiction and spiritual abuse include the following:*[1]

  — stating religious convictions as black and white
  — isolation from people who do not share the same beliefs
  — an absence of grace or mercy because the world and flesh are viewed as inherently evil
  — being obsessive about praying, going to church, reading the Bible, attending crusades, watching television evangelists, sending money to missions
  — excessive fasting
  — hearing messages from God and using them to justify controlling and abusive behavior
  — judging others; often angry and violent toward "heathens" (unbelievers)
  — brainwashing—persistent attempts to persuade family and significant friends to their way of thinking
  — compulsively talking about God and religion or quoting from Scripture
  — conflict of ideology with hospitals and schools
  — discouraged from thinking for oneself, doubting, or questioning
  — sexuality seen as dirty or bad
  — cannot accept criticism
  — suffers tension and stress and often develops physical illnesses, such as eating disorders, depression, and anxiety
  — often stares; goes into trances
  — erratic personality changes

- *Twenty-one erroneous beliefs that can fuel toxic faith:*[2]

  — Security and significance with God depend on my behavior.
  — When tragedy strikes, true believers should have a real peace about it.
  — If you had real faith, God would heal you or the one you are praying for.

— All ministers are men and women of God and can be trusted.

— Material blessings are a sign of spiritual strength.

— The more money you give to God, the more money He will give to you.

— I can work my way to heaven.

— Problems in your life result from some particular sin.

— I must not stop meeting others' needs.

— I must always submit to authority.

— God uses only spiritual giants.

— Having true faith means waiting for God to help me and doing nothing until He does.

— If it's not in the Bible, it isn't relevant (all truth is in the Bible).

— God will find me a perfect mate.

— Everything that happens to me is good.

— A strong faith will protect me from problems and pain.

— God hates sinners, is angry with me, and wants to punish me.

— Christ was merely a great teacher.

— God is too big to care about me.

— More than anything else, God wants me to be happy (free from pain).

— You can become God.

- *Irrational thinking patterns common in religious addiction include the following:*[3]

  — *Thinking in extremes*—driven by an all or nothing, black or white mentality that causes the addict to be very hard on him- or herself and others.

  — *Drawing invalid conclusions not based in reality*—global thinking (using words like *never* and *always*) about life.

  — *Filtering out the positive and distorting reality*—selectively hearing only the negative and so being negative about everything, especially themselves; in response to positive input they say, "Yes, but . . ."

  — *Filtering out the negative and distorting reality*—selectively hearing only the positive to shield their already low self-worth; allowing themselves to do what they would condemn in others, causing a lot of relational wreckage; the weight of restitution can be crushing when they finally see it.

  — *Thinking with the heart*—feelings become the basis for reality because the belief is that one's perception is "certainly accurate."

  — *"Should/ought" thinking*—constant self-condemnation for not being able to measure up.

  — *Co-dependency*—egocentric feeling of being responsible for everything, needing to be in control, always aware of the needs of others at the expense of their own.

**331**

- *Characteristics of a toxic faith system and spiritual abuse include the following:*[4]

  — *"Special" claims* regarding revelation directly from God, a certain manifest destiny, or ministry applications.

  — *Authoritarianism* that is usually seen in a strong and charismatic leader who has a driven personality and little to no accountability.

  — *An "us versus them" mentality*, which creates a sense of being in confrontation with outside entities; any criticism toward the faith group and its leaders is viewed as an attack from an enemy.

  — *Punitive in nature* and the leaders have the authority to discipline and punish followers in an unbalanced way, offered as a distorted form of love and care.

  — *Service-oriented people are taken advantage of* because the system attracts compulsive personalities who are super compliant, will overwork, and are nonconfrontational, which leaves them vulnerable to mistreatment and abuse.

  — *Closed communication* with all information coming from the top-down and a sense of a privileged in-group, while others are kept in the dark.

  — *Extreme legalism*—performance becomes everything and unquestioned obedience is rewarded.

  — *No objective accountability* because no "truth tellers" are permitted or tolerated, and the leader makes it clear he or she is accountable only to God.

- *Toxic faith can take several forms:*

  — *Compulsive religious activity* is rooted in performance and works-based salvation. The future is essentially controlled by the adherent's ability to work hard enough to please their god. Images of self-flagellation and praying multiple times a day may come to mind, but compulsive churchgoing, busyness in church committees, and the replacement of family with religious activities are Westernized, more socially acceptable versions of the same works-based efforts to gain God's favor.

  — *Masking emotional pain* through beliefs, such as "I must follow these five steps precisely to receive a blessing." To escape the reality of the consequences of their actions (or even the actions of others who have hurt them), they hide and try to medicate their pain through rote practices or in finding the "right" formula. Instead of facing their difficulties and working through their wounds with the Lord and safe people, they are convinced there's almost a magical solution that will provide instant results.

  — *Poor financial stewardship* results from unbalanced teaching that giving to the church or religious group will result in great wealth. Many offer their riches and resources with the expectation of being rewarded with greater prosperity. God does bless us for giving to Him, but it is not always in a monetary way and it is never for the purpose of bringing greater comfort through worldly treasure. He understands that our true treasure will be found when we are committed to Him. Neither our faith nor our tithes can bribe God into blessing us, but many still believe that the more they give, the more they deserve tangible blessings from heaven.

— *Self-obsession* robs glory from the Lord because of the demand by religious addicts that God meet their needs and relieve them from their own loads. They may feel entitled to being catered to by God and others. Their self-absorption blinds them to any act of God's grace (undeserved favor) and the needs of hurting people in their life. These individuals feel entitled to be always and only on the receiving end of miracles, service, and blessings, refusing to acknowledge their helplessness without Christ.

— *Extreme intolerance* manifests itself with a strongly biased, black-and-white view of religion. Like the Pharisees in the New Testament, these individuals believe that their form of religious practice is the only right way and they set nearly unattainable standards. Anyone else's way of worship is never appropriate, permitted, or good enough, and their service always has a ritual-oriented glitch that needs to be improved. These individuals will sacrifice relationships, even with people whom they love, for the sake of upholding their man-made ideals.

— *A religious high* is an easy trap to fall into, as spiritual mountaintops are typically more pleasurable than the harsh realities of life. Spiritual high junkies resort to adrenaline rushes (e.g., from religious activities and environments) for stimulation, energy, and relief from pain. The broad-based mood swings offer an altered view of reality—an easier, more digestible perception of truth. Because God seems to be at the center of these experiences, toxic believers do not realize that they are exhibiting many of the same symptoms found in other forms of addiction.

## ASSESSMENT INTERVIEW : 3

*Note:* These questions are taken from the book *Toxic Faith: Understanding and Overcoming Religious Addiction* by Stephen Arterburn and Jack Felton, pages 315–16.

1. Has your family complained that you are always going to a church meeting rather than spending time with them?
2. Do you feel extreme guilt for being out of church just one Sunday?
3. Do you sense that God is looking at what you do, and if you don't do enough, He might turn on you and not bless you?
4. Do you often tell your children what to do without explaining your reasons, because you know you are right?
5. Do you find yourself with little time for the pleasures of earlier years because you are so busy serving on committees and attending other church groups?
6. Have people complained that you use so much Scripture in your conversation that it is hard to communicate with you?
7. Are you giving money to a ministry because you believe God will make you wealthy if you give?

8. Have you ever been involved with a minister sexually?
9. Is it hard for you to make a decision without consulting your minister? Even over the small issues?
10. Do you see your minister as more powerful than other humans?
11. Has your faith led you to lead an isolated life, making it hard for you to relate to your family and friends?
12. Have you found yourself looking to your minister for a quick fix to a lifelong problem?
13. Do you feel extreme guilt over the slightest mistakes or identified inadequacies?
14. Is your most significant relationship deteriorating over your strong beliefs compared to those of a "weaker partner"?
15. Do you ever have thoughts of God wanting you to destroy yourself or others in order to go and live with Him?
16. Do you regularly believe God is communicating with you in an audible voice?
17. Do you feel God is angry with you?
18. Do you believe you are still being punished for something you did as a child?
19. Do you feel if you work a little harder, God will finally forgive you?
20. Has anyone ever told you a minister was manipulating your thoughts and feelings?

# 4 WISE COUNSEL

Religious addicts are faced with overwhelming humiliation once they hit rock bottom. They are caught in the tension of their patterned thoughts and the truth of their circumstances. Most likely it is at this point, faced with the reality of their shattered lives, that they come to you, the helper. Remember that we each have the potential to commit the worst of sins and we are kept from them only by the grace of God.

When addicted individuals take the first step in freeing themselves from a convoluted faith, they will probably experience anxiety, doubt, and loneliness, and they may have second thoughts about walking away from their religion. One of the major reasons for this is that they are abandoning what has been cherished and valued for quite some time. They are leaving the community that "accepted" them, experienced things with them, and even thought for them. Additionally they are facing the humiliation of admitting they were wrong (remember, their confession will probably reach the individuals whom they abandoned to follow their toxic religion).

# 5 ACTION STEPS

Review the section on spiritual applications in chapter 4 at the beginning of this Quick-Reference Guide regarding recovery from addiction because they are applicable to toxic faith and religious addiction. Recovery from any addiction can be a protracted process that requires courage, hard work, commitment, and endurance.

# 1. Consider a Biblical Version of the 12 Steps

- Review the steps given in chapter 4 regarding *Spiritual Applications*. Consider incorporating these principles and biblical precepts in your day-to-day living. Walk them out with a support group and through accountability partners.

# 2. Ask Questions

- Ask a lot of questions of someone in a Christian church whom you trust so that you will gain a broader perspective on what the Bible teaches regarding who God is and what a healthy and balanced faith walk looks like.

# 3. Complete the Following Exercise

- With a paper and pen, go to a quiet space and take a few minutes to get the thoughts about the day out of your head. This may require just writing whatever comes to mind for five minutes.
- For the next two steps, be honest with yourself. Abandon all of the beliefs that you have been pressured to believe about God. Writing about who you think you *should* be will only further cripple you. Instead, answer from how you respond in actual experiences and take as much time as you need.
- How do you feel about God when you are alone, stressed, or anxious? Write descriptive words or phrases that explain your perspective.
- What fears do you have when you think about God? Write descriptive words or phrases that explain your perspective.
- Do you feel that God has wronged you? If so, write about the situations with descriptive words or phrases that explain your perspective of God regarding this difficult circumstance.
- What parts of your heart and life do you resist giving to God? Write down what you are withholding with descriptive words or phrases that explain the reasons you do not give all of yourself to God.
- Open your Bible to 1 Corinthians 13:4–7. Write down the descriptive phrases about love (some Bibles use the word *charity* instead of *love*); copy the passage, replacing the word *love* with *God* (see 1 John 4:16). This will create a short list of some of God's attributes.
- Compare the first lists with the final list taken from 1 Corinthians 13. The more distinction there is between the first two lists and the third, the greater the misunderstanding of God's character and relation to us as His redeemed children.
- The next step may be the most difficult, but it is also one of the most vital steps in healing. This step is confession—being honest about your brokenness not only before God but also before one or more believers who are trustworthy and gracious. In this context, you can experience in a tangible way the love and the grace of God. Bring your answers to a trustworthy believer (perhaps more than one) and talk through your doubts about God. Confess your sin of unbelief in

the true character of God and ask the other believer to pray for you, that you may be healed (James 5:16).

- Integrate confession and community into the foundation of your life. Acknowledge that confession among trustworthy, grace-saturated believers is vital to walking in the greatest plan God has for you—walking just as Jesus walked while here on earth.

# 6 : BIBLICAL INSIGHTS

*You do not delight in sacrifice, or I would bring it; you do not take pleasure in burnt offerings. My sacrifice, O God, is a broken spirit; a broken and contrite heart you, God, will not despise.*

*Psalm 51:16–17*

In this psalm David proclaims that the Lord does not want ritual sacrifices but broken spirits. In other words He does not want a religious practice without a humble acknowledgement of the reasons behind the act (human sinfulness and godly holiness). It is only after we come to the Lord with empty hands that He accepts our religious acts and spiritual disciplines (for example, prayer, Scripture reading, tithing). A broken and contrite spirit and heart is one that relies completely on the grace of the Father and not in self-effort and works.

These verses are a comforting reminder to the individual who has just forsaken the idols of a toxic religion. Undoubtedly he or she will experience spiritual brokenness. This passage is such a consoling reassurance of God's acceptance of the shattered life!

*Blessed are the poor in spirit, for theirs is the kingdom of heaven.*

*Matthew 5:3*

The Greek word for "poor" is *ptochos* and it literally means "lacking in anything," and in this context it refers to being aware of one's spiritual need. This word paints a picture of a beggar with his hands stretched up, pleading for someone to grant him anything that will sustain his life. Jesus calls the individuals who are conscious of their spiritual neediness blessed (meaning happy). These individuals are literally "fit for admission into the divine kingdom" (Thayer's Lexicon). Those who humbly acknowledge their spiritual need for the riches of God are welcomed with open arms, and as they experience His generous grace, they are clothed with blessing.

*Trust in him at all times, you people; pour out your hearts to him, for God is our refuge.*

*Psalm 62:8*

The central statement of this verse is bookended by two phrases that direct our attention to God's stability and the reality that He is the same yesterday, today, and forever. On the front end, we receive the commission to trust in the Lord, which puts us in a position of confiding in Him, setting our hopes on Him, and fearing nothing for ourselves. On the back end, we see that God is a haven to which we can flee and find shelter from the storms of life or danger. It is from this place of recognizing that He really is trustworthy that we can pour out our hearts before Him through the simple act of prayer. God wants our honesty in prayer, to hear our true confessions and the genuine state of our heart. An honest confession exposes the depth of our heart, the very place that needs to be uncovered so that God can give us an intimate knowledge of His love for us.

## PRAYER STARTER : 7

Father, we praise You that You desire to draw all people to repentance and that it is Your kindness that beckons us. Thank You for _____ and Your zealous commitment to draw him (her) into a clearer understanding of Your love and grace. Even his (her) willingness to seek help is evidence that You have been pursuing him (her). Thank You that the blood of Jesus is a sufficient covering by which we can come boldly before You, even though we are broken. _____ needs to have a personal relationship with You, Lord. Set him (her) free from a religion in which he (she) knows about You but doesn't know You. Shine the light of Your truth into any confusion and wrong thinking . . .

## RECOMMENDED RESOURCES : 8

Arterburn, Stephen, and Jack Felton. *Toxic Faith: Understanding and Overcoming Religious Addiction*. WaterBrook, 2001.

Blue, Ken. *Healing Spiritual Abuse: How to Break Free from a Bad Church Experience*. InterVarsity, 1993.

Booth, Lee. *When God Becomes a Drug: Breaking the Chains of Religious Addiction and Abuse*. SCP Limited, 1998.

Bussell, Harold L. *Unholy Devotion: Why Cults Lure Christians*. Zondervan, 1983.

Chrnalogar, Mary Alice. *Twisted Scriptures: Breaking Free from Churches That Abuse*. Zondervan, 2000.

Cloud, Henry, and John Townsend. *12 "Christian" Beliefs That Can Drive You Crazy: Relief from False Assumptions*. Zondervan, 1995.

Johnson, David, and Jeff VanVonderen. *The Subtle Power of Spiritual Abuse: Recognizing and Escaping Spiritual Manipulation and False Spiritual Authority within the Church*. Bethany, 1991.

VanVonderen, Jeff. *Tired of Trying to Measure Up: Getting Free from the Demands, Expectations, and Intimidation of Well-Meaning People*. Bethany, 2008.

VanVonderen, Jeff, Dale Ryan, and Juanita Ryan. *Soul Repair: Rebuilding Your Spiritual Life*. InterVarsity, 2008.

## Websites

Spiritual Abuse Awareness: www.spiritualabuseawareness.com/

Spiritual Abuse Recovery Resources: www.spiritualabuse.com/?page_id=45

Spiritual Research Network: www.spiritual-research-network.com/home.html

# Workaholism and Performance 40

- It was not unusual for Mark to work ninety or more hours every week. His talents gave him a lot of opportunities for various jobs, and he enjoyed being able to use all that God had given him. His efforts were paying off as promotions kept coming throughout the seven years he had been at his company. The affirmation from supervisors was quite motivating and he felt he was using the talents and gifts God had given him. What he wasn't seeing, however, was the slow deterioration taking place in his marriage and in his relationship with his eight-year-old son, Seth.

- The annual Milner family ski vacation was a great time to rest, get away from the noise of daily life, and reconnect with grandparents, siblings, and cousins. Everyone looked forward to the annual trips except for Sharon, who saw getting away from work as more of a hassle than anything else. Instead of relaxing, she became anxious whenever she was in a place where the cell phone service and internet connection were spotty. Even on the slopes, her mind was consumed with unfinished projects and temporarily abandoned assignments. Long after everyone else went to bed, she would link in with her computer and spend hours catching up with the day's activities that were taking place hundreds of miles away. The only true rest Sharon experienced was the "relaxation" that came when she was working.

- "I'm sorry, Mom and Dad, this project just came in today, and I'm the only one capable of completing it right!" Tony and Leila sat at the table, watching their daughter, Rachel. It seemed like the cell phone was glued to her ear, and she was trying to talk with them at the same time, but most of her attention was on the papers spread out in front of her and the calls she was making. Unmarried, Rachel spent all of her time on her job as an advertising sales manager. She rarely socialized with friends because she would never say no to any assignment she was tasked with. Work was her greatest passion and a source of love for her. She turned to her job for a sense of accomplishment and recognition, working tirelessly to remain an indispensable asset to the company.

# 2 DEFINITIONS AND KEY THOUGHTS

- *Married men overwork more than any other demographic*—married women and unmarried men and women. *Unmarried women are second.* According to the U.S. Census Bureau, the percentage of employed American men regularly working more than forty-eight hours per week is higher today than it was twenty-five years ago. Using Current Population Survey (CPS) data from 1979 to 2006, this *increase was greatest among highly educated, highly paid, and older men*, was *concentrated in the 1980s*, and was *largely confined to workers paid a salary* as opposed to hourly wages.[1]

- A new study by the Organization for Economic Cooperation and Development (OECD) reaffirmed that on average people in America are putting in *20 percent more hours of work than they did in 1970*. It also shows that in the same period, the number of hours worked in all the other industrialized countries, except for Canada, decreased.[2]

- The *average workweek* in the United States is *fifty-four hours*, according to a Sage Software Survey in 2007. Typically *only 14 percent of the workforce work forty hours or less*. One-third work fifty to fifty-nine hours per week, and 80 percent work between forty and seventy-nine hours, according to a 2006 study of twenty-five hundred Americans. According to a report by the nonprofit Families and Work Institute in New York City, over *30 percent of all American workers were chronically overworked* in 2004.[3]

- The problem of increased working hours is made more acute by the fact that *fewer workers take time off or use their vacation days* than a generation ago. A recent study by Expedia.com revealed that only 38 percent of U.S. employees are taking all of their earned vacation days. The average employee used only fourteen out of eighteen accrued days. At least 30 percent of employed adults never use all of their vacation days according to a 2005 Harris Interactive poll. Each year Americans hand back 421 million unused vacation days to their employers.[4]

- Research has identified *four distinct workaholic styles:*[5]

  — *The bulimic workaholic* wrestles with perfection and *believes a job must be completed perfectly or not done at all*. These individuals may have difficulty starting projects and then rush to complete them by set deadlines. They work frantically to the point of exhaustion, which usually results in a less than desirable outcome.

  — *The relentless workaholic* represents *the adrenaline junkie* who takes on more work than can possibly be done by one person. They attempt to keep too many plates spinning, work in a hurried fashion, and because of this approach to tasks, the work is sloppy, not very thorough, and/or incomplete.

  — *The attention-deficit workaholic* is the individual who *starts with a flurry of activity, but fails to finish projects* because of boredom, losing interest, or turning his or her focus to the next new project that seems exciting. They love the brainstorming process of tasks and projects but get easily lost or distracted by the details and simply do not follow through.

— *The savoring workaholic* is the type of person who works in a *slow, methodical, and overly scrupulous* manner. Usually they have a lot of difficulty in letting go of projects, do not work well with others or delegate effectively, and prefer to be alone in completing tasks. These workers are *absolute perfectionists* and frequently miss deadlines because whatever they are tasked with does not look or feel "perfect" to them.

- A 2010 study from CareerBuilder that sampled thirty-one hundred people examined various *indicators of workplace addiction* and what workers do to find balance between work and personal time.[6]

  — Over half (52 percent) reported they *worked more than forty hours per week*; 14 percent *worked more than fifty hours*; and 31 percent brought work home at least once per week—10 percent doing so at least every other day.

  — Nearly 25 percent stated it was *difficult to let go of work-related pressures* once they left the workplace.

  — A fourth (24 percent) reported that when they were at home or out socially *they still thought about work*; 19 percent *dreamed* about work; and 16 percent acknowledged that most of their *conversations*, regardless of what environment they were in, *almost always focused on work*.

- Extended workdays and an unwavering focus on business while at home are *taking a toll on family relationships*.[7]

  — Almost a fourth (22 percent) of workers reported they *did not have time to pursue personal interests* because they were always working; 15 percent stated they would rather be working than at home; 12 percent said the amount of time spent on work was causing friction with their family members; and 9 percent were more concerned about approval from their supervisor than their family.

- Workers reported *increased stress levels and health complications* related to work pressures.[8]

  — Over half (51 percent) of workers reported their *workloads had increased* over the last six months; 27 percent had not taken a personal or sick day in the last several years; and 26 percent had experienced health issues directly related to workplace stress.

- *Workaholism* is an *overinvestment in job-related tasks* that exceeds the actual need and drives one to think about assignments, projects, and the to-do list even outside of the workplace.

- Some suggest two different types of workaholism:

  — *Job-involved workaholics*: These individuals have *a high work commitment and have obsessive-compulsive behaviors.* They enjoy their work and avoid activities outside of their jobs.

  — *Compulsive workaholics*: These individual maintain *high work commitments without obsessive-compulsive behaviors* and are more likely to have poor work habits and dysfunctional relationships.

- Spence and Robbins[9] have developed a *"workaholic triad"—work involvement, work compulsion*, and *work enjoyment*. Workaholics are highly involved in their jobs and feel compelled to work yet they do not necessarily gain satisfaction from the work they accomplish. The researchers identified *work enthusiasts* (who scored high on involvement and enjoyment in their work but not compulsion) and *enthusiastic workers* (who scored high on all three measures).

- *A distinction is made between thinking about and being highly involved in one's work*, as well as one's beliefs or attitudes about work. The core of workaholism is both *cognitive* and *behavioral*. This means that the individual's mind, as well as their time, is consumed with work.

- Some people view workaholism positively and view workaholics as more satisfied and productive in their jobs. Still other professionals see workaholics as obsessive, dissatisfied, and annoyances within the workplace. So what is the line between a healthy work ethic and addiction to one's work? *Workaholics are defined by work*—they cannot see themselves outside of their jobs. When they think of their identity, they also think of their job role, function, and accomplishments. *If work is infringing on an individual's health, relationships, and financial or general well-being, there is likely a work-related addiction.*

- Isolation is at the center of most addictions and workaholism is no different. Instead of seeking interaction from relationships, *workaholics fulfill their needs from over-involvement in their job.*

- Diane Fassel has studied workaholism among the individuals who come to her for management consultation. She found three stages of addiction to work:[10]

  — *The Early Stage*: The worker has *chosen to be trapped in chronic busyness.* He or she takes on too many tasks, cannot or will not take time off from work, and works overtime (even unpaid overtime).

  — *The Middle Stage*: The addict begins to *distance himself or herself from relationships* and turns to work for needs to be met. His or her thoughts and emotions are tightly linked to work and winding down becomes difficult. *Fatigue and weight gain or loss* may also be present in this stage.

  — *The Late Stage*: The addict faces *more serious physical symptoms* of workaholism: ulcers, high blood pressure, and ongoing headaches. At this point, the individual is at risk for many other serious health issues, including heart attack and stroke.

# ASSESSMENT INTERVIEW : 3

1. Is work on your mind even after you leave your job at the end of the day?
2. Do you work longer hours than your job description calls for?
3. Do you consistently take on more work than you are required? (*If there is a temporary increase in workload and the individual works long hours during this period, it does not make him or her a workaholic.*)
4. Do any of your relationships suffer because of an over-investment in work?
5. Do you bring work along with you on vacations? Do you work on weekends and during holidays?
6. Do you have trouble switching your brain to off? Do you have trouble sleeping at night?
7. Is resting from work a foreign concept to you?
8. Do you consider work to be relaxing?
9. Do you consider yourself to be better than others? If so, is work a pursuit for success that you use to support your view of yourself?
10. Are the expectations you have for yourself realistic?
11. Do you consider yourself to be a perfectionist?
12. Do you ever feel that you are unable to stop working?
13. When you think about your identity, is work the dominant characteristic that comes to mind?
14. Do you get more excited about your work than about family members or anything else?
15. Are there times when you can charge through your work and other times when you cannot seem to get anything done?
16. Is work the activity you like to do best and talk about most?
17. Do you work more than forty hours per week?
18. Do you turn your hobbies into moneymaking ventures?
19. Do you take complete responsibility for the outcome of your work efforts?
20. Have family members or friends given up expecting you to be on time for functions because of work-related matters?
21. Do you take on extra work because you are concerned that it will not otherwise get done?
22. Do you underestimate how long a project will take and then rush to complete it?
23. Do you believe that it is okay to work long hours if you love what you are doing?
24. Do you get impatient with people who have other priorities besides work?
25. Are you afraid that if you do not work hard you will lose your job or be a failure?
26. Do you get irritated when people ask you to stop doing your work to focus on something else?
27. Do you work or read during meals?
28. Do you believe that more money, influence, or prestige will solve the problems in your life?

# 4 WISE COUNSEL

Below the surface of workaholism, there may lie a poor sense of identity. (The belief is "Who I am is based in what I do" or "My primary value comes from what I do—my work.") Help the client nurture an identity that is based on his or her relationship with Christ and apart from the work that is performed. Workaholism, like every other addiction, is rooted in creating distance from other people. Because of fear, the workaholic distances himself or herself from people to avoid deep or transparent relationships. They use work to fill the void where there should be healthy intimacy with others. The goal of recovering from workaholism involves admitting weakness in this area and the need to be connected with others.

Two key signs that a workaholic is recovering from his or her addiction are the ability to express feelings related to personal beliefs about work stress and the freedom to allow others to honestly do the same. These indicators show denial is decreasing. Recovering workaholics are also able to set appropriate boundaries and say, "No," "Thank you, but I can't," and "It's not worth the price of my health and family."

Addiction is distraction from reality and workaholism is a dynamic used as a form of escape. Unresolved issues may be from childhood (neglect, abuse, trying to prove competence in some manner, rejection) or from a current situation or relationship (stress at home, not receiving support or recognition from anyplace but work, unrealistic expectations). Help the workaholic come to a place of honestly evaluating the negative impact he or she is experiencing when trying to be affirmed only through work.

Often the workaholic struggles with self-deception and faulty thinking. Help the individual see the imbalance and replace false beliefs with truth. For example, one lie he or she may believe is that one's value and significance come from performance alone. This mind-set is frequently found in ministry leaders because it is couched in religious language and combined with unreasonable demands. The fear of man is like a snare according to the Scriptures. However, the truth is that this individual is valuable apart from anything he or she could ever perform or accomplish, because worth is inherent as a creation of God.

# 5 ACTION STEPS

## 1. Triage Daily Events

- Learn how to assess what is going on in your work environment and then prioritize things in a more balanced way. Decide and schedule time for the most important activities, such as time with God, quiet time, family time, sleep time, social and leisure activities.

- Be sure to include relationships among the highest priorities. Many believe it takes intentional and focused time to maintain important relationships. Consider a spiritual retreat with God, a romantic weekend with your spouse, "date nights" with your children, and social activities with friends for extended investments in your close relationships.

- Avoid adding something into your schedule without eliminating an activity that is equivalent in time and energy.
- Create "breathing space" margins by blocking out more time than necessary to complete tasks. Learn the art of the "fifteen-minute vacation" when you allow yourself to take periodic breaks to stretch, take a walk, connect with a co-worker, or shut your eyes.

## 2. Rest before Getting Worn Out

- Author and businessman Stephen Covey suggested four areas for personal renewal. Physically—get proper exercise, rest, and nutrition. Socially and emotionally—make deep, intimate connections with others. Mentally—exercise your brain through reading, writing, and learning. Spiritually—pray and meditate, serve others, and experience nature.
- Remember that God has built rest, the Sabbath, into His creation. The reason for the Sabbath is not simply our weakness and frailty, but to remind us we are not in control. It is God who carries out His kingdom work. We are stewards. We can stop and the world is not going to fall apart. It has been said (tongue-in-cheek) that cemeteries are full of "indispensable people." The truth is, we are not indispensable. It is for God's good pleasure that He raises up leaders. If we die tomorrow, the work of Christ will continue and this helps keep us in a place of humility. We can convince ourselves that we are working for the glory of God, but at what point does it become an addiction?

## 3. Write Your Own Obituary

- Imagine being on your deathbed and think about what would be going through your mind. Would you be satisfied with overworking or lamenting that you had spent too little time with family members and friends? Would you be content with the relationships you have had with your spouse, children, significant others? Would you be happy with what you have accomplished in life or within the kingdom of God? In reality, life boils down to relationships, because they have an eternal impact. Work will come to an end. Careers can end unexpectedly. In the next generation or two, most people will probably not remember your name or contributions you made at work. However, your love for family and others can change their lives and the lives of those they touch.
- In his book *Choosing to Cheat*, Pastor Andy Stanley makes the point that in the balance of work and home, you will always be cheating somewhere. When you choose work over family, you are cheating your family. When you choose family over work, you are cheating at work. Because you will inevitably be "cheating" someone, somewhere, you must decide where it is worth it.

# 6 : BIBLICAL INSIGHTS

*Keep your lives free from the love of money and be content with what you have, because God has said, "Never will I leave you; never will I forsake you."*

*Hebrews 13:5*

Sometimes, the love of money and possessions are the primary driving forces behind workaholism; at other times, it can be fear and anxiety over a lack of provision in life. We wonder whether God will show up in our circumstances. He promises to never abandon us, so we can rest in this with peace, knowing that He is aware of our every need. Otherwise, our pursuit of "things" can put us into spiritual bondage.

*Better one handful with tranquility than two handfuls with toil and chasing after the wind. Again I saw something meaningless under the sun: There was a man all alone; he had neither son nor brother. There was no end to his toil, yet his eyes were not content with his wealth. "For whom am I toiling," he asked, "and why am I depriving myself of enjoyment?" This too is meaningless—a miserable business!*

*Ecclesiastes 4:6–8*

In this passage Solomon says that it is better to live a life of true rest than to expend one's time and efforts vainly on pursuits that ultimately leave one empty-handed. This is a picture of the man who knows no end to planning riches for himself yet has not internalized the truth that his work for wealth is in vain. For the workaholic, this verse is a reminder that work without rest is a hollow enterprise and wealth without contentment in all things is meaningless.

*In vain you rise early and stay up late, toiling for food to eat—for he grants sleep to those he loves.*

*Psalm 127:2*

In this psalm Solomon again writes of the vanity of hard work without rest. It does not matter whether one stays up late or wakes up early—each is dependent on God for his or her daily bread. If you embrace this truth, you will receive rest and peace of mind, instead of chaos and endless striving.

*Whatever you do, work at it with all your heart, as working for the Lord, not for human masters.*

*Colossians 3:23*

In healthy Christianity, there is no compulsive obedience, only obedience born of love, both from the Father and for Him. This verse speaks of where our hearts are focused and in what and in whom we are placing our trust. Let the Lord order your steps and chart your path in work and life. Only then can we experience what it means to be fully free to follow and serve Him with joy.

## PRAYER STARTER : 7

Lord, I want to lift up _____ to You and ask that You give him (her) clarity of focus and a healthy perspective on work and priorities. Bring peace to every anxious thought. We acknowledge that You are our provider and that You will never leave us or forsake us. Help _____ draw close to You for his (her) sense of identity and worth. Bring healing and restoration to any relationship that has been hurt because of the workaholism. Thank You that we can stop trying to control every outcome in life and trust You in all things . . .

## RECOMMENDED RESOURCES : 8

Cloud, Henry, and John Townsend. *Boundaries: When to Say Yes, When to Say No, to Take Control of Your Life*. Zondervan, 1992.

Crabb, Larry. *The Pressure's Off: Breaking Free from Rules and Performance*. Water-Brook, 2010.

Harling, Becky. *Freedom from Performing: Grace in an Applause-Driven World*. NavPress, 2011.

McGee, Robert. *The Search for Significance*. Thomas Nelson, 2003.

Robinson, Bryan E. *A Guidebook for Workaholics, Their Partners and Children, and the Clinicians Who Treat Them*. 2nd ed. New York University Press, 2007.

Stanley, Andy. *Choosing to Cheat: Who Wins When Family and Work Collide?* Multnomah, 2003.

Winter, Richard. *Perfecting Ourselves to Death: The Pursuit of Excellence and the Perils of Perfectionism*. InterVarsity, 2005.

### Websites

Psychology Today: www.psychologytoday.com/blog/wiredsuccess/201203/workaholism-and-the-myth-hard-work

Workaholics Anonymous: www.workaholics-anonymous.org/page.php?page=home

# Chemical Dependency Assessment

_____

_(Name of Practice Here)_

_____

_____

_(Address and Phone Number of Practice Here)_

Client Name: _____

## FAMILY/SIGNIFICANT OTHER(S)

What is your family's/significant other's perception of your drug or alcohol use?

_____

_____

_____

_____

When did your family/significant other(s) become aware of your drug or alcohol use?

_____

_____

_____

_____

How has your family/significant other(s) attempted to address the problem with you?

_____

_____

_____

_____

_____

Please indicate any past alcohol and substance abuse history within your family.

| Family Member | Alcohol: *What kind? How long? How much?* | Substance Abuse: *What drug(s)? How long? How much?* |
|---|---|---|
| Mother | | |
| Father | | |
| Grandmother | | |
| Grandfather | | |
| Stepmother | | |
| Stepfather | | |
| Brother | | |
| Sister | | |
| Stepbrother | | |
| Stepsister | | |
| Aunt | | |
| Uncle | | |
| Other | | |
| Other | | |

# CLIENT SYMPTOMS AND BEHAVIORS

1. There has been a significant change in your attitude toward rules, regulations, parents, siblings, spouse, children, etc. ____Y ____N
2. There has been a noticeable lack of participation in family activities since you began using drugs and/or alcohol. ____Y ____N
3. You have become more isolated. ____Y ____N
4. You have begun to lie more and/or blame others more frequently for your problems. ____Y ____N
5. You have stolen money, other valuables, prescription blanks, medication from home, etc., to support your substance abuse. ____Y ____N
6. You communicate less with family members and tend to be more secretive and/or paranoid. ____Y ____N
7. There have been significant changes in sleeping habits (either too much or too little) since beginning substance abuse. ____Y ____N
8. There have been significant changes in eating habits (either too much or a lack of appetite) since beginning substance abuse. ____Y ____N
9. You have begun to associate with an entirely different peer group. ____Y ____N
10. Your new peers tend to avoid contact with your family when they come to the house or call on the phone. ____Y ____N
11. There has been a significant change in your attitude toward work or school. ____Y ____N
12. There has been a significant drop in your work performance or grades in school (including absenteeism, suspensions, firing, etc.). ____Y ____N
13. There has been a significant change in your attendance at work or school. ____Y ____N
14. You have gone on binges for periods of two days or more during which you were intoxicated or high most of the time. ____Y ____N
15. You have had blackouts or periods during which you cannot recall things that happened while drinking or using drugs. ____Y ____N
16. You have tried to hide the fact that you are drinking or using drugs, sneaking drinks, hiding bottles, drugs, paraphernalia, etc. ____Y ____N
17. You drink or use drugs to avoid feelings of anger, guilt, shame, nervousness, stress, or other negative feelings. ____Y ____N
18. You find yourself almost constantly drinking or using drugs or talking about it with others. ____Y ____N
19. You have experienced hangovers or felt strung out. ____Y ____N
20. You have given up some important social or recreational activity to continue drinking or using drugs. ____Y ____N
21. You have had an allergic reaction or overdose while drinking or using drugs. ____Y ____N
22. You have promised someone that you would stop drinking or using drugs before and then you broke the promise. ____Y ____N
23. You have had frequent arguments or conflict with family and/or friends over your drinking or drug use. ____Y ____N

24. At times you drank or used more than you had intended. _____Y _____N
25. You have been unable to stop drinking or using since you started. _____Y _____N
26. You have thought about taking your own life while intoxicated or using as a result of ongoing substance abuse. _____Y _____N
27. You have set a fire accidentally or intentionally as a result of ongoing substance abuse. _____Y _____N
28. You have driven a vehicle while intoxicated or using or have been ticketed or arrested for driving under the influence. _____Y _____N
29. You have lost your temper and/or have become verbally abusive as a result of ongoing substance abuse. _____Y _____N
30. You have become physically or sexually abusive as a result of ongoing substance abuse. _____Y _____N

# ALCOHOL AND SUBSTANCE USE HISTORY

Please check the appropriate boxes and fill in the "Amount" column where indicated.

### Drug and Alcohol Use in Past 90 Days

| Substance | Never | <1/wk | 1/wk | 2–3/wk | 1/daily | >1/daily | Amount |
|---|---|---|---|---|---|---|---|
| Alcohol | | | | | | | |
| Amphetamines | | | | | | | |
| Cocaine/Crack | | | | | | | |
| Inhalants | | | | | | | |
| Hallucinogens | | | | | | | |
| Heroin | | | | | | | |
| Marijuana | | | | | | | |
| Other Opiates | | | | | | | |
| PCP | | | | | | | |
| Sedatives | | | | | | | |
| Tranquilizers | | | | | | | |
| Other_____ | | | | | | | |
| Other_____ | | | | | | | |

What is your drug(s) of choice?

_____

_____

What substance(s) causes you the most problems?

_____

_____

What has been the maximum period of abstinence for you since you began using drugs and/or alcohol?

_____

What methods do you use to administer drugs?

_____

_____

How old were you when you began using/abusing substances?

Type of Substance                                                Age of First Use

_____

_____

_____

_____

_____

_____

Describe any relapses in the last 6–12 months. What are your triggers?

_____

_____

_____

# SUPPORT SYSTEMS

Do you have family members/significant other(s) who use drugs or alcohol?
____Y ____N

Do you have close friends who offer moral support and accountability? ____Y ____N

What percentage of your close friends drink or use drugs? _____ %

What percentage of your general acquaintances drink or use drugs? _____ %

Do your leisure activities include drinking or using drugs? ____Y ____N

Please explain:

_____

_____

_____

What attempts have you made to quit in the past? How successful were they?

_____

_____

_____

_____

What role will faith, spirituality, or the concept of a "higher power" play in your recovery process?

_____

_____

_____

_____

## Self-Help/Support Group Involvement

| Name of Group | Where Group Met | First Date Attended | Frequency Attended | Attendance Terminated |
|---|---|---|---|---|
| Alcoholics Anonymous | | | | |
| Narcotics Anonymous | | | | |
| Cocaine Anonymous | | | | |
| Celebrate Recovery | | | | |
| Other Self-Help or Support Groups | | | | |
| Other_____ | | | | |

_____     _____

Client Signature                                            Date

_____     _____

Parent/Guardian Signature                            Date

# Notes

## Chapter 1  Disease and Choice

1. Substance Abuse and Mental Health Services Administration Center for Behavioral Health Statistics and Quality, "Results from the 2010 National Survey on Drug Use and Health: Summary of National Findings," U.S. Department of Health and Human Services, September 2011, www.oas.samhsa.gov/NSDUH/2k10NSDUH /2k10Results.htm#5.1.

2. Centers for Disease Control and Prevention (CDC), "Trends in the Prevalence of Alcohol Use," www.cdc.gov/healthyyouth/yrbs/pdf/ us_alcohol_trend_yrbs.pdf.

3. Centers for Disease Control and Prevention, "Trends in the Prevalence of Marijuana, Cocaine, and Other Illegal Drug Use," www.cdc.gov/ healthyyouth/yrbs/pdf/us_drug_trend_yrbs.pdf.

4. Substance Abuse and Mental Health Services Administration Center for Behavioral Health Statistics and Quality, "Results from the 2010 National Survey on Drug Use and Health," www. samhsa.gov/data/NSDUH/2k10Results/Web /HTML/2k10Results.htm#3.1.

5. Centers for Disease Control and Prevention, "Alcohol and Public Health Fact Sheets," October 28, 2011, www.cdc.gov/alcohol/fact-sheets/alcohol-use.htm.

6. Ibid.

7. J. J. Collins and P. M. Messerschmidt, "Epidemiology of Alcohol-Related Violence," *Alcohol Health and Research World* 17 (1993), 93–100.

8. National Institute on Drug Abuse, "Info Facts: Understanding Drug Abuse and Addiction," March 2011, www.drugabuse.gov/publications/ infofacts/understanding-drug-abuse-addiction.

9. H. E. Doweiko, *Concepts of Chemical Dependency,* 8th ed. (Belmont, CA: Brooks/Cole, 2012).

10. C. Franklin and R. Fong, *The Church Leader's Counseling Resource Book: A Guide to Mental Health and Social Problems* (New York: Oxford University Press, 2011), 40–52.

## Chapter 2  Trauma and Comorbidity

1. National Institute of Drug Abuse, "Research Reports: Comorbidity: Addiction and Other Mental Illnesses," September 2010, www. drugabuse.gov/publications/research-reports/ comorbidity-addiction-other-mental-illnesses /what-comorbidity.

2. Ibid.

3. C. Couwenbergh et al., "Comorbid Psychopathology in Adolescents and Young Adults Treated for Substance Use Disorders: A Review," *European Child and Adolescent Psychiatry* 15, no. 2 (2006), 319–28.

4. American Psychiatric Association, *Diagnostic and Statistical Manual of Mental Disorders* (DSM-IV-TR), 4th ed. (2000).

5. L. M. Najavits, "Seeking Safety: A New Psychotherapy for Post-traumatic Stress Disorder and Substance Use Disorder," in *Trauma and Substance Abuse: Causes, Consequences, and Treatment of Comorbid Disorders* (Washington, DC: American Psychological Association, 2007), 147–70.

6. L. Jacobsen, S. Southwick, and T. Kosten, "Substance Use Disorders in Patients with Post-traumatic Stress Disorder: A Review of the Literature," *American Journal of Psychiatry* 158, no. 8 (2001), 1184.

7. Ibid.

8. Ibid.

## Chapter 3  Treatment Protocols

1. Institute of Addiction Medicine, www. ioam.org/statistics.html.

2. Ibid.

3. Ibid.

4. Ibid.

5. D. Mee-Lee, ed., *Patient Placement Criteria for the Treatment of Substance-Related Disorders,* 2nd ed. *(ASAM PPC-2R)* (American Society of Addiction Medicine, 2001).

6. Ibid.

7. Ibid.

8. Addiction Technology Transfer Centers (ATTC), *Unifying Research, Education, and Practice to Transform Lives: Performance Assessment Rubrics for the Addiction Counseling Competences,* attcnetwork.org/explore/priority areas/wfd/getready/docs/rubric5-11-2001-2.pdf (2001), 18.

9. Ibid.

10. C. L. Hart, C. Kasir, and R. Oakley, *Drugs, Society, and Human Behavior* (New York: McGraw-Hill, 2009).

11. Ibid.

## Chapter 4  Spiritual Applications

1. M. Gross, "Alcoholics Anonymous: Still Sober after 75 Years," *American Journal of Public Health 100*, no. 12 (2010), 2361–63.

2. Ibid.

3. Ibid.

4. Ibid.

5. Ibid.

6. Ibid.

7. For information on Saddleback's Celebrate Recovery Program, see C. W. Dyslin, "The Power of Powerlessness: The Role of Spiritual Surrender and Interpersonal Confession in the Treatment of Addictions," *Journal of Psychology and Christianity* 27, no. 1 (2008), 41–55.

8. *Celebrate Recovery Bible*: NIV (Grand Rapids: Zondervan, 2007).

9. Dyslin, "The Power of Powerlessness."

10. Ibid.

11. Ibid, 44.

12. A. B. Murray-Swank, K. M. McConnell, and K. I. Pargament, "Understanding Spiritual Confession: A Review and Theoretical Synthesis," *Mental Health, Religion and Culture* 10, no. 3 (2007), 276.

13. Ibid.

14. Ibid.

15. Contemplative Outreach, www.contemplativeoutreach.org/.

16. Ibid, 831.

17. Mark R. Laaser, "Working with Couples from a Spiritual Perspective," *Sexual Addiction and Compulsivity* 13 (2006), 209–17.

18. Blaise Pascal, en.wikiquote.org/wiki/Blaise_Pascal.

## Chapter 5  Recovery and Relapse Prevention

1. *Everyday Health*, www.everydayhealth.com/addiction/understanding-addiction-relapse.aspx.

2. Ibid.

3. Ibid.

4. www.caron.org/current-statistics.html.

5. Ibid.

6. Stephen Arterburn, "Effective Inpatient and Residential Addiction Recovery Models," *Christian Counseling Today* 16, no. 1 (2008), 34–37.

7. Ibid.

8. Ibid.

9. Alcoholics Victorious, www.alcoholicsvictorious.org/faq/rec-diet.html.

## Chapter 6  Alcohol

1. Doweiko, *Concepts of Chemical Dependency*, 60–71.

2. Ibid.

3. Ibid.

4. NHTSA, "Traffic Safety Facts," last modified March 2008, www.nrd.nhtsa.dot.gov/pubs/810801.

5. P. Stevens and R. Smith, *Substance Abuse Counseling: Theory and Practice* (Columbus, OH: Pearson, 2005), 44–53.

6. U.S. National Library of Medicine, "PubMed Health," last modified March 20, 2001, www.ncbi.nlm.nih.gov/pubmedhealth/PMH0001771/.

## Chapter 7  Caffeine

1. Johns Hopkins, "Behavioral Pharmacology Research Unit Fact Sheet: Caffeine Dependence," www.hopkinsmedicine.org/bin/m/b/Caffeine_Dependence_Fact_Sheet.pdf.

2. Ibid.

3. Ibid.

## Chapter 8  Cocaine and Crack Cocaine

1. Substance Abuse and Mental Health Services Administration, "2001 National Household Survey on Drug Abuse," last modified June 16, 2008, www.oas.samhsa.gov/nhsda/2k1nhsda/vol1/chapter2.htm.

2. Ibid.

3. Ibid.

4. Doweiko, *Concepts of Chemical Dependency*, 131–43.

## Chapter 9  Depressants

1. Substance Abuse and Mental Health Services Administration, *Results from the 2010 National Survey on Drug Use and Health: Summary of National Findings*, NSDUH Series H-41, HHS publication no. (SMA) 11-4658 (Rockville, MD: Substance Abuse and Mental Health Services Administration, 2011).

2. U.S. National Library of Medicine, "PubMed Health."

3. The United States Drug Enforcement Administration, "Depressants," www.justice.gov/dea/concern/depressants.html.

4. Doweiko, *Concepts of Chemical Dependency*, chap. 7.

### Chapter 10 Diuretics and Weight Loss

1. Mayo Clinic, "Diuretics," last modified December 16, 2010, www.mayoclinic.com/health/diuretics/HI00030/NSECTIONGROUP=2.

2. Substance Abuse and Mental Health Services Administration, *Drug Abuse Warning Network, 2009: National Estimates of Drug-Related Emergency Department Visits*, DAWN Series D-35, HHS publication no. (SMA) 11-4659 (Rockville, MD: Substance Abuse and Mental Health Services Administration, 2011).

3. J. E. Mitchell, D. Hatsukami, E. D. Eckert, and R. L. Pyle, "Characteristics of 275 Patients with Bulimia," *American Journal of Psychiatry* 142 (1985), 482–85.

4. J. E. Mitchell, C. Pomeroy, and M. Huber, "A Clinician's Guide to the Eating Disorders Medicine Cabinet," *International Journal of Eating Disorders* 7, no. 2 (1988), 211–23.

5. J. E. Mitchell, et al., "Metabolic Acidosis as a Marker for Laxative Abuse in Patients with Bulimia," *International Journal of Eating Disorders* 6, no. 4 (1987), 557–60.

6. T. Pryor, M. W. Wiederman, and B. McGilley, "Laxative Abuse among Women with Eating Disorders: An Indication of Psychopathology," *International Journal of Eating Disorders* 20, no.1 (1996), 13–18.

7. Mitchell et al., "A Clinician's Guide to the Eating Disorders Medicine Cabinet," 211–23.

8. Ibid.

### Chapter 11 Hallucinogens

1. Doweiko, *Concepts of Chemical Dependency*, chap. 12.

2. Substance Abuse and Mental Health Services Administration, *Results from the 2010 National Survey on Drug Use and Health*.

3. Ibid.

4. Ibid.

5. Doweiko, *Concepts of Chemical Dependency*, chap. 12.

6. Ibid.

7. Ibid.

8. United Nations Office on Drugs and Crime, 2008 World Drug Report (New York: United Nations Publications, 2008).

9. Ibid.

10. Substance Abuse and Mental Health Services Administration, *Results from the 2010 National Survey on Drug Use and Health*.

11. Doweiko, *Concepts of Chemical Dependency*, chap. 12.

12. P. N. Jones, "The American Indian Church and Its Sacramental Use of Peyote: A Review for Professionals in the Mental-Health Arena," *Mental Health, Religion and Culture* 8, no. 4 (2005), 277–90.

13. Ibid.

14. National Institute on Drug Abuse, "Infofacts: Hallucinogens," last modified June 2009, www.drugabuse.gov/publications/infofacts/hallucinogens-lsd-peyote-psilocybin-pcp.

15. A. Fickenscher, D. Novins, and S. M. Manson, "Illicit Peyote Use among American Indian Adolescents in Substance Abuse Treatment: A Preliminary Investigation," *Substance Use and Misuse* 41 (2006), 1139–54.

16. R. G. Carlson, Wright State University Boonshoft School of Medicine, "The Prevalence of Dextromethorphan Abuse among High School Students," last modified May 11, 2011, www.med.wright.edu/citar/dads/letter.

17. Drug Enforcement Administration, "Drug Fact Sheet: Dextromethorphan," www.justice.gov/dea/pubs/abuse/drug_data_sheets/Detromethorphan.pdf.

18. P. Addy, "Facilitating Transpersonal Experiences with Dextromethorphan: Potential Cautions and Caveats," *The Journal of Transpersonal Psychology* 39, no. 1 (2007), 1–22.

19. National Drug Intelligence Center, "Psilocybin Fast Facts," last modified August 2003, www.justice.gov/ndic/pubs6/6038/index.htm.

20. Substance Abuse and Mental Health Services Administration, "2001 National Household Survey on Drug Abuse," last modified June 16, 2008, www.oas.samhsa.gov/nhsda/2k1nhsda/vol1/chapter2.htm.

### Chapter 12 Inhalants

1. Alliance for Consumer Education, Inhalant.org. www.inhalant.org/inhalant/abusable.php.

2. Doweiko, *Concepts of Chemical Dependency*, chap. 13.

3. Ibid.

4. Substance Abuse and Mental Health Services Administration, *Results from the 2010 National Survey on Drug Use and Health*.

5. Ibid.

6. Ibid.

7. United Nations Office on Drugs and Crime, *2008 World Drug Report*, chart, United Nations publication sales no. E.08.XI.1 978-92-1-148229-4.

8. Doweiko, *Concepts of Chemical Dependency*, chap. 13.

### Chapter 13 Marijuana and Hashish

1. Doweiko, *Concepts of Chemical Dependency*, chap. 10.

2. Ibid.

3. Ibid.
4. Ibid.
5. Ibid.
6. Substance Abuse and Mental Health Services Administration, *Results from the 2010 National Survey on Drug Use and Health.*
7. Ibid.
8. United Nations Office on Drugs and Crime, *2008 World Drug Report.*
9. Doweiko, *Concepts of Chemical Dependency,* chap. 10.
10. Ibid.
11. Substance Abuse and Mental Health Services Administration, *Results from the 2010 National Survey on Drug Use and Health.*
12. Ibid.

## Chapter 14  Narcotics and Opiates

1. United Nations Office on Drugs and Crime, *2008 World Drug Report.*
2. Ibid.
3. Ibid.
4. Doweiko, *Concepts of Chemical Dependency,* chap. 11.
5. Substance Abuse and Mental Health Services Administration, *Results from the 2010 National Survey on Drug Use and Health.*
6. Ibid.
7. Ibid.
8. Ibid.
9. Doweiko, *Concepts of Chemical Dependency,* chap. 11.
10. Drug Enforcement Administration, "Drug Fact Sheet: Hydrocodone," www.justice.gov/dea/pubs/abuse/drug_data_sheets/Hydrocodone.pdf.
11. Doweiko, *Concepts of Chemical Dependency,* chap. 11.
12. United Nations Office on Drugs and Crime, *2008 World Drug Report.*
13. Substance Abuse and Mental Health Services Administration, *Results from the 2010 National Survey on Drug Use and Health.*
14. Doweiko, *Concepts of Chemical Dependency,* chap. 11.
15. Ibid.
16. Ibid.
17. Substance Abuse and Mental Health Services Administration, *Results from the 2010 National Survey on Drug Use and Health.*

## Chapter 15  Nicotine

1. MedicineNet, "Nicotine Information," www.medicinenet.com/nicotine/article.htm.
2. Ibid.
3. Ibid.
4. Ibid.
5. Ibid.
6. Ibid.
7. Ibid.
8. Ibid.
9. Ibid.
10. Ibid.
11. Ibid.
12. National Institute on Drug Abuse, "Facts about Nicotine and Tobacco Products," National Institutes of Health, www.archives.drugabuse.gov/NIDA_Notes/NNVol13N3/Tearoff.html.
13. Ibid.
14. Ibid.
15. Ibid.
16. Ibid.
17. Ibid.
18. Ibid.
19. American Lung Association, "General Smoking Facts," 2012, www.lung.org/stop-smoking/about-smoking/facts-figures/general-smoking-facts.html.
20. Champions for Health, "The Facts about Nicotine Addiction," 2012, www.championsforhealth.org/the-facts-about-nicotine-addiction.php.
21. American Lung Association, "General Smoking Facts."

## Chapter 16  Prescription Drugs

1. National Institute on Drug Abuse, "Topics in Brief: Prescription Drug Abuse," www.drugabuse.gov/publications/topics-in-brief/prescription-drug-abuse.
2. Ibid.
3. Office of National Drug Control Policy, "Prescription Drug Abuse," www.whitehouse.gov/ondcp/prescription-drug-abuse.
4. Ibid.
5. Centers for Disease Control and Prevention, "CDC Grand Rounds: Prescription Drug Overdose—a US Epidemic," www.cdc.gov/mmwr/preview/mmwrhtml/mm6101a3.htm?s_cid=mm6101a3_w.
6. Office of National Drug Control Policy, "Prescription Drug Abuse."
7. Centers for Disease Control and Prevention, "CDC Grand Rounds."
8. National Institute on Drug Abuse, "Topics in Brief: Prescription Drug Abuse."
9. Centers for Disease Control and Prevention, "CDC Grand Rounds."
10. National Institute on Drug Abuse, "Topics in Brief: Prescription Drug Abuse."
11. Ibid.
12. Ibid.
13. Ibid.
14. Ibid.
15. Ibid.
16. Ibid.

17. Office of National Drug Control Policy, "Prescription Drug Abuse."

18. Centers for Disease Control and Prevention, "CDC Grand Rounds."

19. Ibid.

20. Ibid.

### Chapter 17  Stimulants

1. National Institute on Drug Abuse for Teens, "Stimulants: What Are They?" www.teens.drugabuse.gov/facts/facts_stim1.php#what_are_they.

2. Ibid.

3. Ibid.

4. Ibid.

5. Ibid.

6. Ibid.

7. Ibid.

8. SAMHSA News, "Stimulants and Delinquent Behavior," www.samhsa.gov/samhsa_news/volumexvi_2/article13.htm.

9. The National Survey on Drug Use and Health Report, "Nonmedical Stimulant Use, Other Drug Use, Delinquent Behaviors, and Depression among Adolescents," www.oas.samhsa.gov/2k8/stimulants/depression.pdf.

10. National Institute on Drug Abuse for Teens, "Stimulants: What Are They?"

11. Ibid.

12. U.S. Drug Enforcement Administration, "Stimulants," www.justice.gov/dea/druginfo/factsheets.shtml.

13. Ibid.

14. National Institute on Drug Abuse for Teens, "Stimulants: What Are They?"

15. U.S. Drug Enforcement Administration, "Stimulants."

16. Ibid.

17. Ibid.

18. Ibid.

19. Ibid.

20. Medline Plus, "Attention Deficit Hyperactivity Disorder," U.S. National Library of Medicine, www.nlm.nih.gov/medlineplus/ency/article/001551.htm.

21. Ibid.

22. U.S. Drug Enforcement Administration, "Stimulants."

23. Ibid.

24. Ibid.

### Chapter 18  Bodybuilding and Body Image

1. Archibald D. Hart, *Healing Life's Hidden Addictions* (Ann Arbor, MI: Servant, 1990), 39–42.

2. Ibid.

3. Ibid.

4. E. O. Guillen and S. I. Barr, "Nutrition, Dieting, and Fitness Messages," Journal of *Adolescent Health* 15 (1994): 464–72.

### Chapter 19  Cutting and Self-Harm

1. Web MD, www.webmd.com/mental-health/features/cutting-self-harm-signs-treatment.

2. J. A. Bridge, S. Marcus, and M. Olfson, "Outpatient Care of Young People after Emergency Treatment of Deliberate Self-Harm," *Journal of the American Academy of Child and Adolescent Psychiatry* 47, no. 9 (2008), 213–22.

3. Web MD, www.webmd.com/mental-health/features/cutting-self-harm-signs-treatment.

4. HelpGuide, www.helpguide.org/mental/self_injury.htm.

5. Examiner.com, www.examiner.com/parenting-education-in-buffalo/self-injury-facts.

6. Web MD, www.webmd.com/mental-health/features/cutting-self-harm-signs-treatment.

### Chapter 20  Eating Disorders

1. The Renfrew Center Foundation for Eating Disorders, "Eating Disorders 101 Guide: A Summary of Issues, Statistics, and Resources," (North Palm Beach, FL: 2002).

2. National Eating Disorders Association, www.nationaleatingdisorders.org/anorexia-nervosa.

3. National Association of Anorexia Nervosa and Associated Disorders, www.anad.org/get-information/about-eating-disorders/.

4. Mayo Foundation for Medical Education and Research, www.mayoclinic.com/health/anorexia/DS00606/DSECTION=symptoms.

5. National Association of Anorexia Nervosa and Associated Disorders, www.anad.org/get-information/about-eating-disorders/bulimia-nervosa/.

6. U.S. Department of Health and Human Services Office on Women's Health, www.womenshealth.gov/publications/our-publications/factsheet/binge-eating-disorder.cfm.

### Chapter 21  Fetishes and Bizarre Interests

1. American Psychiatric Association, *Diagnostic and Statistical Manual of Mental Disorders.*

2. Ibid.

3. Ibid.

4. Tim Clinton and Ron Hawkins, *The Popular Encyclopedia of Christian Counseling: An Indispensable Tool for Helping People with Their Problems* (Eugene, OR: Harvest House, 2011), 313–15.

### Chapter 22  Food Addictions

1. J. L. Fortuna, "The Obesity Epidemic and Food Addiction: Clinical Similarities to Drug Dependence," *Journal of Psychoactive Drugs* 44, no. 1 (2012), 56–63.

2. Y. Zhang et al., "Food Addiction and Neuroimaging," *Current Pharmaceutical Design* 17, no. 12 (2011): 1149–57.

3. WebMD, www.webmd.com/mental-health/mental-health-food-addiction.

4. C. L. Ogden et al., "Prevalence of Obesity in the United States, 2009–2010," www.cdc.gov/nchs/data/databriefs/db82.pdf.

## Chapter 23  Gambling

1. No Gambling Addiction, www.nogambling addiction.com/addiction-statistics.htm.

2. Gambling Addiction, www.gambling addiction.org/index.php/poker/30-gambling -addiction-statistics.

3. *Gambling Therapy*, "What Is the Social Impact of Gambling?" last modified March 2012, www.responsible-play.com/en/what-is-gambling/social-impact-of-gambling.aspx.

4. Alta Mira Recovery Programs, "Surprising Research Shows Gambling Addiction Exceeds Alcoholism," www.altamirarecovery.com/blog/surprising-research-shows-gambling-addictions-exceed-alcoholism/.

5. Gambling Addiction, "What Is Gambling Addiction?" www.gamblingaddiction.org/index.php/poker/25-what-is-gambling-addiction.

## Chapter 24  Hoarding

1. Obsessive Compulsive Foundation, www.ocfoundation.org/hoarding.

2. Psychology Today, "Is Hoarding an Addiction or Purely a Compulsive Behavior?" last modified March 2, 2011, www.psychology today.com/blog/when-more-isnt-enough/201103/is-hoarding-addiction-or-purely-compulsive-behavior.

3. Obsessive Compulsive Foundation, www.ocfoundation.org/hoarding.

4. Ibid.

5. Ibid.

6. Ibid.

## Chapter 25  Internet Use and Gaming

1. Video Game Addiction, "Social Consequences of Gaming Addiction," last modified 2009, www.video-game-addiction.org/social-consequences.html.

2. Ibid.

3. Gaming Addiction, "Facts," last modified June 19, 2012, www.gamingaddiction.net/facts.

4. Ibid.

5. Tech Addiction, www.techaddiction.ca/gaming-addiction statistics.html#.ULAYkqP WqJU.

## Chapter 26  Kleptomania and Stealing

1. *Discovery Fit & Health*, "Kleptomania Overview," 2012, www.health.howstuffworks.com/mental-health/mental-disorders/kleptomania.htm.

2. Mind Disorders, www.minddisorders.com/Kau-Nu/Kleptomania.html.

3. American Psychiatric Association, DSM-IV-TR.

4. *Discovery Fit & Health*, "Kleptomania Characteristics," 2012, www.health.howstuffworks.com/mental-health/mental-disorders/kleptomania1.htm.

5. Mayo Clinic, "Kleptomania: Risk Factors," www.mayoclinic.com/health/kleptomania/DS01034/DSECTION=risk-factors.

6. *Discovery Fit & Health*, "Kleptomania Causes and Treatment," 2012, www.health.howstuffworks.com/mental-health/mental-disorders/kleptomania2.htm.

7. Mayo Clinic, "Kleptomania."

8. *Discovery Fit & Health*, "Kleptomania Causes and Treatment."

9. Ibid.

10. Ibid.

11. Ibid.

12. Mayo Clinic, "Kleptomania: Symptoms," www.mayoclinic.com/health/kleptomania/DS01034/DSECTION=symptoms.

## Chapter 27  Pornography and Sexual Addiction

1. Paul Strand, *Exposing Porn: Science, Religion, and the New Addiction* (Virginia Beach, VA: Christian Broadcasting Network, 2004).

2. David C. Bissette, "Internet Pornography Statistics: 2003," www.healthymind.com.

3. "Pornography Statistics 2003," Internet Filter Review, www.internetfilterreview.com.

4. Safe Families, www.safefamilies.org/sfStats.php.

5. MyAddiction.com, www.myaddiction.com/education/articles/sex_statistics.html.

6. Carol Coleman-Kennedy and Amanda Pendley, "Assessment and Diagnosis of Sexual Addiction," *Journal of the American Psychiatric Nurses Association* 8, no. 5 (October 2002), 143–51, doi: 10.1067/mpn.2002.128827.

7. The Christian Counseling Center of First Presbyterian Church, www.christiancounseling.ws/integritygroup.asp.

8. Web MD, www.webmd.com/sexual-conditions/guide/sexual-addiction.

9. Tuscaloosa Christian Counseling, www.tccounseling.com/#/sexual-addiction.

10. Answers.net, "How to Deal with Your Sexual Addiction," www.christiananswers.net/q-eden/sexaddictiontips.html.

11. Clinton and Hawkins, *The Popular Encyclopedia of Christian Counseling*, 387.

12. Ibid., 386.

13. Ibid., 387.

## Chapter 28  Shopping and Excessive Collecting

1. About.com, www.addictions.about.com/od/lesserknownaddictions/a/shoppingadd.htm.

2. PubMed, "Estimated Prevalence of Compulsive Buying Behavior in the United States," last modified October 2006, www.ncbi.nlm.nih.gov/pubmed/17012693.

3. PubMed, "Compulsive Buying: Descriptive Characteristics and Psychiatric Comorbidity," last modified January 1994, www.ncbi.nlm.nih.gov/pubmed/8294395.

4. PubMed, "A Review of Compulsive Buying Disorder," last modified February 2007, www.ncbi.nlm.nih.gov/pmc/articles/PMC1805733/.

5. PubMed, "Estimated Prevalence of Compulsive Buying Behavior"; PubMed, "A Review of Compulsive Buying Disorder."

6. PubMed, "Cognitive Behavioral Therapy for Compulsive Buying Disorder," last modified December 2006, www.ncbi.nlm.nih.gov/pubmed/16460670.

## Chapter 29  Technology and Social Networking

1. Tech Addiction, www.techaddiction.ca/facebook-addiction-statistics.html#.ULJUg6PWqJU.

2. Ibid.

3. The Telegraph, "Facebook Generation Suffer Information Withdrawal Syndrome," last modified January 2011, www.telegraph.co.uk/technology/news/8235302/Facebook-generation-suffer-information-withdrawal-syndrome.html.

4. Ibid.

5. Social Networking, "What Is Social Networking?" last modified June 18, 2012, www.whatissocialnetworking.com/Addicted_to_Social_Sites.html.

6. Royal Pingdom, "Study: Ages of Social Network Users," last modified February 16, 2010, www.royal.pingdom.com/2010/02/16/study-ages-of-social-network-users/.

7. Ibid.

## Chapter 30  Voyeurism and Exhibitionism

1. Tim Clinton and Mark Laaser, The Quick-Reference Guide to Sexuality and Relationship Counseling (Grand Rapids: Baker, 2010), 313–15.

2. Encyclopedia of Mental Disorders, www.minddisorders.com/Py-Z/Voyeurism.html.

3. Ibid.

4. American Psychiatric Association, Diagnostic and Statistical Manual of Mental Disorders, chap. 11.

5. Ibid, chap. 11.

6. Clinton and Laaser, The Quick-Reference Guide to Sexuality and Relationship Counseling, 171–76.

7. Kids Live Safe, "Sexting," www.kidslivesafe.com/learning-center/sexting.

8. Pew Research Center, "Teens, Cell Phones, and Texting," Pew Internet and American Life Project, www.pewresearch.org/pubs/1572/teens-cell-phones-text-messages.

9. Encyclopedia of Mental Disorders, www.minddisorders.com/Del-Fi/Exhibitionism.html.

10. Clinton and Laaser, The Quick Reference Guide to Sexuality and Relationship Counseling, 171–76.

11. Recovery Nation, "Assessing Voyeurism," Exhibitionism and Stalking, www.recoverynation.com/recovery/w_voyeuring.php.

## Chapter 31  Adrenaline and Thrill Seeking

1. Archibald D. Hart, Thrilled to Death: How the Endless Pursuit of Pleasure Is Leaving Us Numb (Nashville: Nelson, 2007), 23.

2. Psychology Today, www.psychologytoday.com/basics/sensation-seeking.

3. P. Lencioni, "The Painful Reality of Adrenaline Addiction," Leadership Review 5 (Winter, 2005): 3–6, www.leadershipreview.org/2005winter/LencioniArticle.pdf.

4. Archibald D. Hart, Healing Life's Hidden Addictions (Vine Books, 1990), 176.

5. Ibid.

6. Ibid.

7. Ibid., 176–78.

8. Ibid., 181.

9. Ibid., 3.

10. L. I. Meadows, "Adrenaline Addicts Anonymous: Adrenaline Notes," last modified 1995, www.adrenalineeaddicts.org/docs/1.pdf.

11. Ibid.

12. Ibid.

13. Lencioni, "The Painful Reality of Adrenaline Addiction."

14. Hart, Healing Life's Hidden Addictions, 184.

## Chapter 32  Anger and Rage

1. American Psychological Association, "Anger," www.apa.org/topics/anger/index.aspx.

2. Jim Platt, "Crossing the Line: Anger vs. Rage," Dartmouth College, last modified Spring 2005, www.dartmouth.edu/~hrs/pdfs/anger.pdf.

3. D. Richmond, quoted in Chip Ingram and Bruce Johnson, Overcoming Emotions That Destroy: Practical Help for Those Angry Feelings That Ruin Relationships (Grand Rapids: Baker, 2009), 28.

4. Tim LaHaye and Bob Phillips, *Anger Is a Choice* (Grand Rapids: Zondervan, 1982), 14.

5. D. Richmond, quoted in Chip Ingram and Bruce Johnson, *Overcoming Emotions That Destroy*, 33.

6. Ibid., 44–45.

7. Ibid., 50–51.

8. Ibid., 58–59.

9. Ibid., 68.

10. Annie Chapman, *Putting Anger in Its Place: A Woman's Guide to Getting Emotions under Control* (Eugene, OR: Harvest House, 2000), 51–53.

11. David Stoop and Stephen Arterburn, *The Angry Man: Why Does He Act That Way?* (Word, 1991), 67–68.

12. Mayo Clinic, www.mayoclinic.com/health/intermittent-explosive-disorder/DS00730.

13. Web MD, www.webmd.com/mental-health/news/20060605/study-millions-may-have-rage-disorder.

14. Ingram and Johnson, *Overcoming Emotions That Destroy*, 80–82.

15. Mayo Clinic, www.mayoclinic.com/health/passive-aggressive-behavior/AN01563.

16. Ingram and Johnson, *Overcoming Emotions That Destroy*, 17.

## Chapter 33 Anxiety and Worry

1. H. Norman Wright, *Winning over Your Emotions* (Eugene, OR: Harvest House, 1998), 20.

2. Ibid., 20.

3. Anxiety and Depression Association, www.adaa.org/about-adaa/press-room/facts-statistics.

4. Ibid.

5. Ibid.

6. Elyse Fitzpatrick, *Overcoming Fear, Worry, and Anxiety* (Eugene, OR: Harvest House, 2001), 13–24.

7. PsychCentral, www.psychcentral.com/disorders/anxiety/.

8. Ibid.

9. Wright, *Winning over Your Emotions*, 22–23.

10. Richard Dobbins, *Your Feelings: Friend or Foe?* (Sisters, OR: VMI, 2003).

11. Ken Nichols, *Harnessing the Power of Fear* (Forest, VA: Alive Ministries, 1996).

## Chapter 34 Chronic Stress and Self-Imposed Pressure

1. David Hagar and Linda Hagar, *Stress and the Woman's Body* (Grand Rapids: Revell, 1996), 20.

2. Ibid.

3. Archibald Hart, *Coping with Depression in the Ministry and Other Professions* (Dallas: Word, 1984), 37.

4. Hans Selye, "The General Adaptation Syndrome and the Diseases of Adaptation," *Journal of Clinical Endocrinology and Metabolism* 6 (1946): 117–230.

5. American Psychological Association, "Mind/Body Health: Stress," www.apa.org/helpcenter/stress.aspx.

6. Ibid.

7. Ibid.

8. American Institute of Stress, www.stress.org/.

9. American Heart Association, www.heart.org/HEARTORG/.

10. Thomas Whiteman and Randy Petersen, *Stress Test: A Quick Guide to Finding and Improving Your Stress Quotient*, (Colorado Springs: Pinon Press, 2000), 24.

11. Hagar and Hagar, *Stress and the Woman's Body*, 24–25.

12. Richard Winter, *Perfecting Ourselves to Death: The Pursuit of Excellence and the Perils of Perfectionism* (Downers Grove, IL: InterVarsity, 2005), 25.

13. Ibid., 25–26.

14. Ibid., 26–28.

15. Ibid.

## Chapter 35 Co-dependency and Toxic Relationships

1. L. L. Stafford, "Is Co-dependency a Meaningful Concept?" *Issues in Mental Health Nursing* 22, no. 3 (2001), 279.

2. C. A. Springer, T. W. Britt, and B. J. Schlenker, "Co-dependency: Clarifying the Concept," *Journal of Mental Health Counseling* 20, no. 2 (1998), 141. www.search.ebscohost.com.ezproxy.liberty.edu:2048/login.aspx?direct=true&db=a9h&AN=564232&site=ehost-live&scope=site.

3. P. E. O'Brien, and M. Gaborit, "Co-dependency: A Disorder Separate from Chemical Dependency," *Journal of Clinical Psychology* 48, no. 1 (1992), 131.

4. C. Hughes-Hammer, D. S. Martsolf, and R. A. Zeller, "Depression and Co-dependency in Women," *Archives of Psychiatric Nursing* 12, no. 6 (1998), 327.www.ncbi.nih.gov/pubmed/9868824.

5. A. J. Mahari, *Enmeshment, Co-dependency, and Collusion*, www.soulselfhelp.on.ca/coenmesh.html, 2007.

6. P. Stevens and R. L. Smith, *Substance Abuse Counseling: Theory and Practice* (Pearson, 2005), 221.

7. Ibid.

8. Jerry L. Johnson, *Fundamentals of Substance Abuse Practice* (Thomson, 2004), 142.

9. Ibid.

10. Mental Healthy America, "Factsheet: Co-dependency," *Mental Health America*, www.

nmha.org/go/codependency; www.psychcentral.com/lib/2012/symptoms-of-codependency/.

11. Sheer Balance, www.sheerbalance.com/brettsblog/8-toxic-personalities-to-avoid/.

**Chapter 36 Cults and the Occult**

1. E. Stetzer, "Mormonism, Cults, and Christianity," Lifeway Research, last modified October 8, 2011, www.edstetzer.com/2011/10/mormonism-cults-and-christiani.html.

2. J. D. Salande and D. R. Perkins, "An Object Relations Approach to Cult Membership," *American Journal of Psychotherapy* 65, no. 4 (2011), 381–91.

3. Ibid.

4. Ibid., 382–83.

5. Christian Apologetics and Research Ministry, www.carm.org/cults-outline-analysis.

6. How Cults Work, www.howcultswork.com/.

7. Salande and Perkins, "An Object Relations Approach to Cult Membership, 381–91.

8. B. Robinson and E. M. Frye, "Cult Affiliation and Disaffiliation: Implications for Counseling," *Counseling and Values* 41, no. 2 (1997), 166–74.

9. Ibid, 168.

10. Ibid.

11. Ibid, 171.

12. Ibid, 172.

13. Watchman Fellowship, www.watchman.org/index-of-cults-and-religions/.

14. Columbia Electronic Encyclopedia, "Occultism."

15. Ibid.

**Chapter 37 Narcissism and Attention Seeking**

1. Mayo Clinic, "Narcissistic Personality Disorder," last modified November 4, 2011, www.mayoclinic.com/health/narcissistic-personality-disorder/DS00652.

2. Ibid.

3. Ibid.

4. Ibid.

5. American Psychological Association, "Narcissistic Personality Disorder," last modified June 21, 2011, www.apa.org/monitor/2011/02/narcissism-dsm.aspx.

6. Ibid.

7. Mayo Clinic, "Narcissistic Personality Disorder."

8. T. Millon, cited in E. Ronningstam, *Identifying and Understanding the Narcissistic Personality* (Oxford University Press, 2005), eBook Collection (EBSCOhost).

9. Mayo Clinic, "Narcissistic Personality Disorder," mayoclinic.com/health/narcissistic-personality-disorder/DS00652/DSECTION=risk-factors.

10. Mayo Clinic, "Narcissistic Personality Disorder," mayoclinic.com/health/narcissistic-personality-disorder/DS00652/DSECTION=treatments-and-drugs.

11. Ibid.

**Chapter 38 Obsessions and Compulsions**

1. National Institute of Mental Health, www.nimh.nih.gov/health/publications/obsessive-compulsive-disorder-when-unwanted-thoughts-take-over/what-are-the-signs-and-symptoms-of-ocd.shtml.

2. OCD Center, www.ocdcenter.org/about-ocd/ocd-statistics.php; National Institute of Mental Health, www.nimh.nih.gov/statistics/1ocd_adult.shtml.

3. International OCD Foundation, www.ocfoundation.org/O_C.aspx.

4. Ibid.

5. About.com, "Obsessive-Compulsive Disorder," www.ocd.about.com/od/causes/a/OCD_TAF.htm.

6. International OCD Foundation, www.ocfoundation.org/uploadedFiles/MainContent/Find_Help/IOCDF_Scrupulosity_fact_sheet.pdf.

7. American Psychiatric Association, *Diagnostic and Statistical Manual of Mental Disorders*.

**Chapter 39 Religious Addiction and Toxic Faith**

1. Leo Booth, *When God Becomes a Drug: Breaking the Chains of Religious Addiction and Abuse* (SCP Limited, 1998), 17.

2. Stephen Arterburn and Jack Felton, *Toxic Faith: Understanding and Overcoming Religious Addiction* (Colorado Springs: WaterBrook, 2001), 33.

3. Philosophy and Religion, www.philosophy-religion.org/criticism/toxicfaith.htm.

4. Arterburn and Felton, *Toxic Faith,* 134.

**Chapter 40 Workaholism and Performance**

1. *Psychology Today*, www.psychologytoday.com/blog/wired-success/201203/workaholism-and-the-myth-hard-work.

2. Ibid.

3. Ibid.

4. Ibid.

5. *Psychology Today*, www.psychologytoday.com/blog/the-power-slow/201012/are-you-workaholic.

6. Taylor and Francis Online, www.tandfonline.com/doi/abs/10.1207/s15327752jpa5801_15.

7. Ibid.

8. Ibid.

9. J. T. Spence and A. S. Robbins, "Workaholism: Definition, Measurement and Preliminary Results," *Journal of Personality Assessment* 58, no. 1 (1992): 160–78.

10. Diane Fassel, *Working Ourselves to Death: The High Cost of Workaholism and the Rewards of Recovery* (New York: HarperCollins, 1990).

# THE QUICK-REFERENCE GUIDES

The newest addition to the popular Quick-Reference Guide collection, *The Quick-Reference Guide to Addictions and Recovery Counseling* focuses on the widespread problem of addictions of all kinds. Each of the forty topics covered follows a helpful eight-part outline and identifies (1) typical symptoms and patterns, (2) definitions and key thoughts, (3) questions to ask, (4) directions for the conversation, (5) action steps, (6) biblical insights, (7) prayer starters, and (8) recommended resources.

*The Quick-Reference Guide to Counseling on Money, Finances & Relationships* focuses on the ever-growing need for sound counsel on financial issues. It is an A–Z guide for assisting people-helpers, pastors, and professional counselors for formal and informal counseling situations.

For pastors, counselors, and everyday believers, *The Quick-Reference Guide to Counseling Women* will be a unique and welcome aid to bring hope, life, and freedom to women in need.

Providing answers on issues such as sexuality, drugs and alcohol, and parent-adolescent relationships, *The-Quick Reference Guide to Counseling Teenagers* prepares those in the position to advise teens to counsel amidst the rapidly changing youth culture.